MEN OF VALOR AND
ANXIETY

JEWS IN EASTERN EUROPE
*Jeffrey Veidlinger, Mikhail Krutikov,
and Geneviève Zubrzycki,* Editors

MEN OF VALOR AND ANXIETY

Polish-Jewish Masculinities and the Challenge of Modernity

Mariusz Kalczewiak

INDIANA UNIVERSITY PRESS

This book is a publication of

Indiana University Press
Herman B Wells Library 350
1320 East 10th Street
Bloomington, Indiana 47405 USA

iupress.org

First printing 2025

Cataloging information is available from the Library of Congress.

ISBN 978-0-253-07382-2 (hdbk.)
ISBN 978-0-253-07383-9 (pbk.)
ISBN 978-0-253-07384-6 (web PDF)
ISBN 978-0-253-07385-3 (ebook)

To Irad

CONTENTS

ACKNOWLEDGMENTS

I thank friends, colleagues, and students who accompanied me through research and writing. I thank my colleagues at the University of Potsdam, Germany: Magdalena Marszałek, Bohdan Tokarskyi, Fabian Erlenmaier, and Sina Rauschenbach. The conversations with you have been crucial for conceptualizing and designing this project. For several years, I was a member of the Gender/Queer and Jewish Studies Working Group at the Selma Stern Center for Jewish Studies. Jan Wilkens and other colleagues from the group helped me find my way through the rich, but sometimes overwhelming, body of gender studies scholarship. In Potsdam, and during my time at the University of Warsaw, I had the privilege to teach Jewish gender studies for the first time. Students provided me with nuanced feedback, and their curiosity validated my interest in the historical workings of gender.

This book would not have become what it is without numerous conversations with colleagues around the world. I was happy to meet Paul Lerner at the University of Southern California in Los Angeles. Paul has been a wonderful host, and I enjoyed presenting my ongoing research to USC students and colleagues. My stays as a visiting professor at Tel Aviv University and the University of

Haifa have been very enriching. I thank Marcos Silber, Iris Racha-mimov, and Michal Shapira for welcoming me into their classes and for their warm encouragement. I am grateful for the continuous support of Raanan Rein of Tel Aviv University, who taught me how to balance the universal and the particular in the study of Jewish history. It was a privilege to be a part of the dynamic group of scholars who offer new, gender-sensitive approaches to Polish-Jewish history. Emma Zohar, Magdalena Kozłowska, Aleksandra Jakubczak-Gabbay, Zuzanna Kołodziejska-Smagała, and other dear colleagues: thank you for sharing my passion for Polish-Jewish history beyond antisemitism.

This research could not be realized without the financial help of diverse institutions. Initially, the University of Potsdam and the Postdoc Network Brandenburg (Brandenburg Ministry for Science, Research and Culture) provided me with a stable research environment. At a later stage, I had the privilege to become a Humboldtian and spend two years working as an Alexander von Humboldt Foundation Fellow at USC. Also, I thank the German Historical Institutes in Warsaw and Washington, DC, for providing me with research fellowships that facilitated my work in the archives. Also, I express my gratitude to the Emanuel Ringelblum Jewish Historical Institute in Warsaw, the Jagiellonian University Archive, the United States Holocaust Memorial Museum, the College of Charleston Library, and the Grodzka Gate-NN Theater Center in Lublin for providing images and art from their collections.

I am grateful to my husband, Irad Ben Isaak, for being a wonderful and critical support through the research and writing process. Our conversations provided me with so much inspiring food for thought.

Finally, I thank Anna Francis, the acquisition editor at Indiana University Press. It was wonderful to have you guide me through the publication process.

A NOTE ON TRANSLATION, SPELLING, AND TRANSLITERATION

AS THIS WORK RELIES HEAVILY on Yiddish and Hebrew sources, extensive transliteration was necessary. The Yiddish transliteration is usually based on the standardized YIVO transliteration system. There are several exceptions to this system. If a title or a name had an original (at the time of publication) or more easily identifiable transliterated spelling, I followed this spelling. For instance, I spelled the Warsaw daily newspaper as *Unzer Express* instead of *Unzer Ekspres*. In terms of Hebrew transliteration, I followed the simple romanization system elaborated by Pim Ritbroek for Brill ("Hebrew: a simple transliteration system," version 0.3, January 27, 2011). Geographical names appear according to their respective historical names instead of their contemporary forms, unless there is a conventional English equivalent (like Warsaw for Warszawa). Foreign words are italicized only the first time they appear, at which point they are explained. All translations are by the author unless otherwise indicated.

MEN OF VALOR AND
ANXIETY

INTRODUCTION

ZISHE ZATORSKI GREW UP IN a family of Talmud scholars but did not share his father's and grandfather's ideas of male respectability. He did not want to study and grew up to be strong and well built. Maier Czompel looked like a refined young man, but sticking a knife into someone's side was as small a thing to him as eating a slice of bread. These Jewish men remembered by Warsaw Bund activist Bernard Goldstein are not religious, do not value studiousness, have fit bodies admired by non-Jewish workers, and appear distant from a stereotypical Orthodox Jew. Just as little do they stand for the respectability of a diligent salaryman striving for a petite bourgeois lifestyle. To be sure, these men are a radical example of intransigent working-class masculinity, and other groups of Polish-Jewish men followed other masculine ideals. How Zatorski and Czompel lived their lives as men was a product of the social reality of interwar Poland that marginalized its Jewish citizens. Yet they refrained from internalizing notions of Jewish masculine inferiority. Conversely, at different life stages, they asserted their masculinity as normative, be it through economic achievement, religious excellence, or strong fists. Their masculine identities intersected with those of their fellow Christian workers and overlapped with heroic masculinities, achievement-based bourgeois masculinities, and scholarship-based Jewish Orthodox masculinities.[1] Zatorski and Czompel represent interwar Polish-Jewish men who, through everyday practices, demonstrated that the masculinities of Jewish men were not specific to that segment of the population but were in line with wider gender mechanisms valid then in Poland.

This book analyzes how Jewish men in Poland of the 1920s and 1930s adopted and adapted gender models and gender practices and how they made a sense of themselves as men and Polish Jews.[2] Polish-Jewish masculinities crystallized in a relational matrix where both men and women, Jews and non-Jews, negotiated Jewish masculinities and interwove them with other social processes. At the turn of the twentieth century, Jewish men lived in a social reality in which their masculinity was regularly tested, criticized, and redesigned against the backdrop of exclusionary ideologies that prevailed then in Europe.[3] The social and economic changes at the turn of the twentieth century, including industrialization, migration, the rise of radical politics, women's movements, the Great War, and the allure of nationalism, challenged traditional gender roles for Jews and non-Jews alike. In order to tell the complex story of how Jewish men and women dealt with those social changes in a nuanced way, a history of Jews in Poland needs to include the gender regime that operated simultaneously with the political, economic, and national regimes. Following Edward P. Thomson and Howard Zinn, who took as their subject ordinary people and their experiences in Great Britain and the United States, this study looks at the masculinity of ordinary Polish-Jewish men and observes the workings of masculinity through the lenses of class and ethnicity, rather than discussing the lives of community leaders.[4] My study demonstrates that Polish-Jewish men faced oppression and disenfranchisement in diverse social contexts yet continuously asserted their masculine normativity.

In dialogue with scholarship on masculinities in Europe and beyond, this book offers a major rethinking of existing approaches to Jewish masculinities. Unlike previous studies, I frame Polish-Jewish masculinities as far from exceptional but rather embedded in and entwined with general European and Polish gender processes.[5] By demonstrating this embeddedness, this book challenges major paradigms about Jewish masculinities, such as the idea that Jewish and non-Jewish masculinities differed, the idea that Jewish men were emasculated and excluded from gentile notions of masculinity, the idea that Jewish masculinities were flawed or deformed, the idea that Jewish men internalized a sense of masculine inferiority, and the idea that only Zionism has "straightened" Jewish men and "normalized" Jewish masculinities. Rethinking Jewish history through the lens of masculinity theories elaborated in other geographical and social contexts, this book revisits and rethinks these assumptions and paradigms about Jewish men, dismantles them, and verifies to what extent they apply in the context of Polish-Jewish masculinities. By focusing on Polish-Jewish men pushed to the margins of Polish society by antisemitism, yet who continuously claimed their access to local venues of masculine hegemony, I shed light on complexities of masculine concepts and identities. Underscoring the self-perceived normativity of Jewish men and their embeddedness in wider masculine dynamics, my study offers a gloss on historiography centered around Jewish particularism and antisemitism's influence on male gender identities.

The rationale of this book is to make masculinity visible in the history of Polish Jews and to map out masculinity theories in a geographical and cultural space so far relatively unexplored from this research perspective. Whereas, in recent years, a gendered approach to cultural and social history has uncovered diverse facets of Jewish women's experience, masculinity is rarely taken up as a research framework in the study of eastern European Jewish history. Historical books in general do not explore how the experience of masculinity structured the lives of the men they write about, the organizations they created, and the events in which they participated.[6] This is not, however, a fault of only eastern European Jewish studies but rather a trend in history writing in general. As noted by Tosh and Roper, generations of historians excluded women from the public record but, by elevating "public" men as the object of study, also entirely submerged men's gender identity.[7] This book demonstrates that Jewish masculinities were evolving alongside other crucial economic, social, and political processes that Jews were a part of, illuminating aspects previously invisible and having implications for histories of Jewish labor, family, class, national identities, religion, and so on. I study masculinity by looking at spheres of male engagement, such as home, work, and social networks, but I also include nonrelational elements, such as body, and locate masculinity in individual practices and experiences. To historicize Jewish masculinities, I rely on both Jewish discourses and practices ("doing gender"). By seeing gender as an organizing principle of Jewish social structures, practices, and institutions, I reframe the historical inquiry to include the gendered experiences of Jewish men.

This study on Polish-Jewish masculinities is indebted to women's studies scholars who, since the 1970s, fought to redefine Jewish and non-Jewish historiography to foreground female voices and perspectives.[8] In earlier times, *Jewish* usually meant *male Jewish*, but generations of feminist historians allowed us to understand how male and female experiences differed throughout history and how Jewish women strove to claim agency in private and public matters. I follow the scholarship that defines masculinity as relational and informed by notions of femininity. Many Jews in Poland indeed conceived of masculinity as the flip side of femininity, and Jewish masculinities in Poland were embedded in the patriarchal gender order in which men dominated women. Jewish men were anxious and had trouble coming to terms with female claims for equality in a way analogous to non-Jewish men, and their Jewishness did not make them more sympathetic. Importantly, it was precisely the historical research on women that made us aware that men too were and are gendered beings. Male experiences throughout history were traditionally seen as the master narrative, which led to perceiving practices and discourses created by men to be free of gender. Masculinity was thought to be "unmarked" because men did not see themselves as males and scholarship also resisted seeing them as men.[9] Since masculinity receives its validation not from women but from other men, I focus on homosocial spaces, that is, spaces where men are among men, which best elucidate the workings of masculinity.[10] However, women are present across all chapters, and I analyze their prominent role in defining masculinity as well.

This book suggests that masculinities are porous, flexible, and selective and that Jewish men consciously chose from a palette of masculine models and practices to design their own Jewish masculinities. This process was enhanced at the beginning of the twentieth century when masculinity entered into a protracted period of cultural reflexivity and malleability.[11] I study masculinities as models structuring how men act, think, and construct their sense of self that interrelate with personalized experiences of performing one's gender identity in social settings. These models code certain practices, collectives, or ideas as masculine and thus gendered.[12] I suggest that men move within a certain masculine spectrum, that multiple masculinities can be chosen or combined, that masculinities are achieved in a processual way, and that masculinities are fluid and evolve throughout a person's life. However, while Polish-Jewish men shaped their masculine performance on the individual level, they did so within predetermined hierarchical systems of power and gender normativity that they did not choose. In the interwar period, various social bodies (governments, political parties, religious groupings, etc.) promoted competing normative masculinities that individual men and male collectives practiced. Jewish men engaged with normative masculinities as they negotiated and performed their individual gender identities.

Polish Jewry produced masculinities more multifarious than simply mimicking hegemonic gentiles, internalizing the antisemitic vision of "Jewish male deformation," or following a "specifically Jewish" form of masculinity.

JEWISH SOCIAL HISTORY AND THE
HISTORY OF MASCULINITY

Interwar Poland was home to the largest European Jewish community of more than 3.3 million. The majority of Polish Jews worked in commerce, crafts, and small industry. Most Polish Jews lived in small- and medium-size towns, but the share of those residing in the five biggest cities (Warsaw, Łódź, Lviv, Kraków, and Vilna) kept growing and in the early 1930s reached about 25 percent of Poland's total Jewish population. These cities were centers of a culturally and economically influential Polish-speaking Jewish middle class. In many towns and cities, Jews made up 30 percent or more of the population and enjoyed high visibility, while the majority of Poland's citizens (60% in 1931) were usually low-income peasants. Ethnic Poles were the dominant ethnic group (69% in 1931); other ethnicities made up the rest of the population (Ukrainians about 14% and Jews about 10% in 1931).[13] While, in the 1930s, the majority of Polish Jews were still Orthodox, this was an Orthodoxy impregnated with influences from modern partisan politics, sports, and popular culture. More and more Jews belonged to the urban working class.[14] The largest group of Jewish shopkeepers and artisans took part in all-Polish social, cultural, and political developments. The army, universities, factories, religious institutions, and political parties were spaces that also resonated with those Jewish men and women who were not their members. Most Jews in interwar Poland were bilingual and fluent in both Yiddish and Polish. The vibrant Jewish press in Yiddish and Polish interconnected Jews across the class and geographic spectrum and encouraged them to engage with political, social, and cultural processes. This complex social landscape produced the diverse Jewish masculinities that I study in this book.

Traditionally, the interwar history of Polish Jews has been told within a political narrative: Polish Jews suffered as a discriminated ethnic minority and developed forms of political representation (Zionism, Bundism, communism, political Orthodoxy) in order to improve their situation, either in Poland or in a new homeland in Palestine. One branch of this historiography has emphasized Jewish vulnerability and powerlessness in the face of antisemitism,[15] while a revisionist stance stresses the political agency and capacity of Polish Jewry as it attempted to shape its collective fate.[16] Following Salo Baron, I assert that politics was only one of many arenas of the social and cultural life of Polish Jews, and we should strive to unearth their everyday lives hidden behind political pamphlets and partisan press.[17] A gendered perspective, in our case adapted specifically to analyzing the lives, experiences, and values of Polish-Jewish men, allows us to access a more complex and nuanced picture of Polish and Polish-Jewish history. A study of the masculinity of Jews and other minority groups challenges the union of power and privilege with masculinity writ large.[18] Focusing on a discriminated ethnic minority in a European country that first struggled for its independence and later embarked on an accelerated modernization project, this book demonstrates how the links between ethnicity and gender were constructed in a place in which masculinities followed many Western patterns but also had their own local specificity.

At the beginning of the twentieth century, when Polish-Jewish lives were transforming in multiple directions, Jewish masculinities experienced a period of diversification as well. As tradition and religion were losing their monopoly over Jewish life in Poland, Jewish men faced a need to reconceptualize who they were and who they aspired to be. Some chose to do this within a political framework, but to offer a full picture, the study of Polish-Jewish social history needs to also trace the experiences of those unaffiliated with political movements. In a time when men's relationships to institutions such as nation, religion, family, and work were changing, and men and women debated transforming or revitalizing masculinity, the meanings of masculinity had become clearly visible. The anti-Jewish violence, economic deterioration, mass migration, secularization, and rise of nationalism and socialism that defined the first half of the twentieth century had a major influence on how masculinities were conceptualized, performed, and criticized in eastern Europe. Particularly, the effects of industrial warfare during the Great War disrupted long-established masculine conventions of intimacy, honor, and manly sacrifice.[19] In this era of change and instability, Polish-Jewish masculinities became differentiated along the lines of age, socioeconomic status, level of religiosity, place of residence, patterns of exchange with non-Jewish surroundings, and the character of familial relations and were influenced by how non-Jews and the state perceived Jewish men. Importantly, masculine desires and ideals did not always directly translate into experiences. The dreams and aspirations of Jewish men often disagreed with the opportunities and social realities available in interwar Poland.

The marginalization that Jewish men experienced in Poland influenced their perception of masculinity. Since being a self-made man and having agency in one's own affairs were then considered major masculine virtues, Jewish men who faced the limitations of antisemitism as they designed their own fates could and did feel marginalized. Antisemitism had a gendered dimension. For example, when sociologist Józef Chałasiński wrote in 1937 that antisemitism in Poland had resulted from a sense of "powerlessness" in the young peasant generation, he was implying that through antisemitic violence, peasant men sought to gain access to a dominant masculine framework from which they were excluded.[20] As Kenneth Moss wrote, Polish-Jewish men struggled to gain the capacity to determine their own fate and often felt "futureless."[21] Jewish socialism, resilient Orthodoxy, and integrationist subculture in Polish cities were influential, but many Jews felt uncertain about their future and disempowered because of the "ramified politics of enmity."[22] I follow Moss in his underscoring of Jewish skepticism concerning the capacity of Jewish politics to influence the fate of Polish Jews and suggest that these doubts translated into increased masculine anxieties. However, instead of assessing the actual scope of agency of Jewish men, I am interested in how and why Jewish men claimed their agency in the street, the circus, the university corridor, and the media and how they discussed the way the limitations of their agency defined them as men. Antisemitism was only one of many factors that influenced the gender identities of Polish-Jewish men. Offering a broad discussion of Polish-Jewish masculinities, this book does not center on antisemitism, although its influence on Jewish masculine self-images emerges in almost every chapter.

The Polish-Jewish case complicates the models in the scholarship that developed from looking only at western Europe and the United States. Historical masculinity scholarship revealed a model of a bourgeois-hegemonic male that developed in nineteenth-century Europe.[23] The bourgeois model defined individual achievement, self-control, and being a master of one's fate as crucial features of modern Western masculinity. Earlier, the masculine ideal had been defined by a narrow elite of noblemen, and only the social changes of the Enlightenment allowed larger groups of men to be included in the process of making masculinity. In the West, as the middle class slowly took over the reins of power, they had to build a nonaristocratic elite.[24] The new elites also emerged in Poland in the second half of the nineteenth century with the appearance of the working middle class, the so-called intelligentsia, heroic soldiers, and new industrial entrepreneurs. As George Mosse argues, from the end of the eighteenth century, "the manly ideal changed very little," and although the transformation accelerated with time, the dominant masculine stereotype experienced only a slow evolution.[25] The bourgeois model suggested that economic power was a male realm and that women should be subjugated to "male rationality"—goals that at the turn of the twentieth century proved difficult to achieve against the backdrop of growing female emancipation and the new social currents sweeping Europe. I argue that the bourgeois model was central for Jewish and non-Jewish men in interwar Poland. Polish-Jewish men followed, fantasized about, discussed, and put into practice the values of bourgeois masculinity, which invites the historian to explore how models established elsewhere translated into a Polish context.

The bourgeois model, which later mutated into the Western model of hegemonic masculinity, took several forms, and the competition among them validated idealized male behaviors.[26] One of these was the self-made businessman who possessed an entrepreneurial spirit and status-granting wealth. In the Polish-Jewish context, this subtype was represented by Łódź textile tycoons who merged technology, capitalism, and charity in their claim to self-made masculine hegemony.[27] As they transformed into modern capitalists, these Jewish men developed both a new vision of self and a vision of conjugal relationships modeled on the Western bourgeois ideal of a gracious housewife without public aspirations. Men who could not access the wealth of the most successful entrepreneurs also followed the logic of diligence and devotion to work and relegated their wives to the domestic sphere. This approach was characteristic, in particular, for the new class of salarymen, but in the 1920s and 1930s, many middle-class feminist "New Jewish women" also defined homemaking as women's primary task.[28] Since European masculinities experienced their major transitions precisely when modern European nationalism was celebrating its advancements, it was in this context that the subtype of heroic masculinity verified on the battlefield developed. The military institutionalized sports as a part of military training, valorized male bonding and camaraderie, and, it was believed, shaped self-confidence, courage, and perseverance. This was when the ideal combining a strong and attractive body and a trained spirit blossomed. At the end of the nineteenth century, the military also democratized in foreign-controlled Polish lands, so more men had access to the army, which became a venue for testing their masculine virtues.

George Mosse has excellently theorized the bourgeois-hegemonic masculine model and its subtypes in the context of the United States. While this model was valid in Poland as well, the country's nonlinear and complex social and political history made it develop differently than in the United States or western Europe. As Wolfgang Schmale noted, in eastern Europe, the model of hegemonic masculinity developed only partially.[29] Poland's static hierarchical social structures impeded men from the lower classes from joining the hegemonic male elite. In partitioned Poland, the *pańszczyzna*, or serfdom of peasants, was gradually abolished only over the course of the nineteenth century.[30] Peasant men, still constituting around 60 percent of Poland's interwar male population, had barely any chances for upward social mobility and consequently inclusion into hegemonic masculinity in the 1920s and 1930s.[31] Peasant masculinities in Poland were to a certain extent similar to marginalized masculinities in the colonial context in which native men were disparaged as effeminate.[32] In both Poland and colonized Africa and Asia, but also in British-controlled Ireland, marginalized men incorporated certain elements of hegemonic masculinity in their resistance to subjugation. In western Europe, villagers and blue-collar workers were included in the unifying model of masculinity. This process was conditioned by the emergence of a centralized nation-state, the militarization of society, and the development of education and literacy, all of which spread the ideas of hegemonic masculinity to broad sections of society. These developments were not the case in eastern Europe, where there were far fewer spaces where the self-made masculine ideal could be achieved. Polish and Polish-Jewish masculinities formed in a way that made the full application of Western frameworks difficult. Nevertheless, men in Poland operated to a great extent within the same masculine ideals as in the West, even when they could hardly be achieved in Poland.

MASCULINITY STUDIES AND JEWISH STUDIES

Although masculinity only recently became a category of analysis in historical scholarship, the first studies of masculinities began a century ago—in the 1930s. The first theories of masculinity were rooted in sociological deterministic theories of gender essentialism and binarity between males and females. The 1930s sex role identity (SRI) theory argued that only one normative form of masculinity existed and that all men accepted it and attempted to conform to it.[33] SRI theory was soon followed by sex role strain (SRS) theory, which gained great popularity in the 1970s and still affirmed the existence of one normative form of masculinity yet stressed that numerous men could not conform to the norm, which increased their vulnerability.[34] The masculinity within this approach was a static construct, either over time or across social or geographical contexts.[35] Newer sociological theories, formed in opposition to SRI and SRS, speak of multiple masculinities that could be chosen and/or combined and that fluidly evolve throughout a person's life. Scholars argued that masculinities, like all gender identities, were multiple and situational.[36] Since the 1980s, the scholarship on masculinity entwined with the scholarship on patriarchy, which is a systemic male supremacy over women.[37]

In the last thirty years, one influential analytical perspective has been Raewyn Connell's constructivist theory of hegemonic masculinity. Hegemonic masculinity defines idealized ways of successfully "being a man" and in doing so defines other masculine models as inferior.[38] Connell's theory also speaks of alternative masculinities constructed and designed to reinforce the dominant masculinity: complicit, subordinate, and marginalized masculinities. Scholars usually define Jewish masculinities as either marginalized or subordinated. While hegemonic masculinity is a central notion in this book, following gender studies scholar Todd Reeser, I choose to see hegemony and subordination as contextual, historically mutable, and fluid, rather than stable.[39] I avoid putting Jewish men in Poland into an impermeable category based on ethnicity and religion. In Poland, many Jewish men practiced gender identities that were not defined by their subordination.[40] Since I am concerned with how Jewish men themselves defined their masculinities and what practices and virtues they considered valid, I am less interested in locating Jewish men within broad systems encompassing the entire society that are always defined by the non-Jewish majority. By the same token, this work is less absorbed with how hegemonic masculinity and male privilege systemically legitimized the patriarchy and the domination of men over women but is instead focused on how unstable, malleable, and breakable the historical workings of masculinity were. Being aware that Jews embracing gentile notions of masculinity might be understood as acquiescing to the desires of non-Jewish hegemonic masculinity, I suggest seeing Jewish men as active and conscious actors rather than objects in a process of negotiating hegemony and marginality. Looking at Jewish men in interwar Poland allows me to focus on men who oscillated between masculine hegemony and the periphery while making choices and forming attitudes defined by local social discourses around masculinity.

Studies from the 1990s established how antisemitic western European cultures defined the Jewish body and mind as "pathological," "deformed," and "inferior." Sander Gilman demonstrated that the representation of a male Jew with a circumcised penis lay at the very heart of Western Jew hatred. Gilman was right when he wrote that "the greater the identification of the Jew with the goals and values of the broader society, the more impacted the Jew is by the power of such images." The situation in western Europe, with its highly acculturated and nonnationalized Jewish population, was starkly different from the one in Poland, with its strong Zionism and Orthodoxy that produced masculinities confident in their Jewishness. Where Gilman and I differ is regarding the scope of Jewish agency in the light of emasculating antisemitism. Following the antisemitism-focused approach to Jewish history, Gilman discusses Jewish capitulation in the face of oppression. He writes that "no one who identifies, either positively or negatively, with the label 'Jew' is immune from the power of such stereotypes. It reflects the relative powerlessness of the Jew in the Diaspora." Gilman assumes a Jewish internationalization of Jewish bodily difference and pathology that "cannot be underestimated."[41] While in dialogue with Gilman, this book suggests an approach that sees Jewish masculinity as not directly informed by antisemitic stereotypes.

The turn of the twenty-first century was a time when scholars intensively studied Jewish masculinities in the context of Zionism.[42] The Zionist paradigm permeated the historical writing on Jews and remains one of the most valid interpretative frameworks. Zionism, like other modern nationalisms, dovetailed with and reinforced masculinity and heterosexuality.[43] Concerning the history of masculinity, the Zionist paradigm implies that only Zionism has healed "deformed" diasporic Jewish masculinities and given a boost to a new ideal of a Jewish man who is confident and strong in mind and body. While the Zionist approach to masculinity can be seen as a case of marginalized men's agency and a creation meant to repudiate European stereotypes of Jewish men as effeminate, it misinforms us about the masculine self-image of Jewish men beyond Zionism. What is problematic about the essentialist Zionist vision of Jewish masculine recuperation is the premise that something was wrong with Jewish men. The premise that Jewish men either had deformed bodies or perceived themselves as inferior, weak, and unmasculine before the arrival of Zionist ideas is at the least very doubtful. The majority of Jewish men in the European diaspora, just like men all over the world, despite the increasing difficulty in maintaining patriarchal masculinity, saw themselves as embracing the masculine norm. The idea of a corrupt Jewish masculinity was a product of Zionist politics and not of a social reality that the majority of Jewish men in eastern Europe experienced. As Matan Bord demonstrated in the context of pre-1948 Mandate Palestine, lived Zionist masculinities were much more ambiguous than those emerging from Zionist pamphlets and literature.[44] Later in the twentieth century, the Zionist paradigm influenced the emergence of postwar masculine models of tough Jewish men that needed the canvas of a weak diaspora Jewish man to gain validity.[45]

A major turning point was Daniel Boyarin's work *Unheroic Conduct*, which recovered a gentle rabbinic model of masculinity and presented it in opposition to the dominant über-masculine Zionist model.[46] Boyarin wrote that "there is something correct—although seriously misvalued—in the persistent European representation of the Jewish man as a sort of woman. More than just an antisemitic stereotype, the Jewish ideal male as countertype to 'manliness' is an assertive historical product of Jewish culture."[47] Boyarin posited that the *eydlkayt* model (gentle, sensitive masculinity centered on noble studiousness) functioned as a form of resistance to the non-Jewish model and that, in the nineteenth century, Jewish men capitulated by culturally submitting to the external pressures of "being as other men." He speaks of these Jewish men as exchanging their fundamental Jewishness in a desire to become modern by mimicking western European Christian men. Boyarin writes of Jewish masculinity being read outwardly as feminized yet still considered masculine within the internal Jewish hierarchies that valued men who were gentle, studious, and timid. Boyarin's theory was highly influential, but scholars also criticized its shortcomings.[48]

Boyarin's ideas, based on Talmudic research and the study of western European men such as Sigmund Freud, in the twenty-eight years that have passed since his *Unheroic Conduct* was published, came to represent not only the masculinities in rabbinic Judaism or Freudian thought but were often extrapolated to a completely different context: Orthodox Jewry of eastern Europe. Boyarin did not study eastern Europe and did not study Orthodox Jewry in the modern era, but the idea that rabbinic sources were central to Orthodox Jewishness in eastern Europe led to the conflation of Boyarin's theory with modern eastern European Jewish masculinities. I value Boyarin's research for the way it empowered eastern European Jewry by emphasizing its own masculine model, but I do not agree that the Orthodox Jewry in eastern Europe in the first half of the twentieth century conceptualized Jewish men as femininized. Jewish men's mindsets and capabilities as men were informed not only by religious sources that might have valued gentleness but also by rich Jewish discourses that were very far from notions of Jewish effeminacy. As I demonstrate in the chapter on the yeshivot, a substantial share of the male Orthodox elite shared masculine concepts popular among non-Jews and defined them as very Jewish.

Within historical studies, there are two new burgeoning subfields related to Jewish masculinities: Holocaust studies and North American Jewish studies. Björn Krondorfer demonstrated how research on the Holocaust and masculinity had been by and large overlooked in works dealing with Jewish masculinities and called for a stronger inclusion of critical masculinity studies in the study of Jewish history and of the Holocaust in particular.[49] I follow Krondorfer's approach calling for scrutiny toward aspects of Jewish history that so far have rarely been studied through the lens of masculinity, often out of fear that the study of gender might overshadow the significance of ethnicity. In North

American Jewish studies, the work of Sarah Imhoff allows us to see Americanization as a gendered process. She demonstrates how American Jewish males championed a masculinity of self-sufficiency, courage, and health and how they attempted to cast Judaism as an "American religion," that is, a religion promoting the values of rationality and universalism.[50] Miriam Eve Mora's work even more centered on Jewish masculine self-image in the United States and how upwardly mobile American Jewish men responded to emasculating stereotypes about Jewish men.[51] I borrow from Mora and Imhoff the idea that Jewish men strove to shape their masculinities along lines characteristic for the non-Jewish majority but offer a corrective proposing that not only in the United States, but already in interwar eastern Europe, Jewish masculinities did not represent particularity but rather overlapped with gentile masculine models.

Cultural and literary studies were much more productive than history was as far as the study of Jewish masculinities is concerned. Works in literary and cultural studies are important for historians too because they open up new theoretical approaches.[52] For example, literary studies discussing masculinity in the context of World War I preceded the emergence of historical works on this topic.[53] Also, literary studies of Zionist masculinities predated most of the historical works. Scholars of Jewish literature followed in the footsteps of Eve Sedgewick, who, in the English context, examined "the structure of men's relationships with other men" and "male social bonds (rivalry, friendship, entitlement, mentorship, and homosexuality)"—problems also central to social history.[54] In a manner similar to Jewish studies, in Polish studies, masculinity first emerged as a research approach in literary and cultural studies.[55] In the last twenty years, the study of Russian masculinities has become an established subfield of eastern European cultural studies, but we are still lacking studies that tell the history of masculinity in Poland, other countries of central and eastern Europe, and their respective ethnic minority cultures.[56] While this book works with nonliterary sources, I enter into discussion with literary scholars concerning masculine ideals and symbols.

SLALOMING IN THE MASCULINE MATRIX:
POLISH-JEWISH MASCULINITY BEYOND
JEWISH EXCEPTIONALISM

Since this work seeks to place Polish-Jewish men and their experiences and positionings in the center, I decenter external, non-Jewish ideas about Jewish masculinity. This book foregrounds Jewish voices and Jewish debates and, in that way, follows scholars who stress a need for better inclusion of the intersectional agency of ethnically marked or otherwise marginalized masculinities.[57] We need to refocus the discussion about Jewish masculinities to include how Jewish men themselves conceptualized, discussed, and performed their masculinities, instead of focusing on what non-Jews had to say about Jewish masculinity. While Polish-Jewish men were aware of a stereotypical vision of the eastern European Jew who was small in stature, weak in physical constitution, and busily engaged with commerce and speculations, the idea of weakness does not appear to have been internalized. I suggest that the Polish-Jewish case testifies to the blurriness of the boundaries between hegemonic and marginalized masculinities that intersected and amalgamated.[58] As Graham Dawson has claimed, "masculine identities are lived out in the flesh but fashioned in the imagination."[59] In this vein, I posit that Jewish masculine fantasies, that is, hopes that for a variety of reasons could not be lived out, are no less important than their experiences, as the two spheres intertwine with, condition, and inspire one another in a perpetual dialogue.

The shift from external images of eastern European masculinity to self-images and practices is not an easy one. Flawed images of eastern European Jewish masculinities have permeated scholarly and popular writing to the extent that they have become homogeneous with Jewish masculinities. Gender representations and images are powerful and influence how gender identities are discussed, performed, and criticized. Todd Reeser noted correctly that "images can be turned into myths when they become so widespread that culture takes them for granted as a narrative of masculinity. When such images are so widespread, they are taken as universal, and, on a cultural level, come to appear as mythological."[60] This idea about the power of images is also true concerning eastern European Jewish masculinities, in particular concerning features that presumably distinguish them from non-Jewish masculinities. In this respect, I suggest that findings on effeminate Jewish masculinity from other cultural contexts (particularly Germany) and time frames should not be applied freely to interwar Poland. We need a discussion of masculine discourses, practices, and representations in Poland based on the local sources.

A major argument of this book is that Polish-Jewish men considered their masculinities normative, both when they followed the Orthodox masculine model and when they aspired to be included in local non-Jewish notions of hegemony. Like any other men around the world, Jewish men in early twentieth-century Poland strove to imagine themselves as following masculine norms that were specific to a given time and space and did not render themselves passive victims of the local hegemonic masculinity. They slalomed within a masculine spectrum and cumulatively constructed their masculinities by borrowing concepts and practices from several parallel masculine models.[61] In the context of Polish-Jewish masculinities, it means that men chose from elements characteristic of non-Jewish hegemonic masculinities (that is, idealized and recognized ways of being a successful man) and earlier dominant Jewish Orthodox masculinities (that is, strictly adhering to Talmudic and rabbinical traditions of learnedness) to build their own gender identities through a process of selection, appropriation, and borrowing influenced by local Jewish and non-Jewish discourses, mindsets,

and gendered practices. Jewish men elaborating their masculinities balanced between diverse normative masculinities that were,
however, often centered around shared core masculine features,
such as domination, providing, protecting, and respectability.

I suggest that at the beginning of the twentieth century, many
Polish-Jewish men aspired to the hegemonic bourgeois masculinity that they associated with power and privilege. In the modern
era, as Krondorfer notes, "traditional religious models went out of
fashion among other reasons because respect, power and authority were increasingly found in the secular realm rather than in the
ecclesiastic context." This process made Jewish and non-Jewish
masculinities more related.[62] For many Jewish men, the dream
of rising to the middle class and the professional transformation
it entailed was strongly linked with adhering to a bourgeois masculinity model. The new Jewish middle class aspired to be on an
equal footing with the gentile middle class. By adapting the practices and values of the possessors of the masculine hegemony,
they redefined Jewish notions of gender to resemble non-Jewish
ones. For example, while bourgeois men in the West linked wom-
en's professional activities with immorality, the Jewish maskilic
ideal also criticized women's control of the domestic economy.[63]
Also the Jewish left, despite a proclaimed pro-equality policy, de
facto worked to maintain traditional gender roles and thus also
male domination over women.[64] Whereas Jewish historical scholarship has been dominated by a tendency to see Jews and their
history as self-contained, I argue that Polish and Polish-Jewish
history formed a matrix of entanglements and their fabrics were
interwoven, including in terms of gender. As Moshe Rosman put
it, Jews were *of* Poland and not merely *in* Poland, and they were
consequently linked to the social and cultural processes in the
country.[65]

Even though Polish nationalist discourses often excluded Jews
and did not consider them members of the national community,
this does not mean that Polish-Jewish masculinities were shaped

primarily in the context of this rejection. For example, in a time when employment and economic self-sufficiency were hard to achieve in Poland and made the idea of being the master of one's fate illusive, some young Jewish men sought to follow the hegemony-granting and all-Polish model of the heroic soldier or powerful sportsman. Instead of internalizing the Jewish difference, these men built masculine identities that had the potential to move them closer to the all-Polish hegemony. Scholars have devoted much research to the study of antisemitism in Poland but have paid less attention to how Jews resisted it and, all the more so, how antisemitism and resistance to it had their gendered dimensions. I suggest that the rejection from the hegemony on the part of the non-Jewish majority did not translate into a recognition of one's masculine inferiority. Conversely, for many acculturated Jewish men, it translated into ever-stronger attempts to embrace practices and values valid in general society. The examples of Jewish fraternity members who aspired to belong to the male elite of Poland, militarized Revisionist Zionist youth groups, or Jewish soldiers in the Polish military who followed heroic masculinity are evidence that the exclusion they experienced did not result in an internalization of inferiority.

In interwar Poland, due to the size and level of sociocultural autonomy of an almost-three-and-a-half-million-strong Polish Jewry, Jewish masculinities could be negotiated in an inner-Jewish context. In many towns in Poland, Orthodox Jews constituted the majority, and the constant comparisons with non-Jews had a weaker significance for the formation of gender identities. Jewish men in Poland could exercise some degree of hegemony within Jewish society. This aspect was underscored by Maddy Carey and Björn Krondorfer concerning the Shoah but is even more true for the less oppressive time before the Holocaust.[66] I refer here in particular to patriarchal Jewish male authority over women and young people. For Orthodox Jewish masculinity, it was the religious realm, and not the army, politics, or other areas of life identified as masculine outside of traditional Jewish culture, that was a space for performing masculinity. This is how the ideal of the *talmid khokhem* (Torah scholar) emerged, and the yeshiva became a shelter in which the masculine ideal of a religious scholar was constructed.[67] My sources from interwar Poland demonstrate that the modernity altered masculinity of Jewish men in Poland, although it was not a radical rupture with earlier Jewish cultural and gender traditions. While some Orthodox men broke with religion, many others searched for ways of combining it with elements of the hegemonic non-Jewish model.[68] The situation of Orthodox Jewish men in Poland was very different from what Jewish men experienced in western European cities. In the German context, as Sander Gilman explained, "Jews attempted to cope with their marginalization by making their Jewishness invisible to others and sometimes even to themselves. The Jew had but little choice: . . . in his physical being, [he] must try, on one level or another, to become invisible. . . . For visibility brings with it a true risk."[69] In Poland, for many (in particular Orthodox) Jewish men, the "Jewish difference" was not immediately marginalizing or emasculating because they experienced it differently than did acculturated Jewish men in the West. Because, to a certain extent, Jewish men confident in their Jewishness determined what a masculine norm was, underscoring their ethnic and religious difference was not automatically considered humiliating.

While this book does not center on women, it argues that women were central in defining masculinity, particularly concerning men's lives at home. Constructing codes of masculinity also meant constructing a gender boundary. For example, young men who studied in the yeshivot went through apprenticeships into an elite Jewish masculinity that defined their privilege over women. In the mid-nineteenth century, the idea of Jewish men being anxious and vulnerable and women being strong and sexually potent dominated maskilic minds.[70] In the interwar period, the separation of work and home that governed the daily lives of

Jewish salarymen and merchants was central to the perceived "inadequacy" of Jewish men and women in Poland. While I demonstrate how moldable and fluid masculinity was, this book also makes it clear how masculinity was linked with power: men's power over women, the power of older over younger men, and the power of heterosexual over homosexual men.[71] Male power in the Jewish context was modified by Jews' social marginalization, yet, as numerous case studies in the book reveal, the patriarchy permeated Jewish private and public life in a way no different from the non-Jewish context. Through their perpetual referencing of hegemonic masculinity, the marginalized masculinities of Jewish men in Poland helped stabilize male hegemony within the Jewish realm.

BOOK STRUCTURE

The time period under study begins in the 1890s and ends with the Holocaust, which serves as the final caesura of this era of Polish-Jewish history. Whereas the first chapter dealing with yeshiva masculinity explores the decades between the 1890s and 1910s, all other chapters center on the interwar years. The first chapter introduces the religious Orthodox context that dominated at the turn of the century. Later, other identifications considerably challenged Orthodoxy but Orthodox values also permeated the gender identities of many Polish-Jewish men in the 1920s and 1930s, and I make it visible through all the chapters. Geographically, this project looks at areas that between 1918 and 1939 belonged to Poland and before 1918 to the respective partitioning empires. Speaking of Polish Jews, I refer to Jews who inhabited historically Polish lands and became Polish citizens after 1918. I use a variety of historical sources: personal memoirs, advice books, military reports, political pamphlets, works of Jewish scholarship engaged with questions of gender, and literary depictions of masculinity, as well as the Jewish and non-Jewish press. The diversity of source material allows for a complex reconstruction of the social and cultural reality in which Polish-Jewish men lived, but it also makes the research difficult. As Elissa Mailänder noted, it is a challenge to simultaneously investigate masculinities and femininities within and between classes, ethnic groups, and sexual orientations.[72] Also, researching masculine continuities in times of relative peace is more demanding than examining moments of crisis. Sources are relatively silent about continued, uninterrupted processes.[73] Following gender historian Merry Wiesner-Hanks, I use my sources not only as an account of discourses on masculinity, but I see behind the text real men with experiences, desires, agencies, feelings, mindsets, and bodies.[74] Many of the sources I use have already been explored by Jewish history scholars, but I look at them differently. Because we rarely find sources that explicitly speak about masculinity and because Jewish men often blurred the gendered character of their writing, I needed to read between the lines and extract masculinity from narratives that had previously been explored in different contexts. The chapters in this work focus on central areas of male experience in the early twentieth century: breadwinning and consumption, the military, male sociability, and the body and sexuality. While this book includes male experiences from a wide spectrum of Jewish classes and cultures, there are swaths of Jewish social history and the history of masculinities in Poland, such as fatherhood, that are beyond the scope of this book and still wait for their historians.

Chapter 1, "Yeshiva Men: Elite Religious Knowledge and Intellectual Potency," investigates the process of constructing, channeling, and taming yeshiva masculinity at the turn of the twentieth century. I demonstrate that the yeshiva was an institution central to shaping an elite Orthodox masculinity in eastern Europe. After introducing the yeshiva landscape, this chapter discusses education in yeshivot as a mechanism for claiming masculine respectability, yeshiva authorities' engagement in taming

and controlling masculinity, and the intricacies of male bonding and intimacy that defined vulnerability, mutual confidence,
and emotional care as central to the yeshiva experience. Drawing
on memoirs of men who studied in these institutions in their
teens and early twenties, this chapter enters into a discussion
with scholars of Orthodox Jewish masculinity. In particular, I reevaluate Daniel Boyarin's arguments concerning the masculinity
of Jewish Orthodox men in eastern Europe as radically divergent
from gentile notions of masculinity. Yeshiva masculinities, I argue, were to an extent conjoined with non-Jewish masculinities,
rather than essentially distinct.

Chapter 2, "A Jew and His Penis: Circumcision and the Entanglements of Jewishness and Masculinity," examines the
meanings of circumcision and a circumcised penis in the social
and cultural world of interwar Poland. Unlike studies following
the Freudian interpretation that see circumcision as a practice
symbolically emasculating Jewish men and producing a sense
of inferiority, this chapter suggests that, in Poland, circumcision
provided Jewish men with a sense of greater normative masculinity. As exemplified by stories of men who were circumcised
as adults or teenagers, for most Jewish men in Poland, being
uncircumcised—and not the reverse—resulted in a sense of inferiority. Next, I portray the opposition to circumcision from the
side of Jewish freethinkers and Socialists who defined the act
of refusal to circumcise as a sign of masculine consistency and
personal freedom. Finally, I look at how Polish antisemites applied the anticircumcision rhetoric, linking it with brutality and
Jewish "barbarity" but at the same time fearing that a growing
number of uncircumcised Jewish men would make the once ob-
vious distinction between a Jew and a Christian imperceptible.

Chapter 3, "Boys Showing Off: The Working Class, Strongmen, and Corporeality," analyzes the figures of strongman Zisha
Breitbart (1883–1925) and boxer Shapsel Rotholc (1913–1996) in
the context of Jewish working-class masculinity and traces how

their followers discussed, challenged, or rejected Jewish masculinities centered around physical power. This chapter starts with a short overview of the link among Jewishness, masculinity, and corporeality in Europe in general and interwar Poland in particular. Next, I analyze Breitbart's career as a strongman and athlete in the 1920s as well as Rotholc's boxing career in the 1930s. Breitbart and Rotholc exemplify how performances and social modeling of physical strength and fitness became central to defining Jewish masculinities in interwar Poland. This chapter argues that Polish-Jewish men of the working class rarely conceived of themselves as "weaklings" in need of transformation and explores how they perceived bodily fitness as compatible with Jewishness. In Poland, the model of a powerful and defense-ready Jewish man proved to be particularly attractive in the context of the interethnic conflict and antisemitism. Bodily strength was intended to protect Jewish men and their communities and prove to Jews and non-Jews alike that Jewish men were not weaklings.

Chapter 4, "Tender Bonds of Fraternal Affection: Student Fraternities, Homosocial Sociability, and Jewish Respectability," examines all-male Jewish fraternities at Jagiellonian University in Kraków between the 1920s and 1930s. I start by providing a short history of Jewish fraternities at Polish universities and later analyze how fraternities established a system of tutelage to make normative Polish men out of their members and instill the masculine values of obedience and discipline. The study of fraternities reveals how, for many Polish-Jewish men, their fraternity was a venue for raising a claim to masculine respectability equal to that of their gentile fellow students. Next, I look at homosocial sociability within these fraternities, what Kraków's Bar Kochba fraternity described as "brotherly bonding." The last section offers a closer look at how Polish-Catholic men sought to exclude Jewish men from venues and mechanisms that confirmed privileged masculinities. The case of the Jewish fraternities in

Kraków demonstrates how masculine gender orders included both the agency of marginalized groups and the power of dominant groups.

Chapter 5, "Pulling the Trigger: The Military and Jewish Masculinities," explores the involvement of Polish-Jewish men in the Polish military in World War I and the following two decades. First, I discuss the case studies of Władysław Steinhaus (1896–1915), who served in the Polish Legions, and Yankev Kahan (1900–1973), who served in the Polish army in the early 1920s, to demonstrate how some Jewish men found meaning in military service and understood that it helped them validate their claim to masculine hegemony. Later, I explore how both military and antisemitic press discourses emasculated Jewish men by questioning their military fitness. The last part analyzes Jewish war veterans in interwar Poland and their efforts to claim access to respectability and masculine hegemony as related to mythologizing the military. Overall, this chapter sheds light on the workings of gender in the shadow of interethnic relations in the army and shows how notions of violence, sexuality, suffering, disability, and class evolved into complex Jewish military masculinities. The chapter suggests that even some Orthodox Jews embraced military discipline, male bonding, and homogenization, and their Jewishness expanded to include virtues of heroic military masculinity.

Chapter 6, "Leisure and Toil: Masculinity in Profession, Family, and Consumer Culture," analyzes Jewish media outlets in Yiddish and Polish to trace how consumption (cars, cosmetics, clothing) defined middle-class masculinity and explores heated debates about gender roles at the intersection of homemaking and career. The emancipation of women, the experience of World War I that undermined traditional notions of masculinity (such as heroism and bravery), and the economic crisis that crushed the idea of the man as breadwinner all made Jewish and non-Jewish men anxious about their status. However, wealth, self-made success, and business achievement remained valid markers of masculinity in interwar Poland, while men were called to embrace consumerist values as well. The chapter demonstrates how Jewish men defined themselves anew through consuming services or possessing goods and how they engaged in the general evolution of Polish masculinity in the 1920s and 1930s in the realm of consumption. It also shows how the traditional ideal of the man as the provider was increasingly criticized as inadequate and at odds with the needs of a modern Jewish woman who searched for a tender lover and understanding partner.

Chapter 7, "Homosexual Masculinities: Between Crime, Progressive Calls, and Homophobic Subversion," looks at Jewish masculinities beyond heteronormativity. In the 1920s and 1930s, Polish-Jewish self-declared homosexual subjectivities appeared for the first time. Adolescent Józef Halpern from Lviv, the young painter Józef Rajnfeld from Warsaw, and the much older Łódź manager Leon Waks conceptualized their homosexual desire as a major aspect of their gender identities. Following an overview of Jewish expert discussions on homosexuality in Poland, I explore how Polish-Jewish debates placed homosexual men within a semantic realm of deviation and crime and how the male homosexual was defined as a sexual predator threatening normative heterosexual masculinity through seduction. Then, I offer a close reading of Józef Halpern's memoir and demonstrate how the changing notions of male friendship created opportunities for men attracted to men and how nascent homosexual subjectivities began to emerge in 1920s Poland. In the final section, I show how Polish-Jewish men employed homophobic discourses about Muslims and German Nazis to stabilize their fragile heteronormative masculinities. Taken as a whole, this chapter demonstrates that local medical and legal discourses surrounding homosexuality informed and regulated Jewish homosexual masculinities in interwar Poland. Unlike in Germany, within the Polish-Jewish debates, homosexuality and Jewishness rarely appear to be mutually constitutive.

ONE

YESHIVA MEN

Elite Religious Knowledge and Intellectual Potency

IN 1895, A FUTURE GREAT Jewish historian, Ben-Zion Dinur, and his deaf and mute friend, Eli, departed to a yeshiva in the city of Homel. Eli not only followed his friend to realize his dream of studying in a remote yeshiva but took on a role as an intimate friend and protector. Despite his disabilities, Eli was a *gvartan,* that is, a tough, muscular guy. The union between the two teenagers culminated when Eli showed Ben-Zion one finger on each of his hands and connected them, signaling the intimate connection that linked them. During the half year they spent together in Homel, Eli protected his friend from those who wanted to question Ben-Zion's position in the yeshiva. Other students called Eli a gabbai, or a warden, of Ben-Zion, and allegedly some of them attempted to cut the link between the two boys. When they finally managed to convince Eli to reduce his ties with his friend, it was a major source of anguish and distress for Ben-Zion. The intimacy between the two boys was also challenged by Eli's mother, who accused Ben-Zion of "seducing" her son and "neglecting him" in the yeshiva.[1]

The story of Ben-Zion Dinur elucidates the intersection of Jewishness, friendship, and masculinity in the context of an eastern European yeshiva. The last two decades of the nineteenth century and the first decade of the twentieth century saw the flourishing of the major Litvak yeshivot (Jewish religious academies focusing on the study of the Talmud) like the ones in Volozhin, Slobodka, Telz, and Mir.[2] This chapter examines the process of constructing and performing yeshiva masculinity at the turn of the twentieth century. I rely on memoirs of men who studied in Litvak yeshivot in their teenage years and early twenties and reconstruct masculine ideals, values, and practices in the yeshivot. I suggest that we need to rethink Orthodox Jewish masculinity in a way that looks at how its core values conjoined with gentile masculinities, rather than focusing exclusively on how Jewish and non-Jewish men differed. I argue that yeshiva masculinity encompassed some mechanisms analogous to Western hegemonic masculinity: the desire for power and influence, an achievement-based sense of being a master of one's destiny, and a quest for empowering masculine intimacy. To that end, this chapter suggests that eastern European Orthodox yeshiva masculinity, rather than being exceptional, celebrated several masculine ideals and ideas that both Jewish and non-Jewish cultures produced and perpetuated.

I enter into discussion with scholars who have studied historical Orthodox Jewish masculinities. In particular, I seek to reevaluate Daniel Boyarin's arguments concerning the masculinity of Orthodox men in eastern Europe.[3] Boyarin suggests that eastern European Jewish culture developed and valorized *eydlkayt* as a gentle and receptive masculine countermodel to non-Jewish masculinity. Boyarin assumes that sensitiveness was the shared and recognized virtue of Orthodox Jewish men, which he sees as opposing the aggressive, warrior-like gentile masculinity. I, however, argue that men in the Orthodox world of the yeshiva to a great extent shared values similar to homosocial spaces in which non-Jews and acculturating Jews acted as men.[4] Yeshivot, exactly like the army or a university fraternity, defined knowledge, skillfulness, and respectability, rather than the gentleness or receptiveness emphasized by Boyarin, as core masculine qualities. The yeshiva sources reveal a complex reality in which yeshiva men engaged in power struggles, at times violent, and suggest that gentleness was not a celebrated masculine virtue. In his study, Boyarin relied on textual rabbinic sources, but to explore the lacunae of knowledge concerning masculinity in yeshivot at the turn of the twentieth century, we need to look at young Jewish men's perspectives and not only at the ideal and textually normative yeshiva masculinity mediated through religious texts. Only by hearing the voices of yeshiva students can we learn about their subjectivities as men who reflected on and performed their yeshiva masculinities.

The yeshiva microcosm allows us to study Jewish Orthodox gender models in a particularly exclusive Jewish setting. While the world of the yeshiva was not resistant to external influence and was indeed rather porous, its relative Jewish monoculturalism allows us to study Jewish men in a context in which we can hardly speak of a Jewish mimicry of Christian masculine models. Because yeshiva education did not offer major advantages in the Christian world, the men who enrolled into yeshivot chose inner-Jewish mechanisms of constructing elite masculinity. This chapter relies on a selection of about twenty autobiographies and memoirs written by men who studied in the Litvak yeshivot between the 1890s and 1900s. In those years, many Jewish "men [still] swam with the stream" and continued the traditional path of Talmud study.[5] However, autobiographies by men who experienced yeshivot at the turn of the twentieth century were the almost-exclusive domain of those who broke with religion or whose faith transformed beyond Orthodoxy.[6] I borrow from autobiography scholarship the central idea that autobiography directs attention to the dynamics of the process of the crystallization of the self. I do not delve into genre specifics but use the selection of yeshiva autobiographies as a fabric from which I extract aspects related to gender roles and reconstruct the spectrum of yeshiva masculinities.

Figure 1.1. A group of Jewish men in front of the Lublin yeshiva, 1930s, author Abram Zylberberg (?). Photo from the collection of Grodzka Gate-NN Theater Center, Lublin, Poland.

In the following sections, I start by exploring how the yeshiva sought to tame undesired forms of masculinity and channel virtues and behaviors that were believed to be proper. Then I move to elaborating on my central premise suggesting the analogies between yeshiva masculinity and other Western forms of establishing elite masculinity. I analyze the notion of respectability—a key masculine virtue both inside and outside the Jewish religious environment. In the next section, I focus on the importance of knowledge and knowledge competition for establishing masculine power and authority hierarchies. Later on, I explore the meaning of corporeality in yeshivot and suggest that the body was, next to knowledge, a central gender framework that operated within yeshivot. The last section speaks of the meaning of male intimacy and friendship for forming yeshiva masculinities. I argue that friendships offered young men the emotional support they needed in a competitive institution and provided models of being a man.

THE YESHIVA SYSTEM AND TAMING AND CHANNELING MASCULINITY

At the turn of the twentieth century, men studied in yeshivot from their mid- and late teens until the age of about twenty-five, while some were older than that. Most of the yeshivot in that era existed in areas dominated by the mitnagdim tradition, that is, in contemporary Lithuania and Belarus.[7] However, the student body of these yeshivot was geographically diverse and included not only locals but also young men from the Polish lands further west, such as Warsaw and Lublin. Since the Middle Ages, eastern European yeshivot were supported by local Jewish communities. Following the catastrophic pogroms during the Khmelnitsky uprising in the mid-seventeenth century, Jewish communities were increasingly unable to support institutions of higher learning, and many communal yeshivot began to disappear throughout the eighteenth century. The development of the Hasidic movement, which challenged the Litvak tradition of learning, in the eighteenth century exacerbated the crisis of the yeshiva. Hasidism depreciated Talmud study, and consequently, the high status of Talmud scholars diminished and Hasidism could more easily draw young men into its ranks.[8] In the context of this yeshiva crisis, in 1803 Rabbi Hayyim of Volozhin, fearing that the chain of Talmud learning would be broken, founded the prestigious Volozhin yeshiva.[9]

Young men who studied in the yeshivot represented a small fraction of the entire young Jewish male populace in eastern Europe. In the late nineteenth century, most Jewish boys attended only the *heder*, or primary Jewish educational institution. There, they acquired technical literacy in Hebrew, which was not usually accompanied by any meaningful comprehension of the content studied. Most adolescent youths across Jewish eastern Europe studied not in yeshivot but in *batey midrash*, or communal study halls.[10] While only young men studied in yeshivot, batey midrash were frequented by regular townsfolk who turned the building into a synagogue during the prayers.[11] The key innovation of the nineteenth-century yeshiva was the subordination of students to the *rosh yeshiva*, or yeshiva headmaster, which was not the case in batey midrash.[12] In the course of the nineteenth century, the yeshiva landscape experienced diversification. Since the mid-nineteenth century, yeshivot needed to come to terms with the maskilic influences from outside and from within.[13] At the end of the nineteenth century, new political ideologies of socialism and Zionism not only diminished the human capital base of the yeshivot but also transformed yeshivot into centers of Zionist and Socialist agitation.[14] Next to the Litvak yeshivot, interwar eastern Europe experienced the rise of numerous Hasidic yeshivot, which had previously been quite uncommon. In traditionally more Hasidic Galicia and Congress Poland, several Hasidic yeshivot appeared even before World War I, yet it was the transforming experience of the war that led to the establishment of yeshivot linked to Hasidic courts.[15] In the mid-1930s, about twenty thousand young men attended yeshivot in Poland, about ten thousand less than the number of Jewish men enrolled in secular secondary schools.[16]

The yeshiva constructed and maintained Jewish men's patriarchal domination over women. Since the yeshiva was the stage for moving a young man from the familial space into the space of public engagement, such as assuming a rabbinical position, this encourages us to refer also to non-Jewish mechanisms for men to enter the public sphere. The yeshiva as a school of public engagement would then be a classic example of the separate spheres theory, which well into the twentieth century defined home and family as a feminine realm and the public world outside the home as a masculine realm.[17] Just like gentile masculinities, Jewish Orthodox masculinity also contributed to maintaining the patriarchy. It was the young man, and not his sister, who was encouraged to study and succeed in the public realm. The yeshiva offered him a social standing unavailable to most women, and it was the yeshiva that upheld the exclusion of women from access to sources and institutions of Jewish knowledge. Yeshiva-educated men linked power and knowledge, and they exerted control over those outside the elite and marginalized both women and men who did not have access to yeshiva training.[18] Yeshiva studies offered its alumni a limited access to masculine hegemony, which they exercised within the Orthodox world.

The yeshiva at the end of the nineteenth century was a space of masculine geographic and cultural mobility.[19] As the life paths of many men examined in this chapter demonstrate, yeshiva students often traveled hundreds of kilometers, switched their yeshivot, and later in life developed diasporic connections with fellow yeshiva graduates. Mobility also meant leaving the yeshiva for positions outside the religious setting. Many excellent students used the yeshiva as a trampoline for launching their careers beyond Orthodox Jewry, and many were able to combine both worlds relatively smoothly. Some interrupted their yeshiva studies to attend Russian gymnasiums but later often returned to the yeshiva.[20] Since yeshivot at the turn of the twentieth century were shaped as much by modern Jewish politics as they were by traditional Talmud learning, the male networks established there accompanied yeshiva graduates through their lives as politicians, journalists, scientists, and religious leaders. The mobility was less visible concerning the entry criteria—many yeshiva students came from well-to-do Orthodox families who could cofinance their education, and the yeshiva perpetuated, rather than restructured, existing Jewish social hierarchies.

Like other homosocial spaces, the yeshiva was a space where male gender identities were constantly controlled and channeled. The yeshiva was similar to a boarding school, with rosh yeshiva and mashgiach (yeshiva supervisor) adopting the positions of educator and controller. For instance, Leyb Hasman, a mashgiach from the Telz yeshiva, believed that young men were similar to young and fragile trees that could be formed and molded.[21] In many yeshivot, the public and private behavior as well as the reading practices of yeshiva students were under surveillance, as was the rest of their free time and their bodies. The leadership of the yeshiva sought to tame behaviors that did not correspond with the desired yeshiva masculinity. Rav Zalman Isser Meltzer of Slutsk believed that outside of the yeshiva, young men could be exposed to what he saw as "bad culture."[22] Young men were punished when they engaged in relationships with women, and expulsion from the yeshiva was linked to public shaming and exclusion from the Orthodox Jewish world. In Volozhin, rosh yeshiva established a spy group to "check up on the virtues of every yeshiva student."[23] In Mir, the mashgiach used to look through the private possessions of the students in their lodgings.[24] This control was often executed by means of psychological and physical violence. In the Volozhin yeshiva, discipline was maintained by rescinding honors such as being called to the Torah, then by reducing the student's allowance, then by a slap, and finally by expulsion. Between 1890s and 1900s, in many yeshivot, young men received a slap in the face for shaving or removing sidelocks.[25]

The system of yeshiva punishments was intended to exclude those who were rebellious from the tight-knit community of yeshiva men. In Slobodka, students were encouraged to watch each other, and Moshe Reguer felt "constantly followed, with people checking out everything I did and everywhere I went."[26] Reguer recalls that the authorities' suspicion of him placed him on the margins of the yeshiva community, which caused his depression. Unlike other young men, Reguer was forced to wear torn and patched clothing, and his food was poor and meager, "not given with the same generosity with which it was given to the others." Reguer felt an excruciating sense of exclusion, and particularly painful for him was the separation from other yeshiva students: "a pain of an innocent man who has fallen into a pit and cannot defend himself." The exclusion was a public and repeatedly performed act of humiliation and consequently a permanent process of emasculation by the yeshiva heads. The rosh yeshiva violently ruined Reguer's friendship with a promising student: "They used every means to cut the thread of friendship that was beginning to weave us together." Reguer's masculine pride did not allow him to bow his head, since "it would be a matter of spiritual defiance."[27] Reguer's narrative testifies to how *rashey yeshivot* employed discipline and punishment to design behaviors that they considered normative for yeshiva men and how some young men reacted to humiliation with resilience and contestation.

At times, yeshiva students attempted to challenge the authority of rashey yeshivot in what yeshiva memoirists describe as "rebellions."[28] When a Volozhin student named Yeshayahu was hit for cutting his sidelocks, all other students canceled their studies and out of comradely solidarity debated how to react to the offense. They perceived the slaps received by Yeshayahu as something collectively experienced by all yeshiva students.[29] Fellow students decided to make their uprising public, and they made sure it was seen and heard in the entire town. They smashed tables, broke windows and benches, and spilled liquids on the floor. Ultimately, the students were able to force the rosh yeshiva to apologize in front of Yeshayahu and thus restore his honor.[30] Usually, the rebellions or riots were linked to introducing innovations in yeshivot, particularly in the tense time before the 1905 revolution, and led to numerous disruptions in yeshivot in Slobodka, Telz, and Mir.[31] The case of Yeshayahu demonstrates that not only politics and personal conflicts led to the riots but also cases where the respectability of yeshiva youths was threatened. This example illustrates that yeshiva men shared the concept of masculine honor that developed in post-Enlightenment Europe. Offending a member of a male elite group led to expressions of solidarity that aimed to restore the man's injured reputation.

THE YESHIVA AND THE INTRICACIES OF
MASCULINE RESPECTABILITY

For many young Jewish men, the yeshiva was a space providing them with status as members of the masculine elite. The yeshiva was a place where respectability, a core masculine virtue in the modern world, was transformed into a masculine Jewish virtue. A young man who entered the yeshiva could undergo a "respectable transformation," that is, turn into a man respected not for his religiosity but for his scholarly talents and financial autonomy. The Volozhin yeshiva and other yeshivot that began to grant their students regular stipends that helped young Jewish men gain financial self-sufficiency. Meir Bar-Ilan, who studied in the Volozhin yeshiva, recalled, "In Volozhin, a poor boy who felt humiliated because of his situation in the desolate home or a forlorn *beit midrash* could straighten up his back and increase his self-respect." He was "his own lord" (*adon le-atsmo*), or master of his fate, one of the central ideals of Western hegemonic masculinity.[32] Bar-Ilan's words demonstrate that the yeshiva was not a direct extension of the shtetl and its Jewish institutions. It was a transformative space where young Jews could develop and flourish as respected men.

For some young men, just like a gymnasium or university education outside of their hometown, yeshiva studies were linked to gaining independence. Being autonomous and in the subject position appeared in many cultures as a core masculine value projected against feminine dependency.[33] Entering the yeshiva was a rite of passage that included a sense of breaking with the past: a process when a young man becomes a part of the community outside his family.[34] Some yeshiva students remembered traveling to the yeshiva as a rite of passage from dependency into masculine autonomy. It was often their first train trip alone, without accompanying family members, a first-time feeling of having their lives in their own hands.[35] Ben-Zion Dinur felt independent when he traveled alone to the Rakhov yeshiva dressed in a new kapoteh (a Jewish coat) and smoking cigarettes with a golden filter. Earlier Dinur had run away from his home to a yeshiva in Homel: "I wanted to run away from the guardianship of the family, of numerous uncles and cousins. From their opinions and questions."[36] In contrast to the situation among eastern European peasants, Jewish siblings did not usually compete with each other for limited resources (such as land), which would be crucial for their future success. Upward (and downward) mobility among Jews was seen as the result of individual merit and effort.[37] The yeshiva appears thus as a place of transformation into an independent Jewish man—a figure similar to the Western ideal of a self-made man who determined his masculinity through personal achievement.

In the Slobodka yeshiva, its leaders instilled in yeshiva youths a sense of collective pride. This mechanism allowed young men to imagine themselves as members of a superior and exclusive elite and at the same time promoted intragroup solidarity. The principle of *gdolat ha-adam* (man's betterment) stipulated that self-respect and respect for fellow yeshiva students were interrelated. Yeshiva students assisted each other when sick and established support funds for the needy, and for many yeshiva students, those bonds of comradely solidarity and unity were the strongest they had ever experienced in their lives.[38] While eastern European Jewish culture generally praised charitable giving, the practice of mutual help between young males had an additional meaning. The principle "all for one and one for all," which was valid in the yeshivot, is another example of elite masculine virtues that were shared by both the non-Jewish society and the yeshiva microcosm. Similar to members of university fraternities or army comrades, yeshiva students believed that this mutual support would have gender-specific benefits and define them as members of a solidary masculine elite. This attitude developed within the quintessentially Jewish musar movement and was not imported from the surrounding societies. This Jewish-origin logic of elite male solidarity puts into question arguments proposing enforced Jewish mimicry of gentile practices.

In the yeshiva world, as in the army and university fraternity, masculinity centered on shaping desired features and eliminating problematic ones. Self-containment and emotional control were common parameters for measuring one's masculine performance. The control of one's mind and body were closely linked to the idea of (self-)sacrifice. While, in the gentile context of Poland, sacrificing one's health or life for the homeland was the top achievement of heroic masculinity (for instance, during the Polish national rebellions), yeshiva men had analogous practices of self-sacrifice for a "greater good."[39] Moshe Reguer, who spent freezing nights learning Gemarah, felt the "indescribable feeling" of someone "who sacrificed himself on the altar of Torah."[40] Musar ethics advised restricting moments of enjoyment by defining them as improper—a process similar to the Western masculine virtue of self-control.[41] The rhetoric of sacrifice also appears in the account of Menachem Zlotkin, who compared the yeshiva to a monastery: "His situation [as a yeshiva student] was similar to the situation of a monk who, in order to devote himself to godly work in the companion of other monks, has distanced himself from social life and resigned from all pleasures in life."[42] In that sense, discipline, submission to authority, and distance from personal benefit appeared as core yeshiva values. We notice that, while Jews and gentiles might have had different mechanisms for shaping young men's character, the broader logic was very similar.

One of the central mechanisms for increasing the respectability of yeshiva students was their financial independence. For generations, yeshiva youths put themselves in the ranks of the lower class by eating at the tables of the wealthy during their studies. While acting poor might have seemed reasonable at one time, by the turn of the twentieth century, eating like beggars was increasingly linked to shame. The introduction of regular yeshiva stipends, and later dormitories and cafeterias, was to strengthen the self-esteem of yeshiva students.[43] Many students at the prestigious Volozhin yeshiva received regular pay slips that increased their confidence as men who could support their studies without resorting to charity.[44] The issue of yeshiva students' financial independence elucidates the transformation of traditional Jewish mechanisms of achieving respectability. At the turn of the twentieth century, being a studious young man was not enough to grant one the desired respectability. Studiousness needed to be linked with financial independence to produce a respectable Orthodox man. The yeshiva reformers noticed this challenge, and the most renowned yeshivot took care to provide young men with the financial means to feel respected. The stipend system proliferated in the Hasidic and Litvak yeshivas of interwar Poland.[45]

According to Efraim Moszwicki, at the beginning of the 1890s, a yeshiva student preferred to be called a *yeshiva man* instead of a *yeshiva bukher* [yeshiva young man]. Yom Tov Levinski remembered that in the 1900s, yeshiva youths were sometimes called *arim bukher* (poor boy) or *lavke kvetcher* (bank occupier), which emphasized their low status.[46] In Volozhin, to be called a yeshiva bukher was one of the biggest offenses, linked to notions of misery and mercy.[47] Gradually, the perception of a yeshiva bukher as an insult also spread across eastern Europe. In order to challenge the link between unrespectable characteristics such as poverty and inferiority and yeshiva studies and to transform its students into respectable men in linguistic terms, the Volozhin students chose to speak about themselves as *anshey yeshiva* (yeshiva men) or *bney yeshiva* (yeshiva sons). The memoirs of yeshiva alumni demonstrate that they desired to conceive of themselves as respectable men and actively attempted (including on the linguistic level) to be known as successful and self-made and not poor and miserable.

The masculine respectability that yeshivot hoped to foster needed a social background against which their students would appear as members of the extraordinary elite. This was achieved by contrasting them with regular Jewish men who lived in the town where the yeshiva was located but did not have any intellectual link to the yeshiva. Also, the physical separation between the students and other city residents strengthened this division. The yeshiva in Slutsk was purposefully placed on the outskirts of the town to create a secluded space of all-male knowledge and scholarship, separated from the townspeople. Moshe Reguer recalls that it was "below the city and amidst the fields and grass. The yeshiva had been purposefully placed here when it had been founded to remove the students from the noisy city life."[48] The father of Yehoshua Leib Radus feared that his son would come in contact "with mischievous, irresponsible and empty" Kovna boys who did not attend the yeshiva.[49] These examples demonstrate how men who studied in the yeshivot intended to separate themselves from the average Jewish townsmen to achieve and mark their superior status.

Many former Volozhin yeshiva students indeed imagined themselves and their colleagues as learned and sophisticated when compared to the regular townsfolk. The relationship between regular Volozhin Jewish men and students of the yeshiva was conflict ridden, and both groups felt that they were not on equal footing. Menachem Zlotkin spoke of the two groups as if they "did not belong to the same people" due to their difference in status.[50] Don Yichye recalled that yeshiva students "looked [down] from above" at the regular townsfolk of Volozhin.[51] Pinchas Turberg believed that "they [yeshiva men] were the aristocracy of the town" whose voices were respected. The system of financial support liberated students from financial dependency on the townsfolk. While, in some yeshivot, students still "needed to yield before the shtetl inhabitants," in Volozhin, seventeen- or nineteen-year-old boys could feel superior to established and much-older artisans and merchants.[52] The situation in Volozhin demonstrates how masculinity based on scholarly excellence was shaping the hierarchies within Jewish Orthodox society. It was not advanced age, experience, or a communal position that granted men high social status and respectability but membership in the yeshiva system.

Male respectability was linked to marriage and the establishment of a patriarchal family. The Orthodox Jewish culture proscribed men's obligation to marry and defined what marriage and what bride would help the yeshiva graduate establish his status as a member of the elite.[53] Many men believed that as yeshiva graduates, they would have better marriage prospects compared to those who studied in less prestigious institutions or married without an advanced Jewish education. Efraim Moszwicki remembered that yeshiva students had a "very high value" in the eyes of regular shtetl inhabitants.[54] Zvi Scharfstein, a teacher in Galicia in the 1900s, wrote, "The father wishes for his daughter a young man with side-locks, somewhat of a Talmudic scholar, a Hasid; in short: somebody similar to him."[55] Jewish historian Jakub Schall believed that fathers of adolescent daughters often participated in Talmudic discussions run by yeshiva men vacationing in other towns.[56] However, in the early twentieth century, when feminism, Polonization, and education destabilized Orthodox Jewish families, being a yeshiva alumni lost its status to a certain extent. Rachel Manekin demonstrated conflicts between parents and daughthers for whom they arranged a match. As more Jewish women gained access to modern education and a vision of marriage for love proliferated across eastern Europe, the religious excellence of a future husband lost its importance for women.[57] However, only after World War I did arranged marriages stop being the norm, and earlier parents helped maintain the gender system that privileged yeshiva alumni.

These accounts demonstrate that yeshiva studies were a mechanism granting young Jewish men a higher level of inner-Jewish respectability. The yeshiva did not have a major role in non-Jewish social mobility. Choosing a yeshiva over available non-Jewish institutions (such as university, partisan politics, or journalism) suggests that for some Jewish men in eastern Europe, high status valid only in the Orthodox Jewish setting was not only a product of limited options but also something that corresponded with their needs. Respectability had a dimension of financial independence, communal respect, good marriage prospects, and belonging to a masculine elite. The respectability that yeshivot promoted overlapped with many concepts central for Western hegemonic masculinity like self-control, celebration of achievement, and sacrifice. As the next section demonstrates, yeshiva masculinity was negotiated through a process of constant enacting and testing of a superior Talmudic knowledge that determined one's privileged status.

KNOWLEDGE, STATUS, AND THE THEATER OF TESTING

The Orthodox eastern European Jewish culture praised the learning of religious Jewish texts and defined studiousness as a recognized masculine virtue.[58] The importance of religious studies is quite visible in several Yiddish folk song lyrics. In one of them, we read, "Pletslekh mit puter vet men shmirn / in heder arayn vet man im firn / sforim ver er shraybn / a giter un frumer yid / vet er m'rtse hashem blayben" (We will smear him pies with butter / we will lead him into a heder / he will write books and / if God wills / he will remain a good observant Jew).[59] The song underscores the parents' dedication to providing for their son so that he could grow to become a learned man strongly anchored in the Jewish tradition. Jewish men in eastern Europe who after graduating from the yeshivot found the source of their respectability elsewhere, including in a business or in non-Jewish educational or political arenas, continued to esteem religious learning and studiousness. Knowing how their society valued learned men, young Orthodox Jewish men enrolled in yeshivot to claim belonging to a respected masculine elite. While land

Figure 1.2. Yeshiva building in Raduń (Poland before 1939, now Ukraine), 2014. Photo from the collection of the Grodzka Gate-NN Theater Center Digital Library, Lublin, Poland.

ownership, careers in the state apparatus, and blood-based nobility were not available or not effective in the eastern European Jewish context, scholarship and learnedness were useful markers of elite membership.[60]

Within the yeshiva, religious learning was conceived as a process of acquiring knowledge and not as a religious act. In the Mir yeshiva, only a fraction of boys prayed on the Shabbat, while others used the time to chat or trade books.[61] In Slobodka, many students enrolled only after graduating from the Russian state gymnasia, which provided them with the general knowledge they now sought to complement with religious learning.[62] Being religiously observant was not equal to being competent in religious knowledge and being *harif,* or sharp minded. In many yeshivot, only the latter quality was considered a masculine virtue. Moshe Eleazar Eizenstadt and Efraim Moszwicki noticed that, unlike in other yeshivot, in Volozhin, "the prayer was not valued much."

The center of focus, rather, was Talmudic studies.[63] Simcha Asaf, who studied in the Telz yeshiva in the first decade of the twentieth century, added, "The value of every young man was measured according to the level of his knowledge and understanding of the Talmud."[64] In Telz, there were four levels of study, which were not organized according to the time spent in the yeshiva or the student's age but according to the knowledge already achieved, and Telz students were instilled with "intellectual pride" and superiority.[65] These accounts reveal that only studiousness and knowledge made a proper yeshiva man and that regular synagogue attendance was equated with the average Jewish masculinity and not the elite masculinity to which yeshiva students aspired.

The educational process in yeshivot appears similar to other institutions where European men acquired knowledge, such as higher educationor tutelage by experts. The yeshiva was, to a great extent, similar to other masculine cultures centered around the knowledge of classic texts and practices of elite homosocial bonding. Both yeshiva and similar secular institutions assumed that masculinity was something fluid and consequently could be instilled in young men through the process of tutelage, supervision, and homosocial interactions. Leib Jaffe, who graduated from the Volozhin yeshiva and later continued to study at several German universities, was convinced of the similarity of both types of institutions.[66] Like a gymnasium or university, the yeshiva was a place for acquiring hardly accessible knowledge that would raise one's social status. For instance, Don Yichye's memoir moved the Talmud learning process in the yeshiva from the realm of faith to the realm of science. He described one of the rashey yeshiva in Volozhin as a "surgeon" who analyzed the Talmud as a structure that needed to be approached scientifically.[67] Religious knowledge seemed to be like any other form of scientific knowledge: measurable, categorizable, and verifiable.

At the end of nineteenth century, both in gymnasia and yeshivot, knowledge served as a key to unlock control and privilege. Reflecting on the contents studied in yeshivot, Zalman Epstein writes, "They learned Torah, Gemarah, and Rishonim. Not because of piousness and not to fulfill a mitzvah. But because it was the real thing, science, knowledge, something valuable in the life of a Jew, something where reason finds levelheadedness."[68] Later, Zalman Epstein continues,

> They did not investigate too much and did not worry about life goals, exactly as a young European devoted to general and classic studies does not think about his future and does not ask himself why he needs to know Homer poems or works of Cicero, or acquire unuseful general knowledge about nature, history or the sphericality of Earth. The young European knows that these studies will turn him into a man who is socially needed and appreciated. Already growing up he knows how to choose his own way and how to find himself in a specific form of productive life. The perspective of a Volozhin yeshiva student on his future and the meaningfulness of his studies was very similar.[69]

For Zalman Epstein, the yeshiva appears to have the same power that transformed men who acquired a secular education, that is, to allow young men to join the elite. In his memoirs, Epstein suggests that the Volozhin yeshiva was a place where young men from peripheral towns learned the habitus that allowed them to define themselves as men of a higher status. Many yeshiva students knew from the very beginning that they were to be merchants or businessmen, and not religious leaders, yet these students also sought to be recognized as excellent Talmud scholars. Jewish men across the class spectrum perceived the knowledge acquired in the yeshiva as a mechanism for increasing their perceived sense of elite membership.

Religious knowledge was a factor that allowed the categorization and hierarchization of yeshiva men independent of their *yikhus* (pedigree, noble descent) and financial status. While the sons of rich families who did not excel in learning could commission more talented students as private tutors, their status within the yeshiva microcosm was low.[70] When affluent Ben-Zion Dinur arrived at the Slobodka yeshiva, he was glad when the mashgiach told him that he would receive the highest level of financial support due to his own intellectual achievement and not his family's status.[71] In the Volozhin yeshiva, excellence in studies granted young men an extraordinary status: they were exempted from the overarching control of the mashgiach and could themselves design their studies.[72] In Telz, in order to progress to the third study level, one needed to prove "independence and initiative" in understanding the Talmud.[73] Yeshiva leadership attempted to design proper behaviors by employing control and supervision, but men excelling in their studies were given a higher degree of freedom. In that sense, knowledge and initiative were defined as masculine virtues, recognized both by fellow students and yeshiva authorities. Since independence and initiative are classic post-Enlightenment European masculine virtues, it becomes evident how close yeshiva virtues were to the virtues of other European male elites.

Proper yeshiva masculinity was constructed through constant public knowledge testing. Shlomo Zaltsman compared the emotions surrounding tests of religious knowledge to the emotions around sports typical for secular young men: "We, who then in our wildest dreams did not know about football, we found in this intellectual wrestling the same spiritual tension which gymnasia students now experience on the sports field."[74] Moshe Reguer recalls that in the Volozhin yeshiva, "excellent students tested the younger ones . . . the goal was to instill envy among them." These exams introduced a hierarchy in which religious knowledge and skill (*bki'ut*) defined one's status in the homosocial world of the yeshiva.[75] In that sense, a probing conversation in the presence of listeners was not an insult but part of the social graces of the intellectual elite.[76] Ben-Zion Dinur and his brother sought out opportunities where men known for their communal status and religious knowledge would test their knowledge and thus approve of their adolescent masculinity.[77] In Mir, external candidates were examined "without any mercy," not only by rosh yeshiva but also by the students.[78] At the same time, the testing was not intended to humiliate the weak but to praise the excellent. In Telz, more advanced students who did not treat the young ones with respect were subsequently boycotted.[79] This mechanism underscores the solidarity of young men who acknowledged hierarchies based on knowledge yet shared a belief in the equality of chances to acquire this knowledge and the status it entailed.

The mechanism of establishing high social status through knowledge needed to be public and continuously performed to be effective. Yehiel Yaakov Weinberg, who studied in Slobodka from 1901 onward, recalled that in the yeshiva, an "aristocratic regime" ruled, which was maintained via public confirmation of study excellence. Weinberg writes, "He [rosh yeshiva] generously passed to *iluim* and *matmidim* greater amounts of money. He attempted to grant them respect in a way conspicuous and visible for all bney yeshiva."[80] In Telz, Avrahaml Stavisker was a regular guest in the house of the rosh yeshiva thanks to his intellectual capabilities, and he was loved by both the yeshiva authorities and fellow students.[81] On Saturdays, Moshe Reguer regularly dined with the rosh yeshiva in Slutsk, at which time he was publicly tested in his Talmudic knowledge.[82] In interwar Hasidic yeshivot, the achievement of completing the yeshiva was celebrated at public graduation ceremonies.[83] The practices described prior point out how masculine prestige linked to religious excellence was performed in public in order to be collectively recognized.

Attention was given to a student as an award for his talent or obedience. For instance, the attention Rabbi Finkel gave or withdrew from particular students shaped center-periphery relations within the yeshiva.[84] This means that yeshiva masculinity was dependent on the respect and status granted through proximity

to the possessor of the highest religious skills and authority—
the rosh yeshiva. Efraim Moszwicki recalled that rosh yeshiva
Chaim Soloveichik used to walk through the study hall with his
left and right arms holding his favorite students. Then, still-young
Soloveichik appeared to Moszwicki as a "friend and comrade"
of yeshiva students; they used to encircle Soloveichik after the
lecture, and "filled with sympathy and love," he continued on his
way to his house hugged by two boys.[85] These accounts suggest
that intimacy was a tool that rashey yeshivot applied to channel
specific behaviors of yeshiva students while at the same time defining other behaviors as not normative.

Litvak yeshivot established religious knowledge and skill as
a central and desired marker of Orthodox elite masculinity.
The knowledge seemed to have a transformative effect, turning yeshiva students from possibly pious but ignorant boys
into respected Jewish men. Excellency in religious learning
provided yeshiva students with the status of desired and attractive young men. At the same time, yeshivot emerged as a space
were studiousness entwined with another masculine quality:
a beautiful body.

SERAPHS AND *BAALEY BASAR*:

CORPORALITY IN THE YESHIVA

Next to scholarly excellence, other factors, including physical
beauty, played a role in shaping the status of yeshiva men, both
within the yeshiva and in the larger Jewish society. While traditionally the concept of *sheyne yidn* (beautiful Jews) referred to being cultured upstanding members of society and having Talmudic
knowledge, the memoirs of yeshiva students reveal that physical
beauty also played a role in shaping the self-image and external
perception of yeshiva students.[86] For instance, Efraim Moszwicki
recalls that one of the *yishevnikim*, the Jewish residents of villages,
desired to host for the holidays or for a summer study break not

excellent scholars but "good and beautiful boys."[87] Joseph Rolnik remembered that as the son of an affluent householder, he was to choose the boy who stayed with them for the holidays. Rolnik enjoyed the privilege of "choosing whomever he liked" and whomever he fancied as a possible friend. Rolnik recalled that some of the yeshiva guests sang beautifully and filled his house with joy and that his sisters were attracted to young men who spent their yeshiva holidays at their home.[88] These examples evidence that not only Judaic knowledge but also external beauty were seen as social values that yeshiva men appreciated.

The consideration of physical beauty played a role for yeshiva students who wondered about the link between body and spirit. Yitshak Nissenbaum was attentive to other yeshiva men's appearance and bodies. One of his fellow students was tall and *baal basar*, or well built, and comparing his body with that of the other young man, Nissenbaum began to debate what true masculine values were: "I have asked myself. Are the power and body the sense of the thing or is it spirit and talent? Did I lose being short?"[89] Meir Sheli, upon arriving at the Telz yeshiva, analyzed in detail one of the older students regarding his physique: low stature, well-kept long hair, cheerful smiling face, with eyes "thirsty for human interaction."[90] The young man, named Avrahaml Stavishiner and described by other students as an angelic "seraph," caught Meir's attention due to his "eye-raising uniqueness." Stavishiner's figure was strikingly noticeable in the room full of youths, his voice cheerful, penetrating, and blazing. His performance in the study room made everyone look at him, and other youths could barely take their eyes off him. During the study breaks, Avrahaml was surrounded by numerous boys seeking his proximity and was the center of attention. Meir Sheli compared Avrahaml to a sourdough that made the entire community of young men ferment and effervesce.[91] In addition, Ben-Zion Dinur admired one of his comrades in the Korsuń yeshiva: "The guy from Kamionka had a pleasant face, red cheeks, black hair, black and shining eyes

Figure 1.3. Wilhelm Wachtel, *Młody jeszybotnik* (Young yeshiva student), Lviv, 1916. Painting from the collection of the Emanuel Ringelblum Jewish Historical Institute, Warsaw, Poland (MŻIH A-697).

and his voice was sweet and calm. When he was learning aloud, I—and not only I—was truly enchanted by the pleasant tone of his voice. He was a bright, witty and straightforward guy and we became good friends."[92] Those examples demonstrate that yeshiva men paid attention to the appearance and behavior of other students and constructed their own masculinities through admiration or rejection of certain characteristics.

The perception of male beauty in yeshivot was conditioned by broader Jewish conceptions of beauty. For example, the idea of whiteness in the Orthodox eastern European Jewish culture was perceived as attractive, and dark skin was read as unmasculine.[93] Pale skin suggested studiousness, while tanned skin moved one outside of the study hall to the market, blue-collar jobs, and consequently closer to the non-Jewish peasants. One Yiddish folk song read, "Shvarts bist du, shvarts / ober mit khen / far vemen du bist mis / far mir bist sheyn."[94] Blackness, which appears here as a negative feature, was probably related to suntanned skin, which implied physical work. However, eastern European Jewish meanings of blackness and whiteness were complex and translated into nuanced ideals of male beauty. Memoirist Riva Chirurg, who grew up in central Poland in the 1930s, considered whiteness and blackness as complementing each other. When describing her brother Baruch Leib who graduated from the Metivtah yeshiva in Warsaw, she wrote: "[He was] tall, dark-skinned, with large black pupils against a shine silky whiteness. Oblong face, white teeth glistering like a string of pearls."[95]

In some accounts, yeshiva students focus on the ugliness of their teachers and fellow students. Joseph Rolnik remembered the assistant of the yeshiva mashgiach as a "depressed young man, with an unkempt beard and a hat that was always crumpled," which made him seem neglected and weak.[96] Shlomo Kluski, a Warka Hasid born in 1906, argued that a beautiful man was "average … not big and not small … the body should not be fat, it also can't be too delicate, but just fine. … The harmony of inner and outer should first and foremost be visible in one's face … one cannot trouble the body, should keep it beautiful."[97] While, in the Orthodox eastern European Jewish culture, bodily deformations and ugliness could be compensated for via studiousness or high social status, male beauty was not ignored and was a factor in social interactions between men and between men and women.[98]

The yeshiva was a homosocial space where young men observed and mutually influenced one another in terms of desired male appearance. In Volozhin, many big-city guys spread their manners, customs, and ways of talking and moving to their fellow yeshiva students. Zalman Epstein speaks of movements and clothing that evolved during one's stay in yeshiva: "A small-town boy after spending a few years learning in Volozhin turned into another man also in the external sense, with new clothes, a new way of talking, new body language." In another place, Zalman Epstein describes students as "fresh and beautiful young men."[99] As Epstein recalled, a yeshiva student returning to his town as an elegant man with good taste would have a transformative influence on young males who did not have the privilege of studying.[100] His remarks underscore the meaning of corporeality and beauty within a social context that seemingly gave attention only to the power of the intellect. The same dynamic continued into the 1930s. Ben-Zion Gold remembered that he admired his friend who returned from a Lublin yeshiva: "His whole manner has changed, he seems to have become sedate, almost dignified . . . I liked what I saw."[101] Riva Chirurg described her brother arriving in Kielce from his studies at Metivtah yeshiva in Warsaw as "a prince from Wonderland."[102]

Proper clothing had the function of marking yeshiva students' status as members of the elite. The neat dress was supposed to elevate the status of yeshiva students in relation to gymnasium students, who wore impressive uniforms that coded their social status and aspirations.[103] According to one memoirist, the yeshiva student was to be "pleasant, dressed in a respectful way, not expect anything from others, think and express his views, always go straighten up, know how to defend his rights, recognize his individual value and the value of his learning."[104] These recommendations could have easily been taken out of any bourgeois guidebook for young men. Mashgiach Yehoshua Grodzinski of Slobodka made sure that students were well kept, in clean and well-maintained clothes, and bathed regularly. Sometimes he even accompanied students to a tailor to order them new attire.[105] Moshe Reguer, arriving at the yeshiva in Kremenchuk, remembered that for the local students, the "outward appearance and cleanliness, beauty, the attention to particulars of presentation, the preventing of belching, the pressing of the crease of the trousers, the folded decoration of the handkerchief" was of great importance.[106] One memoirist recalled that financial support from the United States allowed some students to order suits in the latest styles and to dress "elegantly and classily."[107] The clothing was linked with masculine respectability and self-esteem. The proper outfit symbolized belonging to the elite and projected high social status. At the same time, the beautiful clothes were understood as an expression of the inner beauty and harmony achieved through studiousness.[108]

The body and its fitness were not neglected in yeshivot, as many Zionist or western European Jewish sources on eastern European Jewish Orthodox corporeality might suggest.[109] In the Volozhin yeshiva, students who did not leave town for the Passover holiday often relocated to the neighboring villages to rest and gain bodily fitness.[110] Efraim Moszwicki recalled that after this retreat, students returned "fat and well-rounded."[111] During the hot summer days, Slutsk yeshiva students often abandoned their studies to "invigorate their hearts and lungs, and to enjoy the beauty of nature."[112] In the summer afternoons, many Volozhin yeshiva boys left "the choking dust of the yeshiva for [the] grass, to dance on it among all the flowering vegetation."[113] Reguer recalls that during his free time, he took baths in the river and had "a chance to straighten my back from the constant bending over the pages of the Gemarah."[114] Shlomo Zaltsman enjoyed nature walks around Mir yeshiva with his close friend.[115] Also, Pinchas Turberg remembered spending summer evenings in the fields and forests, enjoying the fresh air.[116] Other boys continued to discuss scholarly topics during their walks while "inhaling the fresh air."[117] Importantly, the nature trips were done collectively, in the company of other yeshiva students, which strengthened the male intimacy while protecting their health.

Many memoirists speak of shared games and sports as one of the key experiences they had in the yeshiva. In the Łomża yeshiva, swimming belonged to students' key formative experiences no less than their studies. Yom Tov Levinski, who studied there between 1913 and 1914, argues that "there was no student who did not learn to swim while in Łomża." Hundreds of yeshiva students relished their summer days swimming in the Narew River, and many proved to be excellent swimmers. Their swimming excellence was performed in front of other yeshiva boys and other Łomża residents, who arrived to watch a large group of yeshiva youths swim together.[118] As one of the best memories from his time at the Kremenchuk yeshiva in the mid-1890s, Ben-Zion Dinur remembered swimming in the Dnieper River. He recalled, "I loved swimming in Dnieper. To go down there at the beach an hour before the sunset, to remove my clothes, to feel the comfortable touch of the sand, and to swim from raft to raft."[119] The fact that Ben-Zion remembered swimming so fondly suggests that some yeshiva boys were attracted to sports and fitness just like other young men in Europe. After hours of learning, many yeshiva students enjoyed swimming and, as Ben-Zion remembered, were willing to break the yeshiva rule and practice their favorite sport despite occasional bans.[120] The examples of Levinski and Dinur make it clear that yeshivot were complex social spaces that focused not only on the transmission of knowledge but also provided men with venues for developing bodily fitness.

A healthy and beautiful body was recognized as linked with intellectual powers, which for their part defined the hierarchy among yeshiva men. Being out of shape or ill also made it difficult or impossible for students to excel at their studies. In Volozhin, the mashgiach made sure that students who were sick stopped learning and rested. Yeshiva students were expected to take care of their bodies by getting good sleep and nutrition.[121] However, some students neglected their bodies, which resulted in corporeal dysfunctions. Yitshak Nissenbaum remembered a fellow yeshiva youth who could barely speak due to his poor health.[122] Moshe Eleazar Eizenstadt recalled that some students were immersed in day and night learning and neglected their health, which resulted in weakness and hemoptysis. He himself caught a dangerous pneumonia.[123] Ben-Zion Dinur, after long hours of learning, had pains in his chest, and doctors discouraged him from excessive studying.[124] When he was sick and spit blood in the Slobodka yeshiva, his mates "took care of him with friendliness, devotion and love."[125] Some rashey yeshivot advised that excessive learning was counterproductive and complained that students who learned excessively became dull and their minds muddled.[126] The yeshiva system seems to have embraced a holistic vision of a man who took care of both his spiritual and bodily well-being that jointly formed a proper Orthodox man.

At the turn of the twentieth century, yeshiva masculinity became more and more conditioned by external influences. This also included new masculine models that, to a certain extent, challenged the masculinity defined by religious excellence. Yeshiva men commenting on men outside the yeshiva world offered insights into what they admired and rejected in other men. Moshe Reguer praised Bundist and Zionist speakers who "fought with sharpness and vigor."[127] Reguer also envied his cousins, who were immersed in secular Hebrew and Russian currents.[128] Reguer speaks openly about the envy that filled him when he saw men who were allowed to gain knowledge that was forbidden to him. B. Shulman, who studied in the Zhadov yeshiva, remembered the intense interactions between the local Bundists and the yeshiva students, some of whom also belonged to the party. The Bundists had allegedly repeatedly beat up yeshiva students and demanded the right to use the yeshiva for their meetings.[129] Yet yeshiva youths managed to violently expel the young Bundists.[130] The Zhadov incident evidences that men who pursued Orthodox Jewish masculinity were involved in a network of interactions with boys and men outside the yeshiva realm and that yeshiva youths were knowledgeable of violent ways of solving conflicts, which they did not hesitate to apply.

Physical beauty played a significant role in yeshivot and entwined with the central virtue of studiousness. The neat external appearance was to raise the self-esteem of yeshiva men and define them as upstanding and dignified men. Yeshiva students engaged in sport activities, such as forest walks or river swimming, that apart from increasing their fitness also made them toned and physically attractive. In this respect, a mechanism developed in yeshivot praising the harmonious beauty of body and mind—it corresponded with the similar ideal that emerged in the non-Jewish context of post-Enlightenment Europe.[131] Another major dimension of the yeshiva experience were intimate friendships between students.

SOULMATES: MASCULINE INTIMACY
IN THE YESHIVOT

Many yeshiva students searched there for male companions with whom they could share their intimate feelings or experience physical proximity. As contemporary sociological research suggests, adolescence and young adulthood are periods when young men greatly value their close male friendships and see them as central to their emotional well-being. Many male adolescents express a tremendous affection for their male friends; they share with them their deepest secrets and feel loss when their relationship wanes. As Niobe Way demonstrated, adolescent male friendships are as much centered around shared intimacy as on masculine competition.[132] The intimacy, vulnerability, mutual confidence, and caring affect that appear in Way's research are easily identifiable in the turn-of-the-twentieth-century yeshiva memoirs. Former yeshiva students describe their close friendships and devotion to male companions and cry over the separation from their dear friends. The desire for intimate friendships and male bonding that was a constitutional element of Western young masculinity in the modern era was typical also for the yeshiva.[133]

In the yeshivot, masculine intimacy was fostered by the spatiality of the yeshiva. Young men had hardly any private space and were distanced from their families; they thus turned to male companions and created intimate support networks. One of the organizational innovations of the Volozhin yeshiva, which at the turn of the twentieth century was adopted in many other Jewish academies, was arranging for sleeping in shared rooms with Jewish families. While students studying in batey midrash slept there, yeshiva students could spend their evenings in shared rented rooms, which fostered private interactions and offered greater privacy. Moshe Reguer recalls that in his yeshiva, the leadership made sure to appropriately "match" the boys. Those stronger in their studies were supposed to positively influence their less apt roommates.[134] At the beginning of the twentieth century, concern over the dangerous influence "from outside" prompted some yeshivot to establish proper dormitories. While earlier the values of the Jewish street and the yeshiva had seemed identical, in those stormy decades, they became increasingly disassociated.[135] In that context, some yeshiva leaders believed that dormitories, which provided youths with greater privacy and intimacy but also allowed for stricter institutional control, were the best solution. Dormitories were introduced in 1899 in the Łomża yeshiva, in 1919 in the Metivtah yeshiva in Warsaw, and in 1924 in Yeshivat Hokhmei Lublin.[136]

The yeshiva offered young men opportunities to forge diverse forms of male intimacy—for instance, through parties, singing, and dancing. Pinchas Turberg remembered singing, dancing, and whirling until the wee hours with fellow students, their legs moving to the sound of music.[137] Yitshak Nissenbaum and Moshe Eizenstadt remembered that they used to play cards at night, for which they were punished by the yeshiva headmaster who supervised their free time.[138] In Volozhin, students organized friendly meetings in one of the students' rooms, where they not only discussed current affairs but also told jokes, parodied people, and laughed. Aba Blosher recalled that yeshiva students liked to sing and hum.[139] Turberg remembered spending nights in shared rooms with his fellow students preparing their own publications.[140] Other boys were casually chatting and smoking.[141] Menachem Zlotkin's complaints about the lack of space for "hanging out with buddies and friends" suggests that many yeshiva men felt a need for such venues.[142] Although some students noticed that yeshivot lacked spaces where young men could befriend each other, youths used their own bedrooms to develop friendships with other young men. These practices merged play and intimacy and defined the yeshiva as a space where elite masculinity was formed and maintained through homosocial camaraderie.

The intimacy forged by the homosocial closeness of the yeshiva seems to have strongly bound men together. Yeshiva students usually shared their bedrooms with two or three other boys and spent most of their free time with them, and in this narrow space, they got to know their customs and bodies.[143] Ben-Zion Dinur shared his apartment with boys in their early twenties, much older than he. One of them, Nachum, adopted the role of his tutor in matters of manners, social interactions, and studies.[144] Moshe Reguer recalled intimate discussions on Saturday evenings: "We all sat on the floor, one leaning his arm on the edge of the trunk, another leaning his head on the shoulder of a friend. . . . The room was totally dark, and we could not make out any faces. It was a sweet, comradely, and still darkness."[145] In another instance, Reguer spoke about loyalty and a sense of mutual responsibility that united the yeshiva friends. When his best friend was arrested, Reguer "felt horrible that his best friend remained in such a terrible situation, and that all his hopes of relying on me were for naught."[146] Another young man dear to Reguer, Shmuel Dov, cared for him during a period of sickness, and "his soul was bound to his."[147] Joseph Rolnik also remembered "being bound by a thick thread" to his friend Ely. He admired Ely Oshmianski's blue eyes, blond hair, glowing red cheeks, and the blue veins visible under his delicate skin; he developed a strong attachment to him, and they promised each other "eternal friendship, perhaps love."[148] By referring to the biblical story of Jonathan and David, both Reguer and Rolnik demonstrate that yeshiva boys were aware of and sought biblical models of strong male friendship and affection.

Many young Jewish men searched, both inside and outside the yeshiva, for male companions and male intimacy. Joseph Rolnik, shortly after leaving the yeshiva at the age of seventeen, "craved new friendships" and "a young soul to clasp to him." He was attracted to strong and more experienced men. Once Rolnik enjoyed boating with a relative in his midtwenties: "We float silently, but we are both happy: I feel safe in the middle of the river with a big, strong man and he has at his side a young boy, a right-hand man . . . these silent journeys brought us close to each other as if we both had a secret that no one could know about."[149] Soon afterward he befriended another man, named Yaakov Feldsher, slightly older than he. Rolnik was impressed by Yaakov's good looks, and his new friend often accompanied him right to his door, and the whole time they "walked arm in arm."[150] Rolnik also appreciated his cousin's appearance: "tall, handsome, muscular boy and dark as a Moore [sic]." When he stood at the mortar and pounded matzah for mathzah flour, Rolnik's cousin embodied for him a powerful, but also very Jewish, masculinity.[151] It was an image of a strong Jewish man, not fighting on the battlefield or fencing with university fraternity brothers but performing hard physical labor in a Jewish religious context.

The intimacy between youths was conditioned by their need for spiritual and physical proximity. Shlomo Zaltsman recalled that when he entered the Mir yeshiva, he was "attracted by a magical power" to a friendly boy two years older. He described him as a loyal and devoted companion, recognized his enormous influence on him, and spoke of being lucky to have met him.[152] The youths at the yeshivot were mutually dependent on one another. Aharon Pick, recalling his days in the Slobodka yeshiva and speaking about his friend Sisuly, who provided him with hints about women and let him take puffs of his cigarettes, commented, "I needed his friendship. . . . My friendship with Sisuly helped me a lot to reinforce my secure position in the yeshiva." Pick suggests that the yeshiva was a space where men were in competition with one another and a proper friendship could raise one's position. Sisuly was strong and able bodied. He regularly chopped wood for the rebetsin's [rabbi's wife] stove and ran various errands and consequently made good material for a defender-friend.[153] Analogous stories about the importance of friendship appear in other yeshiva memoirs. Moshe Reguer was glad when he became good friends with Avraham, with whom he could share his ideas.[154] Ben-Zion Dinur complained right after leaving the yeshiva that he did not have anyone with whom to share his happiness and yearned for *akh karov, haver,* or *yedid* (Heb. "close brother, friend, acquaintance") such as those he had in the yeshiva.[155]

Intimate interactions between yeshiva students were both encouraged and controlled. As in other Western cultural contexts, both biological families and Jewish society as a whole approved of and encouraged friendships between yeshiva students.[156] Many young men attempted to establish friendships that would both serve as a substitute for a family but also protect them within the yeshiva dynamics defined by rivalry. Yeshiva students developed a language of fraternity and perceived strong attachment to other young men as indispensable for their well-being and personal growth. These "loving friendships" provided yeshiva students with emotional support and were legitimized as a form of male elective kinship. While yeshivot promoted this form of relationship between young men, yeshiva authorities made sure to control and channel students' behavior, including relationships with fellow students.

CONCLUSION

The yeshiva has been the institution central to shaping Orthodox Jewish masculinities that exercised a degree of hegemony
within the Jewish setting of turn-of-the-twentieth-century eastern Europe. The yeshivot provided young Jewish men with a high
level of respectability that translated into their perceived sense of
belonging to the Jewish masculine elite. Yeshiva men saw themselves as superior both to women but also to Jewish men who did
not have access to institutions of advanced Jewish learning. In
yeshivot, religious knowledge was a marker differentiating a man
of the elite from regular townsfolk. Yeshivot were spaces where
not religiosity, identified with the regular Jewish population, but
knowledge was celebrated. In this respect, yeshivot were similar
to non-Jewish educational institutions that provided young men
with high social status and respectability.

Yeshiva celebrated the Jewish Orthodox tradition of religious
learning, but as the memoirs of many yeshiva students reveal,
after the learning there were other values that yeshiva students
strove to achieve. Money and entrepreneurial talent as sources of
status were important for Jews, as they were among Polish and
Ukrainian peasants who lived together with eastern European
Jews. Modern yeshivot provided young men with financial independence that translated into a self-image of a successful man.
Yeshiva funding had a form of excellence-based stipends, and in
that sense, the financial support underscored men's individual
achievement—a masculine virtue analogous to a model of a non-
Jewish self-made man who was master of his destiny. The *yikhus*
(pedigree and lineage), which played a key role as a source of
status among Orthodox eastern European Jews, relied as much
on learning as it did on money and, like masculinity itself, needed
to be performed and reaffirmed in order to be maintained.

Memoirs of yeshiva graduates shed light on how elite Jewish
masculinity was formed in the homosocial setting of the yeshiva.

Young men paid attention to their bodies, evaluated each other's physicality, and developed notions of male beauty that intertwined with the spiritual qualities of an elite Jewish man. Yeshiva authorities, in their attempt to shape normative yeshiva masculinity, guided students on how to dress appropriately. Moreover, yeshivot were venues where masculine intimacy and bonding played a central role. Yeshiva students sought intimate friendships, were often jealous of each other, and longed for proximity to excellent and beautiful students. While some yeshiva graduates saw their studies as a desired liberation from the curatorship of the family, the yearning after intimate friendships demonstrates how vulnerability, mutual dependency, and emotional well-being were central aspects of the yeshiva experience.

TWO

—⁓—

A JEW AND HIS PENIS

*Circumcision and the Entanglements of
Jewishness and Masculinity*

CIRCUMCISION HAS LONG BEEN A sign of Jewish difference applied to distinguish Jewish from Christian men—and early twentieth-century Poland was no exception. For Orthodox Judaism, which was the dominant stream in Poland, the circumcision ritual was a symbol of a covenant between God and the Jewish people as transmitted in the Book of Genesis. Other Jewish religious sources, like the midrashim (biblical interpretations), suggested additional meanings of the circumcision ritual, including a willingness to abandon selfishness or strive for perfection. One of the midrashim reads, "As long as you are uncircumcised, you are imperfect. By performing [a circumcision] you will achieve a new degree of holiness and will be elevated above the laws of nature."[1] In western European modernity, circumcision has been read as a sign of everything from sexual hygiene or a cosmetic alteration to a group identity or a mark of adulthood, all the way to diminishment—or enhancement—of sexual desire and even a form of attenuated castration or patriarchal subjugation.[2]

Jewish circumcision in the modern era has been widely studied in the context of antisemitism and exclusion in western Europe; however, there are major lacunae concerning how Jewish circumcision was approached in the context of eastern Europe.[3]

65

Concerning western Europe, such studies have demonstrated that associating the circumcised Jewish penis with sexual inadequacy, dysfunction, and disease was a major feature of antisemitic cultures. Sander Gilman and Daniel Boyarin argue that antisemitic renderings of circumcision as an emasculating source of Jewish shame later became a common internalized trope among Jews as well, particularly in German-speaking spaces. In his reading of Freud's theory of sexuality, Boyarin argued that the source of antisemitism was the interaction between the "knowledge of a Jew's circumcision" and the "gentile castration complex."[4] Gilman writes that modern western Europe created the assumption that circumcision defined the body of the Jew as a damaged male and was central to distinguishing between health and disease, between Aryan and Jew.[5] Women and circumcised Jewish men became conflated in Germany and Austria, with some scholars developing the idea that even Jewish men themselves shared this position.[6]

In the British context, Noelle Gallagher has shown that eighteenth- and nineteenth-century English culture's particular fixation on the Jewish penis also exemplified a similar trend toward conceptualizing Jewish men's bodies as dysfunctional, deformed, or disease prone. English Christians continued to condemn circumcised Jews and attributed to them such problems as lechery and a range of sexual disorders like difficult, unsatisfying, or impossible sexual performance, including impotence. These contradictory characterizations of Jewish sexuality constituted just one example of what Gilman has identified as the "bipolar" nature of antisemitism: attributing to Jewish men simultaneously a love of "whoring" and an inability to obtain sexual satisfaction.[7] Gallagher has observed an equally paradoxical discourse around circumcision, with the persistent recurrence of epithets like "one of the circumcised," "among the circumcised race," or "a circumcised son of Eve" and alleged pathologies of the circumcised penis.[8]

The attitudes of Polish-Jewish men toward their penises and toward circumcision significantly differed from how circumcision was presented by Boyarin and Gilman, and I suggest that their findings should not be extrapolated to early twentieth-century and interwar Poland. Since 3.5 million Polish Jews were less socially dependent on the Christian sphere than in smaller communities in western Europe, they rarely internalized the antisemitic images of circumcision that circulated in wider society. The majority of Jewish men in Poland had a positive attitude toward their cut penis and believed that only the circumcision made them complete and proud Jewish men. In Poland, where Orthodox masculinities did have access to a limited hegemony within Jewish society and where Zionism was very strong, circumcision was viewed not only as fulfilling the religious commandment but also as perpetuating Jewish gender normativity. Following this type of Jewish reasoning, many Polish-Jewish men identified circumcision in a predominantly positive sense. Unlike the German-speaking Jews portrayed by Gilman and Boyarin, who perceived circumcision as "losing" a part of a man's masculinity, for most Polish-Jewish men, circumcision was about enhancing their status through a masculinizing ritual that turned them into proper Jewish men.

While the largest group of Orthodox Jewish men considered circumcision an act of becoming a Jewish man and linked the ritual with masculine respect, Jewish voices against circumcision appeared in Poland as well. These opponents usually hailed from a minority of the metropolitan middle and upper classes and a fraction of Jewish left-wingers. When speaking up against circumcision, this minority of Jewish men in Poland usually did not speak of shame and humiliation but rather of self-determination and personal freedom. For Polish-Jewish men who considered Jewishness as an ethnicity and not a religion, the expectation that all Jewish newborn boys, in particular their sons, should be circumcised was a form of religious coercion. More and more men decided not to circumcise their sons, and they defined their own sense of masculinity precisely through their resistance and claiming their patriarchal authority over their sons' penises. Furthermore, in Poland, the majority of Jewish men not only did not seriously consider questioning circumcision but held a clearly positive attitude toward it, including when they called for reforming the ritual. As circumcision was medicalized in Poland, the figure of a Jewish doctor performing the circumcision emerged and allowed the ritual to be continued within a Jewish setting, but now regulated by science.

Admittedly, the interconnection between a circumcised penis and antisemitism was also present in Poland, with the term *obrzezaniec* (pejorative for "circumcised") omnipresent in the antisemitic press in the nineteenth and twentieth centuries. Also in Poland, some Jewish men saw circumcision as an "invisible stain" that defined their experience as men and citizens. One of them was Edward Dutlinger, who in 1909 commented, "We Jews . . . are used to this disgusting operation since birth. Circumcision is the initial source of our humiliations; it is a stigma of Jewishness."[9] Dutlinger understood the ritual as the cause of Jewish difference and a cornerstone of a chain of humiliations that Jewish men experienced in terms of their social respectability. However, opinions like Dutlinger's were rare, and the antisemitic link between a circumcised penis and alleged Jewish inferiority was not established in Poland in a stable way. Most Jewish circumcision opponents were far from internalizing any vision of weak Jewish masculinity or circumcision-related shame.

This chapter demonstrates how diverse groups of Polish-Jewish men defined their masculinity through their approach toward circumcision. I start by discussing the attitudes of the Orthodox majority by showing how Jewish men who were not circumcised as infants due to a medical condition perceived it as humiliating and challenging their gender self-perception. I also review how circumcision granted respectability to men who performed the ritual—the *mohelim* and the *sandakim*.[10] In the next section, I analyze the complex relation among acculturated Jews, circumcision, and the medicalization of the discourse surrounding it. I suggest that many Polish Jews wished to maintain circumcision as a measure verifying Jewish masculinity but disassociated from religion and performed by a Jewish doctor. After that, I present the opposition to circumcision from the side of Jewish freethinkers and Socialists who sought to transform the notion of Jewish masculinity in a way that was disassociated from religion. This group of Jewish men defined the act of refusing to circumcise as a sign of masculine consistency and personal freedom. Finally, I look at how Polish antisemites linked circumcision with a broad set of anti-Jewish stereotypes and demonstrate how the antisemitic rendering of circumcision-related shame did not gain much internalization among Poland's Jewish men.

ORTHODOX JEWISH MEN AND THE
NORMATIVE JOY OF CUTTING

The Orthodox majority in early twentieth-century Poland viewed circumcision positively as the ultimate inclusion into the community of men. Uncircumcised Jewish men were considered incomplete males and could not perform Jewish masculine rituals, including in the prayer house, and in that sense resembled women and children. For the Orthodox, the growing secularization of Polish Jewry was a major threat, and circumcision appeared at the center of the local debates about Jewishness in general and Jewish masculinity in particular. In 1911, a Warsaw contributor identified only as B. spoke of assimilated Jewish males as "circumcised antisemites." He saw the circumcision of newborn males from acculturated families as "a drop of comfort" in times "when conversion reached an epidemic character and every day we lose hundreds of young people."[11] The circumcisions of men who returned to the religion, or who marked this return by circumcising their sons, were viewed as strengthening traditional Orthodox masculinity and the normative Jewish family. For instance, in 1934, Warsaw Jews celebrated the *bris* (a Yiddish pronunciation of *brit [milah]*) of twenty-six-year-old Antoni Woźniak, son of a Catholic father and a Jewish mother.[12] Following the same logic, the Warsaw kehillah (a communal Jewish self-government body) practiced "a reparative" belated circumcision of neglected orphan boys, supervised in the community-run institution at 26 Płocka Street. To establish the normative Jewish masculinity of these boys, they were circumcised as soon as they came under the oversight of the Warsaw kehillah.[13]

In Orthodox Jewish circles, regular circumcision of infants turned into a popular celebration that sometimes exceeded the dimensions of a family party. In 1935, "the entire shtetl" of Radzymin accompanied the Kozienicer tsadik who arrived to participate in the brit milah of a local Hasid.[14] When popular rabbis and leaders of Hasidic dynasties performed brit milah for their family members, festivities were particularly robust. In 1922, the town of Falenica near Warsaw was flooded with about four thousand Hasidim from all around the country, and Polish State Railways provided additional trains for Jewish men and boys who wanted to assist in the circumcision of the son of Gerer Rebe Avraham Mordechai Alter.[15] The stream of men was so large that the town needed guards to provide rule and order, and some of the visitors slept in the fields. As is the case with most rituals in Orthodox Judaism, only men attended the festive circumcision, which underscored its male centeredness and its importance for performative reproducing of normative Orthodox masculinity. Orthodox Jews saw circumcision as part of the Jewish life cycle and exchanged postcards (fig. 2.1 and fig. 2.2) that underscored the festive character of the ritual.

Family celebrations accompanied Orthodox circumcisions in Poland, stabilizing its normativity among local Orthodox Jews. The circumcision ceremony was preceded by *shulem zakhar*

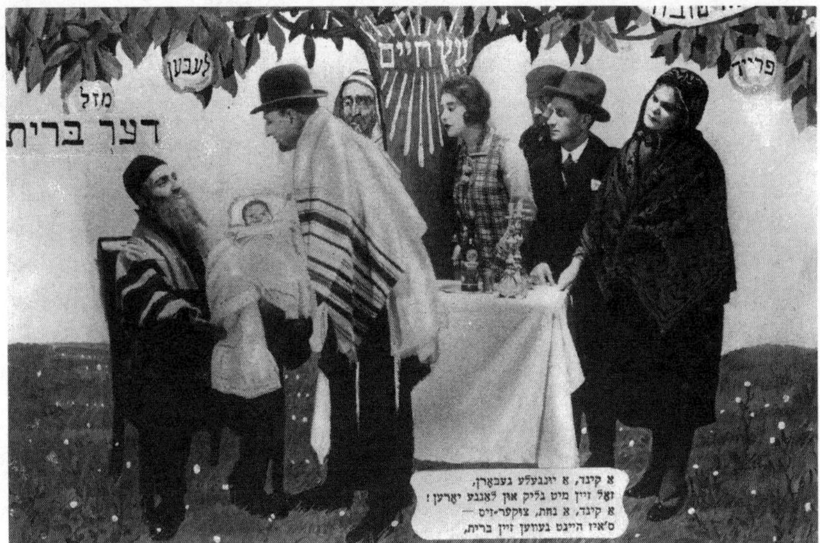

Figure 2.1. Circumcision ceremony, Rosh Ha-Shanah postcard, Poland, 1910s or 1920s. William A. Rosenthall Judaica Collection - Postcards, College of Charleston Libraries.

gatherings several days before and followed by parties known as *brisim*, which Poland's Orthodox Jews called *simkhes*, or happy celebrations.[16] Regina Lilientalowa's ethnographic research on Orthodox Jews in early twentieth-century Poland has revealed a wide array of prayers, rituals, and ceremonies positively valuing circumcision.[17] Before the circumcision of a baby boy, young boys would pray in the room where the newborn was sleeping and ask God and the angels to protect the baby before he entered the covenant with God. The boys' prayers could also be understood as the first instance of including the newborn boy into the male community. The birth of a girl was not associated with an analogous tradition. Also, putting the Hebrew Bible under the pillow of the newborn prior to circumcision was a practice intended to protect him from evil spirits, yet at the same time, it emphasized that literacy in the Jewish texts was then a masculine realm. These folkloric and religious practices defined circumcision as a major event in the Jewish Orthodox life cycle and contributed to marking gender differences between men and women.

The Orthodox understanding of circumcision as constitutive of masculinity is traceable, particularly in accounts of Polish-Jewish boys and men who decided to become circumcised at a later age. These late circumcisions marked their turning into "complete Jewish men" and their inclusion into the community of Jewish men. In 1922, the Jewish daily reported on thirty-year-old Isser-Gershon, whose brit milah was described as a festive act of "yudishn," that is, "Judaizing," and cordially welcomed the "new Jewish man."[18] In a 1923 case of a twenty-year-old man who decided for a brit milah in Warsaw, the Jewish press reported that, prior to the ceremony, the Jewish man "was very happy" and "just jumped onto the [surgical] table." The young man's eagerness to be circumcised communicated his desire to become a normative Jewish man. He did not define his masculinity in comparison to the hegemonic masculinity represented by uncircumcised Christian men but through adherence to the Jewish rituals of masculinization. The to-be-circumcised man proclaimed, "Ikh bin gliklekh vos ikh hob derlebt dem tog vos ikh ver a yid" (I'm happy to have reached the day when I became a Jewish man).[19] The surgery in Warsaw became a point of interest for the community—the courtyard filled with curious men and women. This story illustrates the performative character of circumcision. The ritual was not a private religious issue but rather a public moment of "Judaizing" the penis and granting its owner access to complete Jewish masculinity. Paradoxically, by cutting off the foreskin, Orthodox Jewish men were not "losing" anything but rather, according to the standards they adhered to, were becoming complete men.

For Orthodox Jews, remaining uncircumcised was linked with shame, and the choice not to circumcise a child was often a well-kept secret. In particular, not being circumcised brought into question Jewish men's ability to marry and provided them with a sense of inferiority. A man from Łódź nursed a grudge against his parents for not circumcising him since avoiding the ritual made him non-Jewish in the eyes of the religious parents of his fiancée and hence not a man eligible for marriage.[20] Another man, Yudel Zilbershteyn from Radom, who was not circumcised as a baby due to his family's medical history, "suffered a lot" for not being circumcised. This became a shameful public issue for him in his town and also resulted in him not being able to find a wife.[21] One Kraków Hasid named Haim realized, at the age of sixty, that his circumcision had not been performed professionally and that he was in fact uncircumcised. Following numerous consultations with religious leaders, Haim decided for a second bris and only afterward "felt a complete Jewish man."[22] Missing circumcision made Jewish men nonnormative, ineligible for marriage, and hence disqualified as men.

Remaining uncircumcised led to exclusion from Orthodox Jewish masculinity—an exclusion that, for some boys and men, was unbearable. We observe here a reversed situation of the case of Jewish men being ridiculed by Christian men for not having the foreskin. An example of the exclusion of uncircumcised boys from the Jewish boys' community is the story of the son of a man named Leyb Akerman, who, considering himself a progressive Jew, decided not to circumcise his son. When the boy reached the age of five, the information about his uncircumcised penis got around, and the insults of *sheygets* and *goyets* (non-Jew) became increasingly bothersome for the boy. The discrimination was so painful that eventually the boy "happily jumped on the operation table" and was overjoyed to finally receive a Jewish first name.[23] A thirteen-year-old boy from Warsaw, who was not circumcised because his two brothers died during the bris, wished to become "a fulkomer yud" (a complete Jew), before his bar mitzvah. While the surgery was less important for the boy's father, Moshe Grossman, and his wife, for their son who wanted to be included in the boys' group, it was a crucial matter.

In this boy's case, we also read about a happy boy "jumping on the operation table." Just like men in the military who verified their masculinity through tests of perserverance, also this Orthodox boy considered physical suffering to masculinize him. The boy even asked the doctor not to give him anesthesia since "he wanted to suffer so that his mitzvah [religious obligation] would be greater."[24] This case demonstrates how Polish Jews defined late circumcision as a ritual providing access to Jewish masculinity and as a Jewish "rite of passage."

In addition, acting as a sandak and holding the baby boy at circumcision offered Jewish men the possibility to elevate their status within the Orthodox gender order. In Poland, wealthy Jewish men's desire to be respected by fulfilling the sandak mitzvah was intertwined with poor Jews' desire to receive financial support for the ceremony. The Yiddish term for offering someone the opportunity to be a sandak was *mekhabed zayn*, which meant honoring someone with this function. In many cases, families who did not have the resources to finance the circumcision party approached rich men with an offer to be a sandak and financially contribute to the celebration. Some men explicitly demanded the chance to serve as sandakim at brisim falling on Jewish holidays and actively fought for this privilege.[25] The community intervened when fathers were financially unable to provide a proper setting for the circumcision. In the case of one father living in a shack, the community collected money so that he could rent a flat where the circumcision could be celebrated properly.[26] In Volkovysk, the neighbors of a poor Jewish baker sponsored cakes and alcohol to celebrate the birth of his son and managed to find a sandak willing to donate money for the bris.[27] Not only the circumcision itself included a boy or man into the Jewish gender order but also everything that surrounded the bris, such as being a sandak, upheld male Orthodox hierarchies.

Assisting at a circumcision could stabilize the masculinity of men who due to their nonnormativity were not considered proper Jewish men. In Warsaw in 1939, the perspective of fulfilling a mitzvah by serving as a sandak lured childless Orthodox Jews.[28] Since the Orthodox world considered childlessness nonnormative, and becoming a sandak was believed to raise one's chances of having children, by serving as sandakim, childless men hoped to increase their communal respectability. In Warsaw, a couple of Jewish swindlers named Abraham Zaremba and Itzkhak Tsvaygl, relying on the importance and holiness of serving as a sandak for religious Jewish men, managed to convince several charitable men to make advance payments for circumcision ceremonies at which they were to be sandakim. This turned out to be a swindle, as Zaremba and Tsvaygl took advantage of the benevolence that other Jewish men connected with assisting at the brit milah.[29] Similar stories of abusing the generosity of the wealthy with promises of masculine respectability regularly appeared in Poland.[30] However, assisting at the circumcision of a boy raised by a single mother was not deemed as ennobling as doing so for a family whose reputation was not questionable. For instance, a Białystok rabbi named Rozenbaum refused to serve as the sandak for a single mother who had approached him.[31] Since the Jewish woman transgressed Orthodox moral norms by having premarital sex, the rabbi hoped to maintain Orthodox sexual normativity by refusing to be the sandak of her son.

Numerous Jewish literary sources in Polish and Yiddish featured religious Jewish men defining assistance at circumcision events as a "holy deed" or "holy work." Sholem Ash's renowned novel *Motke Ganef* (Motke the thief) demonstrated how, for marginalized men, assisting at a brit milah was a form of recuperating their communal and gender status. The Blind Leyb enjoyed his honorable role of sandak, which starkly contrasted with his poverty and disability and hence his lack of respectability within the Jewish hierarchy. He said to himself, "What an honorable thing it is to do the bris. One can eat tasty foods, get some vodka, and even money. One becomes a man, becomes respected. What a shame that I can't do the bris every day!"[32] The Blind Leyb compared himself to the other men present in the room, who were either rich or held an office, and noticed how his role in the religious ritual enhanced his masculine status. In the 1910 short story *Skąpiec: Z legend żydowskich* (The miser: From the Jewish legends), its protagonist, Abraham Rzechta, described the circumcision of the firstborn boy in a family as a "święty uczynek" [a holy deed].[33] In Y. L. Peretz's *In alt Khelem (a mayseleh)* (In old Chełm: A tale), Chełm's Polish-Jewish men signaled the communal prestige enjoyed by sandaks and invited the rabbi to assist at the circumcision "of every newborn boy."[34]

Performing the circumcision was linked with policing Jewish gender normativity. The community labeled Jewish mothers refusing to allow their sons to be circumcised as transgressors intruding into the masculine domain. Malke Shtaynberg's fear of the possible medical consequences of the circumcision of her son was identified by the community as a mental disease, and the woman spent several years in sanatoriums and psychiatric hospitals.[35] The mother' wish to independently decide what happened to the body of her son was met with opposition from the Orthodox community, who wished to maintain the bodily standards of Jewish masculinity and the male monopoly over determining Jewishness and masculinity. A similar logic appeared in 1930s Lviv, where one journalist called for making sure to circumcise the extramarital abandoned baby boys of Jewish mothers.[36] The man believed that circumcision would transform these boys into normative Jewish men, including in the case of those who would grow up in an orphanage. When a wealthy Jewish merchant from Chmielnik continued to postpone the bris of his son, the community accused him of being parsimonious and hoping to save money by not organizing a party. The press described the case as "scandalous" and celebrated the return of normativity when the baby boy was circumcised.[37] Also, in a growing number of interreligious relationships, Jewish men perceived circumcision as a mechanism of Jewishly "normalizing" their sons. David Berger, a "half-assimilated" wood exporter from Warsaw, insisted on circumcising his son born by his Christian lover, Marylka.[38] While Berger knew that by having an affair, he had crossed the borders of Jewish sexual and family normativity, he still sought to include his son into normative Jewish masculinity and hoped that his insistence would rehabilitate his own respectability as a Jewish man.

Patriarchal Orthodox Jewish culture favored masculinity over femininity as the preferred gender, and in a Polish-Jewish shtetl setting, there existed rare practices of assigning transgender babies to the male gender. In 1908, Lipa Laykin wrote of a boy who was assigned as female at birth and accordingly named Rachel.[39] When the village began to gossip that Rachel had "turned into a boy," the family and the community began a process of masculinizing the child, now named Eliahu. Rachel-Eliahu was brought to a rabbi, who cut the child's hair short, and his foreskin was removed. Following the custom of asking wealthy men of the community to serve as sandak, local rich man Yehuda Leyb Gurevich performed the duty. After the circumcision ritual, the masculinity of Eliahu was confirmed: he began to pray in the synagogue and read from the Torah "just like any other man" and was married off. While Rachel-Eliahu was probably an intersex person, for the community and the family, it was important to maintain the dichotomous gender order, and the child ended up masculine. The initial confusion was followed by a process of community-run gender reassignment involving the name change from Rachel to Eliahu and ultimately the circumcision that included Rachel-Eliahu into the male religious community. Circumcision was such a clear and powerful marker of Jewish masculinity that even in rare cases of intersex people, it was applied to tip the scale from femininity to masculinity.

IS IT HEALTHY OR BARBARIC? THE JEWISH AMBIVALENCE ABOUT CIRCUMCISION AND ITS MEDICALIZATION

When, in the late 1920s, Polish-Catholic historian Tadeusz Zieliński published his work *Hellenizm i judaizm* (Hellenism and Judaism), Edmund Stein, a Jewish lecturer from the Warsaw Institute of Judaic Studies, fiercely criticized several of Zieliński's assertions. One of Stein's key points was the issue of circumcision. Whereas, for the Catholic Zieliński, circumcision was a matter of shame, for Stein it was a matter of his Jewish masculine pride and male health. Zieliński argued that the circumcision commandment was a "test of ridicule" and that God wanted to "ridicule" his people in front of other nations. For Zieliński, the Jewish ritual of circumcision was indeed ridiculous and ugly. In his response, Stein demonstrated that analogous practices in ancient Egypt and other bodily/sexual religious practices of the Greeks that Zieliński discussed did not receive a pronouncement of being "ugly."[40] For Stein, circumcision was nothing to be ashamed of. Conversely, his text underscored the health benefits of the ritual and presented it as "medically-evidenced."[41]

We may note here that both Catholic and Jewish scholars used the authority of history and medicine to express their own cultural and aesthetic judgments about circumcision. As modern medical knowledge increased among Jews in Poland, circumcision and its importance for Jewishness and masculinity were increasingly put into question, in particular among acculturated urban middle-class Polish Jews. The debates around modernizing and abolishing circumcision expressed a change in beliefs concerning what made a modern Jewish man. While only a minority of Jewish men stopped circumcising their sons, the new figure of a Jewish doctor performing the circumcision emerged in Poland. This new figure allowed acculturated men to still embrace circumcision as a central mechanism for constructing Jewish masculinity, yet in a form that respected their modern beliefs based on science and hygiene. As more Polish Jews approached Jewish-ness in terms of ethnicity rather than religion, the circumcising surgeon appeared more relevant than the traditional mohel.

Two decades before Edmund Stein approached circumcision in a positive light, Poland saw a rise in disagreeing Jewish voices. One of the key Jewish opponents of circumcision in Poland was ethnographer Regina Lilientalowa. In her 1908 brochure, *Precz z barbarzyństwem (rzecz o obrzezaniu)* (End the barbarism: On circumcision), Lilientalowa approached the ritual as barbaric and called on "all those who feel for the child" to abandon it.[42] Cir-cumcision was for Lilientalowa a "disgusting ballast of the past" and "a creation of the wild temptations of the primordial horde" that modern, Zionist-nationalized Jews should eliminate. While Lilientalowa recognized that the ritual had once served specific historical goals, namely to separate Jews more clearly from the people who oppressed them, she did not see its relevance in the early twentieth century. In Lilientalowa's call to halt circumci-sion, we do not find the Jewish self-hatred that sometimes defined anticircumcision attitudes in western Europe. Rather, it is her theory of evolutionism that stipulated that "the symbols of old beliefs and notions" should disappear, since Jewish peoplehood "was not defined by circumcision and other outdated practices."[43] For Lilientalowa, a confident Jewishness was in one's mind and not a bodily mark.

Poland's freethinkers' press had also been calling for the ab-olition of circumcision. In 1908, *Myśl niepodległa* (Independent thought) featured a text titled "Barbarzyństwa judaistyczne" (Judaic barbarities) that presented Jewish voices commenting on a prominent case of a Jewish boy who needed to be circumcised postmortem in order to be buried in Warsaw's Jewish cemetery.[44] In 1927, non-Jewish activist Ludwik Krzywicki published an ar-ticle about circumcision in the freethinkers' journal *Życie wolne* (The free life) focusing on circumcision among native tribes. In this article, titled "Dawne obrzezanie" (Ancient circumcision),

Krzywicki studied the origins of the ritual among the peoples of Australasia and described the ritual as "mutilation," pointing out similarities between "native" practices coded as brutal, disgusting, and inhumane (such as devouring the foreskin) and the origins of the Jewish *metsitsa* (sucking off the penis's blood with lips).[45] Publishing his reflections in 1928 with the same publisher as Lilientalowa, Krzywicki probably aimed to contribute to the ongoing Polish debates about circumcision, and his work echoed that of Jewish proponents of abolishing the ritual. While Krzywicki did not refer to masculinity in his study, his goal was to define circumcision as inhumane and destabilize its positive association held by many Jews in Poland.

Lilientalowa's and Krzywicki's arguments reflected a broader criticism among educated Jewish circles around the world. For example, Ben-Zion Lieber, a Jewish doctor in New York, argued in his 1927 work on human sexuality that, whereas religious Jews should perform circumcision as a religious practice, he opposed inventing seemingly medical reasons for circumcision to be practiced by *fraydenker* (freethinker) unreligious Jews. Referring to the child's right to self-determination, Lieber argued that circumcision violated this right by imprinting the boy with a religious mark. Circumcision was thus a *fargevaltigung*—a word that signifies both violation (of a child's right to religious freedom) and rape. Like Lilientalowa, Lieber suggested that even without circumcision, a boy could grow up as a "loyal Jew in a national sense." He opposed circumcision if not carried out with due medical care and, also like Lilientalowa, linked the ritual with the human sacrifice practiced by the "wild tribes," comparing circumcision with "sacrificing humans."[46] Jewish critics such as Lilientalowa and Lieber disassociated circumcision from any notion of Jewishness or Jewish masculinity and cast it as outdated barbarity.

The debates of the early twentieth century were not the first time Polish Jews considered abandoning or reforming the ritual.

Since the 1840s, the medicalization of the discourse around circumcision grew in Poland, and sporadic Jewish and non-Jewish voices appeared even earlier. Medicalization refers to the process of turning a social phenomenon, process, or condition into a medical matter. In 1842, Jewish doctor Beniamin Rosenblum informed Polish Jews about the health dangers linked to Jewish rituals and called for regulating these rituals in state health policies. Rosenblum believed that circumcision posed diverse medical dangers, not as a Jewish religious practice but as an improper medical procedure. Some mohelim supposedly cut off a fragment of the penis glans, resulting in bleeding, and thousands of children were said to be infected with sexual diseases because the mohelim lacked satisfactory medical knowledge. Rosenblum called on the government to require doctors to accompany every bris and maintain a list of authorized mohelim.[47] Non-Jewish doctors echoed Rosenblum's concerns. T. Belke, head of the hospital Świętego Łazarza in Warsaw, perceived circumcision as one of the main channels for transmitting syphilis.[48] The critical voices seemed to have gained some resonance among Warsaw Jews, and, by the mid-nineteenth century, some Jewish families commissioned doctors to perform the circumcision while a mohel was responsible only for the prayer.[49] For this small minority, science had begun to replace religion as the main tool for explaining the world, and they relegated religious circumcision to the realm of pathology, for which the solution was either its abolition or subordination to medical standards.

In late nineteenth- and early twentieth-century Poland, Jewish doctors appeared at the forefront of circumcision debates and attempted to convince Jewish fathers that circumcision was not only a religious ritual but also a medical procedure verified by science. The combination of these two elements allowed circumcision to become the marker of modernized Jewish masculinity. One of the earliest pamphlets that followed this line of argument and appeared in Poland was *Wieczny związek: Obrzezanie ze stanowiska obrządkowego, chirurgicznego i higienicznego* (The eternal union: Circumcision from a ritual, chirurgic and hygienic standpoint), published in 1883 by a Hungarian-Jewish doctor, Josef Ruff.[50] Twenty-five years later, Przemyśl Jewish doctor Samuel Natan Kutna argued that "circumcision conducted at an early age by a trained hand, that is, according to chirurgical knowledge, is obviously a useful operation beneficial for health that should be considered a preventative rule across the world."[51] Kutna's eloquent and well-researched work also addressed the link between masculinity and circumcision. Refuting the ideas of Christian scientists, Kutna claimed that "circumcision is not a lesser degree of castration, it is rather the opposite of emasculation."[52] Jewish doctors integrated the old circumcision ritual into the new medicalized scientific discourse, and circumcision appeared to be coherent with the sense of modernity that acculturated Jewish men had internalized.

As circumcision became increasingly medicalized, medical experts in the United States and Great Britain also advised prophylactic circumcision among Christians and linked it to improving men's health. While some Polish researchers were aware of these recommendations, the dominant stance in Poland was that proper hygiene was enough to keep men healthy. However, contrary voices were also present. In the 1870s, Catholic doctor Stanisław Janikowski saw traditional Jewish circumcision as "repulsive" yet was optimistic that circumcision could reduce "licentious manipulations," that is, masturbation, which was then seen as detrimental to male health. Janikowski followed American and British arguments praising the ways circumcision could improve health and "morality" if it was more widespread among Christians. Among Jewish critics, we rarely find voices linking circumcision with the taming of male sexuality. The Jewish doctor Kutna challenged the idea that circumcision "lowered exaggerated lust and sinful voluptuousness" and concluded that circumcised men were not less affected than the uncircumcised.[53]

Because circumcision in Poland was rarely conceptualized as a measure to enhance male health or protect men from excessive lust, circumcision remained a mark, or a metonym, of Jewishness, rather than a mass practice that in other countries was intended to produce healthier men.

The medicalization of Jewish circumcision intensified in independent Poland. The Society for the Protection of Health of the Jewish Population in Poland (Towarzystwo Ochrony Zdrowia Ludności Żydowskiej w Polsce) appealed in 1928 for the introduction of a health test and obligatory medical practice requirement for mohelim.[54] In 1934, a Jewish doctor from Nowy Targ named Zachariasz Goldner initiated a debate in which he criticized the standards of circumcision. Local surgeries were allegedly improperly conducted by unprofessional *shokhtim* (kosher butchers) and not mohelim, implying a measure of brutality and carelessness in his comparison. The investigation commission revealed that dozens of circumcisions in southwestern Poland had been incorrectly performed. Seventy boys older than eleven were sent to Kraków to "complete" their circumcision according to newly established medical standards.[55] Addressing a traditional population in Kalisz in 1938, one Jewish doctor named I. Gott argued that circumcision was a hygienic measure, and he embedded the ritual in his wider set of arguments about Jewish superiority in matters of hygiene. Speaking as a medical professional but explaining that the Hebrew Bible was filled with recommendations for good hygiene, Gott strengthened the medicalization argument and made the traditional Jewish population more receptive to modern medical knowledge.[56] These interwar Jewish doctors sought to free circumcision and thus the definition of Jewish masculinity from the authority of religion. While circumcision would remain the sign of Jewish masculinity, it was to be governed by modern medical standards and performed by the mohelim of the modern era—Jewish male doctors.

In the 1930s, medicine was indeed exercising its growing influence on circumcision in Poland. More Jewish parents followed the logic of medicalization and commissioned doctors to circumcise their sons. The weakening position of the traditional mohelim made the Orthodox Jewry fear losing their former monopoly. In 1932, the conference of Polish Orthodox rabbis expressed concern when the Warsaw Jewish hospital did not allow circumcisions for newborns who weighed less than three kilograms.[57] According to statistics provided by the mohelim, in the 1930s, more and more doctors were performing circumcisions while the mohelim were not invited at all. Consequently, the daily number of religious brisim performed by mohelim fell from about forty just before World War I to only about ten in 1935, and the doctors did not follow the religious commandment to circumcise on the eighth day after birth.[58] Importantly, in the early 1930s, about 45 percent of physicians in Poland were Jewish, and the doctors who circumcised Jewish boys were almost exclusively Jewish men. In this sense, circumcision was becoming a male-centered and male-performed process of inclusion into the community of Jewish men in an ethnic sense, rather than a religious act.

To remain relevant in light of the evolving Jewish attitudes concerning circumcision, in 1931 the Warsaw kehillah embraced the medicalization logic and indeed issued a set of rules for licensing mohelim.[59] The kehillah's vice president, Moshe Feldstein, compared mohelim to engineers and mechanics and spoke of them as specialists who needed to have a profound and scientific, up-to-date knowledge of their trade. The new regulations appeared in a joint edition with Mordechai Lensky's medical introduction, in which he explained the basics of antiseptics and human anatomy. The document stipulated, among other things, that mohelim needed to complete medical training and acquire a health certificate. Each mohel was to possess a sterilization device and a glass of antiseptic *jodyna* (tincture of iodine) and to wear a white protective apron. These regulations were not adopted by state bodies but rather by

Figure 2.2. Circumcision ceremony, postcard, Kraków, Poland, 1905. William A. Rosenthall Judaica Collection - Postcards, College of Charleston Libraries.

the Jewish communal self-government in light of a growing number of infant deaths due to medical mistakes, lack of hygiene, or the unprofessionalism of mohelim and also because of the evolving attitudes of parents. Analogous debates took place in other Polish cities.[60] The Warsaw regulations stipulated that older men above the age of sixty-five could not work as mohelim. In that sense, circumcision was defined as a practice to be performed by men in their full masculine power. This change to a certain extent contradicted the patriarchal hierarchy of masculine virtues typical for Orthodox Judaism, which respected the wise patriarch the older he became.[61]

Next to medicalization, circumcision was also becoming increasingly commercialized in interwar Poland where performing circumcisions was disassociated from the religious deed and turned into a profession. More and more mohelim openly demanded money for their services instead of receiving compensation under the table.[62] While some mohelim were eager to perform circumcision for free as a mitzvah, others, especially in the case of circumcisions on adult men, were demanding significant financial compensation.[63] Already in 1912, the Vaad Ha-Mohelim (Mohelim Council) complained that brit milah had "turned into a business" and "a disorder" in Warsaw.[64] Its successor organization, the Agudas Ha-Mohelim (Mohelim Union), saw itself as a community of religious men who performed the brisim as a godly commandment and excluded mohelim for whom circumcision became a source of income.[65] In the mid-1930s, the Warsaw Jewish religious establishment claimed that the issue of circumcision was ruled by "lawlessness" and "anarchy." In 1935, the rabbinate complained that no one was overseeing the circumcision market in Warsaw and that about four hundred mohelim were using forged documents, while other sources spoke of a monopoly by a certain group of mohelim and midwives.[66] If religious circumcision was so corrupt, the reasoning of many Jewish fathers went, they could instead let Jewish doctors circumcise their newborns.

In 1930s Poland, circumcision was becoming a medical intervention rather than only a religious rite. Circumcision remained the mechanism of inclusion into the community of Jewish men but became medicalized and to a certain extent disassociated from religion. This medicalization did not lead to abolishing circumcision but only reformed it. The once separate figures of the physician, representing non-Jewish knowledge, and the religious mohel merged into a new kind of medically certified figure of a circumcising Jewish doctor who enjoyed legitimacy from modern institutions but also maintained the Jewishness of the ritual. Both being circumcised and performing circumcisions found new forms to reassure Jewish masculinity—the circumcised boy was inscribed into a legitimate ideal of Jewish masculinity, and the new figure of the Jewish doctor performing circumcisions integrated modern science with ethnic-understood Jewishness.

SECULAR JEWISHNESS AND THE
MASCULINITY OF REFUSAL

When more Polish-Jewish men began to define their masculinity in terms of the virtues of personal freedom and persistence and formed bourgeois masculine subjectivities, the meaning of circumcision in defining Jewish masculinity in Poland gained particular importance. While secularizing and socialist or communist Jewish men held an ambivalent attitude toward circumcision, this ambivalence only underscored the centrality of circumcision for the sense of being a Jewish man in interwar Poland. First, even when some men wished to disentangle circumcision and masculinity and believed that Jewish masculinity should disconnect from the ritual, the pressure they faced to circumcise revealed the powerful workings of Orthodox Jewish masculinity. Second, for men who refused to circumcise their sons, their decision not to circumcise expressed what they saw as masculine virtues: assertiveness, confidence, self-assuredness, and the strength not to capitulate to external pressure.

In the 1930s, letting boys remain uncircumcised was becoming increasingly common among acculturated Polish Jews. In 1935, the Zionist vice president of the Warsaw kehillah spoke of "hundreds of uncircumcised Jewish children."[67] The government felt urged to solve the situation by issuing a circular obliging the kehillot to issue birth certificates even to uncircumcised Jewish boys.[68] At the same time, many acculturated Jewish men still believed that circumcision was a critical part of marking Jewish masculinity but began to consider the ceremony outdated or inconsistent with their worldview and lifestyle. In one case, a Jewish engineer going by the Polish name Jerzy was "ashamed in front of his Christian neighbors" about circumcising his son, and so the bris ceremony was organized almost in secret.[69] Jerzy was scared that the neighbors would uncover his Jewish identity, so he made sure to lock all the doors and anxiously waited for the end of the operation. Another Warsaw Jewish engineer who had a baby with a Christian woman was afraid of holding the brit milah at his home and attracting the attention of his Christian neighbors. Nevertheless, the engineer still believed that his son needed to be circumcised and therefore hired a mohel and gathered a minyan of Jews and performed the bris in a rented space.[70] While more and more acculturated Polish-Jewish men refrained from circumcising their sons, the examples of these two Jewish engineers demonstrate that acculturation was not automatically linked with a rejection of circumcision. Many men wished their sons to be inscribed into the Jewish male community and believed that the power to decide about a son's circumcision was within the male realm and validated their own sense of masculinity. At the same time, acculturated Jewish men were to a great extent conditioned by non-Jewish imaginations of circumcision that cast shame on the practice.

A major debate concerning circumcision, masculinity, and religious freedom erupted in 1908, when the Warsaw rabbinate refused to bury a ten-month-old boy who was not circumcised.[71] Herman Grynszpan, the father of the boy, considered the decision of the rabbinate an abuse and violation of his freedom of conscience. Grynszpan himself felt very Jewish due to "a shared historical fate and solidarity in resistance to legal and social discrimination," yet he defined his Jewishness very differently from what he described as the "fanatical rabbinate." In his letter published in *Nowa Gazeta*, Grynszpan applied arguments from the anticircumcision debates about the "barbarity" of the ritual. He considered circumcision to be a bodily mutilation and "a barbaric symbol and a remnant of paganism," and in his view, it was not an expression of true Jewishness.[72] The Grynszpan case led to a wide discussion in Warsaw. Some contributors to the debate complained that the kehillah refused to bury the child of a poor man while numerous uncircumcised men from the Jewish elite rested in the Warsaw cemetery.[73] At stake was the question: What was the influence of refusal to circumcise on the construction of Jewishness and masculinity?

One of the central voices in the debate was the young Yiddish writer Sholem Ash, who opposed circumcision as such. Like Grynszpan, Ash saw the procedure as a barbaric act, "a wild operation," and used the analogy of "wild tribes" that had appeared among many abolitionist contributors. Ash's text was met with a public outcry, and some Warsaw Jews denied him the right to speak out. While historian Gershon Bacon contextualized this circumcision scandal in Warsaw in light of the conflict between acculturated Jewish freethinkers and the Orthodoxy, I suggest viewing it in the context of gender.[74] The refusal to circumcise was about not only the question of what constituted Jewishness but also the question of what constituted Jewish masculinity. Grynszpan insisted that he, as a father, had a right to decide what happened to the penis of his son, and in that way, he underscored the Western virtues of independence and persistence that he considered essential for establishing his sense of masculinity. Grynszpan claimed the authority to decide that neither the Jewishness nor the masculinity of his son depended on the ritual and the shape of his penis. Almost all other actors who participated in the 1908 debate were men, and the masculine authority over circumcision was universally recognized. The changing Jewish gender-related significance of circumcision, and its interplay with general European masculine virtues, contributed to the intensity of the debate.

For Jewish Bundist, socialist, and communist men, religious rites were particularly problematic. In 1927, high-profile Bundist leader Wiktor Alter refused to circumcise his son.[75] His objection to the religious rite became a public issue debated in the Jewish and non-Jewish press. For the Orthodox majority, who still controlled the definition of normative Jewish masculinity in Poland, circumcision was tied up with inclusion into both masculinity and Jewishness. Wiktor Alter openly questioned the logic linking circumcision and the validation of Jewish masculinity, and observers noted that he wanted to make his case public to fight the religious coercion and power of the rabbis.[76] When the Alter case emerged in 1920s Warsaw, in eastern and central Poland, Russian regulations on vital records were still in force that authorized the kehillah to register Jewish births. Jewish fathers who decided not to circumcise their sons faced diverse legal obstacles, including rabbis who refused to issue them birth certificates. Wiktor Alter was forced to appeal to the ministry of the interior, and ultimately an exceptional solution was found.[77] While, in a similar German case from 1840s Frankfurt, the central issue was uncircumcised boys' belonging to the Jewish community,[78] in the case of Wiktor Alter in 1920s Warsaw, the issue was graver, since it linked circumcision with the basic registration of birth. Acting from a position of religious freedom, Alter hoped to define Jewishness and masculinity in secular terms. He considered circumcision an oppressive act of religious coercion, which he resisted by expressing a masculinity centered around determination and perseverance.

Another left-wing Jewish man, Sholem Wandel, promised in 1935 to never forgive his wife, who had secretly circumcised their son. The act of circumcision was for him a form of "public shaming" in front of his Communist-minded comrades and another example demonstrating that Jewish men considered their sons' penises key to defining their own sense of resistant and independent masculinity. First, Wandel believed that he had not managed to safeguard his newborn son from a religious practice he considered oppressive. Second, his wife proved to be able to act against his will and challenged the patriarchal hierarchy of power.[79] Similar was the position of Moshe Yaremtshik from Warsaw, who as a leftist did not allow his son to be circumcised despite the protests of his wife.[80] In Sosnowiec, another Jewish man wished to register the birth of his son and, upon being asked if the baby boy had been circumcised, shouted, "I don't believe in this prejudice and

I won't allow them to circumcise my child!"[81] Parents with leftist views who refused to circumcise their children were often described in the Jewish press as *farakshnt* (stubborn) and *fraydenker* (freethinkers). Their socialist or communist beliefs, linked with the rejection of tradition, placed these parents outside normative Orthodox Jewishness. One Jewish newspaper linked communism with criminality, nonspousal sexual relations, and breaking the religious consensus on the male penis.[82] The proponents of Orthodoxy referred with disbelief to the situation in the Soviet Union, where circumcision could have led to legal action or exclusion from the Communist Party.[83] Despite this conservative opposition, some left-wing Jewish men constructed their sense of masculinity precisely around their determination to stick to their worldview and remain consistent.

Socialist Jewish men who refused to circumcise their sons turned into literary figures. In this sense, Yiddish literature evolved into a space for discussing Jewish masculinities in the context of the tension between secularism and Orthodoxy. In Yosef Opatoshu's short story *Printispn* (Principles), we encounter Sonye and Grishe, a young couple with a baby boy named Abrahaml.[84] Grisha was a Jewish Socialist with strong *printispn* that did not allow him to commission a religious circumcision. As in the case of Sholem Wandel, his masculine reputation was at stake. When Sonya insisted on circumcising their son, Grisha answered angrily, "What face would I have in the party if I allowed them to circumcise Abrahaml? You know that I am a man of principles, why do you still insist?" The story pictured two conflicting visions of Jewish masculinity: the Socialist one of Grisha and the traditional one held by Abrahaml's grandfather Shulem. Since his grandson was not circumcised, Shulem felt ashamed in front of his community in the synagogue and stopped attending services. Not being able to enforce the ritual, Shulem felt emasculated as the family patriarch. Shulem and Grisha adhered to competing models of Jewish masculinity and defined their sense of respectability differently, but both felt they were in charge of deciding the fate of Abrahaml's penis and saw this authority as central to marking their own masculinity. Opatoshu's story demonstrates that the issue of shame in a given homosocial environment was a major aspect of being perceived as masculine and could lead to familial clashes. Similar to Grynszpan, Wandel, and Alter, the protagonists of Opatoshu's story also underscored how central circumcision was for defining the Jewishness and masculinity of men who distanced themselves from Judaism.

Early twentieth-century Poland witnessed the emergence of a growing phenomenon of parents refusing to circumcise newborn Jewish boys. While the decision not to adhere to the rite could be conceptualized as a form of subjugation to the norm in non-Jewish society, I suggest that the issue was much more complex. By fighting for their freedom of conscience and religious freedom, Polish-Jewish men underscored their own vision of masculinity. Many of them were confident and proud Jews who nevertheless conceptualized Jewishness through the ethnic and not the religious dimension. Herman Grynszpan, Wiktor Alter, and other left-wing Jewish men considered the decision about circumcision as central to their own sense of Jewish masculinity. They framed Jewish masculinity through notions of assertiveness, confidence, and the refusal to capitulate under pressure. The same masculine logic was true for acculturated Jewish men who, despite the shame that non-Jewish society linked to circumcision, did decide to circumcise their sons and ignore the social pressure.

ANTISEMITES AND CIRCUMCISION: NARRATIVES OF HUMILIATION

While most Jews still viewed circumcision positively, Polish-Jewish interwar attitudes to circumcision were to a certain extent also shaped by how the general society approached the ritual. In Poland's antisemitic print culture, circumcision appeared as a vehicle to socially exclude Jews as foreigners and others. Already in nineteenth-century Poland, Christians perceived circumcision as a violent act. In 1822, Warsaw newspapers reported on one Herszek Arensztajn, who allegedly violently circumcised a five-year-old Christian boy he happened to meet on the street.[85] While, in the early twentieth century, those blood libel–like associations with circumcision disappeared, Polish antisemites developed a discourse in which circumcision was inherently linked with inferiority. The vocabulary pertaining to circumcision depicted it as brutal, unhygienic, shameful, and ultimately emasculating. For example, an antisemitic cover of a Polish patriotic song ran, "Sanacjo, sanacjo, cóżeś ty za pani, że za tobą ida, chłopcy obrzezani."[86] The song linked circumcision with an increased readiness of Jewish men to serve in the military while simultaneously rejecting their claims to hegemonic masculinity. While, for the majority of Jewish men in Poland, circumcision stabilized their sense of masculinity, for antisemites, it acquired a stigma.

Cases of Christian men who underwent circumcision during love-inspired conversions to Judaism emphasized how antisemites linked circumcision with inferiority and emasculation. In one of these cases, a peasant named Franciszek developed feelings for Itka, daughter of a Hasid from a village in the vicinity of Radom, and decided on conversion and circumcision. While we do not know the details, the Jewish newspaper suggested that the man wanted the surgery to please his wife rather than to adjust to the expectations of her parents.[87] In another case of a Jewish-Christian love affair, Dr. S. from Radomsko was circumcised at the age of forty-two in order to marry a local Jewish girl.[88] A similar case from Kraków raised so much interest that even a newspaper from remote Vilna reported about Antoni Semenowicz, a Catholic policeman who converted to Judaism for his Jewish female lover and was forced to retire.[89] Reports from the Jewish and non-Jewish press about circumcisions of converts pictured the ritual as crossing ethnic and gender boundaries. In this logic, Christian men underwent an emasculating and enforced ritual, relinquished their Christian masculinity, and, as the case of Semenowicz shows, lost their former status. The Polish press lamented the physical suffering of to-be-circumcised Christian men and suggested that they had betrayed their ethnic and religious community. While those reports did not explicitly link circumcision with any sexual dysfunction, they did portray it as submitting to the sexual power of Jewish women and thus to Jews in general.

Antisemites and Jewish opponents of circumcision often used similar argumentative strategies. Anticlerical and antisemitic writer Andrzej Niemojewski compared traditional Jewish circumcision with modern surgery in his 1920 pamphlet.[90] While the former was described as being performed by "dirty slobs" who suffered from tuberculosis and syphilis, the latter was conducted by trained doctors wearing gloves and masks who were "responsible to science and the authorities." For Niemojewski, "in light of current knowledge and culture," circumcision was "a barbarism" and "a crime." It was an unhygienic ritual mutilation dating back to the time of "cave dwellers." The antisemite Niemojewski found supporters among Poland's acculturated Jewish elite. In 1923, Polish-Jewish advocate Jan Ruff commented, "The circumcision ritual with its character and symbolism reaches back to the primitive [times] and is conducted in an unhygienic way, is an act of barbarism against the newborn." Ruff complained that 99 percent of unreligious Jews still performed the ritual and agreed with Niemojewski that a *żyd-obrzezaniec* (a circumcised Jewish male) turned into a laughable oddity.[91] This example illustrates that particularly acculturated middle-class Jewish men were aware of non-Jewish antisemitic renderings of circumcision that later shaped their own attitudes toward the ritual. Since they were very much embedded in the Christian society, this group of Jewish men were particularly anxious about their sense of masculinity, and their masculinities were particularly fragile.

For Poland's antisemites, circumcision served as a reason to exclude Jewish men from the community of respectable men. Numerous accounts reveal that mentioning one's circumcision served as a slur, particularly for Poland's riffraff. When, in 1921, an officer from Piotrków decided to get circumcised in order to marry his Jewish lover, one newspaper was sure that "our street urchins will bother him about his sign of the covenant."[92] Writing about obrzezańcy (the circumcised), Poland's antisemites linked the way a circumcised Jewish penis looked with the exclusion of Jewish men from social and cultural life. A particularly strong fixation on circumcision is visible in priest Igancy Charszewski's article criticizing *Wolnomyśliciel Polski*, a publication of Polish freethinkers. Charszewski consistently used symbols of cutting to underscore references to separation and violence in his text. Christian freethinkers working together with Jews, he wrote, were "circumcised from Christianity."[93] One of these freethinkers, Henryk Wroński, writing a negative review of Charszewski's book about satanism, had in fact "circumcised [the book] with the kosher circumcision knife."[94] Charszewski described what he saw as Wroński's misinterpretations as circumcising his words. In this sense, Charszewski fell back on the anti-Jewish stereotype of mendacity and falseness. Charszewski ended his tirade with the following words: "Only the circumcised get fat as pigs, and Poland, which they circumcise in minds and riches, gets thinner and thinner."[95] For Charszewski, circumcision was the source of all Jewish faults.

The antisemites linked circumcision with an alleged Jewish brutality and other anti-Jewish stereotypes. In the antisemitic discourse, the words *obrzezezaniec* and *neo-obrzezaniec* often appeared as adjectives pertaining to Jewish actions and things. Adolf Nowaczyński spoke about "obrzezane talary," or circumcised money.[96] Antisemitic tropes also appeared among Poland's socially critical progressives. For the non-Jewish reporter Wanda Melcerowa, the ritual of circumcision was scary and disgusting, and she complained that the superstition was prevalent even among Warsaw's Jewish elite, who continued to commission "unhygienic mohelim."[97] Some sources presented circumcision as limiting Jewish males' sexual performance. In his drama *Obiad literacki*, Polish-Catholic writer Tadeusz "Boy" Żeleński featured a male protagonist saying that "it could be explained by the fact that, as circumcision decreases pleasure, also the dependency on women decreases."[98] The circumcised penis was thought to be less sensitive and to provide reduced sexual pleasure while also allowing Jewish men to succeed in life since they were less dependent on women than Christian men. This line of reasoning linked an old antisemitic trope of Jewish men losing their sexual ability with a misogynist argument.

The antisemitic press took a particular interest in commenting on Jewish men who were avoiding circumcision. In 1938, the antisemitic *Nowa Rzeczpospolita* wrote about thousands of Jewish men who in recent years had allegedly avoided circumcision by bribing mohels to issue falsified circumcision certificates.[99] While, for Socialist and acculturated Jews, the refusal to circumcise their sons was an expression of their liberation from the tradition and evidence of their ability to determine the source of their masculinity precisely by standing up for their principles, for antisemites, it served as evidence of Jewish hypocrisy and dishonesty. As the title of the article suggested, Jewish men "zlekceważyli" (flouted) their own religious rules. For *Nowa Rzeczpospolita* and its readers, uncircumcised Jewish men posed a threat because "an uncircumcised Jew will always be able to prove that he is not a Jew despite being one." Uncircumcised Jewish men thus became dangerously similar to Christian men and in that sense could call into question the Polish hierarchies of masculine hegemony that marginalized Jewish men.

In answer to the antisemitic fixation on the circumcised penis, in 1936, Jewish writer Roman Brandstaetter encouraged Polish-Catholic nationalists to circumcise. Referring to their fascination with a concentration camp for Arab terrorists that the British had opened in Palestine, he invited them to exchange Bereza (a camp where Poland's Sanacja regime incarcerated its political opponents, including nationalists) for the camp in Palestine. Brandstaetter wrote, "There is one problem. The concentration camp in Palestine is for Arabs only, that is, for Semites, that is, for the circumcised [obrzezańcy]. Our nationalists would need to go through a ritual surgery. Do you want that, gentlemen? With pleasure, you shout. Come inside! *Entre!* High the ritual knives . . . !"[100] By threatening to circumcise Polish nationalists, Brandstaetter attempted to challenge antisemites to submit to a Jewish-produced test of masculinity. In writing about having to endure the circumcision-related pain, he was referring to the masculine virtue of perseverance recognized by Polish antisemites but placed within a very Jewish practice. Brandstaetter suggested that only by making their penises look Jewish could Polish nationalists prove their true masculinity, and thus he challenged the central axis of their masculine and ethnic identity. While antisemites determined circumcision as an almost inborn sign of Jewish otherness, Brandstaetter's subversive text flipped the antisemitic logic. Similar narratives about Jews circumcising unwilling Christians were a trope that continuously appeared in interwar Poland. For example, a 1932 story from Warsaw featured Leybele Kuzmir, who hoped to circumcise an antisemitic Christian clerk and earn some money.[101] While antisemitism pushed Jewish men to the social margins and questioned their masculinity, these stories offered them an ironic counterbalance that projected Jewish masculinity and circumcision as powerful and normative.

CONCLUSION

Circumcision debates in early twentieth-century Poland demonstrated how diverse Polish-Jewish masculinities were and revealed that there was no such thing as a uniform "Jewish masculinity."

Those debates shared a number of topics and arguments with the circumcision debates elsewhere in Europe, but the local Polish context took them in a direction particularly relevant for masculinity. First, while scholars implied Jewish internalized inferiority linked with the fact that Jewish penises looked different from those of the surrounding Christian men, for the majority of Jewish men in Poland, these concerns were nonexistent. Within Europe's largest, traditional, self-sufficient Jewish community in Poland, Jewish men approached circumcision primarily from an inner-Jewish perspective. As exemplified by stories of teenage and adult men who were circumcised at a later age, or by the social respect linked with being a sandak, for most Jewish men in Poland, being uncircumcised—and not the reverse—was what provided them with a sense of inferiority. Since, in Poland, be it in a small town or a Jewish district of a city, Jewish men could live in an immediate environment that was not decisively conditioned by the wider Christian surroundings, they usually internalized and embraced the traditional positive view of circumcision. Within this paradigm, being uncircumcised meant being excluded from the Jewish masculine ideal.

However, in the second half of the nineteenth century, the first Jewish voices seeking to abolish or reform the circumcision ritual in Poland were heard. While some critics, such as ethnographer Regina Lilientalowa, opposed the ritual per se and argued for children's well-being, calling circumcision "barbaric," most other critics called not to abolish but to reform the ritual. In the early twentieth century, those critical voices were increasingly translated into social practice. More and more Jewish fathers, in particular among Poland's Jewish upper and middle classes, decided not to circumcise their newborn sons, and this development raised the concerns of the Orthodox-influenced kehillot. Rejecting the rite was illustrative of the changing notions of Jewish masculinity. For a growing number of Polish-Jewish men, neither the shape of the penis nor the religious rite was central for defining their sense of masculinity, but rather other aspects, such as activism in the Jewish public sphere, professional success, or a sense of personal independence. While, for Orthodox Jewish men, the uncircumcised penis was a cause of personal humiliation, men who did not circumcise their sons located their masculinity in the virtues of consistency, firmness, and personal freedom that came to the fore in their decision to resist religious coercion and Jewish social norms.

Circumcision was discussed not only by Polish Jews but also by gentile doctors and antisemites. Within the Polish antisemitic discourse, circumcision appeared as primitive, unhygienic, and emasculating. *Obrzezaniec* (the circumcised) became a common term to denote almost all anti-Jewish stereotypes ranging from physical oddity and sexual promiscuity to meanness. Cases of Christian men who lost their hegemonic masculinity in the eyes of antisemites through conversion and circumcision, subjugating themselves to the sexual influence of Jewish women, attracted particular public interest. Antisemites used the anticircumcision vocabulary, linking it with brutality and presumed Jewish barbarity, but at the same time feared that a growing number of uncircumcised Jewish men would make the once-obvious distinction between a Jew and a Christian imperceptible. In that case, Christian and Jewish masculinity would become indistinguishable, and consequently, Christian masculine hegemony would weaken or disappear. While a group of acculturated Jewish men adhered to antisemitic logic and began to link the circumcision rite with shame, the majority of Polish-Jewish men followed a Jewish-produced counternarrative that valorized circumcision as central to establishing Jewish masculinities.

BOYS SHOWING OFF

The Working Class, Strongmen, and Corporeality

IN 1936, A LVIV JEWISH journalist commented, "For years we have been told that sport is not merely a matter of physical culture, but a matter of national dignity. When a Jewish team wins a game, it is not just a satisfaction for the team, but for the entire nation. . . . Reading sport news a Jew becomes very happy, as if it was the greatest salvation. . . . As a nervous nation, Jews easily fell into excitement, as if the entire Jewish existence were dependent on the match result."[1] While this quote mocks the exaggerated Jewish interest in sports, the mockery points out the striking importance of the Jewish fascination with sports, fitness, and corporeality in the early twentieth century. The quote makes us consider several questions: Why would shtetl inhabitants, Jewish workers in the great cities, and members of the Jewish middle classes turn into sports fans adoring physical strength, fitness, and sports rivalry? Who were the Jewish sports stars they followed? What do Jewish strongmen and athletes teach us about eastern European Jewish models and ideals of masculinity?

This chapter looks at physical strength as the central concept for defining Jewish masculinities in interwar Poland, particularly among the working classes. My examination concentrates on two case studies—of strongman Zishe Breitbart and boxer Shapsel

Rotholc—and explores how these two figures fit into a larger Polish-Jewish narrative about the body, strength, and masculinity. I focus on strongman shows and boxing, which in interwar Poland represented two popular forms of the public negotiation of masculinity and Jewishness. Telling the story of individuals who gained fame thanks to the power of their bodies, I trace how they negotiated and performed their Jewish masculinities and how these masculinities were received, discussed, evaluated, or rejected. The masculine model centered around physical fitness, while not available to every Polish-Jewish man, had a transformative influence on how Jews more broadly conceptualized masculinity. By following the champions, Polish-Jewish men, particularly those of working-class backgrounds, adhered to an ideal that praised physical power, bravery, and resistance as core masculine virtues.

I suggest that Polish-Jewish men represented masculinities much more diverse than the binary notions of a secular muscle Jewry and a religious and effeminate diaspora Talmud Jewry. These black-and-white divisions are misguided with respect to Polish-Jewish men. I argue that by turning into sports aficionados, Polish-Jewish men rarely conceived of themselves as weaklings in need of transformation but rather sought to enhance their masculine identity through admiring and recognizing a powerful male corporeality that appealed to Jews and non-Jews alike. While only a few individuals reached the level of Zishe Breitbart or Shapsel Rotholc, thousands of Jewish men who followed their performances make it clear that the recognition as fit and able-bodied gained importance across a wide and diverse spectrum of Polish-Jewish men, particularly among men who, like Rotholc and Breitbart, rose from the working class. In that setting, masculinity could be defined by celebrating the domination, bravery, and power of other men with whom one identified. While the spectators might have been anxious about their own masculinity, by associating with the masculine values embodied by Jewish sportsmen, they hoped to validate their own gender identity.

Polish-Jewish men embraced fitness not because they believed that it contradicted who they were but because it corresponded with models of how to be men that were gaining validity at the time. The admiration of fit and sporty men does not need to be linked with a conviction that this ideal is beyond one's reach. Conversely, the popularity of Jewish strongmen and sportsmen suggests that Jewish men in eastern Europe were able to and did follow the masculinity model heralded by the corporeal turn. Although, commenting about the early 1920s, Rotholc wrote, "In hadarim where I learned and, in the courtyard, where I played, no one knew anything about football, tennis, volleyball and for sure not boxing,"[2] the situation evolved quickly, and more Jewish men embraced strength and fitness as key to defining masculinity. This new attitude is clearly visible in the account of one of Poland's Jewish sports journalists. In 1933, sport activist Zelik Rusecki wrote, "Jews, old and young, people who earlier were not interested in any sport, suddenly turned into devout followers of boxing, football and swimming. These followers of 'physical culture' filled out stadiums, circuses, and swimming pools."[3]

The Jewish sports following moves our attention to negotiating male corporeality. Studying how Jewish men in eastern Europe developed and displayed their bodies and how they looked at the bodies of other men tells us a more complex story of Jewish masculinity than that emerging from the study of theoretical and prescriptive texts written by middle-class Zionist Jewish leaders. Without a doubt, programmatic texts by Max Nordau, Max Mandelstamm, and other Zionists influenced the broader Jewish interest in corporeality and its social and cultural functions. In an era when the nascent sports movement excluded Jews, they found empowerment in specifically Jewish sports.[4] Yet the rise of a well-trained body that epitomized aesthetic beauty was a phenomenon characteristic for the entirety of Europe. I suggest that the growing Jewish involvement with corporeal fitness did not appear as a direct consequence of the Zionist ideology but was rather an outcome of social tendencies that circulated then in that part of Europe. Also, in the 1920s and 1930s, the Jewish sports landscape disassociated itself from its earliest Zionist background. In Poland, there were dozens of Jewish sports movements associated with diverse political streams, and they catered not only to the middle class but also to the working class.[5] Jewish sports were linked to nationalism, but I suggest that the link between Jewishness and sports can be conceptualized also from the angle of gender.

This chapter starts with a short overview of the relationship among Jewishness, masculinity, and corporeality in modern Europe in general and Poland in particular. Next, I analyze the 1920s and the career of Zishe Breitbart (Stryków by Łódź, 1883–Berlin, 1925) as a strongman and athlete, and later I move to the 1930s, when Shapsel Rotholc (Warsaw, 1913–Montreal, 1996) becomes our guide. In my examination, I rely on a range of sources, particularly news reports, interviews, cartoons, and memoirs, that allow us to approach Jewish strongmen and sportsmen as individual actors and public figures. I analyze commentaries made by Jews, as well as the inputs of Catholic Poles. These diverse sources allow reconstructing how Jewish and non-Jewish men in Poland reacted to Jewish masculinities centered around the performance of physical power. I conclude that Breitbart's and Rotholc's examples demonstrate how many Polish-Jewish men defined physical strength as central to their masculinity and compatible with local notions of Jewishness. By following famous Jewish sportsmen, Polish-Jewish men, particularly those from the working class, embraced the ideal of a fit and powerful man and believed that, rather than being foreign or inaccessible, it fitted well their Orthodox background and was compatible with who they aspired to be.

Figure 3.1. A group of Jewish boxers (Maccabi) in Kraków, 1937 or 1938. United States Holocaust Memorial Museum, courtesy of Fred Eichner.

JEWS AND CORPOREALITY IN EASTERN EUROPE

Renderings of a dysfunctional, eastern European Jewish masculinity have been repeated so many times that its validity has become self-explanatory. This was the case in the 1990s when cultural studies discussions at the intersection of gender and Jewish studies explored historical antisemitic discourses of "soft" Jewish masculinity.[6] The vision of eastern European Jewish men as unmanly weaklings that developed between the 1890s and 1910s first appeared in the context of western European societies rooted not only in antisemitism but also in inner-European Orientalism. In "Muskeljudentum," published in 1903 in the German *Jüdische Turnzeitung* (Jewish gymnastics newspaper), Max Nordau argued that Jews had been involved in the "mortification of our own flesh."[7] In eastern Europe, we find Zionist leaders who shared Nordau's convictions and engaged in the analogous top-down criticism of eastern European Jewish men who did not belong to the economic and cultural elite. The Kyiv ophthalmologist and Zionist Max Mandelstamm spoke at the 1898 Zionist congress about the "physical improvement" of eastern European Jewish youth who "were of the weak physical constitution and degenerated into distress and poverty."[8] Many western European Zionists believed that poverty and disenfranchisement would make German-style *Turnen* difficult to develop in Poland, Russia, or Romania. However, some proponents of Jewish sports in Germany were amazed at Jewish self-defense groups in Russian Poland. Jewish sports and self-defense served, in their view, the same goal: "straighten [the] Jewish man's body," fill him with resilience and bravery, and thus heal eastern European Jewry.[9] German-Jewish gymnasts followed a Zionist diagnosis about the deformed eastern European Jewish body and psyche and perceived themselves as more experienced allies who could provide the know-how needed for the Zionist bodily transformation in the East.

The approach of German-Jewish gymnasts was hierarchical, and their belief in the effectiveness of sports for transforming the "hunched back" and "pale face" of eastern European Jews spoke more about Zionist western European stereotypes than about the self-perceived reality of Jewish men from Poland or Ukraine. To be sure, Jewish sports organizations in Galicia or Congress Poland that sprouted up at the turn of the twentieth century developed without any German-Jewish financial or organizational support. From the beginning, Jewish sports in eastern Europe were politically (several Zionist streams, Bundism, socialism) and class diverse and included not only gymnastics but also swimming, boxing, football, and light athletics. Local eastern European proponents of sports created their own know-how, rejected elements of the German *Turnen*, and prioritized the pleasure of sport and its Jewish-empowering appeal.[10] We should uncover eastern European

Jewish realities linked to body and fitness from the layers of the Zionist critic. We need to reassess the extent to which eastern European Jews indeed perceived themselves as bodily weak and hence unmanly, or was it merely an external perspective of western European Zionists, members of the eastern European Jewish elite, and scholars who borrowed their vocabulary?[11]

In interwar Poland, the border between the Orthodox masculinity that Zionist and acculturated Jews simplified in the figure of a *Talmudjude* and the Jewish masculine models that challenged it was becoming blurred. Jewish men could and did borrow from a broad repertoire of masculine practices and ideas and created masculine mosaics that sometimes put the black-and-white vision of passive and studious Orthodox men and secular able-bodied Zionist men into question. For some Orthodox men who came of age in Poland after World War I, the importance of fitness was hardly unusual or challenging, as might have been the case two or three decades earlier. Recalling the debates about Breitbart in the early 1920s, the boxer Shapsel Rotholc commented, "About the strongest Jew of our time people spoke in synagogues and on the street, over the food at home and in the *beis midrash* during a prayer. The Jews used to stay a bit longer after the prayer to discuss miraculous stories about the Jewish *gibor* [hero, from the Hebrew root גבר that signifies a man]."[12] This quote demonstrates that the Jewish strongman's victories could be discussed in the synagogue and that these worlds were far from being exclusive. Working-class Jewish men in the big cities, still embedded in the Orthodox tradition yet increasingly shaped by influences from the non-Jewish world, constructed a masculine model in interwar Poland that saw physical power and its public exposure and validation as central in forming masculine identities. The experiences of these men demonstrate how artificial the distinctions that Zionists in western and eastern Europe hoped to establish might have been.

Breitbart and Rotholc embodied masculinity centered on physical competition. Since class disassociated working-class Jewish men like Rotholc and Breitbart from the bourgeois circles, and secularization distanced them from the Orthodoxy, corporeal challenge appeared as a new possible venue for claiming masculinity. Following the French Revolution, more men constructed their identities not by inheriting them but rather by achieving them through challenge. The regulated violence between men became deserving of glory and had the potential to raise one's social position.[13] This logic was valid particularly among men who rose from the working class, such as Rotholc and Breitbart, and who did not inherit social capital otherwise. I suggest that Jewish sportsmen and strongmen tested their bodies to prove their adherence to an ideal centered on physical performance. In the urban context of the early twentieth century, men began to compete in public, and relations between men evolved from bloody violence to sport competition that was measured, domesticated, and regulated.[14] The growing following of Jewish athletes was a result of the transition of masculine models away from those based on brutality and injuring the contestant into those proving one's technical superiority.[15] While men who dueled in earlier decades searched for secluded places, now a crowd of spectators and the professional selection of performing athletes turned Breitbart shows and Rotholc boxing games into popular events.

At the turn of the twentieth century, Polish-Jewish working-class men, exactly like men of other nationalities in central and eastern Europe, began to invest more time and effort into their fitness. In 1935, one Polish-Jewish activist commented, "When the Jew was allowed into a ring, he proved that he fights with reason, power, and bravery. No one could compare a Jew to rattle bones anymore. Boxing, as any other sport, offers a possibility to demonstrate Jewish power and boldness."[16] The quote underscores how natural Polish-Jewish men felt in sports venues despite being newcomers from an ethnic minority. It appears that they were

Figure 3.2. Drawing, "Jacob and Essau," *Di Panorame*, September 24, 1937, 3.

natural sportsmen who waited to be let into the ring. In the 1930s, Jewish fitness was widely normalized in Poland. A satirical column in *Sport-tsaytung* (Sports newspaper) asked, "How is it that Jews excel in the field of sports?" and "How after thousands of years of physical hungering in the Diaspora, we provide the world with sports stars like Baer, Hecht, Rotholc, Witman . . . ?"[17] Also, a cartoon from *Tararam* depicting two disproportionate Jewish men referred to the tension between the power of muscles and the power of mind (fig. 3.2). The blade of satire usually poked at the very real social phenomena that challenged the previous order. The 1920s and 1930s brought the separation of work and free time and the emergence of spaces where Jewish and non-Jewish men could fix, train, and present their bodies. Boxing halls, wrestling rooms, and football fields became part of the urban fabric of Polish cities. New rooms where men exercised in close corporeal proximity, felt each other's sweat, and competed in shared places made the masculine performance more public. Jewish men were aware that Jewish sports were relatively new and evoked tension with the earlier ideals.

Breitbart and Rotholc, both of whom originated in the Orthodox working class, embodied the intersection of working-class Jewish masculinity and physical achievement. Breitbart breaking records of strength and endurance created an epic narrative of overcoming the limits of one's body and economic status. From a poor Łódź circus kid, he turned into a glamorous and successful global celebrity. Rotholc's performances had the power of attracting new groups of spectators who admired him as a fit and strong Jewish man. *Sport-tsaytung* commented in 1939 that his boxing match in Lviv attracted two thousand Jewish viewers and underscored that among them were not only young men, who were the usual admirers of Jewish boxers, but also many women, children, and elderly Jews.[18] Importantly, many Polish-Jewish strongmen who did not achieve the status of Breitbart or Rotholc also epitomized the link between the popular classes and masculinity centered around fitness and physical power. People came to applaud them in open fields beyond towns or in run-down arenas, while the press defined them as Jewish popular heroes. The rise of Jewish strongmen and boxers coincided with the growing involvement of the Polish-Jewish working class in free-time activities. This followed analogous phenomena elsewhere in Europe.[19] For many Jewish boys, Breitbart and Rotholc symbolized the promise of a better life than that defined by their place of birth and class setting.[20]

The specificity of Polish-Jewish fascination with strongmanship and boxing was its ethno-utilitarian character, which might have been less visible among sportsmen from the titular ethnic communities. In the 1920s and 1930s in eastern Europe, the fights of Jewish wrestlers, boxers, and strongmen turned into a mechanism that consecrated the champion and indirectly his entire group of Jewish followers. Being the embodiment and warrantors of masculine virtues, Jewish boxers and strongmen represented all those who recognized themselves in them and believed in the virtues of resistance, bravery, and power. While scholars pointed out that analogous identifications might also have been the case elsewhere in Europe, some Polish Jews believed that the Jewish relationship with sports and corporeality was unique.[21] Jewish sports journalist Sh. Danzig explained the growing fascination with Jewish sports celebrities as a tool to manifest Jewish ethnic pride: "In the history of the Jewish physical movement, from time-to-time shine 'sports stars' who are a living symbol of the awakening of Jewish sports culture. While their achievements in the field of sports are purely individual successes, they increase the prestige of the Jewish sports movement, awaken respect towards the Jews as people of great physical power, and serve as the best propaganda material to spread among the Jews the physical renaissance."[22]

Sports journalist Zelik Rusecki, the leader of the Zionist sport movement, underscored not only Jewish ethnic pride but also the actual Jewish need for defense readiness. Rusecki, who in 1915 cofounded the Polish Maccabi, drew this approach from his own experience when, between 1915 and 1918, the Maccabi organized self-defense units that protected Warsaw's Jews in times of ethnic and economic tensions during World War I.[23] Rusecki commented in 1933:

Sure, everywhere around the world the strong one is respected. Physical power impresses. We notice how the masses bow in front of the strong man. But among Jews, these developments have a special character. A longing for physical strength is so much needed to defend oneself. A Jew lives his daily life in such difficult conditions. He is constantly exposed to the raw power of his neighbors who are willing to use their feasts against him. He suffers from the depreciating attitude of the non-Jewish world. People look down at a Jew from above.... That's why there are such warm feelings towards Jewish heroes.... When a Jewish sportsman wins, an ordinary Jew begins to believe that with some training and in proper conditions, he could also be a winner.... The prominent Jewish sportsman is to a certain extent a guide for the Jewish masses that expect him to serve as an example that one can fight and win.[24]

Both quotes underscore the entanglement of physical performance, nationalism, and masculinity. Polish-Jewish strongmen and boxers were to serve as the evidence that Jewish men possessed physical power, that they were able to defend themselves and their communities, and that their success could be emulated by others; all that stabilized Jewish ethnic respectability and the normativity of Jewish men. Importantly, wrestling and other combat sports served to enhance specific masculine qualities that were less available in group sports. They contained the ritual male antagonism providing a metaphor for the hypermasculine social and political life in the 1920s and 1930s. When Breitbart performed in Warsaw in 1924, regular fights erupted between Jewish and Christian teenagers. In the perception of Rotholc, who participated in them as a child, the fights were not rooted in antisemitism but in a desire to test one's power. The fights followed boxing-like rules and hence served to verify one's masculine virtues.[25] Rotholc and Breitbart individually validated their masculinity by facing and facing off with other men, and Jewish men who admired both Jewish sportsmen followed their vision of masculinity centered around a challenge.

Women do not appear as central for shaping the masculinity of Rotholc and Breitbart. However, as women entered the sphere of Jewish and non-Jewish sports, some Jews in Poland seemed to be worried about the influence of women on highly masculine sports such as wrestling and boxing. Jewish journalist Al. Rekssa wrote that women "led to confusion" in sports and were a "horrible problem" for boxing. Rekssa longed for a ban on women's participation in male fights to "maintain the pure atmosphere of the fight, to avoid polluting it with the female hysteria and femininity in general." Female boxers, he thought, were behaving "against nature," and he even claimed that "women led to the gangrene of boxing."[26] Later, he accused female fans of seducing boxers and ruining their careers. Rotholc's autobiography follows some of the tropes from Rekssa's misogynist text. Rotholc fell victim to sexual harassment by a cabaret actress, Reyzel, who removed her clothes in front of the then eleven-year-old boy. Frustrated after Breitbart rejected her, she attempted to seduce Rotholc, Breitbart's soon-to-be successor: "You're also so beautiful, Shapsel. Take off your clothes, and let's kiss. Let's imagine that you're Zishe Breitbart."[27] While the story from Rotholc's memoir is probably colored up, Reyzel's pushy behavior echoes the fears addressed by Rekssa that women seduce sportsmen and destabilize the sport. At the same time, the story suggested that women found men such as Breitbart and Rotholc attractive and sought their attention. Both Breitbart and Rotholc formed normative heterosexual families, but their sports careers overshadowed their relationships with women. Sportsmen's presumed resistance to women's appeal went hand in hand with the ideal of masculinity centered on self-control. This separation of athletic performance and romantic life with women was typical for sport masculinity not only in Poland but also elsewhere in Europe.[28]

ZISHE BREITBART AND THE STRONGMEN
AND WRESTLERS OF THE 1920S

In 1925, a Jewish photographer put a huge picture of Zishe Breitbart in his shop window at Karmelicka Street in Warsaw. Breitbart posed there sitting on a chair resembling a throne. The Yiddish writer Melech Ravitch, who spotted Breitbart's portrait, noted that the strongman appeared in "a royal pose, with a metal helmet on his head, reddish robe on his shoulders, his iron hands straightened up, holding reins, his eyes controlling everything, eagle-shaped nose—all making an impression of passion and heroism."[29] Zishe Breitbart, who earned his success mostly in Germany, is often analyzed as a figure illustrating social and cultural phenomena in the German-Jewish context.[30] I believe that studying the place of Breitbart in Poland, where he was born, came of age, and was continuously celebrated, could shed light on the issue of Jewish masculinity in 1920s Poland. Even though Breitbart lived in Germany for most of his adult life, Poland's Jewish press followed his life and performances abroad and constructed him as a local, and not foreign, masculine model.[31] Breitbart's following allows us to analyze how physical strength and Jewishness were negotiated in 1920s Poland in terms of gender. How important was Zishe Breitbart for Jewish men who passed down Karmelicka Street? Did they conceive of him as a role model to follow, or conversely, did they reject the way he lived his life as a Jewish man? It is worth asking what message Breitbart sent to spectators during his shows and in his publicity materials. Was this message particular to his male viewers? Was this message directed at Jews specifically? Did Breitbart encourage other Polish-Jewish men to follow him as a man who defines his masculinity via physical strength, or did he want them just to admire him? Breitbart's following in Poland is informative for better understanding the local debates about Jewishness and masculinity.

Who was Zishe Breitbart for the Jewish public in Poland? Breitbart probably perceived of himself as a liminal figure—part showman, part artist, part sportsman. A Lublin poster from 1925 represented Breitbart as a sportsman with an unusual repertoire ("mit zayn oysergevonlekhn sport repertuar") and not as an entertainer.[32] In a 1925 interview, Breitbart spoke of performing "kuntsn" (tricks) and "gvures" (power shows) rather than practicing any sport discipline. In the same interview, he said that he was an "atlet"—that is, a strongman.[33] The perception of Breitbart as the "moderner Shimshon ha-giber" (modern Samson) and "ayzen-kenig" (Iron King) was to a great extent influenced by entertainment tools that Breitbart and his managers had mastered. Yiddish newspapers marveled at his "ayzernen brust shtang" (iron chest), "umzigbare glider" (invincible hands and legs,) and "ibermenshlekhe kraft" (super-human power).[34] However, one Warsaw Jewish newspaper, speaking about Breitbart's shows, referred to "a profession," thus putting into question the innate character of Breitbart's strength.[35] The Yiddish daily *Haynt* wrote of Breitbart "als Shimshon ha-giber," or "appearing *as* Samson," and not about Breitbart "being" Samson. The wording makes it clear that the public sometimes understood Breitbart's actions as a stage performance, possibly separate from his regular life and his regular characteristics.[36] In that sense, Breitbart's masculinity centered around power also could appear as staged and, thus possibly coherent or overlapping with other Jewish masculine models.

Circuses were venues where regular men came into contact with strongmen. In Warsaw, wrestlers and strongmen usually performed the Cyrk Warszawski (the Warsaw Circus), also known as the Staniewski Circus. Erected in the 1890s, the venue in Ordynacka Street was the biggest event space in Warsaw before 1939 and could host up to three thousand viewers.[37] This is where Zishe Breitbart performed in the 1920s. The demand for his shows seems to have been significant: Breitbart offered

two shows each on both Saturday and Sunday, and organiz-
ers hoped that some spectators would buy tickets for all four
shows. The newspaper invitation encouraged visitors that "the
entire Warsaw impatiently awaits the first show of the world-
famous Jewish gibor."[38] One poster for the Warsaw Circus (but
advertising a show in Lublin) spoke of Breitbart as "the world
famous Iron King" ("wszechświatowej sławy Król Żelaza")
and promised that "the public will not forget Breitbart's ex-
periments for 100 years."[39] Strongmen traveled across Poland
to increase their income, and Breitbart visited, among others, Białystok, Lviv, and Bielsko Biała. Another Polish-Jewish
strongman, Leon Majdenberg, sometimes appeared in shacks
that served as sports arenas and traveled to the suburbs of Warsaw and the provinces. The venues in which strongmen performed turned into a space where men and women reflected on
masculinity and Jewishness and where they negotiated valid
models of masculinity.

The entertainment business in Poland was a space defined
by conflict, and Jewish entertainers needed to fight for their
right to perform. Sometimes traveling strongmen were challenged to fight by local men. Occasionally Breitbart appeared
in Poland as a wrestler and not as a strongman, as he usually
did abroad. One wrestling invitation from Radom advertised
the Greco-Roman-style wrestling fight between Breitbart and
Poland's champion, Perkowski.[40] While Breitbart could still
organize his one-man shows and largely maintained his status
as a "new Samson" in Poland, other men there challenged him
to establish a measurable hierarchy of power-centered masculinity. The fact that he engaged in wrestling suggests that even
an international star like Breitbart needed to test his strength,
and consequently also his masculinity, in a direct physical fight
with other men. In 1935, a group of about fifteen men attacked
Leon Majdenberg when he appeared in a rough version of a
circus arena organized in the courtyard of a tenement house

on Nowolipie Street.[41] The attack served as a probe for Majdenberg's masculine powers: the strongman needed to prove that his strength was indeed unique and that he knew how to use it in a confrontation and not only within the limits of a well-prepared show. As the press reported, Majdenberg beat up the entire group of hooligans (probably of Jewish origin) but succumbed when one of them stabbed him with a knife. The fight in the Warsaw courtyard evidences how violence between men shaped the Warsaw Jewish strongmen and entertainment business. While strongmen like Breitbart and Majdenberg usually offered self-curated athletic shows, there were occasions when they needed to prove their prowess, strength, and masculinity in a street fight, which appeared as a ritual of verification.

Breitbart saw his role in Poland in the context of Jewish masculine empowerment through corporeal strength. His 1925 visit had the goal of "making propaganda for Jewish sports" and "having a pedagogical influence" to create a "fight-ready generation of Jews."[42] This encompassed both circus performances and speeches offered at events and for the press. When, in 1925, Breitbart appeared at the Purim party of the Association of Yiddish Writers and Journalists in Warsaw, he not only presented his famous trick and broke thick metal chains but also named himself "a defender of the Jewish people."[43] In granting himself the title of Jewish defender, Breitbart defined himself through the combination of strength, masculinity, and Jewishness. He did not specify to what extent his athletic shows were meant to defend Jews or where the danger was. Yet the message from the Purim party, with a majority of male participants, was clear: only men such as Breitbart—that is, strong, brave, and proudly Jewish—fit into the new era. Breitbart's declaration challenged his spectators to reflect on the values he personified and the values they considered valid. The invitation that Jewish writers extended to Breitbart demonstrates that diverse Jewish subgroups, including those Jewish men, like Yiddish writers, who constructed their masculinities through the power of mind, increasingly recognized physical strength as a value valid for Jewish masculinity.

What makes the Polish-Jewish reports about Breitbart unique is the appropriation of the strongman for Polish Jewry. Breitbart was celebrated as a product of Polish Jewry, and his power and fame were linked to his Polish-Jewish origin. Łódź Jews, as one daily reported, were particularly fond of their "ben-ir" (a fellow Lodzer).[44] When Breitbart briefly returned to Łódź, Jewish newspapers spoke about "Łódź longing after her Shimshon ha-giber" and underscored him being a "lodzer kind" (a child of Łódź).[45] Another newspaper wrote about "our strongman" and "an athlete from Łódź."[46] In Jewish newspaper reports from Poland, we do not find expressions of astonishment concerning the fact that "the strongest man in the world" was Jewish. Emphasizing Breitbart's roots in Łódź, or, as columnist Menachem Kipnis wrote, "him being fed with kugel and tshulent" (eastern European Jewish delicacies), the Polish-Jewish public sphere defined Breitbart as its own child, rather than something drastically diverging from what represented Polish Jewry and Polish-Jewish masculinity. Breitbart was to be a local everyman attractive and unthreatening to men and women alike and an epitome of an uncommon commoner.

In Poland, as in other countries, Breitbart staged himself as a proud Jew. Performing in the Warsaw circus in 1925, he was accompanied by a group of men dressed in white robes with the word "Zion" appearing on their foreheads. The orchestra played Jewish national and folk songs.[47] However, Jews in Poland did not always consider Breitbart as a Zionist. For the prominent Yiddish writer Melech Ravitch, Breitbart's success was not a partisan Zionist success but a general story of Jewish success.[48] Another report placed Breitbart in the world of Jewish Orthodoxy. One *Der Moment* journalist compared Breitbart's train trip to Otwock to a rabbi followed by his Hasidim, who listened to his every word.[49] These two episodes show that Breitbart could be distinctly viewed in multiple Jewish contexts. Jewish men from a variety of backgrounds celebrated him, and interpretations of his figure ranged from Zionist to Orthodox framings of Jewish masculinity. Breitbart symbolized Jewish power and respectability immersed into Zionist iconography, but local Jewish men took his persona in multiple directions.

The Polish-Jewish press included visual representations of Breitbart's performances that linked visual emblems of Jewishness and physical fitness. A picture from *Haynt* from 1925 shows Breitbart dressed in a leopard-print robe revealing his muscled body.[50] The athlete holds in his hands a metal chain that he is about to break. The black-and-white picture makes visible Breitbart's curly and thus distinctively Jewish hair. In that sense, Breitbart's corporeal features corresponded with the title the newspaper gave him: the great Jewish hero. A photo (fig. 3.3) from *Ilustrowany Kurjer Warszawski* shows Breitbart holding heavy stones on his chest. Here we also notice shining curly hair accompanied by a stoic facial expression signaling Breitbart's self-control of body and mind. One Jewish journal praised Breitbart's physical features: "Glorious back structure, charming and good-looking, his external appearance refreshes since he is a man of wide horizons, of a particular uniqueness which not all athletes possess."[51] Another report spoke about Breitbart as "muscular, full-grown, slightly coquettish with his Herculean charm."[52] These references to corporeal aspects evidence that the masculinity Breitbart embodied was a synthesis of spiritual and corporeal elements. In Breitbart, as in the classic Enlightenment ideal of masculinity, the beauty of the mind was reflected in the external beauty of the body. Consequently, Breitbart's masculinity fused his Jewish appearance with the general European masculine self-containment and self-control that more and more Polish Jews embraced as their own.

Figure 3.3. Zishe Breitbart in the Warsaw circus, 1925, *Ilustrowany Kurjer Warszawski*. Narodowe Archiwum Cyfrowe (Warsaw), call number 1-K-12521.

Polish-Jewish young men in the 1920s aspired to be like Breitbart, and it seemed to them quite achievable. Rotholc recalled from his childhood in the 1920s that "Breitbart's royal rule was infectious for us; the boys started to test their power. Can I do the same exercises as the Iron King? . . . There was a kind of Breitbart epidemic which was expressed in regular muscle testing, one just wanted to show off his strength."[53] Menachem Kipnis's story of a little Yankele who "hot zikh farkukt in" (madly looked up to) Breitbart also signalizes that for Polish-Jewish kids, "being like Breitbart"—that is, strong and proudly Jewish—was not an issue of overcoming oneself but rather a very doable thing.[54] Breitbart was a Jewish superhero, not only for the adult men who admired him but also for boys who dreamed of "growing up to be Breitbart." One of them was Mishko Geller from Lviv, titled "an adolescent Breitbart" in the press.[55] Geller was just eleven years old, but his unusual strength allowed him to participate in public power shows. Breitbart's power was celebrated in the Polish-Jewish context precisely because Polish-Jewish men of the working classes, generally speaking, did not perceive of themselves as inferior to Christian men, and following Breitbart was to prove this condition.

The figure of Zishe Breitbart allowed Polish-Jewish men to reflect on various models of masculinity that were available in the 1920s. His strength and international fame valorized Jewish masculinity focused on a fit muscular body and challenged studiousness as a Jewish masculine value. One example that might serve us is a cartoon that appeared in *Haynt* in March 1926. The picture shows a frightened man hiding under a bed with a range of defensive tools. When the man is questioned by his wife, he answers that he is hiding because "[Zishe Breitbart] might want to take revenge on me." The man is captioned as the "sekretarchik," which is a diminutive for a male secretary. This caption suggests that he is probably one of Warsaw's Jewish low-level white-collar workers. The fear Breitbart evokes in the man might symbolize the anxiety of men who followed the ideal of diligent petite bourgeois masculinity when challenged by the Jewishly self-confident strongman masculinity of Breitbart. While the cartoon does not reveal the reason the man hides under the bed, his reaction speaks of the anxiety of Jewish men in times of when masculine models evolved and changed. In the early twentieth century, sportsmen figures evoked references to war and fighting (such as wounds), and the man pictured in the cartoon appeared incompatible with the sport masculinity that Breitbart embodied.

In Poland's non-Jewish sources, Breitbart's strength appeared as something unexpected, possibly fraudulent, and not real. Jewish writer Menachem Kipnis spoke in his reportage (we do not know whether the story is fictional or not) of a certain Christian lawyer who could not stand the fact that the world's strongest man was a *żydek* (Polish pejorative for a male Jew). The lawyer revealed a set of antisemitic expectations concerning how a Jewish man should behave: "A Jew should shout: *handel, handel!* A Jew should shake his head, speculate, combine, but show off his strength?"[56] For the Catholic Pole, it seemed unimaginable that a despicable Jew might show athletic excellence that he himself was unable to achieve. Breitbart challenged the lawyer's gender stereotypes about Jews, and this led to the lawyer's anxiety about his status and ethno-gender privilege. Other Polish satirical newspapers named Breitbart a "pseudo-athlete" or accused him of "sztuczki i machinacje," or tricks and scheming.[57] One well-known Polish antisemitic writer, Adolf Nowaczyński, believed that Breitbart's fame was due to the presumed Jewish influence in the world media.[58] The antisemites were shocked with Jewish power and wanted to cast it as incompatible with "standard Jewishness."

Numerous Polish men embedded in antisemitic discourses attempted to frame Breitbart's strength as "tricks" and questioned his exceptional power and thus also his celebrated hypermasculinity. Exemplary for this approach is Polish non-Jewish wrestler Władysław Pytlasiński. Interviewed by the Polish-nationalist newspaper *Dwa Grosze*, Pytlasiński argued, "Those shows are not athletics. They are just a 'tour de force'—circus shows. I believe that even a mediocre athlete would beat Breitbart in wrestling in just two rounds."[59] For many nationalist-spirited Polish men, it seemed unacceptable that a Jewish man, whom they perceived as an inferior being, would prove a better fighter than a Catholic champion. The *Dwa Grosze* interview served the goal of disassociating Breitbart from being exemplary of Jewish men as such. The interview unfolded as follows: "Journalist: So, Breitbart is in fact not the second Samson, an example of Jewish physical fitness?

Pytlasiński: Of course not. We had a chance to see an example of this Jewish fitness at the tournament in Podchorążówka. Jews (Makkabi) sent three wrestlers who seemingly were very fit, but experienced a total defeat."[60] By linking the Makkabi defeat (not related in any way to Breitbart) against the Catholic wrestlers, Pytlasiński attempted to rhetorically downplay the fitness and masculinity of Breitbart and Jewish men as such. The failure of those Jewish men was supposed to prove that Jewish sportsmen and strongmen were weaklings whose achievements were exaggerated by the press.

Poland's non-Jewish press painted Breitbart as a "Jewish product" that served the respectability interests of Polish-Jewish men. A Lviv satirical journal in broken Polish Jew-speech parodied, "Ale, że un z nasze wiary / Więc go stale podpieramy / Robiąc krzyki między goje/ Że i my też 'mocnych' mamy." The quote speaks of "shouting among the goyim" that "also Jews have [their] strongmen."[61] The journal mocked Jewish efforts to associate Jewishness with physical power and the possibility to extend Breitbart's strength to Polish-Jewish men in general. For antisemites, these efforts were futile because they were supposedly based on Jewish propaganda and not reality. Another satirical text compared Breitbart to a prostitute: "Chodzi Breitbart po ulicy / Ten co rwie łańcuchy / Za nim żydków cała kupa / Niby karaluchy! / Każdy go gdzie może maca / Co mi przypomina / Że ów Breitbart jest czymś takim / Jak lekka 'dziewczyna.'"[62] Speaking of Breitbart as a sex worker, or underlining that he left Poland "with a golden treasury,"[63] highlighted Breitbart's presumed low moral standards and that he was first and foremost a businessman and not an example of Jewish strength. Writing about Breitbart as a prostitute touched by "cockroach-like Jews," the journal openly questioned the masculine gender identity of the strongman. The blade of antisemitic satire turned Breitbart into a woman of easy virtue and disassociated him from any masculine qualities.

Polish antisemitic media outlets portrayed Breitbart not as an athlete successful abroad but as an average Polish Jew and involved him in their antisemitic discourses. *Dwa Grosze* wrote that "the Jewish troublemaker attacks Poles, insults Polishness" ("żydowski awanturnik napada na Polaków, obraża polskość"). The newspaper reported that Breitbart allegedly attacked a non-Jewish man who ridiculed him and his followers, spit on him, and cursed him with the slur "Polish pig." The newspaper portrayed Breitbart as a man without a moral spine who attacked the weak. *Dwa Grosze* described Breitbart as a violent "shaggy fatso" and "guttersnipe" who united the "worst features of a stereotypical Jew."[64] What particularly bothered *Dwa Grosze* (and probably their antisemitic readers) was the visibility of Breitbart in the public space of Polish cities and in the minds of local residents. Since Breitbart's shows transformed into demonstrations for the Jewish Iron King, Polish cities appeared then as particularly Jewish and festive. To destroy the image of Breitbart as a Jewish hero and to compensate for the destabilization of hierarchical gender relations between Jewish and non-Jewish men, the antisemites attempted to cast him as a fight-ready criminal. These renderings were a double-edged sword, however, as an aggressive and violent Breitbart questioned the image of a weak and passive Jewish man.

Polish Jews appreciated Breitbart not only for being a symbol of strength but also for embodying self-made success and the Jewish virtue of charitable giving. Breitbart placed himself within the "from rags to riches" narrative and emphasized his desire to be rich and famous, which spoke to many Polish Jews facing post–World War I poverty. Generosity was another of Breitbart's features that Jews in Poland appreciated. One Łódź journalist described him as sensitive and emotional, particularly concerning his family.[65] Breitbart financially supported his father, despite tense family conflicts.[66] The Yiddish writer Melech Ravitch underscored that Breitbart was generous and "opened his hand easily when someone asked him [for support]."[67] In 1923, *Haynt* wrote about the "hibshe milionen" (beautiful millions) that the entertainer donated to various charitable institutions.[68] In conversation with *Haynt*, Breitbart stressed that he had an innate sense of social justice: As a kid, he allegedly confiscated food from a rich student and distributed it among the poor ones.[69] These examples complicate the image of Breitbart and offer valuable perspectives on ideal Polish-Jewish masculinities. While physical power was admired, a proper Jewish man should also know how to be generous and protective. Melting the traditional ideal of a man as breadwinner and protector with celebrated fitness and physical power, Breitbart's masculinity appeared pluralist and attractive to a large share of Polish-Jewish men in the 1920s.

BROAD SHOULDERED AND SELF-CONFIDENT:

SHAPSEL ROTHOLC AND THE

POLISH-JEWISH BOXERS OF THE 1930S

"Who would years ago believe that among us Jews, 'People of the Book,' boxing would become so important. Jews, by nature softhearted beings, are not able to do this kind of 'work.' So why do Jewish boys not only run to look how someone else beats, but they themselves know how to give a proper bang?"[70] This quote, opening a text about Shapsel Rotholc in a Jewish illustrated magazine, speaks about how, by embracing boxing, Jewish men challenged earlier definitions of Jewish masculinity. In the 1930s, more than twenty years after the establishment of the first Jewish sports clubs in Galicia and Congress Poland, many local Jews perceived sporty Jewish bodies not as an idea for the future but as a partially accomplished reality. Physical fitness became visible not only in sports stadiums but also on the streets. One Warsaw Jewish newspaper commented, "The sports movement in Poland reaches wider and wider circles and attracts more and more people. Sport is now one of the modern manifestations of social life and as such one of the favorite interests of the masses."[71] In 1933, Jewish sports magazine *Sport-tsaytung* casually noted, reporting from a boxing tournament, that "the lion's share of the spectators was, as usual, *ahinu bney Israel* [our brothers Children of Israel]."[72] While sports indeed became a mass movement for both Jews and non-Jews, sports also reflected the class divisions within society. While car racing and tennis were popular among the upper middle class, boxing and football had replaced strongmanship and wrestling as the most popular individual sports.

In the 1930s, boxing began to shape Polish gender orders and was the central arena for performing masculinity based on sports excellence. Independently of religious and ethnic affiliation, young men in Poland admired successful sportsmen and desired to have their bodies, character features, and popularity. Jewish men particularly identified with the Jewish sportsmen who epitomized self-made Jewish success and robust and healthy masculinity. Jewish boxers were part and parcel of the Polish world of professional male sports: Shapsel Rotholc and Leon Rundstein regularly won national championship medals. Unlike football, which underscored cooperative virtues and often did not grant stardom to individual players, boxing echoed masculine attack and defense abilities and was starkly individualistic. Jewish boxers embodied a vision of male fitness conceptually linked with the ability to react and stand up to injustice, discrimination, or violation of one's honor. Even the antisemites followed this reasoning and, to a certain extent, borrowed the boxing-linked vocabulary manufactured on the Jewish street in Poland. This was particularly poignant concerning the term "new Samson." The conservative Polish magazine *Czas* argued that, "in the eyes of Nalewki, Rotholc is the second Samson."[73] While the magazine befogged its message by saying that this was only referring to Jewish residents in Nalewki Street in Warsaw who held these views, the meaning was clear: there was a powerful Jewish boxer, Rotholc, who indeed possessed a ring-validated masculinity and destabilized the local ethnic hierarchies of masculinity.

Shapsel Rotholc was one of the most successful Jewish boxers who gained fame and a following in interwar Poland. Often called by the nickname Szapsio, or Polonized as Stanisław, Rotholc became the favorite of many local boxing aficionados. Born in Warsaw in 1913, Rotholc became the first Jewish boxing champion of Poland in 1933. In 1934, he won the bronze in European championship in Budapest, and in the following years, he represented Poland at numerous international boxing competitions against the United States, Hungary, and Finland. Rotholc fit in well in the Cinderella-like rags-to-riches narrative. Trained as a typesetter and associated with the left-wing Zionist sports club Gwiazda/Shtern, the boxer quickly turned into one of the top stars of Polish and Polish-Jewish sports. In 1934 and 1935, he was among the top ten sports personalities chosen by the readers of the most influential Polish sports journal, *Przegląd Sportowy* (Sports review). The Jewish *Sport-tsaytung* enthroned Rotholc as the best Jewish sportsman in 1936/1937 and the best Jewish boxer in 1938/1939.[74] Rotholc's immense popularity also reached the level of publicly displayed affection. When he won against Antoni Czortek in 1936 in Poznań, the capital of Polish boxing, he was welcomed with "a stream of clapping," and people "tore Rotholc from the hands."[75] Rotholc became a star of Polish boxing and a Jewish jewel that needed to be both protected and displayed with pride.

What differentiated the performance and perception of Breitbart from those of Rotholc was the involvement of the state in the negotiation of power and masculinity. In the boxing ring,

Figure 3.4. Shapsel Rotholc (*right*), after winning, with Czechoslovakia's boxer Fiala, in 1934, *Raz Dwa Trzy*, October 23, 1934. Narodowe Archiwum Cyfrowe (Warsaw), call no. 3/1/0/14/1681/4.

Rotholc appeared not just as a man and a Polish Jew but also as a representative of the Polish state, which in the 1930s understood boxing as an important arena for validating Polish masculinity and Polish ethnic pride. Breitbart rarely appeared as a representative of any nation state, and state authorities in Poland, Germany, and the United States never attempted to capitalize on his power and fame. Also, while Breitbart designed his own shows assisted by his managers, in the 1920s, Rotholc's performances in the 1930s were conditioned by the regulations of the Polish Boxing Association and the influence of its leaders. The latter not only decided whether to allow Rotholc to perform but also pub-licly evaluated his technique and physical condition. Noting the transition from the wild and uncontrolled power of strongmen to the regulated world of boxing, Rotholc explained, "Boxers do not fight just like that, anyone with anyone, a short one with a tall one, an eighteen-year-old with a thirty-year-old, someone who weighs fifty kilos with someone with ninety kilos. Everything is precisely regulated, measured, and weighed. . . . Everyone who belongs to a specific weight is in a specific category. This is how it is around the world and this is how we do it."[76] As sports per-formance became increasingly measurable between the 1920s and 1930s, power-centered masculinity among the working classes in Poland was increasingly subjected to the rules of measurability.

What features have defined Rotholc as a great boxer and a man whom other men looked up to? Spectators and Jewish media praised Rotholc for his hurricane-like tempo, ambition, powerful hands, and "technical repertoire," which combined accentuated physical prowess and personal discipline.[77] The press described Rotholc as a "modest and nice boy," someone who was impetuous when jumping to attack the opponent and had good reflexes.[78] Another report suggested that Rotholc was a "clear, immacu-late amateur leading an abstaining lifestyle."[79] One of Rotholc's trainers described him as "solid and loyal," always ready to fulfill a "citizen's duties."[80] Rotholc himself saw his personality as com-plex, composed of his regular persona and the one he assumed in the ring. He was usually "modest, quiet and calm" and "did not like to stand out, to search for fame or popularity." In the ring, he assumed new features. There, he was "aggressive, full of *hutspe*, pushy and even brutal. A completely different man than in his private life."[81] The quotes from *5ta rano*, one of the most popular Polish-language Jewish dailies in Poland, suggest that journal-ists perceived Rotholc as a man who united both the spiritual and corporeal virtues that were valued in the 1930s. The news-paper underscored the boxer's mental abilities of self-control, cooperation, and ambition while noticing also the moments of mobilizing anger. The Rotholc who emerges from those reports is a man full of the masculine virtues of obstinacy and bullheadedness, which does not allow one to withdraw from a fight.[82] Sport was to allow men to train their characters in determination and stubbornness and in this way to approach the ideal. Societies in the 1930s affirmed masculinities that were more complex than earlier rough models fetishizing muscles.[83]

Rotholc's masculinity was also debated in the context of his corporeality. Press reports analyzed Rotholc's body, which entered into interaction with the bodies of other men: people yanked it from hands to other hands, pulled down from the ring, kissed, and embraced. Fighting with Bernard Jarząbek in 1934, Rotholc "hit him as if he were hitting a training bag."[84] Another report described the body of Rotholc as a machine. Rotholc and Italian boxer Guido Nardecchia were "two powerful machines, with a full impetus; power and energy have thrown one on another."[85] This trope of linking bodily performance with machinery was starkly masculine. In those years, many people perceived machines, cars, and engineering as spheres of masculine engagement. Becoming a machine, Rotholc turned into an über-man. Rotholc's body appeared as a reservoir of masculine energy that could potentially transfer to other men through physical contact. The able body of Rotholc became an artifact that was worshipped by his fellow men independently of their ethnicity. Yet Rotholc himself noted his corporeal vulnerability: "Often my eyes were swollen or covered with blood, my nose crushed and my head had bumps."[86] Rotholc's body appeared thus as adaptable, turning from a machine into a humanlike body.

All-Polish press also examined and praised Rotholc's virtues and achievements. When, in 1934, Rotholc unexpectedly won against the German champion Werner Spannagel, *Przegląd Sportowy* commented, "The result of the fight was decided by the tempo Rotholc imposed, the power of his strikes, his clever tactics and super-human ambition. With true admiration, we look at how he grew from a small unknown competitor into a first-class star."[87] The magazine continued explaining how Rotholc managed to succeed against the odds (unsatisfactory training conditions, the need to have a day job) and praised his talent. In *Przegląd Sportowy* we hardly ever find any reference to Rotholc's Jewishness, only admiration for an ambitious sportsman. Rotholc's example demonstrates that excellent sports performance had the potential to disassociate Jewish men from the antisemitic charge of being weak and effeminate. In that sense, non-Jewish male sports journalists deciding not to speak of Rotholc's Jewishness in a way validated Rotholc's masculinity as governed by the same principles as the hegemonic non-Jewish Polish masculinity. While these non-Jewish men probably still held Jewishness as a deficit, they were ready to focus on other aspects of Rotholc's performance.

It is worth posing the question: What is at stake when a Jewish boxer is a national champion of a country where Polish-Catholic men are the hegemonic ethnic group? Does he challenge the hegemony, and how does this tension influence the masculinity of Jewish and non-Jewish men? I suggest that Polish-Jewish sports journalists and boxing fans celebrated Rotholc's victories because he challenged the hierarchies of the local hegemonic masculinity. Rotholc's masculinity was constructed as linked to the ideal of middle-class masculinity bound up with the idea of civilization (rationality, self-control, and respectability) but at the same time understood as untamed, impetuous, and hot blooded. The latter characteristics, understood as irrational and uncontrolled behavior, were attributed to women, "inferior races," as well as to working-class men.[88] These contradictions in perceptions of Rotholc's masculinity are far from surprising. As Belkin argued, as a normative cultural construction, modern masculinity is structured by a contradiction.[89] Polish-Jewish reports about Rotholc's virtues are far from internalizing Jewish masculine subordination or effeminacy; conversely, they describe Rotholc with a vocabulary traditionally linked with hegemonic masculinity.

While Rotholc's ethnicity might have had only a minor significance for the journalists of the *Przegląd Sportowy* (at least in a declaratory manner), it did matter for many spectators from the non-Jewish working class. When, in 1936, Rotholc beat Catholic boxer Antoni Czortek, spectators favoring his opponent reacted by whistling, which one Jewish newspaper commented on as "unsporty" and chauvinist. The Jewish press openly spoke of Poznań's boxing public as antisemitic and suggested that this antisemitism could lead to a weaker performance by Rotholc.[90] Representing Poland at international tournaments was a particularly tense issue. An antisemitic press, including *Goniec Warszawski*, attempted to disqualify Rotholc, arguing that a "żydek" (Jewboy) should not have "the honor of representing Poland."[91] However, Rotholc's virtues of body and mind seem to have overshadowed his "problematic" ethnicity when the Jewish boxer was successful in fights against Germany. When Rotholc defeated the German Werner Spannagel, he "won the enthusiastic ovation of the until now unsupportive Poznań spectators." Allegedly, several thousand people watched it in the Colosseum theater, and Poznań boxing fans brought Rotholc down from the ring hugging him, even though, three weeks earlier, they had been openly antisemitic during Rotholc's fight with the Catholic boxer Czortek.[92] While beating Czortek, Rotholc appears as a Jewish man challenging the supremacy of Polish non-Jewish men, but when winning over Spannagel, he appears as a Polish man reinforcing the Polish sense of masculine supremacy.

In Warsaw in 1938, Yiddish daily *Hayntige Nayes* printed Rotholc's memoirs, "Shapsel: Di lebens-geshikhte fun shapsel rotholc," in installments.[93] When the first installment appeared in April 1938, *Hayntige Nayes* included a photo of Rotholc in black boxer shorts

Figure 3.5. Shapsel Rotholc's serialized memoir, *Hayntige Nayes*, April 1, 1938, 11.

straightening his left arm in a boxing movement (fig. 3.5). His body is well defined yet not overly muscular. Unlike Breitbart, whose photographs usually emphasized his superhuman power, Rotholc's masculinity appears centered on technique and strength of character. This corresponds with broader European trends: new sport disciplines demanded bodies more diverse than muscular and massive ones. Toned, slim, and more delicate male bodies could now be very masculine.[94] Fighting as a flyweight, Rotholc was a short, slim young man of about fifty kilos. The photo includes a shadow cast by Rotholc, which possibly serves two functions. First, it makes Rotholc seem much bigger and of an impressive posture. Second, it suggests that other men could become Rotholc's shadows, that is, follow his footsteps as a man and sportsman.

The memoir is a first-person narrative telling the story of becoming Poland's most popular Jewish sportsman. Publishing the life story (*lebens-geshikhte*) of the then twenty-five-year-old boxer suggests that Rotholc had already achieved the status of a celebrated hero whose biography was potentially interesting for readers who wanted to know as much as possible about their idol. The memoir was to serve as a guidebook to the fitness-centered male gender identity that Rotholc embodied. Rotholc's memoir promised to reveal the "secrets" of the boxing ring and the "sports world." Revealing the secrets had the potential to allow other men to "become like Rotholc"—that is, Jewish, fit, and successful. The memoir calibrated this message to many young Polish Jews from the working class and poor but modernizing Orthodoxy. Writing about his years in a heder, Rotholc positioned himself as an average Polish-Jewish young man of his generation. Rotholc's narrative centered around his orthodox and working-class background. In the first installment, he writes, "I always came back home with a lot of fame, received flowers, but had no money in my pockets. Until this day I need to work hard for my livelihood and I am proud of it. I am an amateur boxer, and as I always say, for my fights I did not get anything apart from punches."[95] Boxing was a preferred type of sport for impoverished Jewish sport clubs since it did not require a financial investment—conversely, it was bringing the clubs substantial incomes.[96] The memoir demonstrates the divide between working-class and bourgeois sports: Rotholc abandoned his first Jewish sports club because "there were only rich daddy's sons there, they spoke Polish and they looked on me from above."[97] In the working-class club Shtern, on the other hand, he felt at home. While now working-class men also engaged in body- and masculinity-forming leisure activities, the class differences were still strong. The memoirs not only recapitulated Rotholc's rise to the top but had a dimension of mobilizing young working-class Polish-Jewish men to follow his path.

Rotholc used his ancestry to prove his strength as something natural to Polish Jews. Speaking of his father, who was "a short Jew, but strong, healthy as a fir," Rotholc suggests that he inherited his strong body from him. Rotholc and his siblings supposedly were like their dad: "able-bodied, firm, and strong." Shapsel and his brothers used to regularly wrestle at home (*motseven zikh*) while their father enjoyed watching these games and serving as a judge.[98] Rotholc's brother Monis explicitly recommended to him that "a man needs to be strong and have power in the muscles" and suggested he join one of the developing Jewish sport clubs where he could shape his body among other Jewish young men.[99] As a child, Rotholc was thin and weak. His strong and well-built father used to call him a *zdechlak* (weakling) and body-shamed him. His father showed him his own hands and told him, "One should have this kind of hands! Go to work and you will become stronger. In our family, there are no zdechlakes!"[100] The memoirs reveal that Rotholc's Orthodox father praised masculinity based on physical strength and instructed his son that only power made a proper man.

Rotholc's family narrative suggests that in the Polish-Jewish working-class setting, men did not need any external impulse to be strong and hence masculine. They appreciated physical strength even before the advance of Zionist corporeality, were aware of their physical power, and hence did not perceive their masculinity as inferior. The example of Rotholc complicates the conclusions of scholars of American Judaism who underscored that American-Jewish boxers "differed from their parents who kept to the Old-World practices and avoided *goyim naches* [pleasures or activities that only non-Jews value]."[101] Rotholc's old-world father was very much into his son's boxing profession, and in his case, the generational divide seemed not to be that meaningful. Both father and son embraced physical power as constitutive for modern Jewish masculinity. Rotholc's father instilled in his son not only a Jewish pride but also Polish patriotism and differed little from him in terms of their declarative identity choices. The father and the son seemed to embrace an analogous set of gender and ethnicity identity markers.

Rotholc's story illuminates how the Rotholc family challenged Orthodox Jewish gender normativity. While the father wanted Shapsel to grow strong and able-bodied, it was his mother who countered, "What do you want from the child? Why do you want him to be a hero? He should rather have had a good head for learning."[102] The father feared having a weak zdechlak son, which would endanger his own sense of masculinity. In traditional eastern European Jewish cultures, men were praised for their studiousness, but the young Shapsel, and even his father (who still studied Talmud from time to time), seemed to follow a different model of Jewish masculinity. It is the mother who holds on to the tradition and attempts to maintain the Orthodox gender order. Also, Rotholc's time in a heder challenged the classic model of Orthodox Jewish education. While the heder traditionally was an institution that solidified masculinity centered around religious study and established hierarchies of men according to their religious performance, young Rotholc used the heder as a training ground for gender identity centered around physical power. It was a seven- or eight-year-old Rotholc who punched back when the melamed (a heder teacher) attempted to smack him or beat his fellow but older students with *makot retsakh* (murderous hits).

Another stop along Rotholc's track of masculine development was the Polish army. The military was the space where Rotholc the Jewish boxer developed into a man and acquired the "desired learning," as he put it. When writing about learning to drive a car or using a Biks gun, Rotholc applies the vocabulary of submission. He uses the Yiddish word *behershen*, with the Germanic root *herr*, meaning a man. The car that previously behaved as it wanted was, after some training, functioning according to Rotholc's commands. By subduing the machine, the boxer proved himself as technology savvy, which in the 1930s (particularly concerning cars) many people in Poland increasingly understood as a masculine feature. Unlike many young Jews in Poland, Rotholc did not try to avoid conscription to the army, since "knowing the meaning of the assiduous military service, Rotholc was willing to suspend his career."[103] Importantly, military service was, for Rotholc, a space where young men celebrated masculine camaraderie among other men. He does not write about experiencing antisemitism but about spending time with "colleagues and friends" in a soldier's club.[104] It is unclear whether Rotholc did not experience any antisemitism in the army or whether he consciously decided to downplay this experience to present a continuous story of masculine ascent wherein the army played a central role.

The figure of Rotholc allows us to reflect on the intersection of nationalism and masculinity. As *Der Moment* pointed out in 1936, a sports victory was analogous to a military victory.[105] In this combat context, Rotholc appeared as a hero whom Polish Jews needed: "In recent years, Jews in Poland have their own Shimshon ha-giber—Shapsel Rotholc. Polish Jews were proud of him. . . . The little guy! Shapsel Rotholc, the Jew, floors the goy heroes. He will be the source of Jewish redemption."[106] Rotholc saw his fights embedded in the broader respectability struggle of Polish Jewry. Referring to the rising antisemitism, Rotholc argued that Jews needed the ability to fight: "I know this profession very well and I would be very happy when more and more Jews would learn how to give a punch and receive one. It won't not hurt and might be useful."[107] Rotholc wanted young Jews to see in him a role model of a Jewish man who defends his dignity with his fists.

In the late 1930s, Jewish males negotiated their gender identities in the context of antisemitic violence. The discrimination they faced released a lot of anxiety in times when Jewish men were unable to protect their communities. In this context, Polish Jews were increasingly admiring and praising Jewish men who successfully used physical violence against the antisemites. While, in the 1920s, Jews admired Breitbart for showing the power of his muscles in a circus, in the 1930s, they appreciated Rotholc and other Jewish boxers for punching antisemites. The link between Jewish men's boxing performance and their dignity as Jews and men is traceable in the article on Rotholc published in the Zionist Polish-language daily *Nowy Dziennik*: "We need more Rotholcs, more Jewish hard-working, hard, adamant and ironclad Jewish sportsmen, more good results and more Jewish victories. Then we will convince not only the Poznań spectators, the antisemitic press, rickety and unjust sport authorities, we will have on our side those who are now our enemies, we will regain our honor and gain respect even among those who since the cradle grow up in an atavistic Jew-hatred. Through sport victories to recognition and national equality—this should be the motto of all Jewish sportsmen and all Jewish sports and gymnastics associations."[108]

While Jewish defense readiness had been advocated earlier on, Rotholc as a Jewish boxing champion made the link between the ability to fight and masculinity particularly fitting and visible. Other actors also noticed the change. As early as 1922, Jewish journalist Pinchas Katz wrote in a report for New York's *Forverts* that "anti-Semitic newspapers warn that Jews are preparing all day to prove their Samson powers on the Polish back."[109] Katz explicitly linked the development of the Jewish sports movement with the emergence of previously unheard-of Jewish revenge and self-defense: "In one word: everyone found a taste in straightening the bent back, pushing up the sunken chest, hardening the butter-soft muscles, and instead of getting hit, one should now give back. . . . It is in the Jewish nature to do something well if one starts to do it." In 1934, the non-Jewish satirical paper *Wróble na dachu* pictured two young Jews who attempted to gather masculine courage by referring to the recent victory of the Jewish boxer Max Baer over Primo Carnera: "Stupid, what are you afraid of? We won the world championship in boxing."[110] The victories of Jewish boxers served as proof that the collective male Jewish body was healthy and well. Polish-Jewish men who followed Jewish boxers sought to extend the gender dimension of their victories to include all Jewish men.

Jewish masculinity centered around physical power was to be verified by standing up against antisemitism, particularly against Nazi Germany, which embodied it in the 1930s. The strategy of Jewish sportsmen was twofold: either boycotting the tournaments in Germany or winning a fight against a German. For instance, in 1935, several Polish-Jewish sportsmen attempted to avoid competing against the representatives of Nazi Germany so as not to legitimize them. This might have worked against the interests of Polish boxing clubs that attempted to increase their incomes, including even printing swastikas on posters. One Jewish newspaper commented, "WOZB [Greater Poland Polish Boxing Association] is trying to force amateur sportsmen to fight contestants whom they detest and with whom they do not want to have anything in common. Can amateur sportsmen be deprived of this basic human right? Is anyone authorized to enforce competing against a humiliating contestant?"[111] Those Jewish boxers defined their masculine respectability through refusing to compete against men who stood for antisemitic Nazi Germany, and these boxers believed that in this way, they underscored their superiority as decent men and Jews.

Against the voices that criticized him for fighting in the antisemitic country or competing against German boxers, Rotholc believed that precisely demonstrating Jewish superiority in the ring was the best answer to German antisemitism.[112] When, in 1934, Rotholc fought against a German boxer, the press spoke about Rotholc "fighting against the swastika."

One Jewish newspaper compared Rotholc's fight against the German Spannagel to a fight between David and Goliath and celebrated "a Jew who triumphed over the swastika." It was not just a victory but "mangling" and "annihilating" the enemy.[113] Some Polish Jews interpreted Rotholc's victory as a victory over "pure-Aryan führers,"[114] and one Jewish daily described a boxing match in which Rotholc won against a German competitor as a "pogrom."[115] In his memoir, Rotholc extrapolated his experience as a Jewish man and boxer to include all persecuted Jews: "But maybe it is because as a young Jewish boy I shared the experience of the entire nation: the more they hit us, the more resistance we build, become powerful and strong."[116] Fighting with German boxers served as an opportunity to take revenge for the antisemitism experienced by Jews in Germany, Poland, and elsewhere and demonstrated that Jewish men knew how to fight and were on equal footing with non-Jewish men.

When Rotholc decided to participate in the Olympic Games in Nazi Germany in 1936, *Hayntige Nayes* proclaimed that "the Jewish society in Poland no longer considers Rotholc a Jewish sportsman." The daily announced, "We are not interested in their victories or their defeats. For Jewish sports fans, they have ceased to exist."[117] Other voices commented that Rotholc's decision to participate in the Olympics was understandable. *Der Moment* wrote, "Since Poland has relatively narrow chances for 'winning battles,' obviously she could not resign from such a 'tank' as Rotholc." The daily continued in a military-like but excusing tone: "What can a soldier of a Polish army do when he receives a command from a colonel to appear at the platform and wait for a train to Berlin?"[118] Rotholc himself sent a press declaration in which he underscored that he "was forced" to participate in the Olympic Games and expressed his strong loyalty to the Jewish working-class sport.[119] The debate illustrated how Jewishness, masculinity, and sports entangled. According to more radical voices, Rotholc's decision to participate in the Olympic Games in an antisemitic country showed not only a lack of Jewish national pride but also a lack of basic personal dignity. Since dignity and honor were, for many men in interwar Poland, constitutive aspects of masculine identity, not possessing them emasculated Rotholc. According to this logic, Jewish men, particularly a popular role model such as Shapsel Rotholc, should prioritize ethnicity over sports achievement.

The perception of Rotholc in Poland was contextual. While Rotholc as a member of the Bund-affiliated sportsmen of Shtern was seen as a Jew, when representing Poland or Warsaw, he was viewed as a Pole. This latter perception made some Polish Jews very proud: "Far beyond [Poland's] borders the fame of Rotholc does a great propaganda job for Poland. Europe knows Rotholc and is full of appreciation for him," wrote one Polish-Jewish daily.[120] When Rotholc was one of eight Polish boxers who won against the United States, "the radio waves spread his fame around the world."[121] Chosen as one of the ten best Polish sportsmen, Rotholc was a "warrant officer" of the Polish sport, and *Przegląd Sportowy* titled him "a Pole."[122] Baranowski, the head of the Polish Boxing Association, congratulated Rotholc for "making one's mark for the Polish sport" after his victory over Spannagel.[123] Rotholc himself spoke about fighting for Poland with pride: "I was always proud, and still am, that my muscles and fists have brought respect and fame to my home-country."[124] In the context of the growing tensions between Poland and Germany, fans in Poland perceived Rotholc's victories not only as Jewish victories but also as Polish victories. Rotholc came to represent a brave and strong Polish man who defeated the German enemy. Rotholc embodied a form of Jewish masculinity that was self-confident in its Jewishness and its Polishness, and the boxer seemed to embrace both.

CONCLUSION

The case studies examining the following enjoyed by Zishe Breitbart and Shapsel Rotholc in interwar Poland demonstrate how, in the 1920s and 1930s, physical power stabilized as a valid local marker of Jewish masculinity. Particularly, men of working-class background found in Breitbart and Rotholc masculine models adjusted to their class position and available resources, the growing antisemitism, and a general Polish social landscape that elevated the strong body to a residue of modern masculinity. Breitbart and Rotholc enjoyed popularity among secular and religious Jews, which underscores my argument that in interwar Poland, Jewish men moved along a masculine spectrum and utilized an array of masculine elements that fit their needs and the time.

In the 1920s and 1930s, physical power became the object of worship in strongmen shows and, later measured and regulated, turned into a core feature of professional boxing. Breitbart and Rotholc participated in the process of defining power and sports success as central to masculinity. Both men presented a strong body as coherent with their Jewishness or even originating in their Jewishness. Rotholc speaking about how his religious father insisted on him growing strong, or Breitbart proudly exposing his origins in the Jewish working class, sent a message that Polish Jewry naturally produced men who knew how to balance the importance of physical strength and Jewish tradition. Corporeal strength appears to be central not only for the proponents and followers of Zionism but for a much larger number of Polish-Jewish men.

In Poland, the model of a powerful and defense-ready Jewish man proved to be particularly attractive in the context of the interethnic conflict and antisemitism. Bodily strength was, first, to protect Jewish men and their communities, and second, to prove to Jews and non-Jews alike that Jewish men were not weaklings. I suggest that this desire was not linked with a self-identification as weak, deformed, or incapacitated but rather with external non-Jewish discourses of which Polish Jews were aware. An antisemitic Polish press attempted to show that Breitbart and Rotholc were swindlers and thus sought to maintain the ethnic hierarchy of masculinities that saw Poles at the top and Jews at the bottom. Within this complex interethnic cleavage, Jewish and non-Jewish men at large seemed to recognize that physical power had become a virtue that could elevate one's status as a man.

FOUR

TENDER BONDS OF FRATERNAL AFFECTION

Student Fraternities, Homosocial Sociability, and Jewish Respectability

WHEN JOSEPH MENKES PREPARED TO leave for Palestine in 1932, his fellow members of the Jewish fraternity Zelotia in Lviv commissioned a large painting (fig. 4.1) presenting him as a role model of elite Jewish masculinity. The painting pictured Menkes on a plinth, spreading his legs in a pose suggesting his readiness to fight. Menkes held an enormous sword and a protective shield, and a fraternity band with a big Star of David decorated his chest. The painting by Samuel Bikeles, who also belonged to Zelotia, both poked at Menkes's authoritarian methods as a discipline coach, "a terror for own and foreign," and praised his talent for fighting for Jewish men's respectability. While the balding head of Menkes did not echo the ideal of masculine beauty, the painting resonated with the cordial sympathy of fellow fraternity members who admired Menkes's devotion, defense readiness, and fencing competence.[1] The story of Joseph Menkes and his fellow fraternity members illuminates the experience of Polish-Jewish university students who claimed access to elite masculinity in a social context that increasingly pushed Jewish men to the margins.

Student fraternities, or *korporacje* (corporations), as they were known in Poland, emerged in the late nineteenth century as institutions forging a privileged class and gender identity among male university students. In non-Jewish contexts, fraternities were venues for molding and performing masculinity in a setting encompassing a narrow group of men who could study law, medicine, or philosophy. As Sabrina Lausen has demonstrated in her comparative study of Polish and German fraternities and Sonja Levsen in her monograph on fraternities in Great Britain and Germany, in the late nineteenth and early twentieth centuries, fraternities were a phenomenon with similar underpinnings and dynamics across many European countries.[2] The fraternity movement, both gentile and Jewish, expressed a misogynist vision of male supremacy that to a great extent saw women as subordinated, distracting to the process of forming masculine gender identity, and not destined for public engagement.[3] Fraternities epitomized masculine concepts centered around respectability, violence, and defense readiness, and studying them allows us to look at both the idea and the practice of how Jewish and non-Jewish fraternities policed the masculinities of their members and other men. The study of these elitist homosocial gatherings allows us to analyze the patterns illuminating how gender exclusivity was entangled with educating young men into a gender regime that sought to safeguard the patriarchal order and preserve the existing class structure.

The present chapter looks at male Jewish fraternities in Poland, focusing on Jagiellonian University (UJ) in Kraków in the 1920s and 1930s. This university had a significant proportion of Jewish students, which made Jewish self-organization more feasible than in places with only a narrow share of Jewish students, like the western city of Poznań.[4] The first Jewish fraternities in Polish lands appeared in Lviv and Kraków at the very end of the nineteenth century, but archival records of the interwar years represent the bulk of the available source data.[5] The majority of the earliest Jewish fraternities in Poland were Zionist. In Lviv, Kadimah was the first student association, established in 1895, followed later by Emunah (1898), Hasmonea (1909), Makabea (1909), and several others. Operating in Kraków before World

Figure 4.1. Caricature of Joseph Menkes, Lviv, 1930s, reproduced in Harald Seewann, *Zirkel und Zionsstern. Bilder und Dokumente aus der versunkenen Welt der jüdisch-nationalen Korporationsstudententums: Ein Beitrag zur Geschichte des Zionismus auf akademischen Boden* (Graz, Austria, 1994), 4:119.

War I were Przedświt-HaShachar and Hasmonea, while Kadimah and Emunah appeared in 1926. Fraternities represented just a fraction of the bustling Jewish academic life at Polish universities and attracted mostly bourgeois men with a conservative worldview. Broader Jewish attitudes toward university fraternities were ambivalent. In 1926, a contributor to the Zionist daily

Chwila recognized that their hierarchical structure and focus on the code of honor might be outdated, but he still maintained that "brotherhood and discipline" were to be admired. On the other hand, the Labor Zionist Party Hitachdut in Kraków argued that the form of the fraternity was counterproductive in Zionist work and that fraternities were male social clubs.[6] Other left-wing groups were even more radical in their antifraternity stance and saw them as chauvinist.

I focus on reconstructing the value systems that fraternities desired to instill in their members, as well as on how these values were performed and challenged in the public and private spheres. This chapter scrutinizes the documents produced by the Jewish fraternities, such as their correspondence with university authorities and press reports. To that end, this chapter looks at Polish-Jewish fraternities in the context of their Polish-Catholic counterparts. The fraternities were sites of vital young masculinity, and many young men saw these unions as opposition and antidote for the feminized home where old men and women had the upper word.[7] I suggest that fraternities were central for establishing respectable and virtuous elite masculinity for Jewish men. First, Polish-Jewish men sought to achieve masculine hegemony according to the norms valid in the university microcosm and hardly ever saw this desire as enforced or impelling them to make their Jewishness less visible. Second, when studying relations between Polish-Jewish and Polish-Catholic fraternities, it is clear how a group of privileged upper-class Catholic men attempted to build their masculine hegemony on the exclusion of young Jewish men. While the Jewish exclusion from Polish-Catholic fraternities could be analyzed as another case of the antisemitism that defined university life in Poland, I suggest that Polish-Catholic men were particularly seeking Jewish exclusion from the venues and mechanisms of confirming elite masculinity.

BOYS OF PRIVILEGE AND THEIR CRITICS

In the late nineteenth and early twentieth centuries, Jewish student fraternities were common at German and Austro-Hungarian universities. The Jewish fraternity movement gradually expanded eastward to the Galician cities of Kraków and Lviv, which in the first and second decades of the twentieth century became its two major centers in eastern Europe. The local fraternities grew, and the Union of the Academic Zionist Fraternities in Galicia, which boasted about 760 young men, emerged in 1912.[8] The early 1920s saw a wave of new organizations, both in Galicia and in other Polish academic centers. In January 1930, the First Summit of the Zionist Academic Corporations in Poland (Związek Sjońskich Korporacyj Akademickich w Polsce) brought to Lviv about ninety delegates of more than twenty Polish-Jewish fraternities.[9] The university reform of 1933 stipulated that interuniversity student organizations could not exist, which strengthened individual fraternities.[10] The interwar years also saw the reemergence of fraternities outside of key academic centers—in the students' hometowns across Poland. In the 1930s, there appeared many so-called *korporacje synowskie* (sons' fraternities) that were fraternities for male high school students. In Polish cities that belonged to the Russian empire, independent fraternal movement was illegal before World War I.

While Polish-Jewish and Polish-Catholic fraternities were only one of many forms of student associational life, they were conspicuous. Polish-Catholic fraternities were strongest in the northern and western regions where only a few Jews lived and studied. In Poznań in 1927, members of Polish-Catholic fraternities constituted 24 percent of all students, while in much more Jewish Warsaw, Kraków, and Lviv, it was between 4.5 percent and 5.5 percent of all students. In 1927, 2,805 Polish-Catholic fraternity brothers made up 7.3 percent of all students in Poland.[11] Jewish fraternities had a lower total membership, but as far as the average memberships in specific fraternities, they were similar to their Polish-Catholic counterparts and usually numbered between twenty and twenty-five members.[12] In the thirteen years of their existence, Kadimah and Emunah in Kraków accepted more than two hundred young Jewish men.[13] Through a network of personal connections, fraternities provided young men with privileged access to the public sphere, particularly politics and business.

Members of Polish-Jewish Zionist fraternities, in a way similar to their Catholic counterparts, imagined themselves as future members of a national elite—a Jewish national elite. The establishment of Jewish fraternities with a defined nationalist Zionist focus took place in the context of the growing nationalism that defined social life in Poland. Polish-Catholic fraternities developed a nationalist profile that envisioned only ethnic Poles as the true rulers of the country. In this nationalist context, Polish-Jewish fraternities borrowed from their non-Jewish counterparts the ideal of a powerful, defense-ready masculinity linked to knighthood. A reference to knighthood had already appeared in 1913 when Lviv's Hasmonea celebrated its fifth anniversary.[14] The invitation featured an art nouveau–style illustration of a knight, who appears both potent and self-contained, holding a shield with a Polish eagle against the background of Lviv's panorama. The symbols used by the Hasmonea men suggest their strong entanglement in gentile gendered aesthetics and a claim to the regionally valid masculine hegemony. As Polish knights were the elite men of the Middle Ages, so Lviv's Hasmoneans could become (or already were) the male elite of Jewish Lviv. Referring to knighthood and masculine vitality, Polish-Jewish fraternity members created narratives that rhetorically counterbalanced both the precarious Jewish situation in Poland and what they saw as the femininized middle-class household.[15]

Figure 4.2. Żydowski Związek Akademicki "Hasmonea" Lviv, invitation to "Uroczysty obchód dzesięciosemestrowy," 1913. Reproduced in Harald Seewann, *Zirkel und Zionsstern. Bilder und Dokumente aus der versunkenen Welt der jüdisch-nationalen Korporationsstudententums: Ein Beitrag zur Geschichte des Zionismus auf akademischen Boden* (Graz, Austria, 1990), 2:146.

Most Polish-Jewish fraternities were Zionist and embraced the Zionist project of building proud and strong New Jews. The names of Jewish fraternities commonly referred to Zionism and associated fraternities with the Jewish traditions of bravery, prowess, and devotion. Bar Kochba was the ancient Jewish rebel, Kadimah signifies "forward" in Hebrew, and Emunah means "a faith," while Makabea refers to the Maccabees' liberation revolt, which became one of the central pillars of Zionist mythology. So, the Kraków fraternity Bar Kochba underscored its "fondness for tradition" and "resistance to social radicalism."[16] A youth chapter of the Białystok fraternity Arnonia was named Kfirey Arnonia—that is, lion cubs—which underscored the association with the animal known for its power and pride.[17] The character of Bar Kochba in particular was fashioned into a daring and proud Western-style hero, a "fine warrior on the Field of Mars and attentive lover on the Field of Venus," and thus became a key target of masculine reclamation within the Jewish nationalist context.[18] The fraternities' Zionist mythscape was at times intertwined with the immigration to Palestine. In 1933, the union of Polish-Jewish fraternities debated plans for founding a settlement in Palestine as a place where current and former fraternity brothers would live with their families.[19] In 1935, a group of Lviv's fraternity members indeed established the Kvutsat Schiller kibbutz. These initiatives emphasized not only the politics that united the members of Zionist fraternities but also the desire to maintain a tight-knit, cohesive community even after relocating to Palestine.

Jewish fraternities in the United States had similar underpinnings; reflecting the practices and methods used by their European counterparts, they served as a training ground for masculinity. Most non-Jewish American fraternities had the goal of promoting male bonding through rough play, Christian values and service, and the maintenance of the male elite.[20] Jewish-American fraternal organizations developed in the last decades of the nineteenth century as Christian men's fears of losing their homosocial white camaraderie grew in light of new and diverse populations seeking admission to universities. As Miriam Eve Mora argued, by establishing Jewish-only fraternities and mimicking their Christian counterparts, young Jewish males wanted to underscore their proud Jewishness and weave it together with camaraderie and brotherhood. Instead of advocating for admission to general fraternities, they wished to showcase their Jewish identity and recognized the masculine benefits of public Jewish male bonding. Similar reasoning appeared among the members of Jewish fraternities in Poland, who, by establishing fraternities, sought to make their Jewish masculinity visible on campus and in the public space of Polish cities.

The Polish-Catholic fraternity movement was based on ethnic and gender exclusivity. Neither women nor non-ethnic Poles could become members of Polish-Catholic fraternities. The Jewish exclusion appeared in the statutes of these fraternities that straightforwardly announced that one needed to be both Polish and Catholic to apply for membership.[21] While fraternities did not have any class entry criteria, mostly sons of the upper-middle and upper classes attended Polish universities, and consequently, males from these social classes were represented in the fraternities.[22] When a group of females established a *korporacja* in Warsaw in 1930, Catholic fraternity member Tadeusz Doberski wrote a misogynist pamphlet ridiculing these women as "laughable and unaesthetic."[23] For members of fraternities, women were either an object of sexual desire (particularly those from lower classes) or, in the case of older former members, respectable bourgeois wives who were commissioned with coordinating festive luncheons and *komersy* (fraternity parties).[24] Many members of Polish-Jewish fraternities that excluded women would probably agree with the Polish-Catholic frat brother who argued that "fraternities have always been created by men and their goal was to create chivalric, purely masculine types. Founding women's korporacje is thus particularly inappropriate."[25] For Wasiutyński, the gender exclusivity of fraternities was a source of their power. Jewish fraternity member Aleksander Ołomucki complained that Hasmonea, founded in Warsaw in 1915, "did not comply with the rules accepted, the membership was not exclusive, and women were accepted as members."[26]

In interwar Poland, fraternities functioned as insular remnants of male exclusivity and patriarchal privilege, which were increasingly put into question. At that time, most Jewish and non-Jewish academic organizations at the Jagiellonian University in Kraków welcomed women, who from the late nineteenth century onward were increasingly present on campus. For instance, in the 1920s, the number of female members of the charitable Jewish group Ognisko grew from about 30 percent in 1923 to 56 percent in 1926.[27] At the same time, women continued to be underrepresented in positions of power in Jewish university associations. Ideological progressivism and the inclusion of women are not always correlated, and male Jewish students often preferred to exclude women from leadership positions. In 1926, neither board, audit commission, nor peer tribunal of the "Związek" Association of Jewish Socialist Youth (Stowarzyszenie Socjalistycznej Młodzieży Żydowskiej "Związek") included any women.[28] In 1930, of the eight members of the board and peer tribunal in the association of progressive Jewish youth organization Chejruth, only one was female.[29] In Kraków, there were Zionist korporacje that defined themselves as fraternities and were inclusive of women, but most of their members were men, and their documents reveal masculinized language.[30] An exception was Arlosorowja, with almost 43 percent female members in 1939.[31] Against the backdrop of the growing inclusion of women at the Jagiellonian University in general, the Jewish fraternities Emunah and Kadimah were still open to men only and underscored the presumed gender benefits of their all-male character.[32]

In the 1930s, some Polish-Jewish fraternities turned toward the radically nationalist Revisionist Zionism of Ze'ev Jabotinsky. For instance, members of the fraternity Arnonia in Białystok organized an honor guard during Jabotinsky's visit to their town,[33] and the vacation fraternity Hebronja in Stryj named the Revisionist leader an honorary member.[34] While Jabotinsky's physique might not have evoked the strong and proud Jewish masculinity that Białystok Jewish youth wished to emulate, he was a man who encouraged young Jewish men to imagine themselves as descendants of heroic ancient Jewish heroes and hypermasculine protectors of Jewish honor. Revisionist Zionism's focus on shaping men translated into fears about the "damaging" influence of women and a focus on gender separation. The fear of "female masculinization" through politics is traceable in the words of one activist of the Revisionist youth movement Betar: "I would not be exaggerating if I said that all young women in Betar, or, more accurately, in the Zionist movement, are sick with a deep and dangerous psychological illness . . . our young women would very much want, if it was in their power, to turn into men. . . . This is how the popular and well-known spectacle of the she-male was created; according to her sex she is a woman, but according to her character she appears as a horrific mixture of masculine and female qualities."[35] Since fraternities were embedded in the general Zionist movement, they too debated about how to react to the increasing presence of women on campus and in Zionist politics and what influence this might have on the traditional fraternity mission of building elite masculinity.

In the interwar years, many Poles and Jews correctly associated fraternities with economic and social privilege and upper-class snobbery, which translated into a specific gender performance. Jewish and non-Jewish fraternities were aware of how they were perceived by their opponents.[36] In 1925, one Polish-Catholic fraternity member acknowledged that many people thought fraternities were "uncritical copies of German *Burschenschften* and *Trinkvereine*. Fraternities mean [for them] caps, colorful ribbons and weird manners."[37] Many Polish Jews held similar opinions. A Jewish student from Lviv, E. Bienenstock, argued in 1929 that fraternities represented "a conservative, stunted" form of student unions and instead of striving to understand social problems moved young Jewish men to "dancing, bars and duels."[38] Antoni Iwanowski recalled that Warsaw Zelotia grouped the "sons of the most influential

Jewish families."[39] One Jewish member recalled that fraternities welcomed those "who had respect for customs accepted in cultured societies."[40] Magazines of the Polish Fraternity Union (Związek Polskich Korporacji Akademickich) featured forms of leisure typical of a privileged upper class, including skiing in the Alps, festive banquets, opera reviews, and motorcycle trips in France. Pole Stanisław Urbańczyk recalled, "In my social circle the frat boys were unpopular. People laughed at their caps, their dueling mania, their in-file parades on the market square. But many enjoyed their ball parties. Some say that poor boys joined the fraternities to get in touch with the well-off people, to have higher chances for a subsidy and later for a good job."[41] Since fraternities claimed to be democratic, some of them attempted to obscure the fact that they united rich men. For example, in 1931, Warsaw Polish-Catholic fraternities were called to end their lavish banquets in light of Poland's economic crisis.[42]

Socialist groups commonly understood all fraternities as representatives of the conservative capitalist elite. Democratic and left-wing student organizations continuously ridiculed fraternities, particularly the way their members performed as men. As early as 1927, the Union of Independent Socialist Youth (Związek Niezależnej Młodzieży Socjalistycznej) mocked fraternity members whom they saw as careless and nationalist "paniczyki" (lordlings). Another democratic activist spoke of fraternity members as "Sarmatians in parrot feathers" and criticized their exuberant nationalism.[43] The Union of Polish Democratic Youth (Związek Polskiej Młodzieży Demokratycznej, ZPMD) accused fraternities of nepotism, opportunism, and being ponderous and saw them as a destructive force in Poland's social life.[44] In 1933, one ZPMD member mocked the fraternities as violent and primitive: "Since a number of years we notice bunches of lads with little swords in their lapels who cause mayhem at all universities. Bands with sticks and brass knuckles. . . . First you hit your fellow students on their heads, then you hide your cap in a pocket and pretend to be innocent."[45] Socialists underscored the ideological and class coincidence between Polish-Catholic and Polish-Jewish fraternity members, naming them "little blood brothers" and speaking of "cane fights" between lordlings, sons of affluent merchants, and other rich people.[46] By describing vain lordlings or comparing fraternity members to parrots, critics questioned their gender identity and remarked on a frivolous and overly colorful and thus feminized masculinity. By pointing out the brute violence of some fraternity members, their opponents challenged the ideal of a respectable and self-controlling man.

Like the left-wing student organizations, Jewish men within and outside fraternities also attempted to ridicule the nationalist Polish-Catholic korporacje precisely by pointing out that they were indeed based on drinking sprees and upper-class privilege. A short story written by B. Mosiężnik for the Jewish academic journal *Trybuna Akademicka* (The academic tribune) mocked the antisemitism of Polish-Catholic fraternity brothers by reinventing the names of their fraternities, Bijatyka (Brawl) and Pijatyka (Carousal), which reduced these unions to excessive drinking and primitive violence.[47] Mosiężnik's other story laughed at antisemitic frat brothers who, despite the supposedly cordial ties linking members of fraternities, refused to donate blood to their sick friend, while a Jew volunteered to do so. Although the plot was set in Austria, the blade of irony was very much directed at the antisemitism that Jewish students experienced in Poland.[48] By ridiculing Polish-Catholic fraternities, Mosiężnik attempted to minimize their impact on how Jewish men felt and functioned on Polish campuses. If Polish-Catholic fraternities were so embarrassing and detached from the male elitism they put on their banners, Jewish men could feel safe about their status.

A JEW CAN'T BE A FRAT BOY! THE ETHNICIZATION OF EXCLUSION FROM MASCULINE RESPECTABILITY

Following the restructuring of the local fraternity movement after 1918, Polish-Catholic students built their gender identities around the exclusion of Jewish men. From the perspective of increasingly exclusivist Polish-Catholic fraternities, only Polish-Catholic men should have access to the honor and chivalry that the fraternity movement engendered. In that sense, masculinity was defined as something bound to nationality, and access to it was to be sanctioned by men who saw themselves as the local bearers of hegemony. Polish-Catholic fraternities argued that in interwar Poland, one could not be a proper hegemonic man without being both Polish and Catholic. In a society where "demanding satisfaction" was shaping social life, exclusion from the rituals of honor excluded Jews from claiming access to the social elite.[49] The process of Jewish exclusion from the vision of masculine hegemony was not limited to fraternities and encompassed other spheres of professional and social life, such as access to high-level state jobs. Antisemitism in Poland also had gender dimension that impaired men's ability to act as respected providers.

As early as 1923, the Union of Polish Academic Fraternities (Związek Polskich Korporacji Akademickich, ZPKA) excluded Jews from *satysfakcja honorowa*—that is, the right to claim respectability—as regulated by the code of honor.[50] Polish-Catholic fraternity members did not treat Jewish men as respectable or as following analogous masculine norms. This was voiced once again in 1930, when Polish-Catholic fraternity members were called to "limit contacts with Jews to the minimum of politeness" and again refused Jewish men the right to defend their respectability. Catholic fraternity members deemed only those Jews who proved themselves on the battlefield or were officers to be on an equal footing.[51] In interwar Poland, Władysław Boziewicz's *Polski Kodeks Honorowy* (Polish code of honor) was a popular guidebook regulating the solving of conflicts respectably.[52] At the same time, the code had a certain modernizing aspect and extended the category of "respectable men" to include "every male who because of education, personal intelligence, professional position or birth is elevated above an ordinary level of honest man," that is, including Jewish men. By refusing to recognize Jewish men as respectable enough to be a party in honor courts, against the locally valid code regulations, Polish-Catholic fraternity members placed Jewish men in the same category as other marginalized groups, including homosexuals and deserters. The exclusion of Jews from "demanding satisfaction" made the way for the use of brutal violence.[53] While more moderate Polish-Christian men disagreed with excluding Jews from the code of honor, the nationalists had the upper hand.[54]

Jewish men seeking validation of their upper-class masculinity within the fraternities were doubly rebuffed: first through the exclusion of Jewish males from membership in Polish-Catholic fraternities and second by questioning (both rhetorically and via physical violence) the right of Jewish young men to establish their own fraternities. When, in 1924, the Jewish fraternity Monsalwacja applied to the University of Warsaw for registration, Polish-Catholic nationalists were furious: "A group of brazen Jewboy students applied for registration of a newly established fraternity Monsalwacja! And this was approved by the university's Senate.... Monsalwacja! Studious barbarians! Do you know what Monsalwczas is? Monsalvationis? ... Do you realize what kind of blasphemy, what form of anti-Christian contempt these Nalewki Street grabs committed, applying to name a Semite fraternity Monsalwacz?"[55] By naming a Jewish fraternity "Saved Mount," the Monsalwacja members probably were referring to the legend of King Arthur, which served as a prehistory of knightly fraternities. For Polish-Catholic fraternity members, this was an unjust appropriation of what they perceived as their own gender-historic legacy. A year later, the Union of Polish Academic Fraternities spoke about "fighting for the fraternity monopoly," which would allow only affiliated associations to use fraternity caps and ribbons.[56] Polish-Catholic fraternity members attempted to emasculate Jewish men by excluding them from masculine spaces and rituals.

The exclusion of Jewish men from the fraternity gender order is traceable in several songs of Polish-Catholic fraternities that explicitly feature antisemitic content. One of them presented the *narodowcy* (Polish nationalists) as victims of the Polish government's persecution. It spoke of nationalists being incarcerated in the detention facility in Bereza where they would suffer malnutrition and sleep in dark prison cells. Despite these oppressive measures, narodowcy laughed at their destiny and announced that they would "always beat Jews."[57] According to nationalists' logic, conflicts between young Jewish and Catholic men were not to be solved in a respectable manner but through physical violence. One song read, "Our Poland / how shameful it is for us / that you possess so many Jews / that a Jew rules over you, rules over you / sordid and vicious Jew / communists' brother and our enemy."[58] Promising to use violence against Jews, the fraternity members withdrew from Jewish men the access to masculine respectability. For many Polish-Catholic fraternities, nationalism flavored with antisemitism was a constitutive feature. While some Polish-Catholic fraternities claimed not to "differentiate between right and left, between red and white," most of them had right-wing, exclusivist, and nationalist stances.[59] This was translated into discourses and practices of excluding Jewish men from claiming access to masculine hegemony and shifting them to the margin.

THE CAP SCANDAL: EXCLUDING JEWS FROM
ACCESS TO MASCULINE DIGNITY

University fraternities developed a dress code that differentiated them from other young men on campus and in the public space of the city. The central element of the dress code was the *coleur*, a cap called the *dekel* or *czapka korporancka* in Polish (fig. 4.3). In 1925, Polish-Catholic fraternity members claimed that the caps "symbolize our ideology, our mutual brotherhood, and our separate worldview, which might be imperfect, but is truly noble and masculine."[60] The caps had mixed colors and embroidered elements signaling that the wearer belonged to a specific fraternity. Kadimah and Emunah, two Jewish fraternities established in Kraków in the mid-1920s, had from the very beginning allowed their members to wear fraternity caps that proudly highlighted the Jewish character of their organization. Emunah's cap included an embroidered Star of David with a compass, a sign of fraternity movement.[61] Members of Polish-Catholic fraternities believed that Jewish men publicly showing fraternity symbols violated the existing status quo and that establishing fraternities was the sole right of ethnic Poles. "In accordance with our traditional right, we will not agree that Jews should use the symbols of Polish fraternities," quoted one fraternity journal. Jewish men wearing caps and bands were thought to "provoke" and "assault," and this led to "indignation" on the part of Polish-Catholic fraternities.[62]

On February 9, 10, and 11, 1928, members of Polish-Catholic fraternities violently attacked members of Kadimah and Emunah and questioned the Jewish men's right to wear the fraternity insignia. The Kraków attackers shouted to "dissolve the Jewish academic fraternities" and "end the socialism," which suggested their radical nationalist profile.[63] Marek Bolechower, a young Jewish law student and victim of the attack on February 9, testified that he was verbally assaulted by a group of Catholic students. They demanded that he remove his fraternity cap and, when he did not

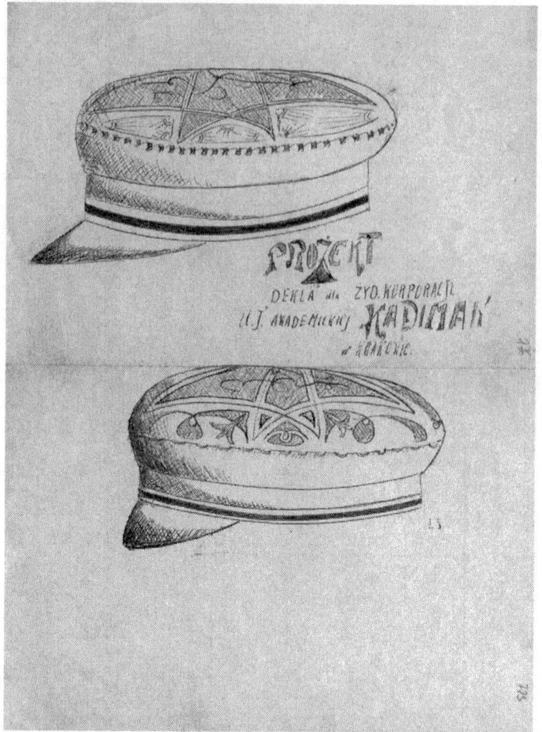

Figure 4.3. Cap of the Kadimah fraternity. Collection Żydowska Korporacja Akademicka "Kadimah" 1927-1939, S II 796, Jagiellonian University Archive (Kraków).

do so, attempted to tear it from his head. Bolechower testified that he called for the police twice and that initially the policemen just checked the IDs of the assaulters and only later took them to the police station on Starowiślna Street. When questioned by the police, the perpetrators were dismissive and contemptuous of the Jagiellonian University Senate, which had allowed Jewish students to wear fraternity caps.[64]

The conflict reached the highest authorities of Jagiellonian University. Initially, the rector refused "to deal with the student attire," which Polish-Catholic fraternity brothers perceived as "unfavorable" since they hoped for rector's ethnic and gender solidarity in limiting the possibilities of Jewish men to claim belonging to an elite fraternity movement.[65] The university called on representatives of Polish-Catholic, Ukrainian, and Jewish fraternities to gather on February 13, 1928, to resolve the conflict.[66] Yet, the next month, rector Leon Marchlewski needed to continue the talks. At that time, the university confirmed that Jewish fraternities were allowed to wear caps and bands, which needed to follow specific design regulations.[67] According to some Catholic fraternity members, Jewish men were "encouraged" by the attitude of the university authorities and were increasingly visible wearing fraternity caps.[68] In April, however, the rector forbade Kadimah members to wear the caps since he "became aware that some of them do not follow the regulations."[69]

These Kraków tensions concerning male student attire echoed discussions and conflicts in Vienna and other Hapsburg cities at the turn of the twentieth century. In 1898, members of the Vienna Jewish fraternity Libanonia appeared wearing blue caps, a privilege previously reserved for Christian German fraternities. Just like in Kraków, violence also erupted in Vienna when Jewish students participated in a regular *Bummel* (a public stroll by members of the university fraternity). In 1902, members of a Jewish fraternity parading in striped bands in the Czech town of Hodonin raised objections from both Jewish and non-Jewish inhabitants.[70] Some fraternities in the Czech lands opted to use ribbons instead of caps in order not to escalate the conflict with Christian fraternities.[71] Analogous conflicts erupted in interwar Poland, particularly in Lviv. On June 28, 1927, Polish-Catholic fraternity members in Lviv approached a group of their Jewish counterparts, demanded that they remove the fraternity ribbons, and finally ripped one off the chest of one of the Jewish fraternity brothers. This was followed by violent attacks, utilizing sticks encrusted with razor blades, that extended out onto the streets.[72] On July 2 of the same year, another member of the

Jewish fraternity was beaten for refusing to remove his fraternity pin, and the rector of Lviv University blamed the victim for "provoking" the attack.[73] In January 1928, Polish-Catholic fraternity members approached the seat of the Polish-Jewish fraternity Emunah, warned its members not to wear fraternal insignia, and later smashed the windows in the building and randomly beat Jewish passers-by.[74]

While verbal and physical assaults on Jewish fraternity members might seem like any other antisemitic attack, they were informative also for the gender dynamics in fraternities. By wearing fraternity symbols, Jewish fraternity members attempted to inscribe themselves in the hegemonic, bourgeois, elite masculinity. In the German context, Miriam Rürup spoke about the "adjustment" that men who represented marginalized masculinities performed to claim their belonging to a hegemonic masculinity.[75] I believe that wearing fraternity caps and bands was, more than an adjustment, a very conscious step in demanding access to the venues and practices of elite masculinity. By trying to force Jewish men to remove their fraternity caps, Polish Catholics tried to protect their exclusive right to define what an academic fraternity is and who is a legitimate bearer of elite masculinity. They did not consider Jews to be men on equal footing but rather an emasculated ethnic minority that should be constantly notified of its inferior status. Jewish fraternity members, on the other hand, did not accept this logic or the masculine subordination that not wearing the caps would imply. The Kraków cap affair reveals the intersection among the masculine respectability of the Zionist Jewish revival, antisemitism, and the protection of masculine privilege.

Polish-Catholic fraternities usually depicted the cases of violence against Jews as a result of "Jewish provocations."[76] While Polish-Catholic fraternity brothers supposedly attempted to keep their temper and behaved with "dignity and measure," it was the Jewish provocations that made them fight back. Following this logic, Polish-Catholic fraternity members were respectable men and used their fraternity caps and bands to mark this virtue in public. Tadeusz Doberski, a member of a Polish-Catholic fraternity, suggested that men not belonging to fraternities were using fraternity caps to pretend to be members. Doberski considered them to be doppelgängers who harmed the reputation of true fraternity men: "The public sees, especially at night and in the evening, suspicious individuals in caps similar to ours, with manners of bandits and pimps."[77] Doberski suggested that men who lacked respectability were using fraternity insignia to claim elite masculinity. Speaking about bandits and pimps, but probably with Jewish men in mind, the Pole attempted to marginalize Jewish men and refute their claim to respectability and masculine hegemony.

The repeated violence against Polish-Jewish young men reveals that Polish-Catholic fraternity members perceived themselves as legitimate defenders of what they saw as their unique right to define elite masculinity. As regulated by the Polish-Catholic interfraternity union, all conflicts between the members of the fraternities and between the fraternities were to be disputed in front of an interfraternity honor court.[78] The use of violence instead of proceedings in an honor court or other mediation body signified that Polish fraternity members excluded Jewish men from a shared ideal of an organized elite masculinity. They used violence to reconfirm their privileged status as possessors of Lviv's and Kraków's public spaces and as the true ruling group in Poland and thus the only real men. As the Zionist daily *Chwila* argued, "Jewish students, just from their sense of national dignity and civil rights, cannot allow themselves to be pushed into the category of second-class citizens."[79] By turning to rectors, administrative authorities, and the police, by making the incidents public, and by fighting with their fists, Polish-Jewish men resisted exclusionary practices that had not only an ethnic character but also gender implications. By casting themselves as dignified victims of unjust and primitive violence, they underscored the upper-class masculine values of moderation and self-control.

For Jewish fraternity members, the right to establish fraternities as elite masculine venues was a source of ethnic and masculine pride. The function of fraternities as a legitimate form of exercising violent Jewish responses to antisemitism was of particular importance. For example, members of Jewish fraternities protected Zionist events from Catholic hooligans, and Jewish fraternity member Feivel Ring was a private guard of the Zionist leader Yitzhak Grünbaum.[80] F. Żelichowski from the Warsaw fraternity Aurora initiated the Jewish self-defense association based in a Warsaw Jewish dormitory. Aurora had another self-defense unit at their seat on 17 Senatorska Street, while frat brothers K. and S. Korman were leading figures of Jewish self-defense at the University of Warsaw.[81]

Some Jewish fraternity members conceptualized wearing fraternity symbols as central to their proud and defense-ready masculinity. In 1928, members of Warsaw's Jewish fraternities proudly paraded through Warsaw with fraternity caps and bands displaying the Star of David.[82] Local fraternity members marched in military formation and donned fencing rapiers emphasizing ideals of knighthood and defense readiness. Jakób Schachter, who was active in Kraków's Emunah and El-Al, wrote in 1937 about the significance of public Jewish appearances in caps and ribbons: "And we, boisterously and cockily, paraded in our fraternity attire, not paying attention to the grumbling of the kind or ill-intentioned elders. We always answered back to everyone and in every direction. People admired us and we were not at all disaffected when in 1927, 1928, and 1929 we needed to fight a battle in defense of our caps and bands. We had street fights under the Sukiennice [in the Krakow market square] and on streets, against much more numerous 'endeks' [members of Polish nationalist parties], alone and isolated from Jewish academic youth."[83]

Joseph Menkes, one of the founding members of the Lviv fraternity Zelotia, took pride in portraying how Jewish fraternity students reacted to antisemitic violence. When Polish Catholics pushed and beat his friend Yehuda Rotenstreich, Menkes organized a group of Jewish fraternity men who violently invaded the lecture hall and beat up Polish-Catholic fraternity members. Menkes recalled that it was "the first of my uncountable fights at the Lviv university and the Corso."[84] In his memoirs, Menkes traced a line of continuous masculine bravery starting from his fraternity days in Lviv and partisan Haganah in Palestine to heading the criminal department of Tel Aviv's police. The fraternity allowed him to develop the boldness that helped him fight back against the antisemitism in Lviv and later for Israeli statehood. Other Polish-Jewish fraternity members who survived the Holocaust narrated their own lives and the lives of their friends in a way that also underscored their success as heroic fighters or respected builders of the State of Israel. Joshua Perec and Mosze Ring praised Aurora members who fought as officers in the Polish army or in the Warsaw Ghetto Uprising, while Alfred Ajzyk Nimcovich eulogized those who fought in the Israeli war of independence.[85] Former fraternity members found it crucial for their perception as men to remember their fellow fraternity brothers as embodying masculine virtues that they themselves hoped to possess.

MAKING REAL MEN: NEGOTIATING AND PRACTICING MASCULINE VIRTUES

As one fraternity report argued in 1928, men's characters "were greatly affected by the postwar era," and most of the fraternities at Kraków's university defined their task of shaping the masculine character of their members in the context of post–World War I gender readjustment.[86] The fraternity was to become a crucible of character formation for young educated men who hoped to stabilize their masculinity against the backdrop of what they perceived as postwar social chaos and the collapse of humiliated heroic masculinity. Fraternities perceived masculinity as something moldable that needed to be designed and formed. The fraternity engendered the collective character of this process—one could achieve the proper elite masculinity only in a process of exchange with other men. Texts from the fraternity context often speak about voluntary subordination to obligations and forging bonds of friendship. The friendship and mutual trust were to become a binding force that would link the frat brothers until the end of their lives and have a permanent imprint on their gender identity. An ideal fraternity member to an extent resembled what George L. Mosse described as a "new fascist man" and reflected male desires and anxieties of the 1920s and 1930s.[87]

Many men who joined the Jewish fraternities believed that their goal was to create a virtuous nationalized type of Jewish man who would also be a good citizen of Poland. A member of Makabea from Lviv suggested that the "discipline and obedience" the fraternity had instilled in their members since 1909 was at the time something "long unseen among Jews."[88] At an event of the Makabea, activist Michał Lingel spoke of an "inferiority feeling," which was the "anomaly" that Zionists sought to cure among assimilated Jewish men.[89] In 1930, Kraków Jewish fraternities argued that "our goal is creating a healthy, national type of Jew and citizen, and counteracting the harmful slogans of social radicalism imported from the East that are disastrous for all nations and poison our contemporary societies."[90] Discipline was to become a cure for what some Zionist men perceived as "Jewish national diseases" and a key concept in the masculine reform that fraternities promised. While these quotes might suggest a certain transformative gender potential, by referring to discipline and public engagement, Jewish fraternity members echoed a traditional masculine model. They aspired to the hegemonic masculinity that their education and privileged class positioning facilitated, which at the same time was challenged by the anti-semitic perceptions of Jewish ethnicity that pushed them to the margins of hegemony. The degree of approximation to hegemony, and its recognition, was what was at stake in debates surrounding Jews and fraternities in interwar Poland.

Fraternities recognized that the Great War had challenged heroic masculine ideals and invested efforts in instilling in their members what they conceptualized as masculinity adjusted to the new era. As one Polish-Catholic fraternity member wrote in 1930, boys in Poland were brought up in an effeminate manner, that is, were taught to shout and cry rather than fight back. Consequently, they lacked what he saw as "masculine virtues." Wojciech Wasiutyński criticized that Poland celebrated "two most unmanly writers" (Adam Mickiewicz and Juliusz Słowacki), which further reinforced the effeminacy of Polish men.[91] Fraternity engagement was supposed to eradicate "character disadvantages" shaped by what he saw as the feminized home. As its core values, fraternity members defined obedience and discipline, a sense of responsibility for one's words and deeds, and a respect for the rule of law. In 1925, Polish-Catholic frat brothers argued that "Poland needs pioneers, people with a manly character, of healthy and noble instincts, for whom devotion and work for others will become their religion."[92] In order to achieve this goal, Polish-Catholic corporations established a system of education that was supposed to make a man out of the new members. It included a strict system of punishments, self-incrimination, and discussing one's moral standing in public.[93] As argued by fraternity members, these rituals were to help "develop a sense of honor and ethical behavior." The Polish-Catholic fraternity Arkonja spoke about "curbing excessive individualism" and condemned "Polish national characteristics," meaning excessive bravery and idealism, and suggested eradicating in men feminine "softness" as well.[94]

Jewish fraternities also underscored discipline, boldness, and defense readiness as their core values. Since character shaping was to be a product of mutual influence between fraternity members, the fraternity imagined themselves to be tight-knit communities where comradely criticism would allow one to grow as a man.[95] Kraków's high school fraternity El-Al spoke of obedience and discipline rooted in both the Revisionist-Zionist worldview and fraternal traditions.[96] Lviv's Emunah attempted to instill in its members a spirit of "fortitude, energy, and ability to defend the Jewish honor."[97] Białystok's Arnonia saw boldness as a feature that characterized the way its members behaved. They were to be in the avant-garde of the "fight of Jewish academics in Poland" and cultivate a sense of honor and national pride.[98] The careful eyes of other men were to allow fraternity members to control and shape their masculinity in the desired direction. The fixation on obedience and discipline reflected analogous calls in the Polish-Catholic setting. Revered Józef Prądzyński, a spiritual leader of one of the Poznań fraternities, believed that fraternities "subdued the stormy rowdiness to the rule of obedience" and preferred "solidarity and brotherhood" over "selfishness."[99] Prądzyński opposed "old-Polish self-interest, romp, unruliness, slave-like, conspiratorial hatred, and Asiatic obsequious duplicity."[100] In that sense, fraternities defined obedience as a core desired masculine value, contrasting with unmasculine individualism, relentlessness, and rowdiness. As much as Zionist fraternities attempted to build a new Jew, Polish-Catholic fraternities attempted to build a new Pole who would not pursue what they perceived as "national disadvantages."

Next to obedience, the brotherhood appeared as the backbone of the fraternity movement. The Zionist fraternity Bar Kochba, next to "spiritual and physical training for work for the rebirth of a Jewish state in Palestine" and "fulfilling obligations toward Poland," defined the goal of fostering the "brotherly binding between members."[101] The summer men's-only camp in the mountain resort Rabka, which Bar Kochba organized together with the "brotherly organization" Emunah, served as a venue for "strengthening the ties between the colleagues."[102] Emunah itself underscored that the fraternity strove to "unite the members with a brotherly knot" while teaching them the value of honor, truth, and civic diligence.[103] Emunah titled its members "brothers," and the organization argued that the "brotherly character" of the organization transformed its members into a support network.[104] Kadimah emphasized that it united young men of diverse political affiliations, bonded by "knots of brotherhood." Due to being a small organization, "all [Kadimah] brothers were truly and comprehensively close-knit."[105]

The homosocial unity and brotherhood between fraternity members was not a virtue specific to Jewish fraternities but was a broader phenomenon across universities worldwide. Polish-Jewish discourses on fraternities were shaped in the context of Polish-Catholic debates.[106] In 1928, Władysław Medyński argued that the brotherhood uniting fraternity members was "something higher than a dry solidarity."[107] In 1935, *Kurier Poznański* suggested that the "strong brotherhood factor consolidates the national upbringing."[108] Unity and brotherhood were to be applied to mold a specific vision of masculinity. For instance, a member of the Polish-Catholic corporation Arkonja argued in the early 1930s that while in England or the United States, students lived together and consequently the university was a place of "shaping the souls and characters under the eye of counselors," in Poland, universities focused just on transmitting content. In that vein, one Arnonia member argued that the fraternities needed to take over education in manners, ideologies, and elite masculinity. Importantly, in the highly nationalized fraternity discourse, brotherhood was something that acquired an ethnic character. When Polish-Catholic fraternity members in Lviv appealed to the police not to intervene against their antisemitic violence, they used the rhetoric of brotherhood that supposedly united ethnically Polish fraternity members and policemen.[109]

Figure 4.4. Komers of the Emunah fraternity in Lviv. *Chwila. Dodatek ilustrowany*, no. 3 (January 15, 1933), 2.

Jewish fraternities sought to establish arenas of male free-time sociability and train their members in the skills they would need as upper-class men. For example, Syjonistyczna Korporacja Akademicka (Zionist Academic Fraternity) strove to "make their members European concerning manners and finesse."[110] In the 1930s, when the political and economic situation of Jews in Poland was becoming more precarious for Jews, male bonding appeared to be especially important. The fraternity Kadimah argued in 1939 that "perfect and truly brotherly bonding between the members even intensified in the light of the difficult situation of Jewish students."[111] So, the fraternity "discussion parliaments" or "literary judgments" were to train the men in oratorical skills that would be needed in professional life and offer them a venue of elite sociability from which they might have been excluded in non-Jewish institutions. At the same time, the biweekly afternoon teas served to integrate the members of the association, and the fraternity used money gathered at these events as loans for the members.[112] Emunah in Kraków organized almost monthly banquets—in fraternity slang known as komersy—or dance parties and several trips to Zakopane, Cieszyn, or Bielsko.[113] One photo (fig. 4.4) picturing the members of Lviv's fraternity Emunah shows that as far as fun was concerned, gender segregation was often ignored. In the photo from 1933 subtitled "komers"—that is, a fraternity party—we see a group of men in fraternity caps; older men, probably former fraternity members, without special attire; and women, who could have been either older men's wives or members of the female chapter of the local Emunah.

Jewish fraternities in Kraków adopted a hierarchical membership structure, typical also for analogous gentile unions. Among Emunah and Kadimah members were *bracia młodsi* (young brothers), *bracia starsi* (old brothers), and *starzy panowie* (old gentlemen) or *filisters* (former fraternity members who are not students anymore). Fraternities believed in tutelage as a principle defining the essence and continuity of the organization but also as a practice of molding the masculinity of new members in a normative direction. Kadimah spoke of fraternity activities as an act of "bringing up" or as the "tutelage" of younger members by the veteran ones.[114] The young brothers had their own *opiekun* (guardian), and each member had his own "fraternity father" as an example the newbie should follow. Jewish and non-Jewish fraternities sought to develop a father-son relationship between the aspiring member and the "fraternity father" that was to resemble a "spiritual union." As one Catholic member explained, "The father should strive to tighten the relationship with the son ... they should spend time together also after the regular meetings so that their relationship (*związek*) will not turn into a fiction."[115] Zionist fraternities in Poland trained their prospective members not only in codes of male propriety but also in Hebrew and knowledge of Jewish history.[116] In sum, the fraternities perceived male identity as something socially and culturally moldable that could be achieved and structured through proper training and examples provided by other men.

The system of fraternal masculine proximity was also supposed to be of help after graduating from the university. Jewish and Christian fraternities circulated lists of former members, who had established careers as lawyers, doctors, engineers, industrialists, or manor owners. In Warsaw, members of Zionist fraternities were proud that their former members sat on the Warsaw City Board (Mateusz Hindes) or in the parliament (Salomon Seidenman, Jakub Rozenblatt, and Mojżesz Koerner).[117] The old gentlemen served as examples of masculine success and life expertise. Many of Emunah's old gentlemen, such as the Zionist leader Leon Reich, offered lectures for the younger members, including on Jewish and European politics and literature.[118] Showcasing the careers of former members, the fraternities established an ideal of masculinity that their current members should follow. Edmund Schechter, a member of the Vienna Jewish fraternity, saw filisters as "ideal role models" for young men, who for their part enjoyed shining at fraternity events.[119] M. Czaskis of the Syjonistyczna Korporacja Akademicka suggested that the institution of *filistariat* linked men with the fraternity for their entire lives.[120] Some fraternity songs mirrored the relations between filisters and young fraternity members. One of them read, "I will make a bet with a filister / who was on an ego trip / I would give away titles and order / for a smile of Venera and a glass of wine."[121] The song suggested that while sex and alcohol were important within the mischievous order, professional success and respect were something that young brothers looked up to in filisters.[122]

BOYS AT PLAY: MALE BONDING AND STRUCTURING THE PROPER MASCULINITY

Jewish and non-Jewish fraternities defined the time spent together in bars or practicing sports as central to establishing masculine identities within the fraternities. These practices were public, structured, and supervised and allowed young men to shape masculine attributes that they hoped to acquire. Members of Jewish fraternities spent time together not only during official meetings but, as Kadimah reported, enjoyed casual walks and cinema or theater outings.[123] Members of Kraków's Makabea appreciated singing in a fraternity choir.[124] Anatol Leszczyński, a former member of the Arnonia fraternity, recalled that members gathered in the club of the fraternity to play chess and *damka*.[125] Apart from the organized fraternity events, their members participated in more private, narrow circle rituals of male bonding. In 1931, four members of a non-Jewish fraternity undertook a male-only trip to France on their motorcycles. They cursed casually, speeding on vehicles that they adored, and after soaking in rain, "tenderly stripped their clothes" to enjoy a moment of camaraderie, wine, and cognac.[126] While we do not have analogous accounts from Jewish fraternity brothers, they probably followed similar bonding rituals. As Randall Collins argued, "encounters make their encountees" and "generate solidarity and symbols of group membership." In our context, the ritualized interactions between men who participated in fraternity beer parties, komersy, sport events, or violence contributed to the emergence of a strong group identity.[127]

The fraternities conceptualized body and spirit as complementing aspects of ideal masculinity and offered their members a space for developing fit and sporty bodies. Jewish members of Warsaw's Aurora and Zelotia were obliged to join the Jewish Academic Sports Association (Żydowskie Akademickie Stowarzyszenie Sportowe), in which the fraternity leaders played a central role.[128] While sports and gymnastics were important as a venue for forming fit bodies, Kraków's Emunah chose to encourage its members particularly to participate in sports linked with elite masculinity, such as fencing. The organization managed to negotiate an exclusive deal with the Jewish Gymnastic Association (Żydowskie Towarzystwo Gimnastyczne), which rented out its sports hall where Emunah members trained in fencing and boxing.[129] Kraków's Kadimah underscored that its summer and winter camps, organized in the mountain resorts of Rabka, Zwardoń, and Szczyrk, were "strictly brothers-only." Instead of joining efforts with other Jewish associations, Kadimah decided that their tight-knit community of young men could be strengthened only when they were just among their "brothers." Since fraternities recognized "health protection" and "bodily development" as their values, Kadimah managed to subsidize members who could not pay to participate in summer camps.[130] One member of Lviv's fraternity Emunah said that "his heart was touched" by the perspective of "being together [with the fraternity brothers], wandering around mountains."[131] These examples evidence how corporeality and sociability were incorporated into the ritualized tool set that fraternities used to shape the social and gender identities of their members. Many fraternity members merged their fraternal and general Jewish sports movements. For example, Szymon Klajer was the goalkeeper of the Warsaw Maccabee football team.[132]

Sports and physical strength became central to performing elite masculinity. In the interwar years, sports competition gradually replaced dueling as a fraternity ritual, yet the link with the one-on-one fight, knighthood, and defense readiness remained stable as a mechanism for claiming masculine recognition. In the 1930s, Kraków's Kadimah, following Emunah and Polish-Catholic fraternities, added fencing and swimming to its regular sports offerings.[133] Fencing was so popular that fraternity members practiced it not only at regular Sunday trainings but also before fraternity meetings.[134] David Feigenberger, member of the Warsaw fraternity Aurora, argued that "individual physical development was the guarantee of national and personal honor, and fencing, which was entirely foreign to the Jewish spirit, was taught because it formed a means of fighting back in forms accepted by others."[135] Some members of the fraternities called themselves "knights" that strengthened the link among fencing, knighthood, and masculinity.[136] Zelotia member Józef Menkes took pride in mastering both an Italian sable and a sword, supervising "most of Lviv's Jewish duels," while being considered one of the best "swordsmen in Poland."[137] The fencing and boxing that fraternity members practiced coded violence as indispensable to fraternity masculinity.

The focus on sports in the Jewish fraternities reflected broader fraternity trends in Poland. In 1925, Catholic fraternity member Wacław Sikorski underscored that "the sport idea must include all fraternities in Poland."[138] In 1928, Polish-Catholic members argued that "sports were a source of a healthy joy of living" that allegedly was stifled when Poland was not independent.[139] In that sense, sports not only shaped the bodily fitness of men in Poland but also improved their mental condition. Reports from fraternity sports events revealed the hypermasculine character of those gatherings. In 1931, the Polish-Catholic fraternity Wisła organized a football game between its freshman and veteran members. Since the sun had recently "awakened the hot temperaments" of the fraternity members, the game was supposed to permit the guys to "tug at each other legally." The game allowed spectators to observe the whole gamut of men of different heights, facial hair, and bodily structures. The fraternity members presented bold and self-confident faces, and one even stripped off his shirt to reveal his impressive chest. Other men with cameras photographed this performance of masculine energy. The journalist contrasted the masculinity of the well-trained "bulls" with Franek, a fraternity member who looked miserable and unmasculine in his shining pumps and white collar.[140] This account demonstrates that fraternity members noticed their bodily differences and that able-bodiedness appeared to be a desired trait.

Communal singing was another important fraternity ritual that revealed the workings of gender within fraternities. The lyrics of fraternity songs underscored the importance of attributes their members glorified: brotherhood, masculine respect, and bravery. Public singing was a means of performing gender identity and affirming national allegiance.[141] One song of a Kraków fraternity, titled "Let Us Love Each Other," suggested sharing a destiny and moments of happiness with one's fraternity brothers: "Let us love each other, dear brothers! / Peace and unity, from this very moment, / from palaces to the village huts, / Let us love each other! / Since, why not, / to live in peace with one's brother, / to play with him, to rejoice with him, to share with him the destiny, happiness, and possessions."[142] The song applauded the fraternity as a source of class inclusivity (which it was not) and intimate male camaraderie that led to collective, brotherly happiness. Also, the anthems of Polish-Jewish fraternities underscored that brotherly cooperation was needed to achieve the common goal. Lviv Zelotians sang about "brothers connecting hands" and "hearts burning with ardency," and this was to help "break the chains of enslavement." Aurora members spoke of their "powerful hands," which were able "to do miracles"—that is, to "end the bad Jewish plight."[143] The vacation fraternity Bar Kochba in Tarnopol sang a song of defense readiness and the ability to fight in the context of Jewish empowerment: "Although we are few, with our deeds / we can cut hydra's head / Although our path is covered with tears, we will reach our goal / Proud of our past and strong in our unity / we will soon reach the goal / Because fighting with faith and not spite / we will defeat the enemy! / So, go Brothers / let's fight bravely as we deserve / and soon we will see the walls of Zion."[144] While some of the songs of German-Jewish fraternities underscored the sense of Jewish shame and the weakness of their ancestors, the Tarnopol fraternity brothers were proud of the past, and glorified the examples of past Jewish bravery.[145] While the lyrics highlighted difficult fate of the Jewish people, the song was an empowering one and underscored the masculine quality of taking things into one's own hands.

Polish fraternity songs suggested two simultaneous aspects of masculinity young men needed to master: one of upper-class respectability and public performance and the other of mischievous, frivolous masculinity rooted in sexual potency and drinking.[146] "Stańmy bracia wraz" (Brothers, let's stand together) called for young men punished for their cocky behavior to stand together: "Brothers, let's stand together / let's make a circle of friends / and let's sing happily / we still have time / Why do you cry, mate? / Laugh, brother, laugh! / Although we are all punished / we are as happy as at a summer camp / Laugh, brother, laugh!"[147] Singing "we still have time," fraternity members were intimating that masculine respectability was something that awaited them only in the future, while now they could and should be rowdy and mischievous. Another song, "Czara wikingów" (Vikings' goblet), suggested that drinking beer would increase a man's power and make him as strong as a Viking knight. Beer was depicted as a nectar that first-year members passed to their more veteran colleagues in a ritual of men's-only collective empowerment.[148] Another song went, "Give the bottle! / Happy is our life / as long as our glasses are full / We need to drink! / We need to drink! . . . a Pole always drinks / even King Sobieski / didn't know the taste of water, he drunk a lot!"[149] The lyrics established here excessive drinking as a crucial part of performing elite Polishness. Drinking was not pictured as something the lower classes did but rather as a frequent activity among members of the elite, including the respected seventeenth-century king popularly known for his bravery. Drinking was a ritual that solidified interactions between fraternity members and shaped a group identity.

Importantly, fraternity members singing their drinking songs were performing their gender identity in public.[150] This added value of drinking was possible only when it was a communal activity, performed with other young men in bars or city squares. Some Polish fraternities recognized that young men were joining their ranks to gain new "beer friends."[151] In Vilna, several bars, such as Maciej, gained the status of fraternity venues.[152] Jan Huber's fancy Winiarnia Włoska (Italian wine bar) in Lviv would become a permanent rendezvous place for fraternity brothers.[153] Similar patterns appeared in other European countries and among Jewish fraternities in Poland. While we do not know whether Kraków's Jewish fraternities sang analogous songs, for sure they frequented local drinking establishments. Members of Emunah designated the Grand café, which attracted the city's intellectual elite, as their regular café.[154] Bar Kochba's anniversary party consisted of dancing in the Pasaż café and drinking in the S. Hendler restaurant until late into the night.[155] Drinking alcohol functioned as a mechanism uniting Jewish men who strove to approach masculine hegemony according to the norms valid within the fraternity microcosm.

At the same time, fraternities struggled with being essentialized as beer clubs. Emunah argued that it was able to offer ideological training without attracting new members with prospects of "beer tipsiness."[156] Others believed that the public perception of fraternities as gatherings of men who come together to drink alcohol was unjust.[157] Anatol Leszczyński recalled that his task as a junior member of a Jewish fraternity was to offer beer to more veteran members.[158] The practice described by Leszczyński underscores the inner fraternal hierarchies. While a drinking spree might seem to be a space where hierarchies lose their meaning, in the case of fraternities, the context of drinking even strengthened the hierarchical relations between men. The komersy of fraternities were venues for performing masculinity centered around alcohol at which veteran members demanded that the younger ones publicly perform acts of subordination and submission. Drinking was not a private issue; it was a public ritual that defined men's status within the fraternal system and granted a kind of masculine charm valid for both Jewish and non-Jewish men.

CONCLUSION

Members of Polish-Jewish interwar fraternities followed a vision of the dominant Western masculinity centered around university education, respectability, wealth, and class privilege. They developed practices and discourses that emulated non-Jewish

fraternities: symbols of knighthood, sports, the idea of brotherhood, and masculine tutelage. The gender separation of fraternities was to help Jewish and non-Jewish men overcome what they
identified as major challenges: the post–Great War collapse of
heroic masculinities, the feminized home, and antisemitic emasculation. As Raewyn Connell noted, it is not always the most
powerful people who are the most visible bearers of hegemonic
masculinity, and marginalized groups co-shape it as well.[159] Jewish men in Kraków's fraternities could strengthen and solidify
upper class and professional hegemonic masculinity without
being fully recognized as its bearers. By adopting the language
and practices of Christian fraternities, Kraków's Jewish students
attempted to perform hegemonic masculinity, but the Catholics
usually contested this with violence. I illustrated this process
with the example of Kraków's cap scandal, during which Catholic bearers of hegemonic masculinity openly questioned Jewish
respectability and the Jewish claim to such hegemony. Polish-
Jewish fraternities created a strong sense of group identity that
allowed marginalized Jewish men to demand access to symbolics and rituals that defined local elite masculinity. Many upper-
class Jewish men embodied a claim to power typical for regional
hegemonic masculinities and, in that sense, strengthened their
gendered agency.

The case of Polish-Jewish fraternities is illustrative for observing the workings of gender at the intersection of ethnicity and
class. As Miriam Rürup noted in her study of German-Jewish
fraternities, Jewish men adopted forms and practices of hegemonic masculinity and gained hegemony within Jewish society,
yet they remained excluded in general society. This was true also
for Polish-Jewish students in Kraków, who were marginalized on
campus based on their ethnicity.[160] The history of Jewish fraternities in Kraków demonstrates how fraternities became institutions for molding elite bourgeois masculinity centered around
respectability, defense readiness, and ethno-national pride. It is

important to look at how fraternity members themselves imagined, articulated, and performed their masculinities, rather than
focusing only on how these concepts and practices were received
in general society. Only by studying these two dimensions together can we fully grasp the masculine dynamics at play in the
early twentieth-century university setting. While Polish-Catholic
fraternity members chose oppression over incorporation, the
case of the Jewish fraternities demonstrates how masculine gender orders could include both the agency of marginalized groups
and the power of dominant groups.

FIVE

PULLING THE TRIGGER

The Military and Jewish Masculinities

IN THE EARLY 1920S, THE Polish army called upon the future famous Yiddish writer Isaac Bashevis Singer (1902–1991) to join its ranks. His visit to the local draft unit was traumatic. Christian draftees cursed the Jewish conscripts, and Singer felt vulnerable stripped naked and harassed with slaps and flicks. At the same time, he noticed that his reaction was not shared by other Jewish young men: "I looked with amazement as the other [Jewish] youths somehow made peace with their situation and did their best to adjust. They quickly assumed a military tone; they even made fun of me on their own initiative. The tall youth with a heroic physique came up to me and said: 'Are you a mama's boy? The army will a make a man out of you.'"[1] Singer's portrayal of Jewish men within the Polish military sheds light on how ambivalent Polish-Jewish interwar attitudes toward the military were. While many Jewish youths identified the military with antisemitism-filled oppression, other Jewish men recognized how the military enhanced their masculinity in interwar Poland and absorbed its gender-shaping logic.

The military conscription that Israel Bashevis Singer experienced was a part of the process by which European states transformed their once-elite military units into massive armies of men from diverse social and ethnic groups. Military service became an initiation rite of inclusion into the national society and the community of men. The hierarchical yet increasingly universal character of the army defined this institution as a space where diverse groups of men negotiated hegemonic masculinity. The military was the venue where "warrior masculinity"—that is, the very core of the masculine gender stereotype—was performed and celebrated. Military service offered men unique resources for the construction of masculine identity defined by emotional control, bravery, physical fitness, self-discipline, and self-reliance but also devotion and camaraderie. Serving in the army often also provided soldiers with high social status, economic security, and physical fitness, thus offering men resources with which to construct and perform their identities in order to reflect the hegemonic masculinity ideal.[2] Military service allowed Jewish men to relate to the core masculine feature of being a protector—an identity element that proved very fragile in the context of antisemitic violence that swept over parts of Polish lands between 1918 and 1920. However, in the post-1918 independence period, the service still allowed some Jewish men to claim their adherence to the hegemonic masculinity centered on power and respectability. While, after 1918, thousands of disabled men warned about the brutality of war, Polish-Jewish men were not immune to the allure of the heroic masculinity ideal.

Polish-Jewish military masculinities developed not in an uncontested vacuum but in a country that praised military achievement and granted military men an elevated status.[3] The army became a space for excluding certain groups of men from the hegemonic forms of masculinity, and military hierarchies often (re)produced class and ethnic divisions as well. In many European countries, most of the officers originated from the nobility and the new upper classes, while members of ethnic minorities faced difficulties reaching the highest army ranks. In Poland, the Catholic and ethnic-Polish majority excluded Jewish men from many venues and, hence, from practices of claiming the hegemonic masculinity, but the Polish army was ambivalent. Jewish men modeled their military masculinities on all-Polish normative military masculinities but imbued them with specifically Jewish sensitivities. Some Jewish men found purpose and meaning in the Polish military, partly because their service offered them access to the resources they needed to construct their masculinity modeled on the hegemonic ideal that praised soldierly toughness, decisiveness, and courage.

The USC Shoah Foundation interviews with Polish-Jewish Holocaust survivors demonstrate that in the 1930s, many young Jewish men desired to join the Polish army and saw their service as constitutive for their sense of masculinity, even when they experienced antisemitic discrimination there. Michał Friedman was devastated when he was not drafted to *podchorążówka*, or cadet school, even though he considered himself to be fit and educated. He recalled that people "fought to serve in the army," which "enjoyed a great sympathy of all social groups."[4] Many other Jewish men felt discriminated against when forbidden from joining the officer school, but their frustration underscores precisely their embracement of the hegemonic Polish masculinity associated with being an officer.[5] After the Holocaust and sixty years after their service, many Jewish men defined themselves through military masculine logic. Henryk Prajs underscored that "having a shapely figure" and "being an elegant and sporty lad" helped him join the cavalry and not the less prestigious infantry where most of his Jewish friends served. He struck up friendships with Catholic, Protestant, and Jewish soldiers and argued that his "smartness and ability" allowed him to enjoy the atmosphere of soldierly camaraderie.[6] Uri Diamant aspired to "be an excellent soldier" in the infantry and used violence to consolidate the respect of other soldiers.[7] Max Brett remembered being treated "as a piece of dirt" and being beaten up, but at the same time, he resented not being allowed into officer training. Brett spoke about abusing other Jewish recruits, which protected his military cred and, in his perspective, paid off.[8] Dozens of similar testimonies demonstrate that Polish-Jewish men who served in the military in the 1920s and 1930s largely embraced a vision of military masculinity that defined fitness, fearlessness, and pride as its central virtues and carried them into civilian life.

Even in societies that attributed inferiority to Jews, some Jewish men were able to benefit from military service. In early twentieth-century Poland, the century-long discussions about granting Jews full civic rights included debates about Jewish military service. By fighting in the army, particularly for Poland's independence, and especially in the Polish Legions, Polish-Jewish men hoped to bolster their perceived masculinity in order to elevate their political rights. Expressing Polish patriotism and a willingness to fight for Poland was also a way to claim masculine agency in public matters. For instance, in 1935, Białystok Jewish veterans complained that Jewish soldiers still needed to fight for recognition of their *pełnowartościowość obywatelska*, or full citizenship rights.[9] A year later, another group of Jewish veterans argued, "We fight against those who want to push us back into the ghetto."[10] The veterans believed that their military service fifteen years earlier granted them full citizenship rights and that the growing antisemitism of the late 1930s was a challenge to their acquired and war-validated masculine dignity. While Polish Jewish men expected their army service to grant them full citizenship, I suggest that they also hoped their service would include them in the hegemonic Polish masculinity.

The gender aspect of Jewish involvement in the military has not yet been properly examined. Jewish service in European armies has mostly been analyzed in the contexts of antisemitism and integration into the respective national culture.[11] The gender of Jewish soldiers has often been overlooked or examined only in the context of male-female relations and the exclusion of women from the homosocial army. Studies on gender and war usually center around majority and titular national groups and are more present in literary rather than historical studies.[12] For example, for David J. Fine, masculinity "helps us to understand Jews as Germans," yet his study largely fails to understand German Jews as men.[13] Fine tells us how Germanness and Jewishness intersected during the war, but he does not incorporate gender as an equally important category of analysis. While scholars such as Christa Hämmerle help us understand the meanings of masculine gender in the army and how veterans conceived of their gender after the war, there is a lacuna of knowledge concerning the interplay of military masculinities and Jewishness.[14]

This chapter analyzes Polish-Jewish military masculinity between the 1910s and 1930s. I shed light on the workings of gender in the shadow of powerful interethnic relations and demonstrate how notions of fighting, violence, sexuality, suffering, disability, and class evolved into diversified and ambivalent Jewish military masculinities. The chapter consists of five parts. In the beginning, I discuss the history of Jewish involvement in the military in central and eastern Europe before 1914. The next section looks at case studies of Władysław Steinhaus, who served in the Polish Legions, and Yankev Kahan, who served in the Polish army in the early 1920s, and shows how these two Jewish men of diverse backgrounds embraced the military logic of heroism and camaraderie. Later, I explore how antisemitic military and press discourses emasculated Jewish men by challenging and questioning their military fitness. The last part analyzes Jewish war veterans in interwar Poland and their efforts to claim access to respectability and masculine hegemony as they engaged in shaping a heroic masculinity and mythologizing the military.

EASTERN EUROPEAN JEWS AND THE

MILITARY BEFORE 1914: AN OVERVIEW

At the turn of the twentieth century, the army was a central space for claiming access to masculine hegemony in Europe at the turn of the twentieth century.[15] Masculinity rooted in military excellence crossed the boundaries of empires and what is defined as western and eastern European Jewry. Jewish men who followed the military masculinity ideal saw the army as a venue where the masculine virtues of discipline, prowess, or sacrifice could be tested and rewarded. In eastern Europe, particularly in Galicia, some middle- and upper-class Jewish men perceived of military service as an honorable platform for turning Jews into proper men. This is clearly visible in, for instance, a 1909 call published by *Jedność* (Unity), a journal of Polonized Jewish students in Galician Lviv, demanding that Russian Jews serve in the tsarist army.[16] In 1909, Russia debated excluding Jews from military service, as Russian nationalists considered Jews unfit to serve in the national army and claimed that Jewish men were "cowards" and "useless soldiers."[17] For Lviv's Jewish men, the Russian discussion about excluding Jews from the military did not mean relief for those unwilling to be drafted but rather their humiliation as men. Such ethnic exclusion would mean emasculating eastern European Jewish men in general, placing them outside the notion of citizenship and impeding their ability to prove their masculinity in the eyes of non-Jewish men. Galician Jewish men gathered evidence proving that Jews, including Russian Jews, were good soldiers and thus capable of fulfilling a masculine military obligation. *Jedność* quoted a Russian officer who praised Jewish bravery in the Russo-Japanese War (1905) as an example demonstrating that Jews were capable of carrying this masculine honor.[18]

At the beginning of the twentieth century, more and more Jewish men in eastern Europe, and Galicia in particular, saw military engagement as a means to inscribe Jewish men into hegemonic military masculinity and as a cure for their presumed pathological effeminacy. In 1918, a Galician Jewish man named B. Zimmerman complained that his fellow Jewish men were effeminate, writing, "The lack of *męskość* [masculinity] is so common among Jewish young men, so visible."[19] Zimmerman argued that, by fighting in

World War I, "the lack of masculinity" would be "at least partially remedied." He continued, "This man, after leaving the army, will not only stop obeying like a soulless slave or commanding with the arrogance of the parvenu, but will emanate with the dignity and freedom of a free man." Zimmerman understood masculinity as "a certain minimal development of muscles, orientation, initiative, decisiveness, independence, and bravery."[20] Whereas Zimmerman's criticism, published in a Zionist journal, might seem to be a typical Zionist critique of the weak diasporic Jewish body, the solutions he proposed were far from Zionist. He did not mention immigrating to Palestine or attending agricultural training in Europe. The military was, for him, the ultimate venue where Jewish young men could rebuild their masculinity. It was enough to embrace an established, well-known model of military masculinity typical of the local upper and middle classes. Zimmerman followed the general European idea that a young man entering the military would leave as a complete, matured man.[21]

In eastern European Jewish history, military conscription, particularly into the Russian army, was usually painted in the darkest hues. Orthodox Jews widely perceived the Russian army as a type of penitentiary, an alien, Christian institution that forced Jews to subordinate themselves to the secular order and abandon their regular religious practice and even presented a danger of converting to Christianity. The impression of the Russian tsarist army as particularly oppressive was rooted in the conscription law that was in force from 1827 to 1874.[22] This law obliged conscripts to perform twenty-five years of service and, until 1859, declared that the sons (aged twelve to eighteen) of former soldiers would be recruited to military schools and become the property of the army as the so-called cantonists.[23] At that time, Jewish communities tended to send heretics, the homeless, orphans, and other "problematic" men into military service and consequently kept the community "safe" from the army's influence, which they perceived as destructive. Scholars have demonstrated how Russian

officialdom was unable to keep track of Jewish recruits, how rabbis did not keep proper track of Jewish vital records, and how
Jewish men attempted to evade service.[24] In interwar Poland,
cantonists served as an emblem of Russian oppression and Jewish resistance. Polish Jews writing about cantonists usually did
not see major continuities between 1920s and 1930s Poland and
tsarist Russia.[25]

As Yohanan Petrovsky-Shtern argued, in the mid-nineteenth
century, the twenty-five years of conscription were not a specifically anti-Jewish measure, and no one in the Russian conscription
pool enjoyed civil freedoms. He demonstrated that unemancipated Jews served together with unemancipated peasants and that
there were no legislative obstacles directed specifically against
Jewish recruits.[26] From the perspective of imperial power, conscription was part of the process of making Jews useful and loyal
Russians.[27] Near the end of the nineteenth century, Jewish attitudes toward the military diversified, and service in the Russian
military became a path to citizenship for some Russian-Jewish
men. The 1874 reform transformed conscription, the army became less of a penitentiary institution (army service was reduced
to six years, with increased religious freedoms), and though Jews
could not be promoted to officers, their numbers in the Russian
army were growing.[28] Despite anti-Jewish counterreforms in the
1880s, the late imperial Russian army offered Jewish men an array
of new possibilities and a means of self-identification.

Jews in the Russian empire gradually changed their attitudes
toward serving in the army, and maskilim openly encouraged
military service to merit emancipation.[29] During the Russo-
Turkish War of 1877–1878, Jewish and non-Jewish journalists
persuaded their readers that Jews were excellent and patriotic soldiers.[30] On the eve of World War I, both liberal Jewish
public opinion and the Jewish religious establishment worked
to present Russian-Jewish men as brave soldiers dedicated to
their homeland.[31] Orthodox rabbis from the Vilna and Warsaw

provinces argued that "Jewish soldiers have never been traitors to their [Russian] motherland; they proved this with their loyalty and self-sacrifice [on the front]," and they projected Jewish men as full of masculine virtues.[32] Books such as M. Usov's (a pseudonym of Moisei Trivus) *Evrei v armii* (Jews in the army, 1911) and the anonymous *Voina i evrei* (War and Jews, 1912) attempted to convince the antisemitic deputies of the Duma (Russian parliament) that Jewish soldiers were not "draft dodgers" but "faithful sons" of the Russian homeland. Such Jewish voices hoped to define Jewish men as following the masculine logic valid then in Russia.

Fearful eastern European Jewish attitudes toward the military found their way into Yiddish literature and reinforced the army's image as oppressive. For example, Sholem Aleichem's short story "Funem priziv" (Back from the draft) pictures a Jewish father attempting to extricate his only son from the draft, and the short story "Gitl Purishkevitsh" tells an analogous story from the mother's perspective. At the beginning of the twentieth century, accounts appeared that portrayed military service in the tsarist army in a much more complex light. While some young Jewish men in the Russian empire prayed not to be drafted, others perceived military service positively in terms of offering adventure, income, and increased matrimonial attractiveness. Fishl Bimko's 1916 collection of short stories, *Rekrutn*, highlights the division within the shtetl concerning the military.[33] Jacob Kreplak's work *Fun kazerme un milkhome* (From the barracks and war) shows the manly camaraderie emerging between Jewish and non-Jewish soldiers.[34] Sholem Ash's *Der Yidisher Soldat* portrays the World War I experiences of an assimilated Russian-Jewish soldier and raises questions around interethnic brotherly bonding in the imperial army.[35] Many personal and fictionalized accounts painted an image of the Russian imperial army in a complex light, merging a claim to military masculinity with memories of ethnic exclusion.[36]

Starting around the end of the nineteenth century, Jews in western and central Europe perceived military service in an increasingly positive light as a means of gaining access (or the illusion of access) to hegemonic masculinity. Scholars often describe Jewish experiences in the armies of western and eastern Europe as being very different. For example, Steven E. Aschheim pointed out that German Jews fighting in the Great War "endorsed the war with an easy conscience," since "the enemy was Russian absolutism; at last, the despotic anti-Semitic heritage could be brought to account."[37] Aschheim suggested that Jews could identify with Germany because that country had offered them more democratic freedoms than Russia had. Aschheim's argument, however, does not consider that some Jewish men made careers for themselves in the Russian army, valued their service time for teaching them patterns of proper masculine behavior, and, despite antisemitism, often shared similar patriotic feelings as German Jews.[38] While Jewish service in central and western European armies came to be remembered as ennobling, the rise to power of the Bolsheviks and the discontinuation of imperial power in Russia impeded the construction of a positive memorialization of Jewish service to the tsar.

World War I, as the first modern mass war, challenged the idea of individual heroism, subordinated male bodies to industrial war strategies, and humiliated heroic masculinity. During the war, about 100,000 Jews served in the German army (12,000 of them lost their lives) and about 320,000 Jews fought as Austro-Hungarian soldiers (about 40,000 perished). Yet the tsarist army also counted 400,000 Jews, about 80,000 of whom died.[39] Across Europe, Jewish metanarratives conceived of the army as a venue of normalization for a previously unstable Jewish masculinity. In post-1918 independent Poland, recognition and high status were reserved for fighters in the elite Polish Legions (Legiony Polskie) or Polish Military Organization (Polska Organizacja Wojskowa), rather than for the much more numerous ordinary recruits who had served in the imperial armies of Prussia, Russia, or Austria-Hungary.[40] Veterans engaged in creating narratives of military glory that in the next two decades wove their way into civil and military discourses.

Following World War I, Poland built a state army that included young men of all ethnic backgrounds. For many of Poland's Jewish men, masculinity was linked with a vision of being a self-made man, hardened through military training, and filled with a self-assuredness built on homosocial camaraderie. Military service during World War I, perceived in Poland as a war of independence, was one of the key pillars defining military masculinity as one of the most validated types of hegemonic masculinity. Ethnic Polish army veterans ruled in the country's national politics, and war-experienced marshal Józef Piłsudski emerged as a symbol of masculine bravery and dedication as well as modesty and moderation. Army veterans and invalids were omnipresent in Poland and functioned as an important interest group that showcased a set of military masculine virtues.[41] The period following World War I saw the emergence of a specific "soldier habitus" that defined Polish culture in the 1920s and 1930s.[42] The importance of the army was maintained through obligatory military service, veterans' public appearances, and other aspects of the militarization of everyday life in interwar Poland. The following sections demonstrate how ambivalent Polish-Jewish approaches to the military were between 1914 and 1939.

WŁADYSŁAW STEINHAUS: POLISH LEGIONS, BOURGEOIS JEWS, AND THE CLAIM TO HEGEMONY

The way young Polish-Jewish men in the upper and upper middle classes embraced the model of military masculinity can be traced in the *Pamiętnik legionisty bł. p. Władysława Steinhausa* (Memoir of the legionary Władysław Steinhaus), published in 1916. Władysław Steinhaus (1896–1916), descendent of an affluent Lviv family, wrote the memoir reflecting on his time as a soldier in the Polish Legions. Steinhaus portrayed himself as any other young soldier and only once mentioned his Jewish origin.[43] The booklet was printed and distributed among soldiers by the Naczelny Komitet Narodowy (NKN, Supreme National Committee), a political body that instigated the Polish Legions to fight alongside the Austrians in the hopes of achieving Polish independence or autonomy through this alliance. Steinhaus's father, Ignacy, was a lawyer, a member of NKN, and a former deputy in the Austro-Hungarian parliament. Władysław's social background is emblematic of a larger group of Galician acculturated and privileged young Jewish men who conceptualized military performance as key to bringing their masculinity closer to the hegemonic ideal. During the first years of World War I, the rhetoric of male military heroism penetrated European societies, and Jews were no exception.[44]

Even before World War I, paramilitary organizations attracted young upper-class Jews from Polish lands who searched for venues in which they could test and prove their elite masculinity. This development corresponded to parallel processes in the Polish non-Jewish upper class. The paramilitary units Towarzystwo. Strzeleckie and Towarzystwo Sportowo-Gimnastyczne "Strzelec" were not massive organizations but rather elite spaces where men who already enjoyed certain class privileges could claim access to masculine hegemony. Such paramilitary units referred to both the gallant tradition of Polish nobility, which historically took upon itself the military burden in Poland, and the Enlightenment ideals of the nobility, whose men not only knew how to fight with a sword but also adhered to concepts of learned and humanist masculinity. In this vision of masculinity, men belonging to the cultural elite, seasoned through military service, would evolve into the patriarchs of the newly recreated Polish political nation.

In this context of reproducing and expanding elite privileges, paramilitary training and later fighting in the Polish Legions meant, for some Polish Jews, a chance for upward social mobility into the ranks of the elite men of independent Poland. From 1912 on, the assimilationist "Unification" Academic Association (Towarzystwo Akademickie "Zjednoczenie") trained Jewish teenage boys to become future soldiers. In Congress Poland, the "Firebrand" Union of Polish Youth of Jewish Origin (Związek Polskiej Młodzieży Pochodzenia Żydowskiego "Żagiew") and Berek Joselewicz scouts organized similar trainings. Many of these scouts later volunteered in the newly established Polish Legions, where about 4 to 5 percent (about six hundred) of all legionaries were Jews.[45] The war galvanized Jewish teenagers in Habsburg Galicia but also in Russia, where some young Jews reportedly have volunteered or, as in the case of Iakov Sharafinivich, run away from home to join the troops.[46] Most of the few available accounts of Jewish men fighting in the legions came from men belonging to the cultured middle and upper classes.[47] Their often privileged class position made it easier to be accepted by fellow legionaries and facilitated their association with Polishness. This group of young Jewish men was particularly convinced that the masculinity tested on the battlefield would allow them to claim belonging to the masculine hegemony and citizenship.

Male agency and fortitude were, for Władysław Steinhaus, the defining features of a military masculinity. Even though Steinhaus was deemed unfit to serve in the infantry, he requested not to be moved to a garrison where he would be responsible for secretarial tasks and have little opportunity for military performance. Steinhaus consciously chose to be where the fate of the war would be decided. The thought of dissolving the legions filled him with anger: "Should I wait for it? To sit alone, separate, without a mission and a goal?" When the legions were indeed disbanded, Steinhaus was frustrated: "I am no longer a legionary! The spider's net of dreams is torn apart and the fairy tale dreams have come to an end. . . . I pity all these thousands [of legionaries] dissolved in Hungary. I pity their ardor, their efforts, and their sacrifices. I pity myself!"[48] Steinhaus seemed to do everything he could to return to the front and in that way claim his belongingness among the top category of men who served on the battlefield rather than spending their time in the barracks. "I finally feel like a legionary. Still not on the battlefield, but already at the front," the young Jew wrote.[49] Steinhaus felt that most of his fellow soldiers shared similar feelings, since "our soldier kids went to fight as though they were going to a party."[50] Steinhaus defined willpower and activism as desired masculine virtues that were supposedly common among the legionaries.

Despite his young age and lack of experience, Władysław Steinhaus imagined himself as a man who had proven himself on the battlefield. His lack of military experience and poor health did not prepare him to be a proper fighter. Yet his discipline and bravery and his death on the battlefield suggested to soldiers who read his memoirs during the Great War that, despite not being physically fit, Steinhaus did what a man should do.[51] His high ambition came into full expression when Steinhaus described the battle of Kołomyja in 1915. Steinhaus did not fear entering the eye of the hurricane and hearing bullets whiz past his ears but rather felt that he was on a mission that he as a man and soldier needed to fulfill. When Steinhaus mistakenly got into a Russian trench, he remained sangfroid and killed two Russians who followed him.[52] In that sense, the young Jewish man showed that what constituted masculinity was not physical fitness but rather strength of character. Masculinity understood as discipline, bravery, and self-containment could fill even a weak body and could be trained and tested in the military. Steinhaus did not perceive his Jewishness as an obstacle limiting his access to those masculine virtues.

Steinhaus argued that the tough soldier life allowed him to forget, or rather disguise, what social class he belonged to and earn respect in a properly masculine, independent way. By fighting as a soldier, Steinhaus proved himself as a potent man who built his success through his achievements and less by benefiting from his class privilege. The military, as Steinhaus wrote, made of him a man also concerning his looks, and his long beard and uncombed hair visually turned him into a "proper front officer." His unkempt facial hair symbolized his military involvement and lack of time for the beauty treatments. Shaving would return him to his "prewar condition" and appeared to a certain extent to be unmasculine and improper while at war. In Steinhaus's perception, his military experiences transformed his body and carved themselves into his face, which he perceived now to look more gallant.[53] Steinhaus embraced the way the military had transformed his looks, and since the bodies of all soldiers homogenized in their neglect, his text resonated with a message of equality available for all men independent of their prewar social status.

Steinhaus's memoir depicted relationships between soldiers as brotherly, and no one questioned that as a Jew, Steinhaus had a full right to be a legionary. Steinhaus himself felt embraced by his fellow soldiers: "I know this regiment so well; I know every screw in the regiment's machine. I just love these boys!"[54] Steinhaus managed to form a supportive community of men with his fellow soldiers and wanted to see the military as a glue that linked Jewish and non-Jewish men. Relations between the soldiers were marked by an interdependence that was necessary within the narrow, closed community of a regiment. Traveling by train, soldiers drank alcohol together, sang songs, and played games.[55] Steinhaus developed cordial relations with non-Jewish soldiers and often admired their masculinity. The most praiseworthy in Steinhaus's eyes was a man named Rylski: aggressive, cursing, challenging the army hierarchies.[56] Rylski symbolized the military masculinity adjusted to wartime, a time when manners seemed to be out of place. Rylski's confident behavior earned him the respect of his colleagues, who admired him as a soldier and a man, and Steinhaus saw his warrior masculinity as a model to follow. Steinhaus's memoir is explicit about the value of male comradeship that included norms and practices that strengthened solidarity between men and in a certain dimension made the hardships of war bearable.[57] It was through relationships with other soldiers that Jews and non-Jews negotiated and practiced military masculinity.

Władysław Steinhaus also appreciated the male beauty of his fellow legionaries. One of his comrades, the "fabulous" soldier named Grzmot, had the face of a baby but was exceptionally brave. In one memoir entry Steinhaus wrote that Orlicz had the "fairytale-like face of a *lisowczyk*," which drew an analogy between the World War I soldier and Polish heroes of the January Uprising of 1863. For Steinhaus, this type of beauty was inherently linked with ancestry and even ran through generations. This was, as Steinhaus put it, "a breed" of beautiful and brave men, many of whom belonged to the nobility and indeed shared a noble pedigree, as well as its ideals combining prowess and a pleasing appearance. Steinhaus concluded, "All faces are strangely beautiful and of good breeding" and admired the inner beauty of the soldiers that radiated from their faces.[58] The attractive faces of the soldiers appeared as an external expression of their masculine virtues.

Jewish men who, like Steinhaus, adhered to the military masculinity ideal sometimes tried to conceal their Jewishness, or at least downplay its meaning. This was clearly visible in the account of Bertold Merwin (born Baruch Menkes), who distanced himself from his Jewishness for the sake of militarized masculinity. Merwin's autobiographical text, *Z życia w Legionach* (Life in the legions, 1918), projects him as any other Polish officer, and his Jewishness is not mentioned at all, nor are other Jewish soldiers featured. Like Steinhaus, Merwin served as an officer and was consequently surrounded by non-Jewish men of noble and upper-class origin. Merwin's accounts describe his fellow soldiers as "bubbling with health" and as a "legionary family" in which the older ones treated the younger ones like their sons.[59] The men "matured" in the primitive war surroundings as they "subdued" soil and forest to serve them.[60] The front lines were also a place where the "virtue of mutual help" crystalized and laid the foundation for future brotherly attitudes in veterans' organizations. Like Steinhaus, Merwin appreciated individual men whom he praised as role models. For him, a man of unique valor was Marian Januszajtis-Żegota, who "controlled his will," analyzed every issue with the "lancet of sharp criticism," and was "fabulously proactive and masculine."[61] Merwin's memoir was published by the NKN and, like Steinhaus's memoir, may have played a certain role as propaganda.

Steinhaus's and Merwin's texts suggest that Jewish men excelling in battles during World War I developed a set of features understood then as masculine and valued by their comrades. Merwin wrote that the war made young men hard working and disciplined: "Where are those days when a young fellow loitered, twiddled his thumbs, was tortured by idleness? . . . Only soldierhood fully engages the young man . . . and teaches him to use every moment. . . . From dusk till dawn the legionary submits to the laws of this iron upbringing."[62] For example, a fellow legionary named Bogumił Rembowski remembered that Jewish Ignacy Hoenich was "overly blustering and mischievous" and would not let others push him around. At the same time, Hoenich was studious, kind, and energetic. Such features laid the foundation for Hoenich's exceptional attitude on the battlefield in the Polish Legions. As Rembowski remembered, Hoenich was able to laugh in the face of danger and prove his recklessness and daredevil bravado.[63] At the same time, gentler men could also be transformed by war into masculine heroes. Adolf Sternschuss, who in prewar Lviv was "always dressed according to the most recent fashion" and was an arbiter elegantiarum of the city, volunteered as a rank-and-file soldier and "died a hero."[64] These sources speak of masculinity as prone to change during the war but at the same time underscore the stability of a certain masculine core that men had long nurtured.

YANKEV KAHAN: WHEN A HASID GETS
STUCK INSIDE A POLISH SOLDIER

While Władysław Steinhaus's narrative might have been typical for a relatively narrow group of acculturated Jewish men, Yankev Kahan's memoir, *Dray yor in poylishn militer* (Three years in the Polish military), is an account of a Jewish man originating from a Hasidic family.[65] Yankev Kahan represented a much larger group of Jewish men whose social background was traditional: Kahan grew up in a working-class, Yiddish-speaking, Orthodox family in Białystok. *Dray yor in poylishn militer*, centering Kahan's service from 1919 to 1922 and first published in 1930 in Białystok, is a complex account with multiple possible meanings. It normalizes military experiences among Poland's Orthodox but quickly modernizing Jewry, exemplifies how Jewish men embraced general Polish notions of military masculinity, and offers a counternarrative to earlier visions of army service as decidedly oppressive and rejected by eastern European Jews.

Kahan's memoir portrays the army as a space of opportunity where a Jewish man could validate his masculinity through internalizing the logic of an institution that was then one of the pillars of hegemony. Kahan's narrative demonstrates how he sought to balance his new military masculinity with his traditional Jewish masculinity. He made sure to emphasize his confident Jewishness but also knew how, with his various talents and strength, to establish a sense of supremacy over Christian men. For instance, Kahan felt superior to numerous peasant men who were barely literate and felt proud when his commanders appointed him a military secretary thanks to his literacy in Polish, which they lacked.[66] Kahan made it explicit that he appreciated the way the

3 יאר אין פוילישן מיליטער

מלחמה-צייכענונג

1919 — 1922

Figure 5.1. Cover of Yankev Kahan's memoir, *Dray yorn in poylishn militer*, Białystok, 1930, reproduced from the 1967 edition.

army remodeled him as a man, and particularly the comradely respect he gradually came to enjoy from other soldiers and officers. He cherished his transition from a "doll-like greenhorn" into a fully developed "beautiful butterfly."[67] After several weeks he felt already transformed: "I was already an old soldier and enjoyed greater trust. . . . I myself became proud and held my head high," Kahan wrote.[68] Kahan was very aware of the transformative influence of the army, and he embraced the evolution he experienced.

Kahan internalized a military logic in which the army was to become his new home, and he was advised to "break with his past" in order to immerse himself in the transformative crucible of the army.[69] Kahan took to heart the military identity that he saw as defined by clean and simple aesthetics and laconic communication: "Shining buttons, clean gun, properly laced shoes are better than academic medals; that simple raw talk is better than rhetoric courses, and turning the brain into a passive organ subjugated to superiors is better than philosophical terms," he commented.[70] Kahan made a clear distinction between the oppressive tsarist army and how he conceptualized the Polish military in the 1920s. "I appeared in front of the draft commission without resistance or fear of the *prizivnikes* [recruits to the tsarist army]," he wrote, adding that he expected to be released due to his poor health.[71] Kahan was convinced that "[for Jews,] serving in the Polish army took a normal form," and he went to the draft unit "free, bold, and without any fear, like a kheyder-boy freed from the rabbi on a holiday."[72] Finally, his battlefield experience enabled young Yankev Kahan to reach the self-perceived peak of his military identity. Bravery at the front, Kahan believed, allowed him and other Jewish men to gain respect and streamline their military careers.[73] For example, Yiddish-speaking soldiers whom Kahan met were proud of having conquered Minsk and Kyiv in the ranks of the Polish military.[74]

Kahan enjoyed the respect of his commanders and comrades, but his memoir also reveals moments of weakness and self-doubt. He wrote about his ailing body: "The backpack tore my weak back and the gun pressed on my left arm. I was covered with sweat and asked myself how I would survive the difficulties yet to come."[75] Elsewhere, Kahan described his inability to keep up with the fast pace of marching—"I tried to maintain the pace, but couldn't"—or falling on all fours during a challenging compulsory army hike in the mountains.[76] On the battlefield fighting against the Bolsheviks, Kahan acknowledged, "I was totally confused, filled with fear and helplessness. I lay down, I was not myself, immersed in thoughts and conversations with myself."[77] At that point, Kahan believed that soldiers were not the heroes but rather the biggest victims of the war. He cried about his young age and did not want to kill anyone. However, speaking about the challenges of a soldier's life often served Kahan as a form of contrast to emphasize his ultimate success in overcoming his limits. Kahan, writing in militarized interwar Poland, was not ready to reject the warrior model that brought wounds, agony, and confusion. Also elsewhere in Europe, the 1920s and 1930s valorized fascist-like military men.[78]

Yankev Kahan's depiction of the army and war includes pacifist lines typical for many former World War I soldiers.[79] Kahan experienced the brutality of war at the Polish-Soviet front, and one of his repeating allegories is a comparison of soldiers to commodities. He wrote about "zelner-skhoyre" (soldier-ware), which needed to be "provided" to the "hungry front-line."[80] In Kahan's analogy, soldiers sometimes did not appear as brave men but rather as perishable human material. During his stay in a military hospital, Kahan was exposed to the injured, who embodied the unheroic face of the war. "It looked like an exhibition of broken parts of a human body, an exhibition of the front hell," Kahan wrote.[81] He saw men with yellow faces and bandaged heads and men crawling without penises. For Kahan, these strong images developed in him a certain anti-war attitude. When his commander encouraged him and the other soldiers to fight against the Bolsheviks, Kahan wrestled with his thoughts—"I don't want to push my bayonet into someone's body"—yet he was aware of the "bloody instincts" that the battle released in men and hence assumed that he would be able to do it when the time came.[82] Kahan's dilemma relates to the "humiliation of warrior masculinity" linked to the experience of World War I when soldiers appeared to be helpless and frightened in front of industrial warfare. At the battlefield, Kahan, instead of bravery and glory, noticed dehumanization that demystified the soldier masculinity.[83]

Kahan's narrative demonstrates that Jewish masculinities in the Polish military were diverse, and he did not consider Jews to have only one shared form of masculinity. Some Jewish men, such as the young soldier who escorted him to his first unit, "behaved so rigidly, army strong, and placed a bayonet on his loaded gun as though he was escorting dangerous criminals."[84] They embraced toughness and violence as desired features of military masculinity. Kahan himself joined in with his non-Jewish comrades when they ridiculed Jewish and non-Jewish "dweebs." Speaking about a young Orthodox Jewish man charged with taking care of the horses, Kahan noted that he "was afraid of his own shadow" and pointed out his feeble, unmasculine appearance and behavior devoid of self-confidence.[85] Perceiving himself as intrinsic part of the military regime, Kahan felt superior to both Jewish and Christian men who were considered to be "oferma"— that is, morons—who "did not know how to hold a gun." Also, he ridiculed conscious objectors from denominations that rejected the military.[86] Kahan stabilized his own military masculinity on the backs of other Jewish men, in particular those humiliated for their religiosity and weak bodies. Disassociating himself from weak, unpopular, ridiculed Jewish men, Kahan hoped to sustain his masculinity built on soldierly respect and camaraderie.

Kahan celebrated the transformative influence of the army on his body. They have shaved his head and his appearance homogenized with that of the other young men. Kahan did not interpret shaving as humiliating. Probably even before the army, he had not been wearing sidelocks or other hair markers of Jewishness.[87] Class and social background seemed to him to lose meaning in the army, and he admired the changes in his body and his assimilation to the uniformed soldier look. When Kahan received his uniform, he and the other soldiers looked at each other, amazed at how the new clothes made them appear as if cut "from the same cloth."[88] He participated in regular exercises and other physical routines that improved his posture and increased his strength. After three years of service, Kahan's comrades have long stopped seeing him as a weak "nebekhdiker bokherl" (wimpy little guy) but noticed in him a soldier with a military posture.[89] For Kahan, his transition into a proper soldier seemed complete and acknowledged by other men. Michael Yosef Salem, another Jewish soldier from an Orthodox background who fought for the Polish army against the Bolsheviks in 1920, came to a similar conclusion. Salem wrote that his "sentimental body" was hardened and accustomed to life in the army barracks.[90] Both Kahan and Salem noted how their civil bodies had transformed into military bodies, along with their characters.

The Polish military interwove masculinity and ethnicity, and Yankev Kahan and probably other Jewish soldiers were aware of this overlap. One example of the implicit masculinity-ethnicity relation is the case in which Kahan humiliated a weak Christian soldier. When both the Christian soldier and Kahan wanted to ride in a cart because they were too weak to march, the antisemitic Christian refused to share a ride with a Jew. Kahan derogatively spoke of the Christian as a "midget," "a soldier-boy" who was smaller than his gun.[91] Kahan attempted to establish his masculine superiority over the Christian soldier by pointing out his own greater physical size and strength that he had learned to view as a valuable masculine asset. Masculinity and ethnicity intersected also when Kahan resisted to subordinate to orders that contradicted his Jewish pride. When a commander ordered Kahan and other Jewish soldiers to attend Catholic mass along with their Catholic comrades, Kahan saw it as an act of oppression and an attempt to make Jewish soldiers assume an inferior and passive position. When Kahan resisted and did not kneel in the church, other Jewish soldiers, whom Kahan saw as "fearful slaves," followed the Catholic majority.[92] Similarly, during the Russo-Polish War, Kahan refused to participate in food confiscations of Jewish homes, while other Jewish soldiers whom Kahan condemned "volunteered" to do it.[93] While discipline was one of the core virtues of military masculinity, Jewish soldiers in the Polish army needed to negotiate it along with loyalty to the Jewish community and their own sense of Jewish pride.

Kahan's memoir demonstrates how military men observed and controlled each other to stabilize masculine hierarchies and shape normative masculine behaviors. Fresh recruits appeared to Kahan as young wild horses who could not find their place in the barracks.[94] Entering the sleeping hall, he noticed how men were casually "spread out wildly" on their bunks.[95] This laid-back masculinity of men immersed in comfortable barracks camaraderie was, however, tamed by military discipline that "seeks to mold reliable bodies and loyal spirits."[96] One officer shouted at the soldiers, "Why do you march so empty-headed like old women? Are you soldiers? You are clucking hens!"[97] Comparing young soldiers to women, the officer tutored the recruits on what virtues and behaviors were accepted in the army and taught that misogyny could be applied to enforce discipline and hierarchies. Kahan and other soldiers sometimes experienced brutal torture. One corporal supposedly approached young soldiers like his "layb-aygene," or serfs, while other corporals treated young soldiers "like machines."[98] When he was on leave in his hometown of Białystok, an officer whom Kahan refused to salute publicly humiliated him.[99] Kahan linked this brutality with army discipline that was supposed to foster soldiers' endurance. Aiming to elevate his status, he promised himself to stop being an army greenhorn as soon as possible, to educate himself in toughness and thus commit to military masculinity.

Yankev Kahan's narrative underscores many moments of experiencing army violence, but he wished not to perceive them as essentially antisemitic in nature. When other soldiers once stole Kahan's food from his backpack, he chalked it up to the mischievous behavior of hungry young men rather than an act of antisemitism.[100] Later on, upon entering the barracks, Kahan heard the cries of a Jewish soldier being beaten and ridiculed. Instead of offering help to the fellow Jew, he attempted to make himself invisible and went to sleep without reacting.[101] Kahan believed that the humiliation other Jewish men experienced was just horseplay by veteran soldiers harassing newcomers or a consequence of the time spent on the front lines, rather than an antisemitic incident. Kahan felt that the army was simply an institution defined by humiliation and rites of initiation that sought to destroy recruits' former identities.[102] Homosocial misogyny, depriving young men of individual agency, and physical violence appeared to Kahan as part and parcel of shaping military masculinity, and he internalized its logic.[103] To strengthen this message, Kahan underscored that many Jewish soldiers had excellent relations with Christians and enjoyed shared walks in neighboring towns.[104] While other sources reveal cases of antisemitic treatment, for Kahan, it was important to downplay them and, in that way, celebrate his achievement and his smooth inclusion into the community of military men.[105]

Sexuality also played a role in shaping Jewish military masculinities. In the barracks, Kahan "listened with interest to the natural and free discussions that were a true pleasure for soldiers' unsatisfied instincts."[106] They nicknamed guns "female lovers," and wounded men sometimes had sex with nurses.[107] While soldiers and officers often made sexual jokes, invited prostitutes, masturbated, or had sex practically in public, Kahan saw himself as still very much conditioned by Orthodox Jewish rules of modesty. "Even though I was a nineteen-year-old soldier, the Hassid was still stuck inside me and he appeared with his virgin-like shame and blushed," he wrote.[108] Kahan considered the soldiers' robust sexuality interesting yet also "premature," and he was fine with waiting for love and sex.[109] Other Jewish soldiers performed their military masculinity more openly, and one of them, named Walkowicz, attempted to bond with Kahan over alcohol and tales of sexual adventures.[110] Some Jewish soldiers liberated from the Jewish community's control began to have extramarital sexual relations with peasant women or converted.

Jewish holidays were the highlight for Kahan, and he anticipated them with impatience. The holidays allowed him to mark his confident Jewishness in an institution that sought to homogenize men. In interwar Poland, local Jewish communities commonly took it upon themselves to organize holidays for Jewish soldiers stationed in the local garrison. Kahan's attitude toward celebrating holidays as a soldier is very telling of how the military transformed his gender identity. When the local Jewish community in Chełm decided to distribute the soldiers among local families, Kahan felt infantilized and unjustly separated from his army friends. While the Chełm Jews wanted to follow a custom typical for yeshiva students who often celebrated holidays with host families, for Kahan, his personal liberty and sense of camaraderie with other Jewish soldiers were more important. He felt uncomfortable as a guest and wished that the community would organize a separate holiday meal just for the soldiers.[111] The military masculinity Kahan had learned in the army produced a need for a new form of respectability, different from the Jewish custom.

The army seemed to somewhat de-Judaize Kahan in the eyes of other Jews, and he felt uneasy about this transformation. In Siedlce, a Jewish girl whom Kahan approached began to shout when she saw him. His military uniform made him look non-Jewish, a representative of state power and void of inner-Jewish kinship.[112] While Kahan wished to combine Jewishness and the military, for many Jews outside of the army context, traditional Jewishness and military masculinity seemed to clash. Kahan insisted on underscoring his past as a "shtibl yingl" (prayer house boy) and filled his memoir with comparisons and allegories mixing military and Jewish traditions. The army draft is described as "being called to the aliyah," referring to the practice of *aliyah leTorah*—that is, rising to read the Torah in the synagogue.[113] Kahan compares army regulations to the Jewish religious code Shulchan Aruch and the humiliation of a soldier by an officer to the humiliation of a heder pupil by a rabbi.[114] These comparisons served various ends. They were both the way he explained the new world of the military to himself and a guideline for his readers who were not familiar with the reality of the army.

Kahan's impressions are not representative of every young Jewish man of his age and background. While Kahan enlisted with relative happiness and high expectations, another soldier of religious background, Michael Yosef Salem, considered his army time to be a forced uprooting from his parents and siblings.[115] Salem, a young Jewish man from Łódź, explicitly mentioned the draft enforcement and revealed that during his first days in the army, he cried at night, suffered from nightmares, and perceived his situation as miserable.[116] When marching out to the front, Salem noticed that also for other Jewish families, the separation was overwhelming. He described his departure to the front as a sad moment without any heroic aspects: "I walked with the Polish biks [a gun] on my arm and backpack on my back, with lowered head, wiping away warm tears that shed from my tired eyes."[117] Marching with his battalion, followed by crying family members, Michael Yosef appears as a man unjustly sentenced to death. Like Kahan, Salem also compared himself and other soldiers to animals sent to the slaughterhouse.[118] He painted the devastating picture of his battalion decimated by the enemy, including his two dear fellow Jewish soldiers, and a moment when he "made the sound of a hunted animal."[119] Whereas Kahan underscored his successful embracing of military masculinity while maintaining his Jewish pride, many Jewish soldiers in interwar Poland felt similar to Salem and perceived their military service as forced and detrimental.

JEWISH WAR VETERANS, DISABILITY, AND MASCULINE RESPECTABILITY

In interwar Poland, the hegemonic masculinity was in the hands of aristocratic and upper-class gentile men who had achieved excellent military records in Poland's recent wars. Many Jewish veterans attempted to situate themselves as close as possible to this dominant gender ideal and acted out their desire to be perceived as full of the virtues typical of hegemonic military masculinity. In a time of growing antisemitism, Jewish veterans utilized their past army experience as a reminder of their heroism on the battlefield to create a self-image as reputable men. Jewish veterans often appeared in uniform in public and created rituals that transformed their military past into a discourse of respectability and merit in times of peace. For instance, during Józef Piłsudski's funeral in Kraków in 1935, several hundred Jewish veterans appeared in uniform and lockstep,[120] and that same year, veteran leaders encouraged their fellow former soldiers to order new uniforms, "since a group of uniformed men walking through the streets evokes respect and appreciation."[121] Militarized Jewish masculinity relied on constantly reenacting Jewish military contributions, educating non-Jews about Jewish wartime heroism and thus fending off accusations of being unsoldierly.[122]

Jewish veteran organizations were not homogenous. The oldest and largest was established in 1922 as the Jewish Union of Invalids, Widows, and War Orphans (Żydowski Związek Inwalidów, Wdów i Sierot Wojennych) and in 1928 had around eighty thousand members.[123] In 1929, the Society of Jewish Fighters for Poland's Independence (Związek Żydów Uczestników Walk o Niepodległości Polski, ZŻUWoNP) appeared, in which officers and upper-class Jewish men were overrepresented compared to the general Jewish population and all former Jewish soldiers.[124] Because of their loyalty to the state and their self-image as Poles of Mosaic faith, as well as their record in the elite Polish Legions,

Figure 5.2. Reunion of the Związek Żydów Uczestników Walk o Niepodległość Polski, Warsaw, 1933. Narodowe Archiwum Cyfrowe (Warsaw), call no. 1-P-1924-1.

the Society of Jewish Fighters enjoyed a listening ear in the Polish government. They claimed to represent the interests of all Jewish men who had fought in the recent wars, yet for men who did not share their class and cultural background, this leadership configuration seemed problematic. A contributor named A. H. Rogowoj, writing for a Jewish Orthodox paper, argued that veterans were too patriotic and was unsure whether they would "find a proper Jewish path."[125] While Jewish men less acculturated to Polish culture and of lower economic status could benefit to a certain extent from the militarized masculinity ideal, its main beneficiaries were those who had been closer to the ideals of the dominant Polish masculinity of that time.

When the war ended, its disastrous impact became visible not only in social and economic life but also in the disabled bodies of the former soldiers. Many Jewish war veterans in different physical and mental conditions suffered poverty and homelessness upon finishing their military service. One Jewish leader described Łódź of 1919 as "flooded" by former Jewish recruits, who only "enlarged the local cadres of beggars and the unemployed."[126] The disability of former soldiers continued to be a burning issue well into the 1920s and 1930s, yet the state appeared disinterested in their painful situation.[127] By 1927, in Kraków alone there lived several hundred Jewish war invalids.[128] According to data from 1934, almost 172,000 recognized war invalids, including 5,000 Jews, lived in Poland. These statistics are problematic, however, since many former soldiers faced difficulties obtaining veteran status and many Jews who registered as Polish nationals of the Jewish religion were ultimately categorized as Poles.[129]

For Jews and non-Jews, the military also became a point of identification in life outside of the barracks and front lines. The veteran leaders created narratives rewarding military effort and achievement, typical for returning soldiers who desired to gain influence in shaping postwar reality.[130] Jewish men hoped that the public gratitude to the soldiers during wartime would transform into continued state support afterward as well. Yet military excellence did not always have a direct positive influence on the status of former soldiers in later times of peace. One of the Jewish veterans complained, "We remember those times when people seeing a combatant were always offering him their seat . . . it seemed [back then] that society would forever remain grateful to those who devoted their lives to defend the country. . . . But the society has quickly accustomed to seeing war invalids . . . and forgotten about their gratitude toward these wretched ones. Returning from the war, they found their possessions destroyed and their place [of work] taken by the young and strong."[131]

Jewish veterans had perceived of their war efforts as an entry pass into the high status and respectable masculinity that the army seemed to promise. War-experienced Jewish men related to protecting as the core feature of the dominant Western masculinity. Yet, when the war was over, they came to conclude that society did not consider their wounds and disabilities as proof of their battlefield-tested masculinity and heroism but rather turned them into obstacles that caused their personal and professional misfortunes. A Jewish veteran named Herman Schwarz lamented in 1928 that the authorities were full of reverence for "the locked graves of unknown heroes" but did not seem to remember the fighters who were still alive.[132]

Jewish veteran organizations appeared as a result of Jews' exclusion from the chivalric ethos of fatherland fighters. One veteran, L. S., commented in 1928 that "initially Jewish men belonged to the general veterans' organization. With time, however, they came to understand that they were not treated there as equal brothers, but as second-class members. The antisemitism of their leaders made all the benefits of belonging to this association illusory."[133] Since gentile associations failed to recognize Jews as equal members, Jewish men decided to form their own associations.[134] Jewish war veterans felt discriminated against in the granting of "concessions"—that is, government leases of specific factories, workshops, and shops to war veterans. In 1928, the journal *Inwalida żydowski* (Jewish veteran) complained that the city authorities of the town of Nowy Sącz "were guided exclusively by antisemitism" in not granting Jewish veterans licenses for running tobacco shops.[135] Activist Jakób Bachner cried in 1928 that "even Jewish men with 100% disability, without legs, hands, or eyes, or totally paralyzed, are not safe [from the discrimination]. The brutal antisemitism does not have mercy on even the poorest cripples!"[136] Bachner underscored that Jewish veterans experienced double discrimination in Poland—both as Jews and as disabled.

Many former Jewish soldiers experienced that gentile soldiers considered them unworthy of the status of war veterans. In 1925, a Jewish veteran named Zygmunt Majer encountered a non-Jewish officer who attacked him in the spa town of Ciechocinek, shouting that "Poland did not resurrect so that he [Majer] could go to the spas." The same antisemitic officer successfully engaged his colleagues to revoke Majer's veterans' pension.[137] In Upper Silesian spas, for example, non-Jewish invalids cursed Jewish veterans as "dirty Jews."[138] Even though the management and doctors protested against the antisemitism, Jewish invalids lobbied not to be placed in Upper Silesian spas and, in that sense, withdrew from spaces of camaraderie where Christian veterans mingled. Spa antisemites wished to turn proud Jewish veterans into outcasts deprived of military masculinity. As World War I became more distant, some non-Jewish veterans put into question Jews' military performance and suggested that they did not fulfill their military obligations. Jewish veterans reacted with rage: "The antisemitic hatred won't stop even before the majesty of death and martyrdom. The truth of the numbers will not be obscured by new attempts of the international antisemitic mafia."[139]

War injuries had an ambivalent influence on how the war veterans related to the core masculine feature of providing and breadwinning. The injuries meant that they were often not able to work full-time, but many Jewish veterans still wished to continue fulfilling the role of family provider in less physically challenging positions. One veteran complained, "People without a hand or a leg, people shot through the head or lungs, deaf or dumb, could not return to their former professions and their health made it impossible to work in physically demanding jobs."[140] Veteran activist Herman Schwarz spoke of former soldiers for whom "work is the highest order" and who "cannot stand the state of idleness," and he saw forcing the war veterans to live from meager disability payments as "excluding them from productive and creative society."[141] Zwi Heller, a Jewish member of the Polish parliament, echoed Schwartz's argument, saying that "we do not want pensions or alms. Jewish veterans . . . demand the opportunity to work."[142] The system of state job redistribution, which was open almost exclusively to non-Jews, excluded Jewish veterans.[143] With state jobs scarce, Jewish veterans launched their own system of assistance with loans and job search help. For example, the Kraków Association of Jewish War Invalids (Krakowski Związek Żydowskich Inwalidów) worked to establish "workshops adjusted to the disabilities of our brothers, [places] where they could work productively."[144] Not being able to provide would mean that disabled veterans had failed in a central masculine realm, and they invested efforts to circumvent this process.

Jewish war veterans perceived themselves as a tight-knit community of comrades and brothers. They expected that the close relationships established on the war front would continue even after the war and help advance the case of war invalids. One veteran activist commented: "As at the front line one was helping his fellow soldier, knowing that one day he might also need assistance, even now, the war invalids need to think not only of themselves, but also of their invalid brothers and their comrades' widows and orphans, all part of one family that has experienced severe hardship."[145] This sense of brotherhood was to serve as a strong protection against the injustice that the war invalids experienced in postwar Poland. Some Jewish veterans perceived their leader, Jakób Bachner, as a fearless defender of the collective rights of Jewish veterans. "He coordinates the entire movement of Jewish war invalids in Poland . . . president Bachner does not know what it means to be tired; relaxation is a foreign word to him . . . for ten years he has worked day and night to ease the harsh fate of Jewish war veterans," his colleagues praised in 1930.[146] For Jewish veterans, Bachner embodied masculine strength and determination, since there was "no barrier or obstacle that he could not overcome," and he was a "mainspring and engine" working hard for the benefit of Jewish war victims. The veterans related to the masculine ideal of a hardworking man devoted to his cause and, in military terms, perceived Bachner as its embodiment. Bachner might even have become an "idol" (bożyszcze) of "all

Jewish war veterans"—that is, an object of admiration due to his virtues and activism.

Jewish veterans in Poland implemented practices intended to reinstate their masculinity by linking up with young soldiers and emphasizing specifically Jewish military male bonding. In the veterans' reasoning, one remained a soldier forever, even long after the war had ended, and military masculinity should be regularly reenacted—for example, by assisting young Jewish recruits. In 1935, Jewish veterans organized a festive Chanukah dinner for more than two hundred Jewish soldiers stationed in Poznań. A choir of Jewish soldiers sang Chanukah songs, and tables were full of sweets prepared by the wives of Jewish veterans. President Henryk Rauch linked the fate of Jewish soldiers in Poland with the story of the Maccabees and argued that soldierhood was key to establishing modern Jewish masculinity.[147] Because it also relied on modern nationalism, Zionist devotion to the Jewish people appeared compatible with serving in the Polish army. The festive Jewish party corresponded to the way non-Jewish veterans celebrated. For example, the Reserve Soldiers Union, Związek Rezerwistów, organized dance parties for New Year's Eve, and Jewish veterans found ways of strengthening their Jewish soldierly bonding in an analogous form. Former Jewish soldiers established their own sites to perform military masculinity that helped them find relief from their humiliations.

Jews wanted to be recognized as virtuous men by fellow Polish veterans and top-ranking politicians, who were the possessors of dominant Polish masculinity. The need for external recognition as decent and virtuous men is clearly visible in photos from 1935 that appeared in one of Poland's major dailies and depicted two Jewish veteran leaders marching at the Constitution Day parade on May 3. By celebrating Polish national holidays and sporting their old military uniforms or elegant suits, J. Tanenbaum and Jakób Bachner linked their soldierly past and projected it as a foundation for their present achievements.[148] When preparing for the consecration of the banner of the Association of Jewish War Veterans in 1935, Jewish men invited not only Jewish leaders but also the mayor of Kraków, Mieczysław Kaplicki; the commander of the Kraków army garrison, Bernard Mond; and the heads of diverse state institutions as well as numerous non-Jewish veterans.[149] In 1926, a senator and the head of the Warsaw City Council Ignacy Baliński attended the summit of the Jewish War Veterans Association. Even though Baliński was a member of the antisemitic party Narodowa Demokracja (National Democracy), Jewish veterans wished to have him attend their yearly summit. Baliński's presence gave Jewish men a sense of reassurance, seeing that even some nationalists did not put their masculinity into question.[150] Using the framework of male bonding they remembered from their army days, Jewish men believed that the recognition from fellow former soldiers and now Poland's top leaders would elevate their status. Celebrating with these men of power and influence, Jewish veterans projected themselves as belonging to the same category of successful men. Hobnobbing with the "highest pilots of the state," Jewish veterans could picture themselves as being on the same level as the gentile leaders.[151]

Some non-Jewish men agreed that Jewish veterans had a right to influence Poland's social matters. For example, a Catholic officer named Tadeusz Zubrzycki, in his book *Żydzi w szeregach polskich w latach 1914–1920* (Jews in the Polish military units 1914–1920), wrote a history of Jewish heroism on the battlefield. The non-Jewish veteran writing about Jewish Saul Pick, who bandaged his wounded hand by himself and continued to fight, or about Emanuel Reiss, who was a *rycerz* (knight) hanged in public by the Russians, recognized that Jewish men possessed the masculine virtues of bravery, honor, and devotion.[152] Some non-Jewish men agreed that Jews could access military respectability. Addressing Jewish veterans, the vice minister of military affairs, General Głuchowski, said in 1936, "Your goal, gentlemen, is to raise your [Jewish] youth to be brave and masculine soldiers in the Polish army."[153] In 1937, veteran and politician Zdzisław Zmigryder-Konopka wrote, "The transformation from Jewish foreignness to Jewish citizenship in Poland started when Jews were called to defend Poland and fight for its independence."[154] This statement conveyed the message that in order to be recognized as full-fledged men, the generation of young Jewish men needed to follow the military masculinity of Jewish World War I veterans.

THE EXCLUSION OF JEWS FROM MILITARY MASCULINITY IN INTERWAR POLAND

While many middle- and upper-class Jewish men in interwar Poland attempted to enhance their masculinity by associating themselves with the military, the 1920s and 1930s saw the emergence of a counternarrative: an antisemitic discourse that emasculated Polish-Jewish men by highlighting their supposed military failures. The Polish army in the 1920s and 1930s was very aware of Jewish recruits in its ranks and saw itself as an actor in Polish ethnic politics.[155] The following section analyzes a wide range of sources, including army reports, military court proceedings, and oftentimes openly antisemitic press caricatures, to demonstrate how real or imagined Jewish military (in)ability began to be conceptualized in Poland not only as an ethnic question but also related to gender.

In independent Poland, the army became an arena for proving one's masculinity, rather than merely proving one's Polishness. After World War I, the Polish military moved from being a national army (*narodowa*) fighting for independence to a state army (*państwowa*) that needed to manage the country's complex ethnic composition.[156] Military service was obligatory for every man twenty-one years of age, but Poland never recruited all men from that age group. The army developed policies and produced knowledge that sought to manage soldiers from ethnic minorities—for instance, by establishing the Nationalities Department (Referat Narodowościowy) in 1921.[157] One of the central mechanisms for controlling access to status-granting officer ranks was a quota system for officer training that discriminated against Jewish and Ukrainian men. The result was that ethnic minorities faced difficulties gaining military respectability as officers and that process excluded them from the hegemonic Polish military masculinity.[158] The exclusion was particularly humiliating to Jewish men who internalized the militaristic logics of independent Poland.

Internal military discussions in the Polish armed forces suggested that Jews were neither physically nor mentally fit for military service. One 1926 report concluded, "The Jewish soldier [is] ready to desert, physically weak, fearful and weakly disciplined, and is not good material for a fighting soldier."[159] Jewish recruits were commonly described as having a *lichy*, or miserable, physical constitution. One report used this adjective to refer not only to the health condition but also to the average height of Jewish men, which was lower than that of other recruits.[160] The arguments appearing in military sources defined Jewish men as unfit for the army due to their ethnicity.[161] This reasoning followed racist anthropological theories fashionable at the time. For instance, anthropologist Jan Czekanowski maintained that Jews were inferior soldiers: "The value of a soldier depends first of all on his physical constitution and special psychological qualities. Everyone knows that Jews present themselves the worst in the physical dimension and that they make the worst soldiers."[162] The so-called nationalities report prepared by the Polish army generalized about Jewish recruits, presenting them as clever and hard to tame but also as a group that the army could not discipline easily: "Moral standing satisfactory. Intellectually mostly well developed. Easily comprehend information. Average intelligence. Cleverness and understanding are highly developed. Culture at a low level, with no sense of order or cleanliness. . . . Since they are characterized by a strong resistance to moral influence and are lacking any love for the service, which they perceive as an unavoidable, temporary evil, military service among this group has a small influence on their intellectual development."[163]

Jewish men in the Polish army faced an array of humiliations that not only singled them out as Jews but also restricted their access to hegemonic masculinity. Numerous reports demonstrate how their comrades bullied Jewish soldiers. In 1919, when non-Jewish soldiers repeatedly beat Jewish soldiers in the Tarnów garrison, these acts of violence were ignored by the officers. In 1920 in Kalisz, officers commanded their soldiers to sing the antisemitic song that portrayed Jewish men as unfit for the army; the officers were later punished. In 1924, Jewish soldier Lejba Milgrom drowned in the San River after his fellow soldiers threw him into deep water and waterboarded him.[164] Numerous commanders complained about how "physically weak Jews fall victim to harassment by comrades."[165] Pinkas Rosengarten, the military rabbi, spoke of the "malicious remarks" and "distress" that Jewish soldiers experienced in the military and concluded that antisemitism had infiltrated the Polish army.[166] While military authorities usually investigated bullying, they usually sentenced the perpetrators with minor penalties.

In the all-male world of the barracks, bullying marked the process of establishing hierarchies that merged masculinity and ethnicity. While the army embraced much of the civilian stereotypes about Jews, in the military context, they gained another gendered dimension. One report from Łódź suggested that Jewish men withdrew from camaraderie and male bonding in the army and linked it to a presumed "caste character" of Jewish recruits.[167] The result was that rituals of all-male military bonding often excluded Jewish men. Beating or otherwise humiliating a Jewish man in front of dozens of other men had a gendered character. It pushed Jewish men into a position of victimhood and subordination and allowed Christian soldiers to imagine themselves as powerful, violent, and at the top of the hierarchy. However, the harassment did not mean that Jewish men internalized the subordinate position that the Christian bullies sought to impose.

Some Jewish men in Poland, for a variety of reasons, hoped to avoid the army. A 1927 Yiddish booklet titled *Militer-pflikht* (Military obligation) explained the rules of service to young Jewish males but paid particular attention to how to "enjoy the postponement of service," how to be released from service, and punishments for not fulfilling military obligations.[168] One post-Holocaust testimony suggests that most of Jewish parents and Jewish draftees welcomed the military administration's hesitance concerning recruiting Jews.[169] Court records reveal a variety of argumentative strategies and methods that young Jewish men used to avoid the draft. In 1919, a young Jew named Zygmunt Sterngast asked another Jewish man to appear instead of him in front of the Kraków military examination board.[170] In 1927, Lejb Goldenberg from Dęblin paid 1,000 złoty to middlemen Dawid Sztajnbuch and Wolf Ajger, who procured a false medical attestation for him.[171] Other Jewish men asked others to denounce them as communists, left the country illegally, or drank immense amounts of coffee to deprive themselves of sleep and appear weak in order to be deemed unfit for service.[172] While ethnic Poles made up the bulk of draft dodgers in terms of absolute numbers, the army and antisemites focused particularly on ethnic minorities when discussing attempts to avoid conscription. While initially the share of draft evaders was high, particularly among non-Poles, from the mid-1920s onward, their numbers fell and oscillated around only 1–10 percent.[173]

Parallel to the military discourses around Jewish men's "incongruity" with or "maladjustment" to the army, the antisemitic press often questioned the right of Jewish men to serve as soldiers. In 1923, journalist Tadeusz Mścisławski wrote in his antisemitic booklet that Jewish officers in the army were a "fatal heritage of the Austrian army and the Legions" and globally accused Jewish soldiers of treason, spying, and the desire to control

Poland and its army. Mścisławski's tirade listed the soldierly virtues of honor, selflessness, and chivalry that Jewish men were supposedly lacking. Speaking about the virtues, Mścisławski not only questioned the ability of Jews to serve in the army and expressed antisemitic prejudices but also challenged Jewish men's adherence to a dominant masculine ideal.[174] Polish antisemites created narratives that sought to challenge the heroic narrative Jewish army veterans had constructed in interwar Poland. In 1936, one Polish weekly wrote, "A soldier and a Jew, these are two contradictions."[175] Another antisemitic author demanded the dismissal of Jewish officers from the army, including Christians married to Jewish women.[176] In particular caricature appeared as a space where anti-Semites put into question Jewish military masculinity.

One antisemitic caricature printed in *Szopka* in 1924 presented a Jewish officer and a Jewish private.[177] The bodies of the two men appear deformed and ugly. Their posture is awkwardly bent, far from upright and masculine. Their bellies are prominent and add to the disproportionality of their frames. Both the officer and the private have big noses, which are supposed to define them as Jews, as was the convention in antisemitic caricatures across Europe. The officer is holding his hands wide open in a gesture of surprise or helplessness, a stance that appears effeminate. The uniforms of both men seem to be oversized, sending a message that men of that deformed physical constitution just do not fit into Polish military uniforms. While uniformed bodies were supposed to differentiate between the civil and military realms and "emphasized musculature, supported the posture, expressing self-control and tempered vitality,"[178] the caricature suggests that this mechanism did not work in the case of Jewish men. On the textual level, the caricature infantilizes the soldier, naming him Aronek, a diminutive of the Jewish name Aron. Furthermore, the officer, "kapytan Rewolwer," is far from representing a gallant officer. He does not work in a combat division but in the "intendentura," or supply division. The captions misspelled his military rank in broken Polish "Jew-speech" (*kapytan* instead of *kapitan*). The title of the drawing, "Machabeusze w wojsku" (Maccabees in the military), intends to ridicule Jewish aspirations of following the glorious ancient example of Jewish military excellence. The punchline and message are clear: no matter how Jewish men try to fit into the army and prove themselves capable of service, their bodies will reveal that in fact they are deformed weaklings and essentially lack the masculinity it takes to be Polish soldiers.

Discussion about cutting Jewish men's sidelocks or beards was another mechanism excluding them from military masculinity and soldierhood. Antisemites located Jewish masculinity in those external features and criticized presumed Jewish unwillingness to adjust to the military canons of male "beauty" and "hygiene." An antisemitic text published in the Polish magazine *Kabaret* ridiculed the very presence of Jews in the state army.[179] Proclaiming "how beautiful the army would look if even half of the Jewish soldiers had sidelocks" and describing "Yoyne, who feels bad sitting on a horse without his *peyes*," the sarcastic sketch seemingly sympathizes with Jewish recruits only to laugh at them later. In another example, following the obligatory haircut, a Jewish man did not recognize himself without his sidelocks and, almost heartbroken, demanded that those symbols of Jewish Orthodox masculinity be accepted in the army. The caricature includes two drawings: one showing a self-confident Jew with sidelocks and another a miserable version without peyes now sporting a military uniform. Naming the protagonist Mojsze Kurduppel (which means Moshe the Half-Pint in Polish), the antisemitic caricature takes another jab at the Jewish body: the presumed lower-than-average height, which is again defining Jewish men as insufficiently masculine and unfit for military service.

Figure 5.3. Caricature, "Machabeusze w wojsku" (Maccabees in the army), *Kalendarz tygodnika humorystyczno-satyrycznego Szopka na rok 1924,* Warsaw, 1924, 65.

Cutting beards and sidelocks was a mechanism of humiliation that merged emasculation with antisemitism. While Jewish recruits could and did expect that their Jewish facial hair would be removed, at the turn of the 1920s, Polish soldiers at times also attacked and shaved random Jewish men they met during military maneuvers. As Dariusz Konstantynów suggested, the enforced shaving of beards by Polish soldiers was a characteristic of the first months of Polish independence in 1919.[180] These acts of violence and intimidation by ethnic Polish soldiers (particularly from Haller's brigade) combined antisemitic violence and conscious emasculation. Unlike smashing windows or beating passersby, cutting beards addressed Jewish men specifically and deprived them of the most visible marker of Jewish masculinity. Antisemitic soldiers attempted to assign to Jewish men a gender identity that was divergent from their own military masculinity, and this act of humiliation demonstrated how linked gender and ethnicity were.

In a 1919 antisemitic caricature, female cartoonist Maja Berezowska commented on current events of forced beard shaving. Berezowska presented two Jewish men and two Haller's brigade soldiers.[181] The soldiers are holding the beards of the two Jewish men and pulling them with force. The Jewish men are pictured with open mouths trying to escape the torture. The Haller soldiers, on the other hand, are laughing, suggesting that the act of violence might be, for them, an expression of lawlessness and playfulness. This impression is strengthened by the embrace between the two non-Jewish soldiers. Hugging each other while harassing the Jewish men sends a message of a collective Polish masculine identity seeking to destroy the Jewish sense of masculine respectability. The caricature's caption reads, "The beards in our hands," suggesting that Jewish masculinity depended on the grace of the Christian possessors of military masculinity. Polish-Jewish and Polish-Christian masculinities appear here to be in conflict, incompatible and exclusive. While many former Polish-Jewish soldiers clung to their military masculinities and built self-images as respected men, the Orthodox men from the caricature seem helpless and detached from any military ethos.

CONCLUSION

Military service carried ambivalent meanings for Polish-Jewish men. Some of these men integrated well into the army, including the army's propaganda mechanisms, and may have internalized its logics. Embedded within broader Polish mechanisms of claiming masculine hegemony, Jews took part in militarized writing and reproducing images of military masculinity. As shown in the examples of Steinhaus and Kahan, some Polish-Jewish men found meaning in military service and understood that it helped them validate and stabilize their claim to masculine hegemony. Since the Polish army and the Jewish community were far from homogenous, the experiences of Jewish men varied and depended on the time, military leadership, the geographic location, their class background, and the ethnic composition of their unit. I have demonstrated how Jewish men embraced the idea of masculine heroism in individual struggles against the enemy but also how this belief began to crumble in the light of mass war and postwar discrimination and sometimes channeled into short-lived pacifist ideas.

While Polonized upper- and middle-class Jews found it easier to embrace the military as a venue for defining their masculinity, even Jews from a traditional setting sometimes found the army useful and embraced discipline, male bonding, and homogenization. Jewish men in the Polish military were aware of its transformative influence on their bodies and minds and were sometimes anxious about the army's de-Judaizing consequences. The example of Yankev Kahan demonstrates how a Jew who identified as a Hasid began to function according to the army's gendered logic and developed not into a Polish soldier but into a self-confident Jewish soldier in the Polish army. In his case, not abandoning Jewishness but expanding it with virtues of military masculinity helped Kahan define himself as a man. However, other Polish-Jewish men did not adhere to the ideal of militarized masculinity and, like many Jewish men earlier in the Russian empire, attempted to be exempted from service. Many Jews experienced army violence and humiliation that intended to emasculate and subjugate them.

While Polish masculinities in World War I differed from their western European counterparts because Polish military masculinity and the state dissociated, in the post-1918 period, the construction of masculinity, the military, and citizenship were closely connected. The masculine respectability that Steinhaus and Kahan epitomized was also of core importance to Jewish veterans in the 1920s and 1930s. Jewish veterans explicitly raised a claim to masculine respectability and state recognition of their merit based on their past military performance. Importantly, both Jews and non-Jews engaged in discussions around Jewish military masculinity, and interwar Poland saw the emergence of antisemitic discourses that openly challenged the idea that Jews could identify with the masculine virtues of heroism, self-control, and devotion to the army. Antisemitism was embedded in military policy, and the military perceived Jewish men as a challenge. Being aware of these processes of exclusion, many Jewish men continued to imagine the army as an oppressive institution.

SIX

—⚯—

LEISURE AND TOIL

Masculinity in Profession, Family, and Consumer Culture

IN 1931, POLISH-JEWISH STATISTICIAN Jacob Lestchinsky praised the "intelligence, energy, agile spirit [*rirevdiker gayst*], and entrepreneurial dexterity" of Białystok Jewish manufacturers who were more adaptive and innovative than their non-Jewish competitors and managed to maintain their businesses in a time of severe crisis in the garment industry.[1] Lestchinsky explained that the "central factor was the psychology": their rirevdiker gayst and risk tolerance allowed Białystok Jewish men to develop their businesses. Thanks to their enterprising spirit, they also managed to safeguard their position as self-made and accomplished middle-class men. Very similar were the characteristics of the *Lodzer-mensh*, an energetic, feet-on-the-ground, unstoppable, and sometimes cruel Łódź business-man.[2] This Polish-Jewish male trader emerged as an ambivalent figure, both attractive and repulsive, and could serve as the model of a man who was intellectually agile, enterprising, and creative.[3] Both the Lodzer-mensh and the businessman with a rirevdiker gayst celebrated an entrepreneurship-based masculine model that in the 1920s and 1930s became increasingly challenged by a model applauding pleasure-centered leisure and consumption.

226

In this chapter, I look at consumption, which is the process of acquiring goods and services by exchanging money, as well as its intersection with professional and family life, two areas that demonstrate how middle-class masculinity dovetailed. I suggest that in interwar Poland, middle-class Jewish salaried workers and businessmen engaged in specific forms of consumption that were a new arena in which masculinity was negotiated. I analyze how Jewish men transformed into consumers, that is, active seekers of goods and services, and the impact of consumption on masculinity. Jewish males in Poland were members of an ethnic minority that was often excluded from all-Polish notions of male hegemony. However, following Connell in her reassessment of the initial model of hegemonic masculinity, I suggest that marginalized male groups, such as Polish-Jewish men in the 1920s and 1930s, constructed their masculinity to embody the claim to power typical of regional hegemonic masculinities.[4] In the period examined here, men and women accepted profession, wealth, and self-made success as valid means of claiming hegemonic masculinity in Poland, and those ideals influenced the identities of Jewish men as breadwinners and heads of households.[5] While marginalized Jewish men facing difficulties providing for their families could appear as "impotent patriarchs" and "emasculated both at work and home,"[6] in interwar Poland, many Jewish men strove to hold on to the markers of hegemonic masculinity relating to work even when they faced major challenges.

The consumer society that developed in the first decades of the twentieth century was a society in which powers of consumption determined social position and "consumable objects played a disproportionate role in creating meaning or shaping individual or group experiences."[7] Poland, including its major cities, experienced a late industrialization and a comparatively late emergence of a consuming middle class, but the 1920s and 1930s marked the explosion of consumer culture.[8] In 1939, a Jewish banker named Joachim Zylberszpic argued that "the growth of consumption is a sign of a nation's wealth" and complained that men and women in Poland did not consume enough. Zylberszpic called for a shorter workweek that would allow people to spend more time in cinemas and restaurants, which would lead to "creating a man of greater needs"—that is, a consumer.[9] Following Salo Baron, this chapter explores the "flow of everyday life" and centers ordinary Jewish experiences embedded in the wider all-Polish reality.[10] While the Polish-Jewish social and economic history of the 1920s and 1930s has been rendered as a lachrymose history of decline and consolidated into a beggar-like figure of an eastern European Jewish *luftmentsh* (impractical person without a definite business), a sizable group of Jews from the biggest urban centers could and did shape consumer lifestyles. In 1938, almost a fifth of Poland's population belonged to the statistical categories of the petite bourgeoisie and intellectual workers, and this share was even higher among Jews, who were more urban than the average Poles.[11]

Evolving consumption patterns intertwined with professional changes, new notions of domesticity, and gender relations. For example, a rise in the number of Jewish men in lower-level white-collar professions resulted in new consumption needs and influenced the way these men performed their gender.[12] At the same time, the dominant articulations of masculinity centered around production, work ethic, and providing for the family were still valid.[13] Professional and economic success was still central to the dominant masculine ideal in Poland, independent of ethnicity. An example of this logic is the article titled "How to Become a Millionaire?," picturing men such as Henry Ford and John Rockefeller. Writing about American millionaires, the Jewish daily *Nasz Przegląd* suggested that the careers of such men were based on an entrepreneurial spirit, self-confidence, and endurance, which Polish-Jewish men should develop in order to become as successful as wealthy American men.[14] Similar motives were behind the media celebration of Jewish ethnic achievement showcasing figures of Jews successful in business, such as Łódź textile tycoons. This ideal of the self-made man who was a good provider became fused with the model of a consuming male. Companies marketed their products and services to this group of men, who shared a dream of Jewish professional accomplishment, and attracted them with motifs of individual masculine success, mobility, and expansionist and conspicuous consumption.

Research on the interplay of gender and consumption in the twentieth century has focused on women as consumers.[15] However, as historian Mark A. Swiencicki has demonstrated, men were indeed a very large and important consuming constituency in the early decades of the twentieth century.[16] Advertisements in numerous general-interest magazines of the period evidence that early twentieth-century advertisers highly courted men. Swiencicki has demonstrated that men have been overlooked as consumers since the emphasis on the acquisition of goods, rather than on consumption itself, overemphasized women's role. Women's control of the household did lead to control over the purchasing of domestic goods, but this did not translate into control over the larger process of consumption. Swiencicki shows that portraying consumption as largely alien to men reinforces the stereotype of consumption as "feminine." Following Swiencicki and Christopher Breward, who researched the figure of the "hidden male consumer," this chapter seeks to unveil how Jewish male consumption and masculinity entwined.[17] Swiencicki studied white American men who actively took part in lavish consumption and consumerism via drinking parties, well-equipped sporting activities, and visits to male-only saloons, variety theaters, and brothels. I explore whether and how Jewish men in Poland followed a similar pattern, in particular concerning how middle-class men's consumption intersected with their fears and fantasies. I review a wide selection of Polish-Jewish dailies and magazines in Polish and Yiddish, as well as sample of pamphlets and cartoons.

Class and masculinity are intertwined, and we need to be attentive and approach consumption as a gendered class issue, not just a class issue. The 1920s and 1930s maintained the link between masculinity and the ability to provide, which traditionally defined men as producers and breadwinners—and women as consumers. Though the hyperinflation of the early 1920s, the economic crisis of 1929, and the growing anti-Jewish economic discrimination challenged the feasibility of masculine economic success in Poland, professional achievement and ability to provide still remained a valid and stable ideal.[18] Importantly, as demonstrated by unemployment data from 1931, blue-collar workers were more threatened by unemployment than were low-level white-collar workers.[19] In Poland, Jewish consumption intersected with nationalism, as producers and importers called on Polish Jews to support both local Polish and Land of Israel industry through consumption, be it of Jewish-produced Palestinian wines or razor blades or through patronizing Polish tourist resorts. Importantly, male consumption often took place outside the home, which often appears as the ultimate site where consumption occurs. Since early twentieth-century men spent so much time and money outside of their homes, we should look closely at their nondomestic consumption of consumer goods and services. Next to middle-class men who were involved in consumption related to personal pleasure, men of the working class also embraced the opportunities and freedoms of modern consumer culture in venues such as eateries, barber shops, and bars that catered to urban bachelors.

PROFESSION, CONSUMPTION, AND
THE FEAR OF CHANGE

In interwar Poland, Jewish men and women intensely discussed what and how a middle-class Jewish man should consume and the impact of consumption on professional life, domesticity, and gender. Hegemonic masculinity is not transhistorical and has not remained stable throughout history. Rather, the very definition of hegemonic masculinity evolves and varies depending on the time and place, and consequently the performance of hegemonic masculinity linked to consumption, leisure, and professional life is specific to the given setting.[20] In that sense, the mechanisms of achieving and verifying hegemonic masculinity in interwar Poland were specific to that era and context, rather than just to Polish men who were also Jewish. Since the greater part of the local Jewish middle and upper classes was Polish speaking, interethnic exchange concerning gender and consumption patterns was commonplace. Importantly, masculine ideals featured in advertising content often contrasted with what was available to them in interwar Poland. For example, the ideal of a self-confident, self-made, tasteful man was undermined by the unhealthy male bodies addressed by advertisements for products healing sexual dysfunctions that plagued men in Poland.[21] In this respect, the situation in interwar Poland bore out Graham Dawson's assertion that "masculine identities are lived out in the flesh, but fashioned in the imagination."[22]

The association between the masculine ideal and the ability to provide needed to be publicly performed and recognized. Aspiring Jewish males in Poland created spaces where their financial achievements could be presented in public. In 1930, in the midst of the world economic crisis, about thirty Jewish businessmen met in Lviv to discuss how the Jewish economic situation in Poland could be improved. The conference, initiated by local Jewish parliamentarians, gathered about sixty men, all of them dressed in elegant suits and bow ties. All but three were smoothly shaven or sported a mustache.[23] The same year, Lviv Jewish bankers celebrated at the Bankers' Ball, presenting a picture of fashionably dressed men and women. Prosperous Jewish bankers could afford to throw fancy parties, buy jewels for their wives, and sport fashionable attire. Writing about them in its financial section, the Jewish daily *Chwila* projected a fantasy of Jewish masculine accomplishment in the consumption and profession realm.[24] Also, Łódź's *Ilustriter Poylisher Manchester* regularly printed eulogic texts about Jewish entrepreneurs and celebrated the business talents of Jewish men who created the prosperity of the local textile industry. Their celebrated accomplishments encouraged a generation of young Jewish men to seek out white-collar and business professions that sold the illusion of future wealth. Polish-Jewish men who aspired to be socially mobile considered menial work inferior. When, in 1928, the ORT organization (Association for the Promotion of Skilled Trades) offered professional courses for Jewish students as a way to finance their studies, many students felt ashamed of doing menial jobs even for a short time.[25] Despite the difficult economic situation in Poland, the ideal of self-made middle-class masculinity was the most attractive for many.

Jewish media channels in interwar Poland established professional success as a measure of one's achievement as a man and encouraged men to display it through new consumption patterns. For example, the yearly almanac of *Nasz Przegląd* printed portraits of men who ran the most successful companies. A photo of "Director Maksymilian Raszkes celebrating his fifty-year jubilee in Warsaw's Meilseil Steinberg and Rittenberg Silk Ribbons Factory" depicted an elegant mustached man with a tie.[26] Some pages earlier, almanac subscribers read about and marveled at the entirely male management of the Łódź textile giant Widzewska Manufaktura portrayed in elegant photographs.[27] The almanac proudly spoke of the "entrepreneurship and activity" of these well-off Jewish men, and their development of foreign trade in the port of Gdynia was presented as a particular achievement.[28] These men were Jewish male role models: professionally successful, proudly Jewish, tasteful, and strong. These images, commisioned by men who achieved self-made success, defined professional white-collar prosperity as a new and desired form of Polish-Jewish masculinity.

Masculinity linked with probity and a strong work ethic was constructed in line with bourgeois femininity reified in the ideal of the homebound housewife. For example, *Nasz Przegląd*'s yearly almanac established a set of norms on how middle-class Jewish women should approach their husbands' professional life: "Listen attentively to what he has done in the office, factory or any institution he works in," "Do not downplay his work or refer to it with contempt or aversion," "Do not complain about his professional failures," and "Do not dampen his spirits being pessimistic about his professional plans."[29] Another illustrated journal advised men and women how to deal with finances in the shared household. Although the magazine recommended that a woman manage the household herself using funds assigned by her husband, but men "by their nature tend to control and calculate," women should not be bothered when men intervene in household expenses.[30] The feminist Zionist weekly *Ewa* agreed that the household was a sphere of female engagement and published meal plans and discussed the "rationale" for buying produce and cooking. Middle-class Jewish women were encouraged to respect men's professional lives and be perfect housewives and exciting lovers who did not question men's leading positions.

In interwar Poland, women were expected to fulfill traditional gender roles, such as being homemakers, wives, and mothers. Men, on the other hand, were expected to be active in the public sphere (which included religious performance) and, often, to approach domesticity as a female-only responsibility. Changing relationships between men and women in the 1920s and 1930s also encompassed the intersection of gainful employment and child rearing and evoked ambivalent feelings. For example, two illustrations from the Krasiński Garden in Warsaw printed in a Yiddish illustrated magazine from 1937 demonstrate how uneasy men felt with childcare and women's professional activity.[31] The first photo shows an Orthodox man holding a sleeping little boy on his lap. The man looks at the camera with confusion and unease. Sitting among elderly Jewish men, he might have felt unsure whether childcare in a public place corresponded with the model of masculinity he considered to be valid. The second photograph shows a man dressed without any markers of ethnicity feeding a little boy from a bottle. The *Idishe Bilder* caption was explicit: "When the mother is a breadwinner, the father is a nanny." While we do not know whether or not the family in the picture is Jewish, the Yiddish caption is informative of how Polish Jews approached the changing division of labor. For the editors of *Idishe Bilder*, the image of a man feeding a boy in a park was unusual and needed to be photographed as a curiosity. While it was women who were considered to be responsible for child-rearing, in the Orthodox world in Poland, women were also considered breadwinners. The wife probably assigned her husband the childcare while she was working outside the home. Importantly, analogous caricatures mocking female emancipation that undermined the traditional division of labor appeared in the non-Jewish press as well.[32] Both Jewish and non-Jewish men were anxious to see how new notions of femininity, profession, and child-rearing would influence gender relations.

Women and men in interwar Jewish Poland were constructed as two distinct types of consumers. Satirical journals presented women as vain and easy to "conquer" with lavish gifts, while men were more rational and practical in their choices. The female author of a journal article about male methods of seducing women mentioned giving expensive gifts, getting her drunk, and declaring love.[33] A cartoon from 1938 presented a woman carefully inspecting the ring she received from her boyfriend, where she seemed more interested in its value than in the man's feelings.[34] Even women's journals repeated the idea of a woman satisfying her husband through proper consumption choices that would stabilize his sense of masculinity. In 1938, *Ewa* advised, "The cabinet of the master of the house should be colored in red, brown or dark blue, according to the profession of its owner. Motifs of an antenna or

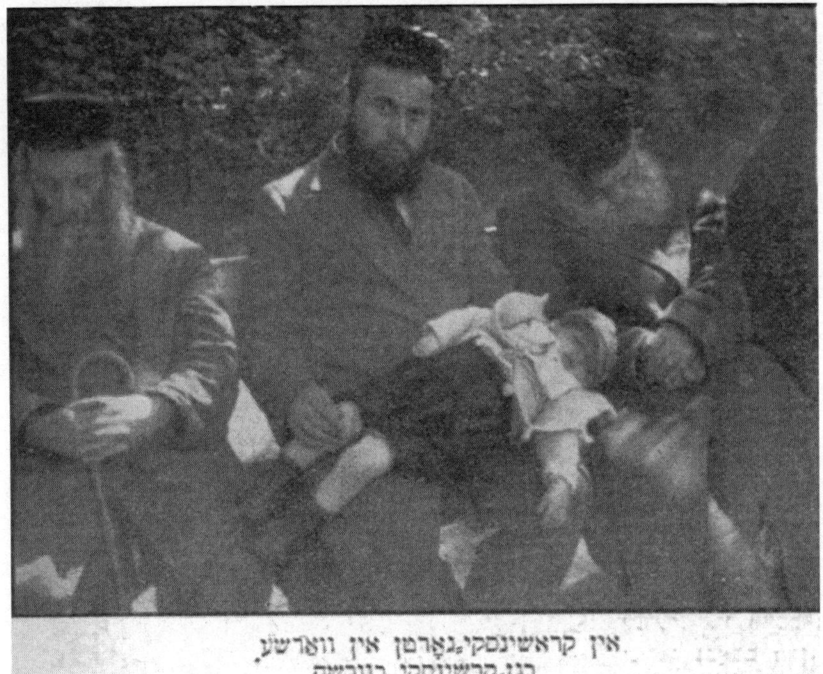

Figure 6.1. Orthodox men with a sleeping boy, *Idishe Bilder*, no. 6, 1937, 20.

spiral, which might be proper in the room of an engineer, do not correspond with the preferences of a writer or doctor."[35] While the weekly encouraged women to take the initiative, this was still to take place within the domestic sphere and reflected the idea that men and women differed in their aesthetic preferences and consumption patterns. Jewish magazines in Poland promoted consumption through their espousal of the "cult of domesticity," similar to those in other European countries and the United States.[36]

Advertisements catering to Jewish women conveyed a message about the ways Polish-Jewish women approached their spouses and their vision of a good husband. One ad from the daily *Nowy Dziennik* shows an image of a man sitting comfortably in an armchair dressed in an elegant shirt and vest. The man smiles with satisfaction, supposedly because his wife has kept his clothes clean and neat. The caption reads, "A satisfied husband avoids

Figure 6.2. A man with a baby in a Warsaw park, *Idishe Bilder*, no. 6, 1937, 20.

going to bars. Marital happiness depends to a great extent on maintaining an exemplary household. It is hard to imagine it without cleanliness in every way. So, esteemed ladies, do not save on the soap!"[37] The ad emphasized (and possibly evoked) Jewish housewives' fear of their husbands spending time in bars, where they could strike up flirtations, overspend their shared money, or fall into drunkenness. A woman in another ad for washing powder proclaimed, "The one who brings me Radion powder would be a perfect husband!"[38] An impeccable household was supposed to keep the man at home and prevent him from venturing into male adventures that middle-class women considered detrimental to bourgeois marriage. While interwar Poland saw the inclusion of women into the public sphere and women served as members of city councils and worked as lawyers, the producers of household items still reduced women to housewives devoted to the household, constantly afraid that their husbands would have an affair.

In the post–World War I years, many upper- and middle-class Jewish men began to believe that bourgeois masculinity was experiencing unprecedented challenges. Since the nineteenth century, embourgeoised men defined their masculinity through their exclusive access to profession, education, and wealth. In the context of growing female access to various jobs, as well as the social ascent of people from the lower classes combined with the economic uncertainty of the early 1930s, many Jewish males feared that their privileged gender-social status might decrease as new groups claimed their rights. World War I and its impact damaged the credibility of prewar notions of masculinity. The cataclysmic loss of life and injury left men physically and psychologically scarred.[39] Polish lifestyle journals for men increasingly used anti-feminist tones and hoped for a return to what they considered the traditional gender order. For example, in 1932, *Współczesny Pan* complained that "emancipation brought so many disappointments," and in 1936, it noted with satisfaction that "a healthy instinct turns women back to practical things, to professional schools," promising to make universities again a male-only space.[40]

In 1927, Polish-Jewish law student Aleksander Ołomucki denounced universities as "factories" recruiting students who only wanted a good job as a lawyer or doctor. Ołomucki complained that, in the post-1918 era, the university had turned into a platform for economic success ruled by "cold, almost primitive calculation."[41] He starkly criticized what he saw as socially dangerous "democratism" and called to limit access to the liberal professions. A similar opinion concerning the *karierowiczostwo*, referring to the perception of professions as a mere tool for ascending to the privileged social class, voiced another young Polish-Jewish lawyer, Seweryn Cynsztang: "We cannot accept that the Jewish academic youth see their studies as a mere fragment of their future [career] path, and ignore things that do not help them get a job!"[42] Cynsztang complained about young Jewish men who were snobbish and focused more on "parties and fun" than on more meaningful "cultural work." Ołomucki's and Cynsztang's texts demonstrate how the perceived decreasing exclusivity of elite professions induced Jewish men's fears about their status.

In the 1920s and 1930s, sports and parties indeed seemed to be increasingly accepted venues for defining one's middle- and upper-class masculinity rather than the old ideal of work.[43] The growing importance of the consumption of goods and free-time services made young Jewish men who attempted to live the ideal of diligent, educated professionals feel marginalized. Criticizing these new developments in 1927, Elchanan Lewin complained about the "hypertrophy of sport" and "dancingomania," arguing that next to socialism, "the ball and dancing were two fetishes of our times."[44] According to Lewin, the press devoted too much space to "well-fed and well-built sportsmen" and neglected young men who pursued distinct ideals. While he focused on the consumption of entertainment services, Lewin's tirade was a critique of new ideals of masculinity that he was not able to follow. Measuring a mere 158 centimeters, skinny, and with a history of diseases, Lewin felt that he did not fit into the new ideal of the Jewish man who concentrated on pleasure-focused and mixed-gender consumption of leisure. Lewin clung to education and profession-based status as anchors of traditional upper-class masculinity and refused to accept the changing times. Mocking men who danced, Lewin also complained about men succumbing to women and the domesticity they embodied. Lewin's views demonstrate the anxiety that the evolving leisure patterns, professional life, and notions of masculinity evoked in men.

The model of a Jewish man who made a career in business and used his money for consumption evoked negative responses from men who criticized karierowiczostwo and wealth as a recognized

דער הער דירעקטאר איז צוריקגעקומען פון
דער פאריזער אויסשטעלונג, און, זעהט,, ער האב
זך פֿלייסיג גענומען צו דער שווערער ארבייט.

Figure 6.3. Drawing, "Der her direktor nebekh" (The poor mister director), *Di Panorame*, November 5, 1937, 5.

form of performing masculinity. Satirical images of well-fed and elegantly dressed Jewish executives and directors derided their laziness and vainness, but their meanings were more ambivalent. One caricature pictured a Jewish director with his legs up on a desk; he had just returned from a trip to Paris and, as the caption noted, "returned to his hard work." Pointing out his trips abroad and his distance from any physical or intellectual work, the caricature both derided a model of masculinity distanced from any diligence and defined it as something many Jewish men dreamed about. Since top positions in the state apparatus were off-limits to Jewish men in Poland, the private economy appeared as the only valid venue for personal economic success. Many caricatures poked fun at the high aspirations of Poland's Jewish middle class, which often contrasted with their actual financial abilities and economic uncertainty. The lazy director was thus an ambivalent figure: criticized for being unproductive but also admired for being able to engage in travel for pleasure and other forms of consumption. The growing importance of consumption complicated the ideal of work and providing as a masculine gendered marker, but economic independence still maintained its validity.

As Jewish men and women were marrying later in interwar Poland, some young Jewish men enjoyed the privileges of "young adulthood," a concept that had not been popular before the early twentieth century. For those men, not their career but rather the freedom of being a young single man was particularly attractive. In I. Oberzhanek's 1936 Yiddish satirical text, we encounter a man who did not dream of a quick career, arguing that "going to work should [be for] horses and married men. They need to go in a harness and work, but a *bukher* [bachelor]? A bukher should eat and drink, and sleep until midday. . . . I made my life with my *bukhershaft* [bachelorhood]."[45] The man in the story presents himself as the antinomy of the diligent Jewish traders and businessmen whom he saw as half-enslaved "draft horses." The narrator, dressed in fashionable white pants and free from a job, was one of the few males who had time on workdays and enjoyed his popularity with women while vacationing at forest resorts near Warsaw. There, he celebrated the personal pleasures of consumerism and metropolitan bachelor culture. However, the story ends with the man marrying one of these women and subduing his bukhershaft for her. This conclusion echoes fears expressed in all-Polish men's magazines that saw heterosexual marriage as caging men in, contradicting their natural robust sexuality.[46] Oberzhanek created a narrative about how women femininized Polish and Jewish culture and spoke about male anxieties around this process.

CONSUMING FASHION AND TECHNOLOGY

In the 1930s, fashion was an important sphere for structuring middle-class masculinities in Poland. Journals such as *ABC Mody: Miesięcznik poświęcony kulturze stroju pani i pana* (The ABC of fashion: A fashion monthly for a lady and a gentleman) and *Współczesny Pan* (Contemporary gentleman) informed men about current fashion trends and how to dress according to the occasion. These magazines, like *Esquire* in the United States, commercially orchestrated and structured both masculinity and femininity.[47] In 1930, the Polish women's journal *Bluszcz* (Ivy) wrote, "The male fashion is also evolving. It is not a constant transformation as in the case of women, but from time to time it brings new recommendations which gentlemen happily follow."[48] *ABC Mody* added that "male attire does not change often, yet demands a lot of neatness," and concluded that concerning fashion, "men are more conservative than women."[49] Male fashion in interwar Poland aligned with a vision of conservative masculinity: rooted less in innovation and more in stability and moderation and exposing the masculine virtues of self-containment and practicality. At the same time, since middle- and upper-class aspirations were relatively new for most Polish Jews, the advice on masculine normativity in fashion consumption had a transformative dimension.

Fashion and sartorial journals discussed the intersection of class and gender and encouraged men to define their status through proper clothing. An *ABC Mody* contributor commenting on male fashion argued that men in Poland were blindly following diverse fashions and consequently dressing chaotically and badly.[50] In that sense, the virtue of masculine moderation, which was also to be expressed in fashion, did not find proper expression in Poland. Fashion supposedly failed to express class in Poland: "It was hard to tell the difference between the director's wife and her cleaning lady," the *ABC Mody* contributor continued. In a section discussing men's suits, the monthly added, "Tell me where you buy your clothes, and I'll tell you who you are." In that sense, clothes were expected to expose both a man's social status and his inner masculine virtues.[51] For example, masculine moderation in fashion was praised in *ABC Mody* in its examination of Józef Piłsudski's uniform. The country's leader's clothes were first and foremost comfortable, allowing him to pursue another masculine value—the devotion to work.[52] Journals both responded to and created a culture that expected men to become fashion consumers and see a validation and enhancement of their status, image, and masculinity in a tasteful consumption of clothes. Using a tone of friendly fashion advice, the journals encouraged men to look to the attire of very successful men in their surroundings in order to avoid being overdressed and ridiculed.

Non-Jewish journals for men such as *Współczesny Pan* advertised both non-Jewish and Jewish tailors, including Herman Lipszyc's parlor in the Warsaw opera house.[53] The gentlemen's clothing store of M. Rajnfeld, also located on the heavily Jewish Nalewki Street in the capital, advertised itself as offering the greatest selection of male fashion favored by its loyal customers "from the spheres of capital's male elegance."[54] Jewish female and male journalists took part in the discussion about male fashion covered not only in fashion journals such as *ABC Mody* but in regular Jewish magazines as well. For example, Jewish journalist Paulina Appenszlak welcomed the fashion freedom men could enjoy, "liberated to a certain extent from the earlier obligatory black."[55] The illustrated Yiddish magazine *Velt-shpigl* (World mirror) and the Polish-language *Nasz Przegląd* published recommendations for male fashion and underscored the values of elegance and correctness. Jewish textile producers also joined the debate and, through advertisements in Jewish journals, sought to create a new group of male fashion customers. For example, one undergarment company proclaimed in a Łódź Yiddish weekly, "Now the man too has recognized the value of soft, silk underwear."[56] Men in these ads were depicted as consumers of fashionable clothes for practical and utilitarian reasons rather than through vanity or gullibility.[57] Commodity consumption was constructed as offering the potential for individual fulfillment without undermining traditional values or the gender order.[58]

In contrast to Appenszlak, who believed in the liberating potential of male fashion, most voices in Polish-language Jewish media used fashion texts to stabilize traditional gender norms and stereotypes. The almanac of *Nasz Przegląd* wrote in 1938, "A man does not succumb to the caprices of fashion, he is not distracted by details and instantly recognizes the entire concept."[59] Later, the almanac criticized men who "are very sensitive to anything connected with fashion, they know all its shades and recognize things that were in fashion last year. But we do not go around with this kind of pretty boys."[60] While previously women were in charge of the family's clothing, the modern male consumer was to take care of his clothing himself. Since women appeared to be too easily manipulated to be trusted with making rational fashion choices for men, advertisements encouraged men to take care of their own closet in a masculine way, which would ensure that their gender identity would not be undermined. Men appeared rational, competent, and able to come to proper conclusions concerning fashion. A vision of a binary gender order can be seen in which men consuming fashion did not transgress gender boundaries but acted "as men should." The desire to maintain the conservative gender order in fashion was typical for bourgeois milieus in Poland across the ethnic and religious spectrum.

In interwar Poland, masculinity was strongly linked with technology, and middle- and upper-class Polish-Jewish men were encouraged to follow the latest technological developments, embrace them through consumption, and in that way frame their notions of masculinity. For example, the men's magazine *Współczesny Pan* linked technological innovation with men's desired and supposedly gender-appropriate role in society.[61] Polish-Jewish media outlets regularly updated their readers about world exhibitions and the recent chemical or biological discoveries, presented portraits of scientists, and sent the message that modern men should be knowledgeable about the newest technological developments. This knowledge, often presented in language common to male camaraderie in a casually familiar tone, appeared as a masculine feature that women were supposedly lacking. For example, the almanac of *Nasz Przegląd* suggested that "it is commonly known that a woman is completely lacking the discovery instinct, that she is not interested in technology, that diverse improvements in daily life have been a product of male hands and of the male mind."[62] The consumption of male-associated technology would differentiate between men and women and clearly mark male gender in a consumer society that still linked consumption with femininity.

Interwar Poland saw masculinity increasingly defined by the consumption of objects that projected a message of being up-to-date with modern technology. For example, the ad for the Cyclosport bike shop on the heavily Jewish Nalewki Street in Warsaw encouraged readers that "every tourist, biker and sportsman uses motorbikes, bikes and parts of the premium label Metro" and promised "quality and precision."[63] Such ads linked the changing professional landscape and the new idea of free time with an affinity to technology framed as masculine. Another ad in *Nasz Przegląd* promised to provide accounting systems offering the highest "rationality, transparency and economy," suggesting that the qualities of the device reflected masculine virtues.[64] Even goods and jobs commonly associated with the female sphere, when linked to technological development, were advertised using male figures. For example, a 1913 ad for vacuum and air cleaners included a man proudly holding the advanced device in a way that reminded readers of a phallic figure.[65] The woman next to him was depicted in a position that underscored her role as servant and cleaner. The elegant man appeared as a knowledgeable scientist, and his air cleaner promised to "kill" bacteria, while the woman looked like a passive beneficiary of the manmade household appliances.

The modernist fascination with technological progress intersected with a vision of men as the fathers of technological advancement. While Poland was a relatively backward country then, new infrastructural investments promised to stabilize the position of men as guarantors of progress. When the first skyscraper was built in Lviv, the Jewish daily *Chwila* proudly presented both its investor, Jojne Sprecher, and its architect, Ferdynand (Feiwel) Kassler, underscoring the entrepreneurial talent and technical expertise of Polish-Jewish men.[66] The 1930s were the era of electrification in major Polish cities, and the Polish-Jewish press linked this technological advancement with male consumption and professional life. For example, *Chwila* printed an ad showing an elegantly dressed man sitting at a desk, working on something resembling an architectural sheet or bookkeeping register. The caption above reads, "A monotonous office work is easier and more effective with proper lighting. Good lighting means a 10-lumen bulb."[67] The ad projected a vision of a Polish-Jewish man who was well off, educated, elegant, and willing to make his life more comfortable through consumption. While the figure sitting over a book might resemble a traditional Jewish man bent over religious books, in *Nasz Przegląd* we encounter a male figure suggesting an alternative path for a modern Jewish man to work, dress, and consume.

Men of working-class backgrounds also embraced consumption artifacts associated with the middle class. When *Idishe Bilder* printed an article about the boxer Shapsel Rotholc, it also included a picture of the boxer and his wife listening to the radio. Both are elegantly dressed; Shapsel wears a suit and his wife a dark dress and leather shoes.[68] Although, in 1938, a relatively small group of 880,000 subscribers had access to a radio in Poland, the journal portrayed the couple sitting by a big wooden radio decorated with Rotholc's sports trophies. The magazine noted that Rotholc still worked as a typesetter and his wife as a seamstress, but their photographs projected a relatively well-off middle-class couple. The photographs evoke middle-class domesticity, the heterosexual family, and economic stability, which were valued and considered normative in Poland. Staging Rotholc as a symbol of middle-class propriety, the illustrated magazine merged diverse models of masculinity that were than valid in Poland: the fit sportsman and elegant member of the urban middle class. Also, images of more religious Jewish men were employed to increase sales of specific products. For example, an ad for Ceres coconut oil included a picture of a bearded Orthodox Jewish man advising his wife to bake only using Ceres. The caption merged the religious vernacular with a commercial context: "My dear wife! Do you feel the atmosphere of the Shabbat? Shabbat is our only comfort. Do you want to truly enjoy the charm of Shabbat? Then bake only using Ceres, sweet Ceres!"[69] The Orthodox man turned into a figure who took responsibility for the household and the Shabbat celebration. However, the ad maintained the traditional gender order: the woman serves food to her husband, while he is immersed in a religious book. While working-class and Orthodox men were not major groups featured in male-centered advertising, their figures were employed to increase the sales of many products.

CONSUMING BEAUTY AND HEALTH SERVICES

Beauty products and hygiene practices advertised in Polish-Jewish media outlets reinforced the binary gender order. Beauty products appeared as a gendered means to love and romance that Jewish women could use to attract men. An advertisement for

Figure 6.4. Erco face powder ad, *Di Panorame*, March 4, 1938, 2.

Erco face powder (fig. 6.4) featured a man and a woman in an intimate pose and defined the consumption of cosmetics as a feminine activity. The man says, "I have the most beautiful wife. With such wonderful skin." The woman answers, "And I have the cleverest husband! You recommended I use only Erco powder."[70] Similar sexist tropes had existed already earlier. A 1934 Nivea face cream ad promised that smooth skin would guarantee "love from the first sight."[71] An elaborate 1912 ad for Floreine face cream, soap, and powder shouted, "A beautiful face is already half a dowry!"[72] Beauty seemed to be the new dowry with which Jewish women could attract men. These ads reinforced the gendered order of the man as the sole provider and the woman as vain and dependent on her husband. The ads defined beauty as the female asset recognized by men and encouraged women to invest in beauty treatments so that men would maintain their sexual interest in them. Also, since cosmetics in the early twentieth century were linked with chemistry and science, both ads presented men as up-to-date with the newest technological developments in the beauty industry.

At the same time, men were encouraged to invest more time into their appearance, which would strengthen their masculine identity and make them more attractive to women. For instance, Helena Brzezińska, writing about male beauty treatments in her "cosmetic-medical institute," spoke of male "rational care of face and hair," which was to be "a condition of success not only among women, but in life in general."[73] Brzezińska sought to attract Jewish male customers by referring to the masculine virtue of rationality. Other companies followed. One cologne ad presented the product as a rational and obligatory "necessary element of everyday hygiene" and thus similar to bread.[74] In another ad, Eau de Cologne 4711 appeared as an "indispensable assistant of any sportsman." The ad differentiated between the cultural meanings that cosmetics would have on men and women. While men using the cologne were supposed to be better sportsmen, women who used it were able to "protect their charm and beauty."[75] We notice that while, for men, the cosmetic was to enhance their masculine qualities mediated through sports, for women, it was to protect them from losing their femininity, which physical activity could undermine.

An artifact that transmitted a message about changing notions of Jewish masculinity in the context of beauty was the razor blade. The razor label Polonia advertised itself in dozens of Jewish newspapers in Polish and Yiddish and promised to be luxurious, produced in Poland, and made of quality Swedish steel.[76] The characteristics of the razor blades spoke to different masculine ideals: their manufacturing in Poland was related to patriotism and supporting the local economy, while defining them as luxurious sent a signal that they were exceptional and available only to a narrow category of successful men. Being clean shaven was becoming more and more popular among Polish Jews and was identified with male beauty. For example, the ad for Nivea shaving cream in the Yiddish yellow daily *Hayntige Nayes* suggested that Jewish men beyond the cultured elite also were called to shave.[77] The ad portrayed a handsome, clean-shaven young man, with a razor blade in his hand, singing happily while shaving. The ad claimed that the cream could "make the skin strong," thus underlining the masculine qualities of strength and practicality versus the feminine delicacy and emotion that often appeared in ads for women's cosmetics. The very practice of clean shaving signaled new ideas about Jewish masculinity. In contrast to Orthodox Judaism, where a thick beard symbolized patriarchal authority, in 1930s Poland a growing group of Jewish men shared the belief that a modern Polish-Jewish face should be clean shaven. Cognizant of this transformation but also inducing it, producers of razor blades and shaving cream hoped to define their products as indispensable to masculine hygiene.

In the same vein, in interwar Poland, male health performance at work and home became increasingly subjected to medical critique that highlighted male health deficiencies. In a Jewish magazine in 1937, acclaimed Jewish doctor Paweł Klinger criticized that "a man does not care about his health since he sees attentiveness and concern about health as a sign of weakness. His pride does not allow him to stay in bed when he gets a cold. He prefers to see himself as a man of iron, in front of whom nature is helpless. He overexploits his body, disregards the warnings nature sends him." Later on, Klinger criticized the diet of many men who "enjoy eating many fat dishes and washing them down with strong drinks" and "spend entire days behind the desk and do not move around in the fresh air."[78] Klinger accused middle-class Polish-Jewish men of neglecting their bodies and blamed excessive consumption and office work for leading to health problems and premature deaths. This text underscores how evolving professional life and consumption and their influence on men's health became a social matter. In interwar Poland, men were encouraged to buy medicines and supplements to make their bodies work properly. Jewish and non-Jewish middle-class men faced similar problems, including sexuality. For example, the non-Jewish men's magazine *Współczesny Pan* included ads of exclusively Jewish Warsaw doctors who treated *niemoc płciowa*, or impotency, and other diseases. In this respect, the Jewish doctor and his fellow-man guidance were tasked with improving the health and sexual performance of all Warsaw men.

While Klinger was critical and prescriptive in his tips concerning aging and the unhealthy male body, many commercials in the Jewish media used a casual tone of male camaraderie. For example, an advertisement in *Nasz Przegląd* selling herbal medicines for digestion problems showed three elegant middle-class men observing a male doctor who was explaining the digestion system.[79] It suggested that liver and kidney diseases, as well as "hemorrhoidal suffering," could be eased with Dr. Lauer Harz's herbs. Those diseases appeared here as of particular interest to men, who, thanks to the medicine, could continue with the unhealthy diets that for many men still expressed the unhesitating and steadfast masculinity to which they aspired. At the same time, the figure of a male doctor underscored the link between masculinity and science. Another ad for cod-liver oil pictured a devastated man who, as the caption read, suffered from "tiredness and weakened life energy." The oil was to help regain healthy fitness, which was expected from a man despite his unhealthy habits.[80] These ads suggested that while men suffering from health problems did not appear to fulfill the criteria of robust and healthy masculinity, the advice of a competent fellow man could bring them back on track.

Ads in Jewish media outlets reflected the need for men to also be normative in terms of sexuality. The Western code of masculinity proscribed men to be vigorous, even brutal, lovers.[81] Those men who failed to sexually dominate women were anxious that they did not conform to the dominant masculinity model and searched for diverse solutions. In 1912, a Yiddish newspaper advertised a medical product intended to increase male sexual energy. The ad went, "Why try to awaken through spirits, tobacco, or strong tea, when you know that it won't help you, but make you more nervous, weak and deflated?"[82] The ad linked concern for male health with the bad health habits of aspiring white-collar men: overworking and spending too many hours sitting resulted in "sexual weakness" (*geshlekhtlekhe shvakhkayt*) and unmasculine effeteness. Men were called to fight against "weakness," which the ad defined as a major problem, contradicting the masculine call for vigor in every sphere of a man's life. Potency products were continuously advertised in Poland between the 1900s and 1930s. In 1913, one Yiddish magazine advertised Stimulol, a French product for "sexual weakness."[83] An ad from 1937 encouraged men to buy a new potency product: "Mobilization of all men . . . Married or single, old or young, poor or rich—every man should possess the invention of the era. Only then will he be able to say that he is a real man. Our invention does not break down; you can use it for your entire life. It will give you the greatest satisfaction."[84] Using the discovery of Warsaw laboratory Chemitor supposedly allowed one to remain a real—that is, sexually fit—man, even into old age. All these ads suggest that many Jewish men suffered from weakened sexual performance and searched for solutions to improve it. They merge consumption and masculinity by recognizing the centrality of robust sexuality for constructing virile masculinity.

Many ads for men's medical products mentioned *nerven krankhayt*, which is a nerve disease. Neurosis or hysteria was associated with women in the early twentieth century, and thus men suffering from nervous disorders appeared effeminate.[85] Nervous disorders, many ads suggested, could have numerous symptoms, including distraction, fears, migraines, insomnia, and stomach problems. Some men linked nervous problems with "sexual deficits" within marriage.[86] Advertisements for "nerve medicines" appeared in provincial Yiddish newspapers, such as *Pinsker Shtime,* as well, which suggests that the idea of mental weakness as a gendered disease had also begun to spread among more traditional Jews.[87] Jewish and non-Jewish doctors rushed to assist men who felt that their "nerves" might be unstable. One doctor advertising in a Łódź Jewish monthly described his health guide as "a health gospel," which was probably something similar to contemporary self-healing therapy. After carefully reading the book, "nervous" patients were to find "a calming joy in life."[88] While the ad did not address men specifically, it included two male faces: one symbolizing psychological distress and the other satisfaction. The combination of text and image sent the message that a normative man should have control over his mental health, which would help him avoid the weakness that deprived men of power and emasculated them. Texts in the Jewish media that spoke of men's mental, corporeal, or sexual deficiencies inform us about the anxieties that Jewish men faced. Men and their social surroundings expected them to be self-assured and full of certitude. At the intersection of antisemitic exclusion and economic slowdown, these expectations were hard to meet for many Jewish men.

MEN CONSUMING LEISURE AND FREE TIME

Jewish and non-Jewish men were addressed as consumers of free-time activities such as sport. While sports have been widely examined in the context of masculine identity formation, not only performing sports but also consuming sports-related goods and services shaped masculine ideals and fantasies. At the beginning of the twentieth century, Polish-Jewish newspapers not only showcased the success of Jewish sportsmen and encouraged youth sports but also defined masculinity through possessing the proper sports equipment. For example, an ad from 1913 for the

Vigor "hand apparatus" suggested that the sports equipment was "the only way to become strong." The gadget was sold together with tables and drawings showing a wide array of gymnastics figures, and the ad itself included several professional sketches. The ad sent the message that Vigor was a major accomplishment of the male technological mind and would allow all men to enhance their strength. Importantly, the ad addressed not only secular men who were discovering the benefits of sports but also explicitly the hadarim—that is, Jewish religious elementary schools.[89] Particularly young men were summoned not only to be sporty but to be sports-aware consumers. A good example of this is an ad in a Yiddish daily advertising Nivea face cream (fig. 6.5). The photo shows a man offering the cream to a woman, both in winter attire on a ski slope. The caption reads, "Every professional skier and *taternik* [Tatra boulderer] knows that before going out, he needs to protect his face and hands with a Nivea cream or oil.... Nivea protects from painful sunburns and intensifies the suntan."[90] The ad combined the recent trends in middle class leisure activities with the expected performance of gender. The man offering the cream to the woman stands as an expert in the science and chemical industry and as farsighted and well prepared for the tough weather conditions in the mountains. Using the face cream does not appear as a feminine beauty practice but denotes being thoughtful, prepared, and knowledgeable. The very activity of skiing presents the man as in line with current sports trends, and his love for the Polish landscape paints him as patriotic. Ads for sports programs and products dotted the pages of Polish-Jewish newspapers, convincing Jewish men that by buying those products or signing up for sports classes, they were embracing a model of masculinity centered around fitness.

I suggest that we can expand the meaning of Jewish sports beyond ethnic empowerment to include the intersection of gender and the consumption of sports services. For example, Jewish law student Zygmunt Braude's contribution about skiing presented

Figure 6.5. Nivea cream ad, *Hayntige Nayes*, January 4, 1935, 7.

it as a proper sport for aspiring middle-class men. A young fellow returning from skiing holidays was "almost a gentleman," Braude suggested. Skiing was central to constructing an ideal of a man who was attractive not only in his bodily fitness but also in his attire, including a snow-white pullover and hat. Skiing allowed young urban Jewish men to signal their masculinity centered around leisure and build it against notions of femininity. Braude believed that women on the slopes "were merely decorative" and that young men needed women around to confirm their masculinity.[91] He argued that the goal of skiing was less to keep fit and more to appear to "rule" in the Polish spa towns through masculine elegance and fitness. In a similar tone, Lviv's Jewish *Chwila* commented that the sports attire in the mountains "is principally characterized by its manliness" and underscored the male character of skiing.[92] Women fond of sports could, however, "through a series of additions and improvements," neutralize what was perceived as the "severe" look of the ski uniform. With colorful outfits, women who "went out of fancy hotels in Chamonix or Sankt Moritz" were seen to express their cheer and vivacity but essentially also their female beauty. The images of men in the mountains were in line with the all-Polish vision of a taternik as "not exactly clean, badly shaven, even shabby," yet fitted with the proper mountain attire.[93] Skiing was framed as a gendered activity that merged consumption with the portrayal of an energetic sporting man.[94]

Also, cars and driving established a link among middle-class masculinity, technology, mobility, and personal freedom. Initially, car ownership was still a relatively new phenomenon and was largely limited to the upper class and urban elites and did not become a mass phenomenon in Poland before the 1970s. The first group of car lovers, the Automobile Society of the Kingdom of Poland (Towarzystwo Automobilowego Królestwa Polskiego), was founded by prince Zdzisław Lubomirski, count August Zamoyski, and other noblemen.[95] In the 1920s and 1930s, a growing number of middle- and upper-class men allowed themselves to buy cars, but becoming motorists remained a marker of the privileged professional status of businessmen, doctors, lawyers, and engineers. This is clearly illustrated in a 1939 lecture about driving and car maintenance organized by the engineers' association in the city of Radom. Engineers were some of the few local men who could afford cars.[96] However, apart from being status symbols and representing male success, cars started to be understood as tools to prosperity. A company from Radom trained drivers, declaring, "Profession means money. The profession provides the livelihood!"[97] While we do not know whether the company was Jewish owned, they decided to cater to Jewish men when choosing their publicity venues. Jewish men in Poland were not immune to the allure of cars, and as other men in Poland, they also saw cars as a way to assert their masculinity and modernity.

Cars and driving in the early twentieth century were assigned to the masculine domain, and many Jewish men considered them indispensable to modern masculinity. Some accounts compared cars to women, turning them into men's possessions, through which men defined their sense of domination. This link is clearly visible in a satirical text by a certain "Ch." The Jewish Ch. wrote that men needed to invest their money in car maintenance, just as they needed to spend money on fancy clothes for their wives. The fanciest cars were streamlined in their construction and thus resembled "female bodies."[98] Through establishing the link with women, Ch. defined cars as central to masculine identity but also revealed a misogynist approach to women who presumably sought male gifts and attention. While the importance of driving cars for constructing masculinity could be underscored by comparing cars to women, it could also be done by pointing out the desired masculine features that "united" men and their cars. For example, in 1928, Kraków's daily *Nowy Dziennik* wrote about the yearly car race that was to pass through major Polish spa towns, noting that the participating cars were to be measured for their speed and durability.[99] Jewish poet Juljusz Witkower, in his poem "Chłodne miasto" (A cold city), imagined cars to be "steel and masculine."[100] Thus, cars' durability and performance became, for the men driving them, a way to prove their high durability and performance. Cars could appear as either masculine or feminine and could strengthen the masculine identity of their drivers by resembling the men they idealized or the women they desired.

Driving destabilized the former class distinctions between men. Earlier, the rich traveled in carriages driven by the poor, but in the early twentieth century, the ability to drive a car appeared to be an indispensable skill for upper-class men. In 1925, the association of Polish-Catholic students asked veteran member Bolesław From to offer driving courses to the other members. *Korporant*, a journal of Polish-Catholic fraternities, offered the following take on the significance of driving for men in Poland in the 1920s: "The growing speed with which the car has conquered the world in the recent years, pushing away other forms of mobility, makes it necessary to get to know this not that new, but still intriguing sport. The car has conquered the world and, according to the proverb 'homo sum et nil humanum ad me alienum esse puto,' one should know how to hold the steering wheel. Abroad, hardly anyone has chauffeurs these days, and one takes care of his machine himself."[101] The journal conveyed the message that a modern man drives and repairs his own car. While some men still associated driving with the lower class, the new times suggested that controlling the technology and "the beautiful art of driving" made one more masculine. Such was the message of F. Grętkiewicz's driving school in Łódź, which in a Jewish weekly advertised "special gentlemen's driving courses" that separated driving students into groups, helping maintain the class division among drivers.[102]

Cars were increasingly advertised as a new masculine status symbol associated with mobility and success. This link was further reinforced by marketing in Polish-Jewish journals advertising not cars but other goods, using images of cars to make the sale. For example, an ad for rubber coats by PPG depicted a man and woman wearing elegant coats and fashionable automobile hats with built-in goggles.[103] Next to them stood a car illuminating the scene with a bright light. The PPG coats were supposed to be luxurious, affordable, and water resistant, which coincided with the images of driving as a sport and the car as a desired material good. While the ad included a mixed-gender couple, the body language suggested that it was the man who had invited the woman to the masculine world of driving. The ad entangled the coat's and the car's symbolics, and the overarching message was that consumption did not undermine, but rather enhanced, male heterosexuality, practicality, and stability. At the same time, Jewish Poland also saw more ambivalent voices about driving. One satirical newspaper blamed cars for the accidents that greenhorn Jewish drivers experienced.[104] However, the positive association between driving and elite masculinity was dominant.

Masculinity and driving were interwoven in Jewish literary texts as well. For example, the short story "Szofer" by L. D. Berkowicz featured a young Jewish driver, a man of about thirty years old, with a "brave, honest and shining face." His face showed a visible scar, which "lent him masculinity and bravery," while his car was "neat and shining." The beauty of the man and the car seemed to intertwine. The driver sitting in the car "ably" started the engine while shaking his hair in a "brave masculine way." The masculinity of the driver was expressed in his total control of the machine; the car "was obedient to his every move." The control was not brutal, but delicate, "as though driving were like 'playing the piano.'" The Jewish driver compared his car to "a blue eagle" that allowed him to explore Palestine and tenderly wiped away the dust to make it shine after the ride. The driver was "attached to the winged machine" and was proud of his profession.[105] Berkowicz's story equated cars with a desire for freedom and an exploratory spirit and presented them as a vehicle allowing men to both travel and signal masculine virtues.

In an era in which the binary gender order was reinforced by countless popular and scientific accounts, consumption of certain products identified with pleasure and free time, such as chocolate or cigarettes, also appeared as a gendered activity. For example, Plutos, a Jewish-owned chocolate producer, was cognizant of how to approach its diverse consumer group—women, children, and men—while both benefiting from and reinforcing the gendered logic. The producer advertised that chocolate did not result in weight gain and was particularly nutritious for children but when eaten by men would have a completely different effect. Plutos understood its male consumers as men who strove for success: "The guarantee of a successful life is hope and a good mood. Plutos Chocolate kills the pest of sadness or deflation and is an injection of energy and optimism."[106] While this ad, as many others published in Polish-language Jewish print outlets, did not cater specifically to Jews, it says a lot about the gendered nature of Jewish and non-Jewish consumption in interwar Poland. Not distinguishing between Jewish and non-Jewish consumers, and presenting the face of a happy middle-class man eating chocolate to invigorate his spirit, the ad strengthened the ideal of consuming masculinity that was gaining popularity among Poland's middle-class Jews.

Smoking cigarettes was another gendered leisure activity that had a high importance in interwar Poland. Smoking was then linked with the urban classes and wealth. Statistics from 1927 reveal that the least developed eastern regions had a lower number of smokers compared to the richer western ones.[107] Sharing a cigarette was for many men a ritual of masculine bonding with other men, independent of ethnic or class boundaries. For example, reportage from a Jewish dormitory in Warsaw mentioned male students playing cards in clouds of smoke.[108] Smoking cigarettes was a gendered activity. First, as argued by one contributor, smoking was considered one of the *bahurshte vidatkes,* or male expenditures,[109] and second, offering a cigarette to a woman was a sign of urban male courtesy. Cigarettes were usually advertised in Polish-Jewish newspapers using male figures. For example, an ad from 1938 included an elegant middle-class man surrounded by cigarette smoke as he read a newspaper, sending the message that a cigarette stood for masculine achievement and pleasure.[110] A cigarette factory in Białystok introduced the label "Boy," underscoring its desired male clientele.[111] However, the rituals of smoking were evolving. In 1939, a Jewish almanac noted that tobacco consumption had become universal: "Smoking has become a necessity and a civil right. A cigarette, a cigar, or a pipe is not a luxury anymore. . . . Everyone smokes, and in the blue smoke they find a comfort for their tense nerves that symbolize our time."[112] Women challenged the idea that smoking cigarettes belonged to the male domain. For example, Blanka Hollendrowa in her vacation report wrote about offering a cigarette to a traditional peasant in the mountain resort of Zakopane.[113] It was a cigarette offered by a urban middle-class Jewish woman introducing the traditional Christian man to her modern ideas about femininity and consumption.

MEN, WOMEN, AND MIDDLE-CLASS
SEXUALITY AND ROMANCE

In interwar Poland, masculinity was continuously defined by its relation to femininity. As the patriarchal culture was losing its power due to both female emancipation and the erosion of traditional venues of masculine validation, Polish Jews were conscious of the growing gender evolution and discussed it in newspaper articles, readers' letters, and satirical cartoons. Against the backdrop of social changes, Jewish men who held on to traditional anchors of masculinity (breadwinning, power, and domination over women) experienced a downgrade if they were unable to provide for or satisfy the modern consumer or romantic needs of their wives. While, for most Jewish men in early twentieth-century Poland, social mobility was limited, popular culture still sold the dream of becoming a rich and respected self-made man. At the same time, their patriarchal and work-centered masculinity was challenged by women who now expected a different kind of man and considered patriarchal, both traditional Orthodox and secularized middle class, masculinity inadequate. In that context, a figure appeared in Poland of a consuming Jewish man who better corresponded to the materialistic, leisure, and romantic needs of Jewish women.

Satirical journals offer a perspective on relationships between men and women in the context of consumption. A man who appears successful there is relatively distanced from old-fashioned courtesy and diligence. Jewish satirical journals such as *Tararam* (1934) and *Mehabel* (1928, 1935–1936), as well as the humor sections of regular Polish-Jewish dailies, with their focus on male-female relations, are very informative for exploring the intersection of gender and consumption. Jewish males and females appear in those satirical papers as consuming beings: enjoying holidays at the suburban cottages, spending time at one of Warsaw's Vistula River beaches or in the cinema. These entertainment venues were spaces where men and women negotiated gender relations against the backdrop of new popular consumption trends. Jewish women appeared particularly associated with leisure activities, from which busy Jewish men were to some extent excluded. Many cartoons parodied the growing incongruity between notions of Orthodox Jewish masculinity and the new Jewish femininity in Poland.

For example, a skit published in 1934 reads, "He lies in the workshop, she on the beach / He is bone-tired, she gets massages / He works hard, but she also not less / He goes to the debt collector, and she goes with a boy / He is covered with sweat, she with kisses / He eats dry bread, she cookies and sweets / He fell asleep a long time ago, she is still awake / He is already sick, she does not have any problem / He works like a horse, she just takes the money / He lies in the ground and she in the field with non-Jewish lovers."[114] The man portrayed in the skit appears to be exploited by his wife. While he sought to provide her with financial stability and was overworked, the woman appeared to be vain, spoiled, and expecting her husband to provide for her comfortable life. The diligent man was not attractive to his wife, who preferred summertime consumption pleasures: massages, outings, and good food. The idealized practical Jewish businessman who strove to provide for his wife and children was juxtaposed with female needs for free time, pleasure, and romance. Work-based masculinity was increasingly insecure, and men who followed this ideal were anxious about the recognition of their efforts of material accomplishment.

Women and men appeared in the Polish-Jewish satirical press as two distinct poles along the spectrum of consumption. Jewish women were often dressed according to the latest trends, aware of fashion, and very much involved in consumption, while Jewish men were presented as conservative, dressed in traditional Jewish garb, and not compatible with consumerism. Jewish men and women appearing in satirical drawings and stories were

Figure 6.6. Drawing, "Oyf der plazhe" (On the beach), *Tararam*, June 1, 1934, 6.

constructed as incompatible. One skit reads, "He is small, thin, broken / a godly grace little Jew, people call him / His woman, Sore Keyle is her name / is his contradiction: healthy, fat, with broad hips and tall / He reaches only to her chin."[115] Many caricatures derided vain women who focused on consumption, which contrasted with the previous ideal of a devoted and selfless Jewish mother. One caricature included a woman who wanted to show off a fancy hat she had bought, not noticing that she was blocking others' view in the cinema. The woman radiates beauty, wearing makeup and jewels, while her male companion is boring, wears glasses, and looks average.[116] Satirical texts and cartoons presented men as submissive *shlimazels* (consistently unlucky persons) and their wives as stuck with a husband who did not correspond to their aspirations, whom they did not love, and who felt oppressed in their marriage. As one text suggested, men felt continuously anxious that a richer or more handsome man would start up a flirtation with their girlfriend or wife.[117]

I suggest that the mockery in satirical Jewish journals spoke of the emasculation of old Orthodox Jewish men by a generation of younger men who perceived themselves as distinct from their fathers. While the majority of Polish Jews were still Orthodox in the 1930s, the generational divide was quite sharp. Laughing at Hasidic or Orthodox Litvak men, the editors poked fun at men whose identities were defined by their Orthodox religiosity. For many young Jewish men embedded in the all-Polish cultural codes, the Judaic learnedness lost any respectability-granting character. Satirical columns, such as those about Orthodox men founding their own football clubs or skiing in a Hasidic kapote, presented Orthodox men as not fit for the challenges of the era.[118] To strengthen the message of older men as incompatible with the modern day in many satirical texts, women accused their husbands of not showing them genuine love or understanding their feelings and needs. Particularly stories of Jewish women being unfaithful and cheating on their traditional partners pre-sented those men as emasculated and unable to exercise pa-triarchal control over their wives. While most Orthodox men were anxious about the new female expectations, Polish men's lifestyle magazine *Współczesny Pan* celebrated "a new type of a man" who "borrow[ed] the best female features, not forsaking the male ones."[119] This new ideal man who was to be an elo-quent partner, a tender lover, and a good husband and father was difficult to meet for many men in Poland. As the feelings of inadequacy intensified between Polish-Jewish men and women, Jewish newspapers ran advice columns about family and love. In the late 1930s, for example, Róża Jakubowiczowa had a column, *Man, froy un familyen-lebn* (Husband, wife, and family life), in the daily *Hayntige Nayes*.

One characteristic that differentiated between the two generations of Jewish men was their attitude toward sex and romantic love. While Orthodox Jewish rites prescribed premarital purity and considered extramarital sex a taboo, the social reality was different and Jewish men were approached as consumers of paid sex and pornographic publications. One ad in a Jewish daily encouraged men to buy booklets such as *Miłość zboczona* (Pervert love) or *Miłość zboczona, lezbiska, masochyzm, gwałt* (Pervert love, lesbianism, masochism, rape) or nude photos.[120] Men bought calendars with *tluste dovtshipen*, or erotic jokes,[121] and Kavanose, a French medicine against syphilis that was advertised in Warsaw Yiddish dailies.[122] Since public morals did not allow for the regular sale of pornographic publications, customers were encouraged to order them by mail. Despite a growing acceptance of premarital sexual relationships, interethnic relationships evoked tension. Jewish men fancied non-Jewish women, and non-Jewish men had affairs with Jewesses, yet these relationships were still considered to cross a certain social boundary. One song included the line, "Blonde loken hot Marianna, oygen bloye. Nor ikh bin a yidisher yingl, zi a goye," which presented interethnic relationships as impossible.[123] Another caricature presented a woman who listened to daily agricultural news following sex with a non-Jewish lover in a field.[124] The woman appears as both promiscuous and interested in recent technological developments such as the radio. Sexual life in interwar Poland appeared to function as "women's tool of resistance": now women had the power to admit (or not) men into the world of sexuality.[125] While, in the early twentieth century, Poland was still a place where rape, particularly of women of lower classes, was very common, Polish and Polish-Jewish cultures produced a gender order in which women could, to a certain extent, regulate not only their own but also men's sexuality.[126]

Traditional (but not only Orthodox) Jewish men seemed unable to meet the expectations of their wives concerning romance,

זי צעברעכט די לוחות...

Figure 6.7. Caricature, "Zi tsebrekht di lukhes" (She breaks the command-ments), *Tararam*, May 18, 1934, 1.

appearance, and consumption patterns. To address this tension, satirical journals invented the figure of a *przyjaciel* ("a friend" in Polish). Unlike the husband, the przyjaciel was fashion conscious, elegant, freshly shaven, and successful. While the przyjaciel may or may not have been Jewish, he always appeared in opposition to the husband, who appeared outdated, unromantic, and focused on his business or religion. One caricature from 1934 shows an attractive woman deciding between her religious husband and a handsome przyjaciel. Her head turns to the przyjaciel, who seems to better answer her ideal of romantic love and modern masculinity. The woman holds the Ten Commandments, which suggests that she is aware of the Jewish religious condemnation of cheating, yet she seems to have already made up her mind to follow her heart and engage with a man who would provide her with romance and attention. The figure of the przyjaciel also appears in the text "A kredens mit a pomotsnik" (Cupboard with a helper) from 1934.[127] The female narrator desires to buy a cupboard, which, apart from its usual function, would come with a male helper as a bonus. Speaking about the "helper" as though he were furniture (the word indeed had a double meaning, pomotsnik could mean a small side table), the woman says to the carpenter, "I don't know how one can live without a helper." She desires a helper who will be "massive, stable, and fresh" so that he can serve her substantial sexual needs. The subtext is clear: a pomotsnik is a lover. These satirical texts both mock traditional Jewish men who cannot satisfy the sexual needs of their wives and present women as smoothly combining the world of middle-class consumption and emancipated sexuality. The text does not judge the morality of the woman, and the blade of irony is directed at the husband, who has no idea that his wife merges her visits to a furniture shop with affairs with other men. These two examples demonstrate how masculine gender identities based on providing are challenged by alternative models and women's desires and how men appear not to retain agency over their marriage. Traditional Jewish men appeared to lose the power over their wives and were anxious about their status.

In the 1930s, Jewish discourses in Poland created a figure of a Jewish women who was more attracted to men who could be passionate lovers and sensitive friends than to those who were good providers. In numerous cartoons and satirical texts, Orthodox Jewish men appeared as unable to function within a social setting that valued romantic love. Polish-Jewish men parodied in the press seemed to fulfill some of these criteria, but hardly ever all of them. One article commented, "There are women . . . who after the wedding attempt to maintain platonic friendships with other men. They are sure that there is nothing wrong with it. . . . The husband is now too busy with his businesses. He needs to provide for his wife and children. He does not have a mind for youthful games! But a woman has more time and misses the compliments of the past, which she does not hear from her husband and expects from another man."[128] While the woman appreciated the financial stability that her diligent husband provided her, she longed for a man who could act as both a provider and a gentle and romantic lover. This contradiction is visible also in a text in which a grandfather advises his grandson how to conquer women. According to the older man, an attractive man should possess "beauty, eydlkayt (gentleness, nobility) and fine speech" and be "funny, interesting, and showing one's intellectual horizons." At the same time, the grandfather was sure that women were vain and interested in the "sound of gold."[129] The recommendation seems to equip the young man with the ability to serve as a "sensitive friend" but stops short of addressing all the expectations of modern Polish-Jewish women. The critique that emerged from Polish-Jewish newspapers was clear: Jewish salaried men and businessmen lacked gentleness and were self-focused, while more romantic lovers had the physical beauty and sensitivity but could not provide the financial security to fulfill female class aspirations.

The blade of emasculating irony targeted Orthodox men in particular. These men were depicted as unable to adjust to modern times and new female expectations. In a social setting where Orthodox studiousness and religiosity were losing their importance as masculine assets, men who represented religion and tradition needed to confront men who represented male fitness and romantic flair. For example, a cartoon appearing in *Tararam* in 1934 shows a Nalewki merchant who walks assisted by two strong athletes. This assistance by men who are strong and can defend him appears to be the only possibility for him to claim his debts and thus maintain the economic stability of his family.[130] A collage on one Yiddish magazine cover mocked a Galician Hasid having trouble mastering skiing—an activity desired for a "new Jewish man."[131] Another cartoon (fig. 6.8) presents a traditionally dressed husband who discovers his wife with a lover.[132] The

‫ס'איז געשעהן אום תשעה־באב...‬

Figure 6.8. Caricature, "S'iz geshen um tish b'av" (It has happened around Tisha b'Av), *Tararam*, July 27, 1934, 1.

husband opens his hands in an expression of surprise and looks defeated. The other man is younger, dressed in an elegant suit and clean shaven, and appears as a total contradiction of the orthodox husband. Jewish women in Poland were increasingly independent in romantic life, and fictionalized stories and cartoons criticizing *laykhtzinike froyen* (thoughtless women) who betrayed their husbands underscored male anxieties about growing female sexual freedom. These cartoons reveal male Jewish fears of inadequacy and weakness in the context of an evolving gender order. Dozens of other cartoons depicted Orthodox Jewish men with peyot failing at fulfilling the role of provider, lover, or family father.

Particularly summers spent at suburban cottages were thought to be a space where women were unfaithful to their husbands who stayed in the city. These stories linked Jewish women's affairs with other men with their consumption of leisure services. In one story, stylized as a wife's letter to her husband, the wife reports from the resort of Krynica and speaks of her *powodzenie* (popularity) with men and about the "Hasids, Germans, and Litvaks" lying in front of her.[133] Women in the resort appeared to attract the attention of adult and adolescent men, who literally "ate them with their eyes."[134] In another satirical text, a certain "faithful Zośka" reported from the spa town of Świder to her husband that the local social games included male-female couples hiding in the barn and adolescent boys running after girls into the forest.[135] At the same time, urban men were portrayed as having affairs with their servants while their wives were vacationing. A man featured in the story "Az man shikt s'vayb keyn Ciechocinek" (A man sends his wife to Ciechocinek) was "a soft Jewish man with a rich pocket, a fat wife, a daughter, and a beautiful servant."[136] Paying for his wife's holidays in the spa town of Ciechocinek, he created for himself a space for sexual affairs with the servant. Satirical texts about Jewish women having affairs illustrate a male fear of free female sexuality and loosening bonds of patriarchal masculine power. Men who attempted to upheld bourgeois masculinities based on male providing and heterosexual monogamy experienced major challenges in retaining their gender identity and patriarchal domination.

Next to cartoons that presented the sexual emancipation of Jewish men, many Polish-Jewish media outlets celebrated female professional achievements at home and abroad. The women's weekly *Ewa* printed stories of accomplished women, and illustrated magazine *Velt-shpigl* included a section on *froyen-derfolgen*, or women's successes. However, in times of growing emancipation of women, traditionalist voices also appeared in Poland that criticized the way notions of femininity and masculinity were evolving. Emancipation posed the danger that distinctions between the male and the female would disappear. One satirical text featured a woman "with a male head"—that is, a woman who "plays cards when a player is missing, rolls a cigarette when one needs one, when one needs to give a speech, she is ready to speak, when one needs to rule, she rules."[137] This model of a new Jewish woman was increasing the anxiety around new gender roles. Men's journals, for their part, criticized what they saw as the effeminacy of men who were apathetic and passive in public matters that traditionally were a male sphere and more active in female-associated realms of entertainment and romance.[138] Conservatives mobilized both men and women to return to the traditional gender order.

One of the Polish-Jewish women who called for a return to the traditional gender division was Klara Lewin. Lewin criticized how gender roles had changed after World War I and argued that strong and independent women were not happy since men naturally searched for women who were obedient and submissive. She inferred, "We long for the times of knighthood. The chivalric spirit still lives in us. A man's chivalric relationship to a woman was a normal expression of the will to fight for a beloved woman. Both the man and the woman enjoyed this game, since he behaved as a man should behave, and she reacted as a woman should react."[139] Lewin continued arguing that contemporary men had less *lebenslust* (love of life) and added that men's preoccupation with social and political questions resulted in "men adopting a passive role toward women." Klara Lewin underscored that "even the cleverest woman wants to be ruled by a man and look up to him" and that men need the feeling of conquering women to succeed in other fields of life. These conservative voices about gender expectations toward men attempted to reinstate traditional gender relations, which were increasingly questioned by the young generation of Polish Jews. While Lewin hoped to recreate the "lost" gender order, her diagnosis concerning masculinities was compatible with criticism emerging from the cartoons and satirical papers: Jewish men struggled to come to terms with new social and cultural dynamics that translated into apathy, anxiety, and failures.

CONCLUSION

Jewish consumption in 1920s and 1930s Poland revealed the growing tension between the previous ideal of a middle-class man as a breadwinner, who embodied the values of enterprise and temperate respectability, and the new model of a consuming male subject. The earlier model put forth the ideal of hardworking masculinity, which dictated that men should deny themselves in order to provide for their wives and children.[140] The emancipation of women after World War I, which undermined traditional notions of masculinity (such as heroism and bravery), along with the economic crisis that crushed the idea of the man as the sole breadwinner, all made traditional men anxious about their status. However, wealth, personal accomplishment, and business achievement remained valid markers of masculinity in interwar Poland, while men were called to embrace additional qualities and values to adapt to the new era. Benefiting from a pattern of later marriage, bachelors in particular were called to find themselves in a culture that gave more freedoms to women, strengthened domesticity, and challenged previously all-male realms.

Jewish masculinities in Poland were part and parcel of these Western transformations. Jewish journals defined men as consumers, and producers of goods and services quickly recognized the economic potential in approaching men and developed advertising strategies geared specifically toward men. They created a message merging practicality, technology, health, and sex appeal to cater to heterosexual men who searched for anchors of masculinity in times of economic and gender transition. Since consumption was so strongly linked to femininity, it was risky territory for men who hoped to establish a solid, stable masculinity.

Jewish and non-Jewish journals orchestrated a masculinity defined through the consumption of fashion, cars, pastimes, and products that would improve men's health while making sure not to undermine their masculinity but rather enhance their robust heterosexual vigor. The salaried and petite bourgeois Jewish man fit in with general Polish and European tendencies, rather than presenting an exception.

The evolution of masculinity models was accompanied by changing gender relations between men and women. The traditional ideal of the man as the provider was increasingly criticized as inadequate and at odds with the needs of the modern Jewish woman. As women were searching for men who cherished shared free time, consumption, and romance, more traditional men felt increasingly anxious about their wives striking up flirtations with other men. The growing incongruity between men and women became a topic of countless cartoons in Yiddish and Polish Jewish media outlets, and Orthodox men in particular turned into a subject of mockery. Men who held on to the earlier ideal of the husband-provider faced difficulties embracing new practices and virtues that they perceived as effeminate. In this context, Jewish Poland witnessed more conservative voices calling for a return to the old gender order.

SEVEN

HOMOSEXUAL MASCULINITIES

Between Crime, Progressive Calls, and Homophobic Subversion

IN 1926, A FIFTEEN-YEAR-OLD POLISH Jew named Józef Halperin dreamed about building a life in Palestine with his sweetheart, Olek. At the time, homosexuality was not only a social taboo in Poland but also a crime punished by the Austrian laws then still in force in Halperin's home city of Lviv. While young Józef Halperin desired Olek, who was also Jewish, he was very aware that their affection needed to be kept secret from family and friends. Halperin wrote explicitly about his love to Olek and was familiar with the term *homosexual* but felt reluctant to use it to describe his sexuality. Halperin's writings illustrate his nascent homosexual subjectivity: he experienced himself as a sexual being, was aware of his sexual desire, and began to build an identity around being a man attracted to men.[1] His memoir demonstrates how homosexual desire was entangled with a vision of male friendship centered around emotional and physical bonding. Within the normative friendship between two young men, Halperin sought to create a space for a relationship defined by tenderness, jealousy, and same-sex love. Halperin's case also shows how the notion of homosexuality became widespread not only among cultured elites but also among regular young Polish Jews like Józef and Olek.

The secrecy and shame that Józef Halperin linked with homo-sexuality were omnipresent in the experiences of homosexual men in interwar Poland. Polish-Jewish homosexual masculinities in the 1920s and 1930s developed within a framework that com-bined what David M. Halperin called pre-homosexual categories, namely effeminacy, active sodomy or pederasty, friendship or male love, and passivity or inversion, with modern homosexual subjectivities.[2] Polish medical experts and yellow newspapers approached, with increasing interest, what was then often called *pederastja* (pederasty) or *zboczenie* (sexual deviation) rather than homosexuality, and men attracted to men were socially os-tracized. Jews and non-Jews in Poland approached male homo-sexuality in a twofold manner: either as a criminal affair or as something one needed to hide from the outer world—or both. Moreover, in a social context that discriminated against Jews, heterosexual Polish-Jewish men developed homophobic strate-gies that attempted to marginalize homosexual men and, in so doing, stabilize their fragile heteronormative masculinity. I sug-gest that Jewish and non-Jewish approaches toward homosexual masculinities in Poland were to a great extent analogous and had similar roots and should thus be discussed together. Within the Polish debates, homosexuality and Jewishness rarely appeared to be mutually constitutive. Jewish difference in Poland was very visible in language and attire and often proudly displayed by Jew-ish men and women. In that context, the Christian majority usu-ally did not resort to effeminizing Jews in order to exclude them and mark them as homosexual and thus other.

In late nineteenth-century Germany, Jewishness and homo-sexuality had parallel and interlocking histories, and gentile het-erosexual bourgeois masculinity was fashioned around these two "countertypes."[3] Local thinkers such as Karl Heinrich Ulrichs spoke about "female souls in male bodies" or "half-men" when they addressed human phenomena that we today locate somewhere along the nonheteronormative spectrum. The emancipation of

Jews coincided with the emancipation of homosexuals, so anti-semitic and liberal imaginations reached a level of phantasmic associations between the two groups.[4] Jews and non-Jews in Poland who were familiar with German culture were aware of German discussions around sexuality and Jewishness. For instance, Hans Blüher's theory of "sexual inversion" and Otto Weininger's ideas of Jewish and female inferiority attracted significant attention in Poland.[5] Like in Germany, homosexuals in Poland often appeared effeminate, wearing makeup or cross-dressing. This was the case of male prostitutes who "moved in the feminine way and imitated female voice" as they actively searched for clients on the streets of Warsaw.[6] In the late 1930s, the Polish Far Right sometimes attempted to link Jewishness and homosexuality. In 1939, Alfred Łaszowski, a writer and member of the radical Obóz Narodowo-Radykalny (National Radical Camp), complained that Warsaw homosexuals were at the front of solidarity with Polish Jews.[7] However, beyond the radical Right, the linking of Jewish men with homosexuals that prevailed in Germany did not find stable ground in Poland and did not translate into a coherent associative framework.

Early twentieth-century Poland did not see as many organized forms of homosexual lifestyles and sociabilities as Germany, but homosexual subjectivities did begin to emerge in Poland as well.[8] In Germany the scale of homosexual infrastructures and homosexual subjectivities channelled into anxieties and resistance among the general society, whereas in Poland the weak visibility produced a weaker opposition.[9] Poland decriminalized consensual sex between men in 1932, while in Germany and much of western Europe, it remained penalized well into the post–World War II era.[10] Large Polish cities featured cruising areas, bars, and cafés frequented by the homosexual public but lacked homosexual organizations and media outlets. Queer life in Warsaw in the 1920s and early 1930s appears to have been more integrated in the mainstream culture without a clear division between queers and heterosexuals.[11] We can speculate whether the early depenalization in Poland might have contributed to a lower need for self-organization and separation. Nevertheless, the invisibility of openly homosexual men had a much more complex background. There are no accounts of specifically Jewish forms of organized homosexual sociability.

This chapter reconstructs how Jews in interwar Poland approached the issue of male homosexuality, in particular how homosexuality became entangled with Polish-Jewish notions of masculinity. Though my access to first-person narratives was very limited, I was able to locate a memoir by Józef Halperin—a young homosexual Jew who struggled with his same-sex desire—as well as the personal letters of Józef Rajnfeld—a Warsaw-born homosexual and Jewish painter. Additionally, I analyze court testimonies of Jewish and non-Jewish men that include first-person narratives about same-sex sex. Instead of focusing on how Jewishness and homosexuality were imagined in non-Jewish representations, I shift the focus to the Jewish perspective and show how, in a world defined by antisemitism and homophobia, Jewish actors articulated their own positions and ideas. My study demonstrates that 1930s Poland saw the emergence of the language of modern homosexual subjectivity. Jewish men were a part of this development but only rarely conceptualized their Jewishness and homosexuality as mutually constitutive. Figures such as Mordechai Langer from Prague—who constructed modern homosexual Jewish identities, battled antisemitism within the emerging homosexual movement, and argued that same-sex desire was at the heart of Judaism—were an exception and not the rule.[12] It was more commonly the case that the "intersectional invisibility" of homosexual Jewish subjectivities defined the social reality of early twentieth-century Poland.[13] The marginalized masculinity of homosexual men was an anxious one, and these men maneuvered to maintain an illusion of heterosexuality that allowed them to benefit from the patriarchal dividend, that is the advantage men gain from their dominance in society. Moreover, I demonstrate that by placing homosexuality outside of the social norm, some Polish Jews attempted to present Jewishness as free of what was then considered a homosexual malady.

I start by offering an overview of expert discussions, fore-grounding input from Jewish doctors and lawyers, concerning homosexuality in Poland. The next section explores how Polish-Jewish debates placed homosexual men within a semantic realm of deviation and crime and established a category of marginalized homosexual masculinity. Next to press reports, I rely on criminal trials involving homosexual men. Taking into account its judicial character, this type of source demands particular care when judging the statements with regard to their underlying perspectives and intentions. This section emphasizes how medical knowledge began to influence societal approaches and how Jews and non-Jews defined a homosexual man as a sexual predator threatening heterosexual masculinity through seduction. Then, I offer a close reading of a memoir written by Józef Halperin, a young Jewish homosexual man. Halperin's case demonstrates how changing notions of male friendship created opportunities for men attracted to men and how nascent homosexual subjectivities began to emerge in 1920s Poland. In the final section, analyzing a number of articles from the Jewish press, I underscore how Polish-Jewish men employed homophobic discourses about Muslims and German Nazis to stabilize their fragile heteronormative masculinities.

POLAND, HOMOSEXUALITY, AND
THE JEWS: AN OVERVIEW

In the Polish-Jewish popular discourse of the 1920s and 1930s, men attracted to men were often considered criminals and deviants who negatively transgressed societal, medical, and legal boundaries. In that highly homophobic time and place, homosexuality appeared as a pathological sexual behavior, not a sexual orientation, and hence police reports jointly discussed homosexuality, incest, bigamy, and prostitution. The association of homosexuality with crime and deviation was a product of hegemonic medical and legal prescriptions that aimed to suppress homosexual desire and regulated the lives of homosexual individuals.[14] The exact spread of ideas related to homosexuality in Poland is difficult to trace and was rather uneven. Though the press and prominent cultural figures used the word *homosexuality*, the average reader was probably unfamiliar with the concepts behind this notion. Unlike medical and legal authorities who followed pathologizing interpretations of homosexual desire, regular men and women sometimes took a much more nuanced approach and occasionally even acknowledged the validity of a commitment between two men.[15]

Before Poland introduced its own penal code in 1932, the homophobic regulations of Russia, Austro-Hungary, and Prussia were still valid in the country after its independence in 1918. This meant that in Warsaw, the 1903 Russian penal code was in force, in which paragraph 516 concerning homosexuality was placed within the notorious section 27 (prostitution and procurement) together with pedophilia, incest, and rape. In parts of Poland that belonged to Prussia before 1918, the infamous paragraph 175 penalized homosexual relations between men. In former Galicia, the Austro-Hungarian penal code—with its paragraph 129 criminalizing "widernatürlicher Unzucht," or "counternatural fornification"—was enforced. These laws considered homosexual intercourse between men a sexual offence, and until 1932, the Polish courts—still following Russian, Prussian, and Austro-Hungarian regulations—sentenced dozens of homosexual men each year. In 1925, courts sentenced fifteen men for "lewd acts, *pederastja, sodomja*," in the Warsaw region, sixteen in the Białystok region, twenty-two in the Lublin region, and twenty-four in the Lviv region (there, specifically for pederastja and sodomja).[16] Sometimes, like in one case from 1922 involving

Kraków dentist Aleksander Skuta, courts sentenced men for "public indecency," not homosexuality.[17] The Polish Police included a vice brigade (Brygada Obyczajowa) that was responsible for homosexuality along with other sex-related cases.

The logic behind depenalizing homosexuality in newly independent Poland in 1932 was complex and can be summarized as a consequence of some progressive legal and medical theories that had spread among the small group of Polish experts who designed the new penal code, along with their desire to project an image of Poland as a modern nation, in opposition to the imperial powers that had partitioned the country earlier.[18] The experts who prepared the new Polish penal code, such as the head of the codification committee, Julian Makarewicz, embraced the progressive legal and psychiatric proposals concerning homosexuality. At the beginning of the 1930s, when the depenalization of homosexuality was being discussed in Poland, several articles in widely read dailies addressed different aspects of homosexuality.[19] While this medical and legal knowledge first emerged in western Europe, only in Poland did the political circumstances allow for the decriminalization of consensual sex between men as early as the 1930s.

The inter-European circulation of medical and legal knowledge included not only its progressive dimension but also positions that defined homosexuality as a disease and a social problem. Lawyers and psychiatrists in Poland were embedded in repressive international discourses around homosexuality and promulgated these via popular science. Numerous international works were translated into both Polish and Yiddish and also reached traditional and religious segments of the local Jewish community.[20] As early as 1876, Catholic doctor Konstanty Grodzki warned that male anal sex was "animalization in search of sexual satisfaction."[21] In 1911, the Polish translation of Friedrich Wilhelm Foerster's book brought to Polish discussions the idea of homosexuality as a "monstrosity" and of homosexuals who "permanently seek to subdue and seduce a normal man."[22] Sexological discourse in Poland accepted the Western idea of inborn and acquired homosexuality that translated into sexual behaviors. For example, the 1930 translation of a French book on "pervert love" claimed that "when the pervert practices homosexuality from birth, he never abandons the passive role."[23] Such books and their translations into Polish and Yiddish brought to Poland a medicalized homophobic discourse concerning homosexuality. One of the few exceptions was psychiatrist Stanisław Mikulski, who in 1920 was one of the first Polish scholars to define homosexuality as a sexual orientation and called for its depenalization in newly independent Poland.[24]

With time, medical and legal ideas about an active "true homosexual" and his heterosexual victim translated into judicial practice. Some men in homosexuality trials attempted to present themselves as heterosexuals who had fallen victim to "truly" homosexual men. These men used the trope of "the homosexual predator and his straight victim" and attempted to prove their innocence in criminal trials. Stanisław Pańczyszyn, a twenty-seven-year-old waiter from Kraków, admitted in his 1937 testimony that he had engaged in sex with Gustaw Galos in a number of Kraków hotels but described himself as a victim of Galos, who had taken advantage of him. Even though Pańczyszyn was an adult man, he noted the significant age difference between him and Galos and revealed how Galos threatened to reveal to his friends and employer that "he gives himself" to another man.[25] Similarly, in a trial against Wawrzyniec Sikora from Kraków, the prosecutor and judge perceived Sikora as a "true homosexual" while his adolescent and homeless sex partners were "forced into prostitution."[26] These examples emphasize how the figure of a homosexual predator—a figure then already widely acknowledged among legal and medical experts—appeared as a mechanism used by homosexual men who hoped to be released from charges in homosexuality trials. At the same time, this strategy stabilized heterosexuality as the only valid form of male sexual desire that was recognized even by marginalized homosexual men.

In interwar Poland, some men had a well-developed sense of homosexual desire and had formed homosexual subjectivities. Some homosexual men in Poland reached out to dailies and magazines in search of sexual, romantic, or life companions. In 1929, the magazine *Ilustrowany Kurjer Codzienny* published a call from a man who wanted "to surround with a son-like or brotherly feeling a man of unusual character, cultured, who with a bit of financial support and possibly also shelter for several months would help me to accomplish my musical studies in Kraków, Warsaw, or Lviv. I am young, handsome, have a pleasant appearance."[27] Other editions included notes like "handsome man seeks a soulmate"[28] or the ad by a man hiding behind the pseudonym of "Wilde"—perhaps referring to the English writer and coded homosexual icon Oscar Wilde—searching for a "cultured, intelligent, financially independent friend."[29] In the early 1930s, big cities in Poland featured a homosexual scene with regular meeting places, and the men's magazine *Współczesny Pan* (Contemporary gentleman) initiated a debate about homosexuality, printing the voices of homosexual men who were calling for more tolerance. Homosexual men who took part in these early efforts sought to carve a niche for themselves within Polish notions of gender and sexuality. This is when terms such as *mniejszości seksualne* (sexual minorities) spread out around Poland's cultured classes and when homosexual men were first defined as a community.

Polish Jews largely shared the same fixed ideas about homosexuality as their non-Jewish neighbors, and the same was true for progressive medical discourses. Jewish doctor Paweł Klinger, using Mikulski's arguments from the 1920s, was one of the key advocates for normalizing homosexuality in 1930s Poland. Klinger underscored that "from the biological point of view, you can say anything about them [homosexual men], but not that they are committing a crime."[30] Klinger declared, on the topic of homosexuality, that "no one's interests are violated—neither an individual nor the society suffers if two adult people have intimate relations upon mutual consent."[31] Klinger progressively argued that any problems homosexual men faced were in fact related to homophobia and the criminalization of homosexuality. Klinger pointed out that homosexuality-related blackmail, suicides, fake marriage, and homosexual prostitution were not related to homosexual desire itself but were a consequence of the social oppression that homosexual men encountered. Klinger called the oppressive measures against homosexuals "atrocities," even while still referring to homosexuality using the derogative term *zboczenie* (deviation), which was common at the time when writing about homosexuals. The following present his opinions on the subject:

> The lion's share of homosexuals are completely normal and healthy in body and spirit, despite the generally accepted opinion that a pederast is a degenerate, a criminal, etc. A closer examination demonstrates that homosexuals do not show any signs of degeneration or hereditary burden; they are people no different than any normal human being. If they show a certain nervousness later in life, it is only as an outcome of negative attitudes toward them from the side of law and public opinion.[32]

> Nothing oppresses the unfortunate *urnings* [homosexuals] more than the terrible odium of the public opinion, which has for them an ineffable hatred and contempt, even more than for the worst criminal offender, including sexual murderers. This phenomenon [of homophobia] is psychologically incomprehensible. Society has a lot of sympathy for the murderer when it sees him defenseless in court, is interested in his further fate, and expresses a certain, admittedly unhealthy, curiosity about him even if he is the most dangerous sadist. However, when it comes to a homosexual, disgust and contempt—these are the feelings of normal people toward this unfortunate man.[33]

> Meanwhile, it is the duty of enlightened people and scientists to fight the public opinion that is unfair to homosexuals, and this

can only be done by making society's masses aware of the essence of this problem as far as possible.[34]

In the face of the oppression that homosexual men experienced daily in Poland, Klinger believed that the task of the "enlightened classes and medical experts" was to provide the wider society with medically verified knowledge. Due to his acculturated background, the Łódź doctor did not focus much on questions of Jewish identity. Like the German-Jewish doctor and homosexual activist Magnus Hirschfeld, Paweł Klinger also concentrated on homosexuality itself and did not imply any particular link between Jews and homosexuals.[35] However, Klinger engaged in proliferating his progressive ideas about sexuality through several Jewish media outlets, such as *Nasz Przegląd* (Our review). His work *Vita sexualis: Prawda o życiu płciowym człowieka* (Vita sexualis: The truth about human sexual life) was republished several times in the 1930s. Calls by Jewish and non-Jewish experts like Klinger indeed led to the decriminalization of homosexuality in Poland, and this progressive understanding of homosexuality spread around Poland and reached parts of its Jewry. However, Klinger's work still had a limited impact and largely did not transform the oppressive Polish-Jewish discourses around homosexuality.

Jews across Poland discussed the major legal reform and the 1932 depenalization of homosexuality. In 1934, Alfred Klaften, a medical student in Lviv, offered a lecture on homosexuality and discussed the topic with his fellow Jewish students.[36] In 1936, the Yiddish daily *Unzer tsaytung* noted that "as is well known, the new penal code does not punish engaging in homosexual acts. This, however, refers only to when a homosexual uses his abnormal sexual proclivity with adults of legal age."[37] The yellow Warsaw Jewish daily *5ta rano* presented the legal change as one of many legal measures that reflected the social change and served to "remove the unneeded ballast [of the law on citizens' lives]." The daily commented, "The authors of the new law adopted the view that pederasty is not an atrocity but a disease, and that pederasts are not harmful to anyone."[38] The news of the decriminalization of homosexuality also reached provincial cities such as Rivne in Podolia. Haim Sheptil, who was an advocate trainee there, disclosed in a long article to local Jews the changes brought by the new penal code. Concerning the depenalization of homosexuality, Sheptil wrote, "Also, homosexuality is not a crime according to the new penal code. The only exception is when the abnormal homosexual sex relations are performed for profit." While Sheptil agreed that homosexuality was "nothing else but an abnormal sexual desire," he welcomed the idea that same-sex intercourse for profit would be penalized as a criminal felony.[39]

Such examples demonstrate how the modernization of the Polish legal order reached Jewish citizens as well. Even though Paweł Klinger and other Jewish authors hoped to inspire less repressive attitudes, sometimes even supportive Jewish contributors still continued to use discriminatory language.[40] For example, the author of the 1928 *Nowy Dziennik* article that reflected on Magnus Hirschfeld's progressive attitude toward homosexuality did not refrain from using exclusionary vocabulary. Even though he was sympathetic toward homosexuals, he still perceived of them within a context of deviation, writing that Hirschfeld "allowed [us] to understand the tragedy of people suffering from sexual deviations."[41] Even though homosexuality was no longer considered a crime after 1932, for the majority of Polish Jews, homosexuality still remained outside the social norm. Even after the depenalization, the Jewish press in Poland proliferated the idea of homosexuality as a crime, and homosexual men struggled to find a framework for their romantic and sexual desires.

HOMOSEXUAL MEN AS "DEVIANTS" AND "CRIMINALS"

In the early 1930s, a yeshiva student using the pseudonym HBD wrote in his memoir about the time he told his sister of a romantic and sexual relationship he had previously had with another young Jewish man. Twenty-one-year-old HBD lived in a small town near Białystok in eastern Poland. Religious Jewish men like HBD, who had less access to popular scientific discourses that transmitted knowledge about human sexuality, explored the ways homosexual desire could be placed within a pre-homosexual framework of a regular friendship between men. In his autobiography, HBD mentioned a seventeen-year-old man who "fell in love with him," accompanied him everywhere, caressed him, and "covered his face with kisses." While HBD pointed out that he was not knowledgeable about sex, he underscored that he "was subconsciously attracted to him." HBD turned into his "closest" and called their relationship love (albeit in quotation marks). HBD continued to exchange letters with his lover and suffered whenever they were apart, and they switched to another yeshiva where, according to HBD's account, "love seemed more important to them than learning."[42] Using words typical for the yeshiva setting ("my closest," "my dearest," *mayn noenster* or *mayn trayster*), the author framed his feelings within a vocabulary of nonromantic male affection that he knew from the yeshiva.[43]

HBD's sister was not understanding of his feelings, and her reaction probably led to a major change concerning how HBD understood his romantic and sexual life. With the passage of time, HBD began to see his sexuality as deviating from the norm and himself as a victim of homosexual seduction. His relationship ended. Recalling their "sexual orgies in the depth of the forest," HBD called his partner a "degenerate" and emphasized that the man was three years older than him.[44] For HBD, homosexuality now appeared to be "infectious," and, reflecting on his sex with other men, he called it "the period of boiling sin" and "unnatural desire."[45] HBD was now armed with homophobic arguments and sought to "liberate" himself from homosexuality, but he continued to have sexual relationships with men. HBD spoke of his inability to control his "burning desire," while he carried on with hugging and kissing another young man in the Kletsk yeshiva.[46] When his new lover abruptly left the yeshiva, HBD believed that their relationship was the reason he left. HBD's reaction demonstrated that he was already aware that homosexuality was a major social taboo not only in the yeshiva but in Poland in general. Later, HBD developed relationships with women and probably forced himself into heteronormativity.

HBD's example demonstrates that homosexual Orthodox Jewish men in Poland might have been unfamiliar with the latest discourses around homosexuality, even when they were actively involved in homosexual relations. In that way, his experience might have been similar to the experience of one Polish peasant who, in the early 1920s, claimed before a court that he presumed that men could have sex with each other.[47] HBD's case elucidates how young Jewish Orthodox men searched for opportunities to develop same-sex romantic and sexual relationships within a Jewish religious environment. HBD's memoirs reveal that he and his partner formed a same-sex relationship based on romantic love and mutual sexual attraction. However, as knowledge about homosexuality reached within the walls of his yeshiva, HBD began to conceptualize his desire as a sin and a deviation. His biography demonstrates that while he initially believed that his love was something pure and beautiful, he later saw his sexual desire as breaking social and cultural norms and hoped to repress it. Echoing the tropes familiar in repressive legal and medical discourses in Poland, he blamed his partner for "seducing" him and "infecting" him with homosexuality, depicting himself as both a victim and a heterosexual.

Autobiographies of young Jewish men include Jewish-produced repressive narratives on homosexuality. One of the few firsthand accounts concerning homosexual desire was Der Stormer's autobiography submitted for the YIVO autobiography contest in 1939.[48] Der Stormer, who grew up in a small town near Łódź, wrote of his yeshiva companions who engaged in sexual activity while sleeping with him in the same bed. While he felt very comfortable beside the two young men, the moment he noticed them having sex was the end of their close relationship. The men attempted to invite Der Stormer to join them, yet he refused: not because he did not want to, but because "I was still young and had little understanding of those things." Writing in retrospect, Der Stormer considered the homosexual attraction between the two men, and its direct and public expression, "a homosexual madness." Der Stormer's reaction demonstrates that as an Orthodox young man in 1930s Poland, he knew what homosexuality was, had internalized homophobia, and believed that sex between men was beyond the social norm.

A similar approach defining homosexuality as a perversion appears in A. Greyno's autobiography from 1934. Writing of the late 1920s and his neighbor named Yosele, Greyno called the neighbor "a homosexual with a vain, suggestive manner" and underscored that Yosele used to dress in a bizarre way to attract attention from everyone. This memoir is one of the sources where we learn about a Jew accused of same-sex desire toward Jewish adolescents. In Greyno's memoir, Yosele appeared as a madman who "lured boys of my age and exploited them for his homosexual purposes." In Greyno's narrative, homosexuality, pedophilia, and madness all merge into one, and Greyno defined Yosele's sexual preferences as "a perversion." His account was exemplary for the blurred discursive borders between homosexuality and pedophilia typical for the 1920s.[49] Connecting homosexuality with mental illnesses, Greyno referred to medical discourses that relocated homosexual men from the prison to the psychiatric ward.[50] Yosele's homosexuality did not appear as an external influence that destabilized the normative Jewish world but instead appeared as almost organic to the small-town Jewish community in a shtetl close to Kielce. Yosele might have been a shtetl example of lower-class homosexuality that openly played with femininity though extravagant accessories and female dress.[51] He was not a member of the metropolitan artistic bohemia that in the early twentieth century was identified with homosexuality but rather a man from a small Polish-Jewish town.

While HBD left a detailed account of his struggle as a homosexual, the lives of other Polish-Jewish homosexual men were mediated only through isolated media reports. In 1927, Khaye Anter informed the Warsaw police that her nineteen-year-old son, Aren, had left home, taken his mother's jewels, and vanished into thin air. The police launched an investigation and reached the conclusion that Aren Anter had been arrested with a large group of homosexuals. Anter's arrest was part of a major roundup of Warsaw vice police against the local homosexual scene. The police arrested men looking for same-sex pleasure around Warsaw's main train station and in gay cafés in the city center. The Yiddish daily *Der Moment* described the group of arrested homosexual men as "a gang of degenerates."[52] The daily portrayed the men as particularly prone to crime—not only were they homosexuals, but they had also forged identity documents and were probably assisting in female trafficking. Jewish media across eastern Europe commonly spoke of homosexual men as criminals, degenerates, and psychopaths. Such demonizing depictions were in line with non-Jewish portrayals that, commenting on the 1927 arrests, spoke of "disgusting dives" where homosexuals gathered and described young homosexuals as prostitutes immersed in the "swamp of the capital."[53]

Throughout the 1920s and 1930s, homosexuality remained semantically linked with crime, and the decriminalization of homosexual intercourse in 1932 hardly changed the broader societal approach. The Jewish press participated in proliferating a repressive sexual understanding of homosexuality. In 1934, the Yiddish daily *Haynt* reported how a young man accused postal clerk Henryk Zalewski of seducing him for several years and "forcing youths into homosexuality."[54] Importantly, as the title suggested, the defendant was supposedly tried "for homosexuality," implying that even within the new legal order, the public opinion perceived homosexuality as a crime. Following the request of the defendant, the court commissioned a sexologist to verify whether the young plaintiff was not homosexual himself. By reporting on the sexologist involved in the trial, the Yiddish daily embraced the dominant logic at that time in Poland: homosexuality was a medical condition and decriminalized but still needed to be repressed since a relationship between two men resembled prostitution or sexual exploitation. The idea of mutual same-sex attraction and affection had not yet gained any traction in society.

Both before and after the legal reform, the Yiddish media in Poland promulgated the idea that homosexuality was a form of promiscuity and a flawed form of sexuality that led to both crime and sexually transmitted diseases. When Antoni Kuchta was arrested in Warsaw in 1934, the Yiddish daily *Der Moment* called him "a degenerate" who had not only had sex with *yinglekh un manslayt* (boys and men) but also infected them with sexual diseases. "Degenerate" became one of the nicknames for homosexual men, although it could also refer to pedophiles and sexual murderers. For *Der Moment* journalists, it was clear that as a homosexual, Kuchta was "a degenerate" even before the trial. While the daily reported that sixteen men had accused Kuchta, it was only Kuchta himself who appeared as "a degenerate homosexual," while the men who had engaged in sex with him were depicted as victims of his evil desire who were "lured into his apartment under different excuses."[55] *Der Moment* relied on the powerful image of a homosexual predator and presented Kuchta as destroying the health and morality of the young men he allegedly seduced.

The 1936 story of Kazimierz Radkiewicz demonstrates how the Yiddish press defined homosexual men as particularly prone to crime.[56] In 1936, the Yiddish daily *Unzer Express* ran a story of a man stabbed in Łódź by his homosexual lover. Radkiewicz presumably ran away to Łódź from his hometown of Żyrardów to escape the "trap" of the homosexual. Within the stereotype of the "brutal homosexual," young men were particularly vulnerable to homosexual aggression. The man who stabbed Radkiewicz appeared as a sex criminal (*seksueler farbrekher*) even though stabbing was not a form of sexualized violence. The newspaper transposed the sexual nature of the relationship between the two men into the criminal act of stabbing. Underscoring the violence of the relationship between the two men, *Unzer Express* strengthened the association between homosexuality and crime. Since Jews and non-Jews in Poland struggled to find the vocabulary to describe homosexual relationships, journalists often presented sexual or romantic relations between men using heteronormative terms. Reporting on Radkiewicz, the Yiddish daily wrote that Radkiewicz was a *kokhanke* (a Yiddish term for a female lover) of the stabber. *Unzer Express* relied on the prevailing theory of active homosexuals and their passive victims and rendered only one of the men as a homosexual, while the second was his kokhanke. Homosexual men appeared to overstep the limits of normative masculinity and, perceived as women-like, were moved to the margins of masculinity.

The Yiddish media in Poland commonly conflated homosexuality with pedophilia. When an eighteen-year-old man from Warsaw supposedly raped a five-year-old boy, the Yiddish newspaper report repeated the popular belief that the young child had been seduced by a malevolent homosexual. A title reading just "Homosexuality" blurred the distinction between the sexual orientation and the criminal act against the minor.[57] A similar rhetoric appeared in the Jewish *Nowy Dziennik* report about a certain Janek M. who had allegedly raped a five-year-old boy. While the "pervert's sick instincts" were directed against a minor, the daily chose to emphasize the perpetrator's homosexuality.[58] The title again suggested that the crime was not the rape of a minor but rather the homosexuality itself. In a 1929 case from Chełm, a nineteen-year-old Christian man named Stanisław Sitarz was tried for attempting to rape a Jewish teenager named Wolf Pech.[59]

The local Yiddish newspaper emphasized the nonconsensual nature of the sexual act by the river and the young age of the Jewish adolescent. While both Sitarz and the Jewish teenager engaged in the sexual act, the Yiddish daily recognized only the older man as homosexual. Such cases demonstrate that, for Poland's Jewish media, it was not the homosexual act itself but being prone to sexual violence that defined one as a homosexual.

The case of Sitarz and Pech is one of the few available criminal trial records that help us trace how not only the Jewish media but also involved men, representatives of the Polish judiciary, and witnesses spoke about homosexual desires and practices. After Sitarz was spotted by a local and later arrested, the police officer from Chełm wrote to the prosecutor in Lublin that Sitarz had "attempted to commit an act of pederasty" with Pech. The Jewish teenager himself spoke about Sitarz's violence at the riverside and his attempt to commit anal rape. Sitarz did not acknowledge that he had "committed acts of pederasty with Wolf Pech" but described the accusation as "Pech's maliciousness." Using the word *pederasty* did not essentially prove Sitarz's familiarity with the notion but was most likely a repetition of the vocabulary used by the interrogator. While Sitarz was probably sexually attracted to men, the only description he used was the legal term of *pederasty*. Pech's sexuality was not discussed at all. The court focused on the sexual violence and saw pederasty as its form. Pederasty appeared as something that one could commit and not as one's inherent feature or gender identity. The district court in Lublin sentenced Sitarz to a year in prison.[60]

The 1938 case of Józef Gruszczyński reveals how Christian and Jewish homosexual men began to form homosexual networks.[61] Twenty-six-year-old Gruszczyński, who was a worker in a factory owned by the Łódź Jewish industrial magnate Izrael Poznański, introduced an affluent Jewish man, Leon Waks, to young males who then had sex with Waks in Gruszczyński's apartment. Gruszczyński was accused of "facilitating prostitution" of young men for Waks and other men of means. While the court focused on Gruszczyński's alleged facilitating of prostitution, the Łódź case provides many details about Łódź's multiethnic homosexual milieu. Trial witnesses who had engaged in sex with Waks revealed that the YMCA swimming hall, football courts, Poniatowski park, and Malinowa and Europejska cafés were venues where they met Gruszczyński and other homosexuals and sometimes had sex. Catholic Gruszczyński, Jewish Waks, and dozens of younger and older Łódź men of different denominations were interconnected in a system of relations in which homosexual sex intersected with friendship and mutual affection mediated through gifts and time spent together. For instance, Gruszczyński used to visit one of his lovers during the holidays, and they took erotic photographs of each other.

Homosexual men involved in the Gruszczyński case began to construct homosexual subjectivities. Jewish Leon Waks spoke openly about his homosexuality: "What connected me with Gruszczyński was that concerning sexuality we liked the same thing." Also, Gruszczyński's sense of homosexual subjectivity was clear: "I had sex with some of the boys and often I am jealous [about them]," elsewhere adding that "he broke up" with some of the men he hung out with or that as a teenager, he had been humiliated due to being perceived as homosexual. During the hearings, Gruszczyński, following trending ideas about "acquiring homosexuality," stated that "he became homosexual seven years ago" and admitted that he had "introduced boys to men who practiced pederasty." Waks described Gruszczyński as his dear friend, and supporting him financially and introducing young men to each other seemed natural to him. In his appeal, Gruszczyński's lawyers underscored that precisely these shared "sexual preferences" made Gruszczyński facilitate Waks's meetings with other men. Gruszczyński and Waks appear as self-aware homosexual men who knew their own sexual desires

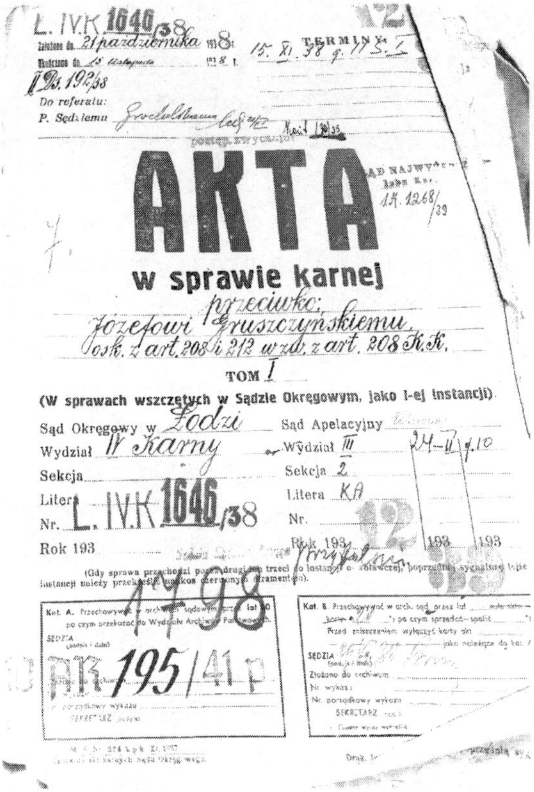
L. IV.K 1646/38
Do referatu:
P. Sędziemu
AKTA
w sprawie karnej
przeciwko:
Józefowi Gruszczyńskiemu,
osk. z art. 208 i 212 w zw. z art. 208 K.K.
TOM I
(W sprawach wszczętych w Sądzie Okręgowym, jako I-ej instancji).
Sąd Okręgowy w Łodzi
Wydział IV Karny
Sekcja
Litera
Nr. L. IV.K 1646/38
Rok 193
Sąd Apelacyjny
Wydział III
Sekcja 2
Litera KA
Nr.
Rok 193
1798
AR 195/41 p

Figure 7.1. File cover, Józef Gruszczyński 1938 homosexuality trial.

and established a network of homosexual men that facilitated consensual sexual encounters.

Gruszczyński was sentenced to three years in prison. The judges did not consider any form of homosexual networking to be legitimate and instead criminalized it as "facilitating prostitution." In the verdict we read, "It would be hard to believe that Gruszczyński would facilitate satisfying sexual desires [of Waks and other men] merely out of solidarity with other deviants." Homosexuality was, for the district court in Łódź, an "addiction," and for the appeals court in Warsaw, a "counter-natural fornication." The Warsaw court presented the case as though only Waks and Gruszczyński were homosexuals with "a deviant sexual drive" while their presumed victims were seduced heterosexuals. Male judges feared that the young men's characters might have been deformed through the interaction with "true homosexuals." This shows the preoccupation of heterosexual men with protecting what they saw as normative masculinity, which homosexual men supposedly put in danger. While the court intended to frame the relationship between homosexual men as one of procurement, one of the young men testified that he had engaged in sex with Gruszczyński "because it was pleasurable." The Gruszczyński case revealed that Jewish and Christian homosexuals in 1930s Łódź networked to establish a community of homosexual men and that their desire to form support alliances centered around sex and trust found little recognition among the outside world.

Jews in interwar Poland, both before and after the depenalization of homosexuality, conceptualized nonheteronormative sexual and romantic behavior as a criminal deviation from the gender norm. In a few cases where men discussed their homosexual subjectivities openly, the self-perception and the wider debate usually took a repressive approach intending to marginalize men who loved men. The Jewish media conflated homosexuality with sexual violence and pedophilia, and homosexual men needed to maneuver to find opportunities to embrace their sexual desire and have sexual and romantic relations with men. For the heterosexual majority, homosexual desire appeared to threaten the normative masculinity, and homosexual men were often accused of "seducing" seemingly heterosexual men. Against the backdrop of this oppressive and homophobic atmosphere, Jewish and non-Jewish homosexual men began to shape their homosexual subjectivities and develop a language to speak about their sexual identity in terms of same-sex love. One of these was a young Jew from Lviv, Józef Halperin.

JÓZEF HALPERIN AND ADOLESCENT
HOMOSEXUAL DESIRE

Józef Halperin's memoir from the years 1926–1932 is a unique source that offers insights into the inner world of a young Jewish man who struggled with his sexuality.[62] Halperin, born in 1911 in Lviv, spoke openly about his homosexual desire for a young man named Olek. Both Halperin and Olek were active in a Zionist youth organization, and the organization became a space for their exploration of romantic and sexual relations. While the relationship with Olek was the only homosexual relationship Halperin mentioned in his memoir, his attraction to the male physique was well defined. For example, Halperin was amazed at the beauty of a fellow *shomer* (member of a leftwing Zionist youth movement) with crow-black hair and shining eyes, an envoy from Palestine whom he described as *śliczny* (cute), and a boy with "wonderful lips" whom he saw in the hospital.[63] At the same time, Halperin was still exploring his sexuality, unsure whether he was attracted to men, women, or both. His coming-of-age narrative mixes Zionist ideals, questions about his adult life, and evolving notions of friendship and sexuality. In one entry, Halperin declared, "I would love to live with him [Olek] a national life in Eretz Israel."[64]

Halperin's diary reveals his passionate feelings for Olek, which he explicitly defined as love. In one entry, Halperin wrote openly, "Today I will write about my love to Olek."[65] The two young men spent a lot of their time together and engaged in intimate activities, including kissing and hugging. When on holidays in Zielona near Lviv, Halperin wrote, "I lie close to Olek and Olek lies close to me. We can embrace and kiss. Ho, how much I enjoy our kissing. . . . Sometimes I try to make Olek hug me and when he does not do it, I feel sad."[66] Even when Halperin began to understand that their relationship was nearing its end, he conceptualized them as a couple. He then asked Olek, "Do you want to break up with me (*zerwać ze mną*) completely?"[67] The thought of being abandoned filled Halperin with fear: "And if he won't come? What then? I lack any explanation, an abyss opens in front of me."[68] Speaking about his love to Olek and his need for same-sex intimacy, Halperin formulated his homosexual subjectivity. Particularly telling is a scene where Halperin visited an ill Olek at home. Their mutual attraction rose and almost ended in a feverish kiss. Halperin wrote,

> I sit and look at him. His face seems so cadaverous and tightened. His eyes are shining and throw a ray of light. Only now one can see his gorgeous big eyes; his entire face is shining from the feverish sweat. . . . I feel good when I sit next to him. I touch his hot hand, we hold our hands, we release them once his mother enters the room, but when she leaves, I notice that he is glad that he can again give me his hand to hold it. . . . We sit like that about half an hour and then his red lips . . . begin to pull me to kiss them. I bend and slowly place my hands on his hands and I feel a shiver. . . .
>
> Today I also visited him . . . we held our hands like yester-day and I looked into his eyes all the time, asking him in my thoughts: please look at me, I love you. And then my face got closer to his face, our lips were very near, and I already felt his breath and then suddenly I got up.[69]

This scene portrays two young males still unsure about their sexuality. Halperin decided to make the first move and initiated holding hands and yearned to kiss Olek. Though Olek did not initiate any sexual or romantic intimacy, he reciprocated, or at least consented to, Halperin's expressions of love and desire. However, in an earlier diary entry, Halperin suggests that Olek too initiated intimacy: "The thought of embracing him did not cross my mind and then suddenly I felt Olek's hand on my neck. I shivered but recalled that it was Olek lying close to me and I was extremely happy. I moved closer to him, he hugged me strongly and began to kiss me. I reciprocated his kisses and I would remember this until the end of my life."[70] While, in general, it was Halperin who expressed his homosexual desire, Olek seemed to enjoy exploring his sexuality along with his friend. Both young men used the opportunities that changing notions of male friendship offered them in 1920s Poland. While their relationship appeared, from the outside, to be a normative friendship between young men, from the inside, it was filled with same-sex tenderness and love.

Though sexuality played a major role for Halperin, he wanted to see his relationship with Olek not only in sexual terms but in romantic terms as well. Halperin repeated in his diary, "I love him, he loves me, we love each other," signaling that their love was mutual and emphasizing that love, not just sex, was the focal point of their relationship. In one entry, Halperin describes how they expressed their feelings: "All I can tell is that I love him for all he does. . . . The greatest evidence of his love for me and my love for him is holding hands on the street . . . I love, I love, I love."[71] Halperin's romantic involvement with Olek also expressed itself in his constant bouts of jealousy. When Olek greeted another boy with a friendly cheer, it was "heart-wrenching" for Halperin, and he described a jealousy he could not resist.[72] Halperin's love became visible in his permanent longing to be near Olek, and he could not sleep without his friend and lover.[73] Reflecting on his own feelings, Halperin wrote, "I always come to the same conclusion: I constantly long for something. For what? I don't know, possibly for Olek."[74] The relationship that Halperin intended to form with Olek was akin to the ideal of heterosexual marriage: exclusive and based on love and intimacy.

The oppressive heteronormativity of 1920s Poland forced Olek to abandon Halperin and strike up flirtations with girls. While the two were in Lviv, Olek sought Halperin's attention, but at a summer camp in Zielona, Olek was suddenly spending more time with other youths. Olek's intensifying contact with girls made Halperin jealous. He considered breaking up with Olek but could not do it: "It is impossible. I would not be able to survive without him."[75] While Halperin wanted Olek to be intimate with him, Olek increased his distance and became uncommunicative. Finally, Olek told him, "Your hugs disgust me."[76] Olek's subsequent rejection of Halperin with the phrase "I cannot live with such a man" revealed both Olek's fear of being in an intimate homosexual relationship as well as the romantic framework of their relationship that was clear to both young men.[77] While previously Olek had possibly been less familiar with the pathologization of homosexuality, his decision to abandon Halperin suggests that he had committed himself to heteronormativity.

Hearing that Olek did not want to continue their same-sex intimacy-filled friendship, Halperin was devastated but still in love with Olek: "What to do now? Should I now live without Olek? No, it is impossible. I can't imagine that. Should I talk to him or not? Shall I come to him and tell him that I can't live without him? No, I can't. I love him endlessly and how could I think that I won't be with him anymore?"[78] After several months, Halperin was still deeply in unrequited love:

> When I think about it now, I feel in my heart some abnormal movement, as if someone has pressed it. What does it mean? Ho! I want Olek here with me! I want to grab him and pull him towards me, I want to kiss him on those hot lips of his, which squeeze ever stronger when we kiss. I want to look in his eyes from a close distance. I would like to kiss his beautiful shining eyes with my lips. Whoever has seen them once cannot forget them. I long for the touch of his palm. Ho, how great I felt when I slept with him, how happy I was when he embraced me and pulled me towards him.[79]

Even after the two young men broke up, Halperin continuously fantasized about Olek, his body and his touch. He loved a man who, as he wrote, "hated him." Olek continued to be "part of his soul, his 'only man' and 'hear-and-spirit support.'"[80] By 1928, Halperin was convinced that Olek was frustrated with his love and did not want to continue their relationship: "He won't understand my attitude towards him."[81]

Halperin's story demonstrates how modern medical and legal notions of homosexuality regulated and influenced the lives of individuals. As young men between the ages of fifteen and seventeen, Halperin and Olek were already cognizant that affection between men was forbidden, and they knew that they could not hold hands when Olek's mother was around.[82] When Halperin kissed Olek for the first time in public, he had ambivalent feelings about what he had done: "We were waiting in the courtyard for the sports class, I looked at him, my heart shivered, I grabbed and kissed him. For the first time ever, he pushed me away. . . . Later during the class, I thought that I should be ashamed of what I did and feared that this public display of affection would discourage Olek."[83] The happiness that filled Halperin following the public kiss merged with pangs of guilt concerning the erotic involvement that was then socially unacceptable. Halperin was afraid that publicly showing his feelings would challenge their friendship and create distance between them. Olek, who refused to see himself as homosexual, decided to react with violence to this sign of affection to safeguard his public heterosexuality.

When reflecting on his affair with Olek from a distance of about a year or two, Halperin revealed that his possible nonheteronormative sexuality filled him with great fear. He began to perceive homosexuality as a pathological deviation. In a longer entry discussing his sexuality, Halperin wrote,

> During the time when I was afraid of homosexuality, I lived with the thought that if I could imagine myself with a woman, I could see if her body attracted me sexually, if it received me or not. In these fantasies I saw myself having sex with a woman and it aroused me sexually.
>
> . . . I fought with myself without any success, I succumbed to lasciviousness. I began to fall into absent-mindedness, fears, I began to ask myself if I hadn't turned into a halfwit or become dull. Along with that, I had the fearful thought that I was a homosexual, meaning a pathological type. In great despair I asked myself: Am I different from other people in this respect as well? Meaning that I am a loser. . . .

The second symptom of this awareness was that I publicly humiliated girls—even though I admired girls' entrepreneurship, endurance, and ferocity.

I still struggle with one big question. Should I do anything or just let it go? Would all this disappear with time? And if not—how to fight against it?[84]

Halperin's entry reflects several contemporary stereotypes concerning homosexuality. Like the witnesses in the trials discussed earlier in this chapter, Halperin linked homosexuality with an aversion to women. He planned a number of "reparative" strategies that were supposed to "cure" him of his homosexuality. He forced himself to imagine being engaged in sexual intercourse with women and hoped that those imaginations would overshadow his homosexual fantasies. Also, reflecting on the then popular idea of a detrimental influence of masturbation and homosexuality on the psyche, he saw his sexuality as lascivious and causing his absent-mindedness and fears. Halperin wrote in Polish, which was his strongest language, and probably acquired his knowledge about homosexuality from Polish books or newspapers. Jewishness seemed not to play a major role in the way he conceptualized his sexuality or romantic love. Since his sexual knowledge was shaped by repressive scientific discourses around homosexuality, Halperin desired the ability to embrace heteronormativity.

Halperin did not feel ready to live life as a homosexual man and decided to abandon his desires and forget about his involvement with Olek. When, a few years later, he was questioned about his sexuality by his soon-to-be-boss, pedagogue Janusz Korczak, eighteen-year-old Halperin wrote, "I answered: Through self-observation I can say that I do not have any deviations. I have not yet started any sexual relations."[85] Halperin indeed began to spend more time with girls, but he still fantasized about Olek. About a girl named Minusia, he wrote, "Her figure fully resembles Olek." In another entry, Halperin wrote, "Would Rachel be enough for me? No! I need to have Olek," assuring that his attachment to Olek was stronger than to two girls with whom he had spent time and hoped to see as a "cure" for his homosexuality and unrequited love.[86] This allows us to speculate whether Halperin's sexuality was fluid or if, more likely, being unable to have a relationship with a man, he searched for women who would remind him of Olek. Speaking about "having" or "possessing" Olek again underscored Halperin's strong romantic and erotic involvement with the young man and his nascent homosexual subjectivity.

While Halperin did not link his homosexuality and his Jewishness, Polish-Jewish painter Józef Rajnfeld (1908–1940), three years older than Halperin, exemplified a man who developed a modern homosexual subjectivity entangled with anxiety about his Jewishness. Rajnfeld, although distanced from Orthodox Jewishness, was familiar with its cultural references, such as the figure of the dybbuk (a wandering soul in Jewish folklore). Struggling to draw the boundary between friendship and sexual attraction, Rajnfeld saw this anxiety as a dybbuk that had gotten hold of him and elsewhere spoke about "a constant fear of Jewishness" that resulted in a sense of inferiority.[87] Jewishness evidently evoked Rajnfeld's anxiety. The painter perceived his youth in Poland and the "family dirt" as responsible for his inferiority complex and the reason he set his life in motion and ventured to Paris. Rajnfeld feared that when visiting Poland, he would see "just its Palestinian [that is, Jewish] part," and being in Warsaw in 1932 was an oppressive experience for him, as he felt bothered by the "Jewish accent" of people he met and what he saw as their stupidity and misery.[88] However, other fragments from his letters demonstrate how Rajnfeld's homosexuality and Jewishness had become entangled. Visiting Tunis, Rajnfeld amazed at the beauty of the local Jewish men, who could not believe that he was Jewish too. His encounters in Tunis and his longing for "a homey and Jewish atmosphere" in Poland and to taste a good herring or matzah with ham elucidate the complexity of his relationship to his Jewishness.

While Halperin was anxious about his nascent homosexual desire, Rajnfeld himself approached the much older writer Jarosław Iwaszkiewicz when he was twenty years old and, knowing that Iwaszkiewicz was queer, hoped to join the homosexual scene around the writer. In his letters to Iwaszkiewicz from his trips around Europe, Rajnfeld wrote openly about having male lovers and his predilection for "Germanic" and "Southern" men. Rajnfeld was preoccupied with his sexual orientation and saw it as harmful for his psyche and body. "I believe that pederasty is the reason for my incompleteness with everything," he wrote, blaming his homosexuality for his "physical and moral softness," bad health, and clumsiness.[89] Elsewhere, Rajnfeld joked that his homosexuality was a "madness" that "would not allow the other forms of madness to develop."[90] Rajnfeld was anxious about his sexuality but had affairs with men all over Europe and described his studio as a "bordello."[91] As Iwaszkiewicz's financial support was supposed to save him from "becoming a slave of pederasts and impoverished Germans," the painter was financially dependent on the older Polish writer.[92] Rajnfeld's letters demonstrate how a young Polish-Jewish homosexual subjectivity dovetailed when not repressed as in the case of Halperin. Both young men approached their sexuality differently and together exemplify the diversity of the gender identities that nonheteronormative interwar Polish-Jewish men constructed.

JEWISHNESS, HOMOSEXUALITY, AND THE STABILIZING POWER OF HOMOPHOBIA

So far, we have discussed the dominant homophobic view of homosexual men as criminals or deviants who threatened the heteronormative masculinity, sporadic cases of homosexual subjectivities such as that of Halperin, and progressive ideas about homosexuals as victims of societal intolerance. However, Jewish Poland also produced and consumed an array of other imaginings of homosexuality. For example, some Polish Jews started to define homosexuality as a "disease" that was characterisitc for the Middle East. They linked homosexuality with the idea that Muslim Middle Eastern men were particularly lustful and lecherous. Polish-Jewish men took part in this Orientalist and homophobic discourse that projected homosexuality onto men considered to be beyond the European tradition. This strategy allowed them to frame European men, including eastern European Jews, as heterosexual. As early as 1903, Polish-Jewish doctor Samuel Natan Kutna wrote that "the lust and outgrowth of sensuality among circumcised Turks, Arabs, and Persians is particularly blossoming."[93] This goes along with Ofri Ilany's findings concerning the Yishuv (Jewish population in Palestine before 1948), where immigrant Jewish men from Europe also saw homosexuality as an "Oriental vice" common among Arab men.[94] Ideas transposing homosexuality onto those from the Muslim communities in the East circulated between Poland and Palestine thanks to press contributors who submitted their impressions of the Middle East to be printed in Poland's media. In 1935, Aron Spiwak, in his report from Tel Aviv for the Polish Zionist journal *Trybuna Narodowa*, commented in a strong anti-Arab tone, "In Tel Aviv there are no robberies, be it when an Arab would rob a Jew on the beach or would rape his wife. In Tunis and Alexandria murders are a daily occurrence. In those barbaric ports homosexuality flourishes, while in Tel Aviv it is nonexistent."[95] The Jewish city of Tel Aviv was reported to be free of the "Oriental vice" that supposedly was a commonplace in Arab cities. The idea of defining other ethnicities as particularly prone to homosexuality merged with the vision of homosexuality as a crime, which was popular then in Poland.

An analogous idea of Arabs as homosexuals appeared in the memoir of Arje Koczer, who as a "Prisoner of Zion" spent some time imprisoned alongside Arab inmates in British-controlled Palestine. Publishing his memoir, Koczer also contributed to the circulation of homophobic, as well as anti-Muslim, prejudices in Poland. Koczer wrote in 1939, "There is no such place on Earth where homosexuality would be more widespread than in the prisons of the East—most of all—in the 'Holy Land.'"[96] Koczer referred here both to the idea that homosexuality was acquired or practiced in spaces absent of women and to the idea of Arab men as particularly interested in same-sex lust. As such, Koczer continued, some Arab prisoners were happy in a prison, a place that provided them with an established framework for homosexual sex. Koczer's narrative defined any instance of homosexual affection as impossible. Writing about prison *przyjaciele*, or boyfriends, Koczer put the word *przyjaciele* in quotation marks, doing the same with the word *romantic*, thus suggesting that same-sex romantic feelings were not valid among Arab men. Later, Koczer cried about the "hideous dealings"—that is, rape between men—suggesting that consensual same-sex intercourse was impossible, which contradicted his earlier thesis about Arabs explicitly looking for homosexual sex in prisons. In his memoir, Koczer portrayed Arabs as men who rape Jewish youths in Palestinian prisons, and in that way, he defined Arab men as violent predators and Jewish men as innocent victims. Consequently, Jewish men who had sex with men did not appear as homosexuals but merely as victims of Arab corruption and deviation. Koczer protected the illusion of Jewish masculinity as decidedly heteronormative. In times of growing antisemitism in Poland, this narrative appeared to stabilize the fragile masculinity of anxious Jewish men.

Jewish debates in Poland connected homosexuality not only with the contemporary Muslim world of the East but also with the ancient polytheist civilizations of the Mediterranean. Like elsewhere in Europe, Polish Jews discussed homosexual masculinities in the context of ancient Rome and Greece. The association of homosexuality with antiquity served both homophobic and antihomophobic discourses and actors. Usually, the examples of prominent homosexual men such as Plato were used to prove that homosexual desire was something natural and present throughout human history and provided a language with which to speak about male homosexuality. However, some Polish-Jewish men applied such examples from antiquity to also argue for Judaism's "purity" from homosexuality and thus its superiority. One of the most striking examples is historian Mateusz Mieses, who used homophobic arguments to claim Jewish moral superiority. While Mieses's 1912 book spoke out against the growing chauvinism in Europe, it did not hesitate to mark homosexuality as abnormal and immoral. He wrote,

> The ancient world did not know the postulates of sexual ethics. Hedonism was an everyday matter. The classic love was not an androgynous sentiment merging two opposing kinds into a higher unity, but a vulgar rambunctiousness, a perversion directed at the being of the same kind. Plato's love is a homosexual love. Also Apollo, Herakles or Poseidon were shining examples of pederasty. The pederastic adventures of Zeus with Ganymede were praised by poets and artists.
>
> Athens in the era of Lucian was a center of boys' love. All Roman poets apart from Odious had a sexual life a la Eulenburg. The best Romans: Caesar, Antonius, Trajan all adhered to this despicable sport. No ancient moralist condemned this perverted excess of the natural [sexual] instinct. Nowadays, we Aryans and non-Aryans alike feel disgust and an instinctive aversion to that rambunctiousness. And this approach is a product of the Jewish legal framework of ethics which, through the Church, had entered the veins of Europeans. Understanding the reasonable expedience of the universe, the monotheistic religion has consistently judged any misdemeanor against the norm of nature, every purposeless excess, every perverted sexual [activity] which does not serve the continuity of our species, as reprehensible.[97]

Also, the Polish-Jewish Judaic studies scholar Edmund Stein wrote in his 1929 article of the homosexuality-free "purity" of ancient Jewish sexual life. Stein, quoting ancient texts by Philon and Joseph Flavius as well as texts by modern historians, discussed the "sexual deviation of homosexuality" that "filled Jews with fear and disgust" and led to a Jewish sense of superiority over the Greeks and Romans.[98] Leon Gutman, praising the ancient Jewish revolt against the Greeks, wrote that Greek political thought destroyed individualism and "tolerated the far-reaching rule of homosexualism."[99] Stein, Mieses, and Gutman were the modern historians whom the historian of homosexuality David M. Halperin saw as responsible for weaving the "thread that connected ancient Greek pederasty with modern homosexuality."[100] Their arguments about Jews being purer in a sexual sense compared to other ancient civilizations were continuously repeated in interwar Poland and helped define homosexuality as something to which Jews were immune.

As ideas and notions about homosexuality circulated around Europe, in the late 1930s, Jews in Poland created a self-defense strategy that ridiculed German Nazism by referring to the alleged homosexuality of its followers. The Polish identification of Germany with homosexuality increased in the 1930s, but these tropes were already visible in Polish discussions much earlier and drew on knowledge of the bustling homosexual scene in Berlin. For example, as early as 1907, a Polish Socialist newspaper in Silesia wrote about a "pederastic Prussian government," while another magazine concluded that "the dirt of Prince Eulenburg kind . . . is absent in the Polish society."[101] After World War I, the Polish far right, in particular, exploited the idea of the "German vice" that they juxtaposed against "Polish purity." For example, in 1927, a radical nationalist daily reported that the "leprosy of [homo]sexual perversion" was brought to Warsaw by Germans during the World War I.[102] A similar framing of Germany as a homosexual other was also common in France, where homosexualism was known as a "German deviation."[103]

Such homophobia-inspired discursive mechanisms are also clearly visible in numerous Polish-Jewish press reports, in particular from Polish-language Jewish media outlets. *Chwila* or *Nowy Dziennik* journalists, who often saw themselves as modern but catered to the conservative Jewish bourgeoisie, took part in shaping this homophobic discourse. Their reports conveyed the message that Nazism brought a moral decadence to Germany and local homosexual life served as a perfect example of Germany's moral collapse. The idea of Nazis, Germans, and antisemites in general as homosexuals was interwoven with the understanding of homosexuality as a crime and social malady. Already in 1932 Ludwik Oberlender wrote in *Miesięcznik żydowski* that "homosexuality plays a prominent role in this [Nazi] system of brotherhood, discipline and love for the leader" and described it as a "moral deficit" of Nazi ideology.[104] When, in 1938, the Polish-Jewish Zionist weekly *Trybuna Narodowa* protested the expulsion of Polish Jews from Germany, it underscored the alleged general moral decay of that country.[105] Comparing criminality rates in Germany between 1906 and 1936, the weekly mentioned not only incest but also a substantial rise in trials against homosexual men (630 vs. 5,321). While the number of prosecuted men grew because of the persecution that homosexual men experienced under Nazi rule, *Trybuna Narodowa* implied that it was the Nazis themselves who brought about the maladies of incest and homosexuality. In the final years before World War II, the link between homosexuality and Nazi Germans remained stable in the Polish-Jewish media. In 1938, Polish-Jewish doctor Paweł Klinger believed that "Germans excel at homosexuality."[106] In February 1939, *Chwila* wrote that, in Germany, "the cases of pederasty among the youth have increased by a factor of eight," explaining it as an outcome of the "state upbringing" in the Third Reich.[107] An analogous contextualization of homosexuality as "a German Nazi problem" could be found in Jewish publications across eastern Europe.

The strategy of defining homosexuality as a sexual deviation common among the Nazis consolidated following the 1934 postmortem trial involving Nazi leader Ernst Röhm.[108] In 1934, the Zionist journal *Divrey Akiva* poked at the antisemitic German propaganda that was blaming Jews for Germany's recent failures. Subversively appropriating the Nazi rhetoric, the journal suggested that Jews caused "sexual deviance" in Germany, in that way deriding the Nazi propaganda that saw Jews responsible for other phenomena that were incongruent with the Nazi vision of society: atheism and social democracy.[109] In 1937, *Nasz Przegląd* reported on Heinz Ruthe, one of the leaders of the German minority in Czechoslovakia and a major Nazi propagandist.[110] The journalist reported that Ruthe "demoralized the youth and encouraged them to pederasty" by organizing educational meetings that turned into male-only sex orgies. *Nasz Dziennik* revealed the affair with palpable satisfaction. A German Nazi turned out to be homosexual, which cast him in a negative light as a sexual pervert. Presenting the Nazis as scorned and mocked homosexuals, the daily turned them into a laughingstock.

The 1934 wave of texts on Nazi homosexuality appears as an almost coordinated propaganda campaign. One particular example of a homophobic counter-antisemitic strategy was an article about Ernst Röhm published in the Yiddish daily *Haynt* in 1934. A. S. Lirik (the pen name of Arn-Levi Riklis) presented Röhm's sexuality and execution as "proof" that Germany suffered under the immoral influence of homosexuality. The members of the Sturmabteilung (SA, Nazi paramilitary units) units were portrayed as *lustknaben* (pleasure-boys) who satisfied the "pathological" desire of the SA leadership. The Jewish journalist used the presence of homosexual men among the Nazis as "proof" that the ideology heralding a moral rejuvenation of Germany was in fact pathological, since homosexuals there had so much influence. Lirik, who was Germany's correspondent for Warsaw's *Haynt*, concluded, "We do not know how long Hitler will stay in power, but morally—Hitlerism is already dead. The 'lustknaben' have dug a grave for themselves and for the entire [Nazi] party." Lirik emasculated the SA men, writing, "They are monkeys and not men. They engaged in *mishkav zakhar* [homosexual intercourse] in wild orgies."[111]

Writing about Germany succumbing to homosexuality, Lirik constructed an idea of Jewish purity, which was free from homosexuality, and of Jews' moral superiority, which was to counterbalance the Nazis' antisemitic renderings of Jews as immoral and pathological. The German men who conceived of themselves as the heroes of Nazi Germany and the new moral foundation of the *Volk* proved, according to the homophobic logic that Lirik embraced, to be homosexuals and hence abnormal and immoral. I suggest that the strategy of presenting German men as homosexuals sought to emasculate men who, for Polish Jews, represented antisemitism. Polish Jews constructed their own masculinity as a pure heterosexual gender identity, and to do so relied on the figure of a homosexual Other—be it the Orientalized Muslim or the German Nazi. Speaking from a position of marginalized men, Polish-Jewish male journalists attempted to stabilize their own masculinity by showing how the alleged hypermasculine Nazis were in fact homosexual and thus not normative men.

In 1934, the Polish-Jewish satirical journal *Tararam* published a picture on its cover of a heterosexual couple dressed in fur coats surrounded by a group of journalists.[112] The Yiddish caption read, "Journalists have seen a Hitlerite on a date with a girl, and not with a young man." Since homosexuality was supposedly so widespread among German Nazis, an instance of a male follower of Hitler on a date with a woman appeared as a major social event that needed to be reported by the press—or so the caricature implied. In the image, the journalists seem confused about this unusual scene and are making notes with great diligence. The caricature mocks Nazi supporters as homosexuals and generalizes about the widespread homosexuality among Hitler supporters, exemplifying how Polish-Jewish anti-Nazi resistance operated with homophobic arguments and sentiments.

Texts linking homosexuality with Nazi Germany appeared across Poland, including outside of the capital. Lviv's Polish-language Jewish daily printed an anonymous article burning with satisfaction that Nazis proved to be "morally deviated" and "physically degenerate." *Chwila* wrote that homosexuality was hereditary in Germany and could reach as much as 12 percent of German society. German racists who spoke of "racial purity" turned out to be "uncurable deviants and psychopaths." Nazis were supposed to be not only men with inverted sexual instincts but to suffer from fetishism and sadism and practice zoophilia with imported exotic animals. Homosexualism was "the illness of this movement" and thus inherent to Nazi ideology. Titling its article "Homosexualism—a Hitlerite Illness," *Chwila* turned to a homophobic strategy of combating antisemitism. Facing racist discriminatory discourses in Poland as well, *Chwila* journalists hoped that revealing how Nazis "lost mental stability" and the "ability to control their animalistic instincts" would allow them to picture their antisemitic ideology and its Polish followers in a negative light and demonstrate that German racial superiority was a lie.[113] Dozens of similar articles in *Chwila* or *Nowy Dziennik*, including those challenging the idea that Hitler was "a normal man" concerning his sexuality, convinced Polish Jews about homosexuality as specifically a Nazi malady.[114]

Picturing German Nazis as homosexuals, defining Arabs as prone to homosexuality, and claiming that Judaism was free of homosexuality, Polish Jews proliferated homophobic discourses with which they hoped to stabilize their own heteronormative, but very fragile, sense of masculinity. Since both Jewishness and homosexuality placed one on the social margins in interwar Poland, heterosexual Polish-Jewish male journalists and scholars created homophobic narratives that attempted to define Jewishness as free from homosexuality and thus more normative. For Jewish men who suffered from the growing antisemitism, shifting the presumed homosexuality to other ethnic groups appeared as a

Figure 7.2. Cartoon, "A sensatsye in Daytshland…"
(A sensation in Germany), *Tararam*, July 13, 1934, 1.

reasonable normalization strategy. This effort to a certain extent resembled the gendered process of making Judaism an American religion that Sarah Imhoff explored.[115] By picturing Arabs or Nazis as "true homosexuals," Jewish actors from Poland hoped to define Judaism as compatible with heteronormative notions of Polishness.

CONCLUSION

Early twentieth-century Polish-Jewish masculinities included the masculinities of men who loved and were sexually attracted to men. In the 1920s and 1930s, we observe the first appearance of homosexual subjectivities. The adolescent Józef Halperin from Lviv, the young painter Józef Rajnfeld from Warsaw, and the Łódź manager Leon Waks were all aware that they were attracted to men and that they had homosexual desires. While young Halperin was afraid to define himself as a homosexual, forty-seven-year-old Waks saw himself as a man sexually attracted to men and participated in homosexual networking. The case of Waks reveals how Jewish homosexual men in Poland attempted to shape their scope of agency and create opportunities for themselves in an environment that marginalized them as social outcasts.

Jewish homosexual masculinities in interwar Poland were informed and regulated by local medical and legal discourses surrounding homosexuality. The idea of an active "true homosexual" and his passive heterosexual victim spread widely among Poland's Jewish and non-Jewish doctors and lawyers and, with time, turned into an accepted social assumption about homosexual predators who seduced or forced heterosexual men into homosexuality. My review of Poland's Jewish press demonstrated how homosexuality was rendered as a deviation and a crime, and average nonexpert Jewish readers had problems understanding it as a valid sexual orientation. Heterosexual Jewish and non-Jewish men engaged in protecting heterosexuality as a feature central to masculinity and continued to marginalize men who were homosexual. The decriminalization of homosexuality in Poland in 1932 was a progressive step that preceded similar developments in western Europe yet did not dramatically change broader societal approaches to homosexuality.

Polish-Jewish men created a set of homophobic narratives that attempted to present Jewishness as free of homosexuality. First, the idea that Middle Eastern men were particularly lustful and prone to homosexuality found its way into Polish-Jewish discussions about homosexuality. Second, numerous texts framing the Nazis as homosexuals facilitated Polish-Jewish men in building a sense of superiority over the Nazis, now characterized by a sexual pathology. When the Nazis disempowered Jewish men in Germany, placed them on the social margins, and deprived them of any masculine respectability, in the light of this major social crisis, Polish-Jewish men created homophobic counternarratives to reassure their sense of normative masculinity.

—∿—

EPILOGUE

Jewish history has its dimension aspect. I have demonstrated how, in the 1920s and 1930s, Polish-Jewish men acted as gendered subjects in a social matrix where gender, ethnicity, religion, and class were interwoven. Reading between the lines and rethinking the everyday experiences of Jewish men, this book demonstrates how the gendered perspective modifies our understanding of Polish-Jewish history. By shedding light on the lived social experiences of Jewish men and on Jewish-produced self-images, practices, and discourses, this shifts the study of Jewish masculinities from external representations to lived Jewish experiences, assertions, and self-perceptions and opens up some finer lines of inquiry to scrutiny. My research on historical Polish-Jewish masculinities demonstrates that in interwar Poland, Jewish masculinities shared their core values and practices with non-Jewish masculinities and thus were far from being particular or exceptional. Despite their marginalization and antisemitic attacks that questioned their gender identity in the military, the university, professional life, and other spaces, many Jewish men raised a claim to masculine hegemony and upheld the dominant masculine normativity. At the same time, Orthodox Jewish men had their own system of stabilizing masculinity that celebrated

313

religious studiousness. Orthodox men in interwar Poland were less conditioned by non-Jewish masculine norms, but, as Polish Jewry became more secular and Polonized, Orthodox masculinities in Poland also increasingly overlapped with wider masculine ideals based on heroism, physical power, economic achievement, and respectability. Similar, in a way, to contemporary North American and Israeli Jews, most interwar Polish Jews considered their masculinities normative and heterosexual, and, in spite of antisemitic exclusion, they did not internalize the vision of Jewish masculinity as deformed and undermined. Polish-Jewish men reflected on what kind of men they were and what kind of men they wanted to be and clung to gender norms that they believed to be valid through performative practices in the private and public spheres. By letting Polish-Jewish men speak through sources, this book underscores Polish-Jewish men's assertions in shaping their fates and gender identities. Not only ethnicity and antisemitism, but also gender, shaped the Jewish experience in interwar Poland.

The Holocaust dramatically redefined Polish-Jewish masculinities, and Jewish men incarcerated in ghettos across Poland lost the mechanisms that had validated their masculinities prior to 1939. As Maddy Carey has demonstrated, the gradual deconstruction of lives was key to the inability of many Jewish men to practice strong masculine identities in the ghettos.[1] Masculinities were deconstructed as Jewish men lost their jobs, their right to socialize in certain ways, and their role as providers and protectors. This ghettoization forced eastern European Jewish men into positions of passivity and inaction that conflicted with their traditional ideas of male gender identity as active and created the damaging and emasculating gendered environment in which the deconstruction took place.[2] At the same time, as Sebastian Huebel has demonstrated, marginalized Jewish men struggled to adhere to a set of traditional practices of hegemonic masculinity in providing for and protecting their families and being caring husbands and fathers. The Holocaust undermined practices of Jewish masculinity, so Jewish men altered gender roles that counted on a prewar gender codex concerning work and domesticity. The hypothesis that oppressed Jewish men no longer felt like men is premature: many of them resisted the attack on their gender identities by taking a proactive stance.[3] After Germany annihilated Polish Jewry in the Holocaust, Israel and the United States emerged as two major Jewish centers, and certain Jewish masculine continuities became visible between those places and pre-1939 Poland.

The study of pre-Holocaust Polish-Jewish masculinities opens up new vistas for contemporary questions of gender and ethnicity. As the Polish-Jewish men who appear on the pages of this book were shaped by general gender norms and the workings of ethnicity, so were and are contemporary American-Jewish and Israeli-Jewish men. As Sarah Imhoff and Miriam Eve Mora have demonstrated, Jewish men in the United States Americanized their masculine values and practices in the course of the twentieth century.[4] The Americanization of Jewish masculinities encompassed men's ambivalence about the interplay of their Jewishness and masculinity. This process was engendered by works of literature and cinema, such as Philip Roth's *Portnoy's Complaint* (1969), which showcased figures of self-depreciating, nerdy, and nervous Jewish men. These American men, like Polish-Jewish men in the 1920s and 1930s, struggled to find a balance between values cherished in the Jewish world and those valid in general society. They felt compelled to follow the Nice Jewish Boy ideal of a man who was brainy, gentle, and class appropriate while at the same knowing that this model defined Jewish men as lacking the confidence, spontaneity, and romance that were associated with all-American masculinity. The countermodel of a "tough Jew" found many representations in American culture, but it never dethroned the Nice Jewish Boy as the strongest local Jewish masculine archetype.

As interwar Polish-Jewish fraternity members claimed access to rituals and markers of hegemonic masculinity, so did American-Jewish men after the Holocaust—for example, in campus Greek life.[5] The ideal of a correct, middle-class Jewish man on equal footing with non-Jews gained major importance in the 1940s and 1950s. Earlier in the twentieth century, American-Jewish men were marginalized because their masculinity was considered incoherent with the masculinity of white Christian men, but when Jewishness turned from being associated with the periphery to being identified with whiteness and privilege, several characteristics of the Nice Jewish Boy ideal also experienced a valorization, even among non-Jews. While Polish-Jewish men fantasized about accessing male hegemony and oriented themselves to this elusive ideal, for Jews in America in the second half of the twentieth century, it became a reality. American-Jewish masculinity became linked with upward mobility, professional achievement, self-assured respectfulness, and sensitivity. With time, the ideal of the gentle and responsible Nice Jewish Boy mutated from someone awkward into someone sexually and romantically attractive. More recently, a Jewish bro masculinity has appeared, as some young American Jews fantasize and work to be tough, sporty jocks, often in a process of interethnic borrowing from the Black hip-hop masculine ideal. Recently, Jewish rapper Lil Dicky negotiated in his lyrics the insecurities of a Jewish man shaped by the middle-class Nice Jewish Boy archetype who ventures into a hypermasculine Black music environment. As Jews moved from the margins to the center and as white male privilege experiences new challenges, Jewish masculinities in the United States continue to evolve.

In the late twentieth century, the high social mobility of American-Jewish men often mutated into misogyny and sexual harassment, and a Jewish male sexual predator became the main face of the American #MeToo debates. Local Jewish communities began to dismantle the paradigms of American-Jewish masculinity that defined Jewish men as safe for women. Like earlier in Poland, here the non-Jewish context and the rise of feminism were also key. Following societal debates about sexual harassment, American Jews began to reflect on how masculinity shaped their communities. For example, Kavod, a progressive Jewish community from Boston, established its masculinities group in the light of a "hyper-visibility of powerful Jewish men perpetuating the violence," and the group was part of a larger Western movement in which men came together to reflect on how masculinity shaped their lives and overlapped with misogyny.[6] The Nice Jewish Boy ideal blurred the idea that Jewish men might be aggressive harassers, might represent violent and emotionally illiterate toxic masculinity, and might be misogynist in the hope that performing this gentle masculine subtype would grant them access to women's bodies. Several commentators weighed in, suggesting that the Nice Jewish Boy ideal might be damaging and debilitating for men. Some American Jews began to perceive the patriarchy as also dangerous for men, in particular for those who fail to fit into the heterosexual middle-class ideal.

While, in the United States, post-Holocaust Jewish masculinities were shaped by Americanization and inclusion into white privilege, in Israel, they were molded by Zionism. Secular eastern European Zionist Jews who founded the state of Israel desired to transform a diaspora Jew into a modern Hebrew. The Zionist diagnosis that Jewish men in the eastern European diaspora were weak, nebbish, and devoid of confidence and activism was their propaganda mechanism rather than a reflection of the self-image of regular Jewish men in the region. The Zionist fantasy included not only imagining a New Jew but also creating a diaspora Jew not from Jewish realities across Europe but from local antisemitic imagery. Zionism, from its inception, had two goals: resettlement in Palestine and reversing the stereotype of diasporic Jewish men as feminine. The Zionist Jewish man would be muscular and heterosexual and would engage in manual labor, becoming the

European explorer in touch with the land and with his body. The Zionist cultural domination over Mandate Palestine and later the State of Israel produced the ideal of a hardened, militarized man that is still valid in Israel today and is embodied in the hypermasculine Sabra—the native-born Israeli. The Zionist culture and later Israeli hegemonic culture has been male dominated, but it has also involved a construction of the feminine as the binary opposite of the male New Jew.

What differentiates Jewish masculinities in America (and earlier in Poland) from those in Israel is the fact that in Israel, Jewish men constitute the majority and define the masculine norm. While, in Europe, gentile masculinities were sometimes constructed in opposition to the Jewish and nonheterosexual "Other," in Israel Zionist masculinity is constituted through the force of the exclusion of the queer, the Mizrahi, and the Palestinian male "Others."[7] Zionist masculinities were shaped by discourses of breeding children and racial improvement that valorized Ashkenazi heteronormativity. Unlike in Poland and the United States, in Israel, Ashkenazi Jewish men enjoyed the privilege of not being marked as an ethnic group and thus imagined themselves as the norm. In Israel, the army is the main agent of socialization into the hegemonic masculinity. Despite the ideal of the hardened man that the army celebrates, in Israel, as Danny Kaplan has demonstrated, the army is also a venue of relatedness and intimacy between men endorsing physical action and intellectual sociability.[8] Israeli men have been sexualized in popular culture, and their supposed muscular sex appeal often appears as their main masculine characteristic, overshadowing their inner insecurities.

Next to Zionist hegemonic masculinities, like in interwar Poland, contemporary Israel also encompasses alternative masculine models with its own normativity.[9] The Israeli TV series *Shtisel* (2013–2021), featuring a local ultra-Orthodox community, has attracted much attention concerning the lives of Jewish women within traditional Jewry, but it also allows us to reflect on notions of masculinity as well. While *Shtisel* characters are fictional, they are illustrative of real masculine dilemmas among Orthodox Israeli men. Shulem Shtisel appears as a family patriarch concerned as much with his professional achievement as a heder headmaster as with the cohesion of his family. Like the Polish-Jewish men examined in this book, *Shtisel* characters also slalom between several masculine normativities. They acknowledge the validity of religious learning, keep to an ultra-Orthodox dress code, and celebrate the heterosexual family. At the same time, both Shulem and his son Akiveh strive for romantic love, and Akiveh allows himself to venture into the world of art. While Shulem and Akiveh might follow the traditional ideals of a respectable Orthodox man and Shulem hopes to maintain his patriarchal authority, their lives challenge this ideal and show how insecure and unstable masculinities are. A set of secondary characters present Orthodox men as violent and corrupt and eliminate the fantasy of a respected and studious paterfamilias. Orthodox masculinities in Israel, like those in Poland before the Holocaust, maintain their own normativity, but they intertwine with the dominant Israeli Zionist masculinity.

What contemporary American-Jewish and Israeli-Jewish masculinities have in common with Polish-Jewish masculinities a hundred years ago is their malleable and pluralistic character, their embeddedness in general gender norms, and their intersectional overlapping with ethnicity, class, and age. Interwar Polish-Jewish and contemporary American-Jewish and Israeli-Jewish masculinities alike are shaped as much by fantasies as they are by lived experiences. As interwar Polish-Jewish men could find both the military and the yeshiva enhancing their perceived sense of masculinity, so do American-Jewish and Israeli-Jewish men of our day. While Israeli Zionist and Orthodox masculinities might appear to contradict one another, they also remain in dialogue, overlap, and often mutually reinforce each other—mirroring the interactions between diverse Jewish masculine ideals in interwar Poland. Jewish men over the last hundred years have aspired to belong to their perceived masculine normativities, resisted antisemitic attempts at marginalization and emasculation, and applied practices, markers, and discourses to stabilize their gender identity. Studying history through the lens of masculinity allows us to uncover the gendered layers of inequalities that Jews and other ethnic minorities experience in the modern world. Ethnicized men's responses to these inequalities demonstrate how, within a contested masculine territory, individual actors manifest their insecurities, but also their assertions and hopes, about what it means to be a man.

NOTES

INTRODUCTION

1. Bernard Goldstein, *Twenty Years with the Jewish Labor Bund: A Memoir of Interwar Poland* (West Lafayette, IN: Purdue University Press, 2016), 72, 105–107.

2. Since the word *Jew* denotes both males and females, in order to speak about the experience of Jewish men, I use the term *male Jews* or *Jewish men*.

3. Pablo Dominguez Andersen and Simon Wendt, introduction to *Masculinities and the Nation in the Modern World: Between Hegemony and Marginalization* (New York: Palgrave, 2015), 2.

4. Staughton Lynd, *Doing History from the Bottom Up: On E.P. Thompson, Howard Zinn, and Rebuilding the Labour Movement from Below* (Chicago: Haymarket Books, 2014). In the Polish context, history from below has been productively used in the context of peasantry: Adam Leszczyński, *Ludowa historia Polski* (Warsaw: WAB, 2020); Michał Rauszer, *Bękarty pańszczyzny: Historia buntów chłopskich* (Warsaw: Wydawnictwo RM, 2020).

5. I follow David Biale, who demonstrated that Jewish sexuality was determined not only by an autochthonous Jewish tradition and "splendid isolation" but was also open to influences from the larger societies among whom Jews lived. David Biale, *Eros and the Jew: From Biblical Israel to Contemporary America* (Berkeley: University of California Press, 1997), 9.

6. Michael Kimmel, *Manhood in America: A Cultural History* (New York: Free Press, 1996), 2–3.

7. Michael Roper and John Tosh, "Introduction: Historians and the Politics of Masculinity," in Michael Roper and John Tosh, eds., *Manful Assertions: Masculinities in Britain since 1800* (London: Routledge, 1991), 1.

8. See, among others: Natalie Zemon Davis, "'Women's History' in Transition: The European Case," *Feminist Studies,* vol. 3, no. 3/4, 1976, 83–103; Joan Kelly-Gadol, *Did Women Have a Renaissance?* (Boston: Houghton Mifflin, 1977); Gerda Lerner, *The Majority Finds Its Past: Placing Women in History* (Chapel Hill: University of North Carolina Press, 1979); Ruth A. Fager, *Sweatshop Strife: Class, Ethnicity, and Gender in the Jewish Labour Movement of Toronto, 1900–1939* (Toronto: University of Toronto Press, 1992); Paula Hyman, *Gender and Assimilation in Modern Jewish History: The Roles and Representation of Women* (Seattle: University of Washington Press, 1995); Judith R. Baskin, ed., *Jewish Women in Historical Perspective* (Detroit: Wayne State University Press, 1998); Harriet Pass Freidenreich, *Female, Jewish, and Educated: The Lives of Central European University Women* (Bloomington: Indiana University Press, 2002); Kathie Friedman-Kasaba, *Memories of Migration: Gender, Ethnicity, and Work in the Lives of Jewish and Italian Women in New York, 1870–1924* (Albany: State University of New York Press, 2002); Iris Parush, *Reading Jewish Women: Marginality and Modernization in Nineteenth-Century Eastern European Jewish Society* (Waltham, MA: Brandeis University Press, 2004); Melissa R. Klapper, *Jewish Girls Coming of Age in America, 1860–1920* (New York: New York University Press, 2005); ChaeRan Freeze, Paula Hyman, and Antony Polonsky, eds., *Jewish Women in Eastern Europe* (Oxford: Littman Library of Jewish Civilization, 2007); Miriam Peskowitz and Laura Levitt, *Judaism since Gender* (New York: Routledge, 1996); Rachel Elior, *The Unknown History of Jewish Women through the Ages—On Learning and Illiteracy: On Slavery and Liberty* (Berlin: De Gruyter, 2023).

9. Björn Krondorfer, "Hiding in the Plain View: Bringing Critical Men's Studies and Holocaust Studies into Conversation," in Björn Krondorfer and Ovidiu Creangă, eds., *The Holocaust and Masculinities: Critical Inquiries into the Presence and Absence of Men* (Albany: State University of New York Press, 2020), 30–31.

10. Pierre Bourdieu, *Masculine Domination* (Stanford, CA: Stanford University Press, 2001), 52; Kimmel, *Manhood in America,* 7.

11. Natalya Lusty, "Introduction: Modernism and Its Masculinities," in Natalya Lusty and Julian Murphet, eds., *Modernism and Masculinity* (Cambridge: Cambridge University Press, 2014), 7.

12. Jürgen Martschukat and Olaf Steglitz, *Geschichte der Männlichkeiten* (Frankfurt: Campus, 2018), 58.

13. Yankev Leshchinsky, *The Last Years of Polish Jewry*, vol. 1, *At the Edge of the Abyss: Essays, 1927–33*, ed. Robert Brym (Cambridge: Open Book, 2023), 1–17.

14. Bina Garncarska-Kadary, *Żydowska ludność pracująca w Polsce, 1918–1939* (Warsaw: Żydowski Instytut Historyczny, 2001).

15. See Moshe Landau, *Mi'ut yehudi lokhem: Ma'avak yehudey polin ba-shanim 1918–1928* (Jerusalem: Zalman Shazar Center for Jewish History, 1986); Emmanuel Melzer, *No Way Out: The Politics of Polish Jewry, 1935–1939* (Cincinnati: Hebrew Union College Press, 1997).

16. See Kamil Kijek, *Dzieci modernizmu: Świadomość, kultura i socjalizacja polityczna mlodzieży żydowskiej w Polsce międzywojennej* (Wrocław, Poland: Wydawnictwo Uniwersytetu Wrocławskiego, 2017); Daniel Kupfert Heller, *Jabotinsky's Children: Polish Jews and the Rise of Right-Wing Zionism* (Princeton, NJ: Princeton University Press, 2017); Rona Yona, *Niye kulanu halutsim: Tnuat ha-avoda ve-ha-aliya me-polin 1923–1936* (Jerusalem: Magnes, 2021).

17. Salo Baron, "Newer Emphases in Jewish History," *Jewish Social Studies* 25, no. 4 (1963): 245–258.

18. Krondorfer and Creangă, *The Holocaust and Masculinities*, 3.

19. Lusty, "Introduction," 7.

20. Quoted in George L. Mosse, *The Image of Man: Creation of Modern Masculinity* (Oxford: Oxford University Press, 1996), 29.

21. Kenneth Moss, *An Unchosen People: Jewish Political Reckoning in Interwar Poland* (Cambridge, MA: Harvard University Press, 2021), 25.

22. Moss.

23. Alain Corbin, "Wprowadzenie," in Alain Corbin, ed., *Historia męskości*, vol. 2, *XIX wiek: Tryumf męskości* (Gdańsk: słowo/obraz terytoria, 2020), 5–9; Mosse, *The Image of Man*, 7–55.

24. Mosse, *The Image of Man*, 134; Kimmel, *Manhood in America*, 11–56.

25. Mosse, *The Image of Man*, 3–4. John Tosh sees masculinity as a "structure particularly resistant to change." John Tosh, "The Old Adam and the New Man: Emerging Themes in the History of English Masculinities, 1750–1850," in Tim Hitchcock and Michelle Cohen, eds., *English Masculinities, 1660–1800* (London: Longman, 1999), 218.

26. Kimmel, *Manhood in America*, 13–42.

27. See Marcin Jakub Szymański and Błażej Torański, *Fabrykanci: Burzliwe dzieje łódzkich bogaczy* (Warsaw: Wydawnictwo Zona Zero, 2016).

28. See Heidi Hein-Kircher, "Debating Social Change and the Jewish Nation: The Polish-Jewish Weekly Ewa on Jewish Families and Birth

Control (1928–1933)," *Journal of Family History* 48, no. 3 (2023): 278–292; Eva Plach, "Feminism and Nationalism on the Pages of 'Ewa: Tygodnik,' 1928–1933," in *Polin: Studies in Polish Jewry*, vol. 18, *Jewish Women in Eastern Europe*, 241–263 (Liverpool, UK: Liverpool University Press, 2005).

29. Wolfgang Schmale, *Geschichte der Männlichkeit in Europa 1450–2000* (Vienna: Böhlau, 2003), 153.

30. In the Prussian partition starting from 1811, the Austrian partition in 1848, and the Russian partition in 1864.

31. Alicja Szuman, "Przeobrażanie struktury społeczno-zawodowej ludności Polski w XX wieku," *Ruch Prawniczy, Ekonomiczny i Socjologiczny* 61, no. 3–4 (1999), 189.

32. Andersen and Wendt, introduction to *Masculinities and the Nation*, 7–8.

33. Talcott Parsons, *The Structure of Social Action* (New York: McGraw-Hill, 1937).

34. Deborah S. David and Robert Brannon, *The Forty-Nine Percent Majority: The Male Sex Role* (Boston: Addison-Wesley, 1976); Joseph Pleck, *The Myth of Masculinity* (Cambridge, MA: MIT Press, 1981); Joseph Pleck, "The Gender Role Strain Paradigm: An Update," in *Toward a New Psychology of Men*, ed. Ronald F. Levant and William S. Polack, 11–32 (New York: Basic Books, 1995).

35. David D. Gilmore, *Manhood in the Making: Cultural Concepts of Masculinity* (New Haven, CT: Yale University Press, 1990).

36. Andrea Cornwall and Nancy Lindisfarne, eds., *Dislocating Masculinity: Comparative Ethnographies* (London: Routledge, 1994), 3.

37. See Ivan Yablonka, *A History of Masculinity: From Patriarchy to Gender Justice* (London: Penguin, 2022); Judith M. Bennet, *History Matters: Patriarchy and the Challenge of Feminism* (Philadelphia: University of Pennsylvania Press, 2010); Pavla Miller, *Transformations of Patriarchy in the West, 1500–1900* (Bloomington: Indiana University Press, 1998); Jeff Hearn, *The Gender of Oppression: Men, Masculinity and the Critique of Marxism* (New York: St. Martin's, 1987).

38. Cornwall and Lindisfarne, *Dislocating Masculinity*, 3.

39. Todd W. Reeser, *Masculinities in Theory: An Introduction* (Chichester, UK: Wiley, 2011).

40. See Maddy Carey, *Jewish Masculinity in the Holocaust: Between Destruction and Construction* (London: Bloomsbury Academic, 2017), 41.

41. Sander Gilman, *Freud, Race and Gender* (Princeton, NJ: Princeton University Press, 1993), 51.

42. Michael Brenner and Gideon Reuveni, *Emancipation through Muscles: Jews and Sports in Europe* (Lincoln: University of Nebraska Press, 2006); Daniel Wildman, *Der veränderbare Körper: Jüdische Turner, Männlichkeit und das Wiedergewinnen von Geschichte in Deutschland um 1900* (Tübingen, Germany: Mohr Siebeck, 2009); Ofer Nordheimer Nur, *Eros and Tragedy: Jewish Male Fantasies and the Masculine Revolution of Zionism* (Boston: Academic Studies, 2014).

43. Andersen and Wendt, introduction to *Masculinities and the Nation*, 5.

44. Matan Bord, "Creating the Labor-Zionist Family: Masculinity, Sexuality, and Marriage in Mandate Palestine," *Jewish Social Studies* 22, no. 3 (2017): 38–67.

45. Paul Breines, *Tough Jews, Political Fantasies and the Moral Dilemma of American Jewry* (New York: Basic Books, 1990); Warren Rosenberg, *Legacy of Rage: Jewish Masculinity, Violence, and Culture* (Amherst: University of Massachusetts Press, 2001).

46. Daniel Boyarin, *Unheroic Conduct: The Rise of Heterosexuality and the Invention of the Jewish Man* (Berkeley: University of California Press, 1997).

47. Boyarin, 3–4.

48. Davison noted that "Boyarin's Rabbinic masculinity functions well only as a sine qua non of male Jewishness unaltered by the effects of modern movements." Neil R. Davison, *Jewishness, and Masculinity from the Modern to the Postmodern* (New York: Routledge, 2015), 14–15. Rosenberg, in his critique of Boyarin, underscored that his revision of the Jewish masculine ideal ignored heroic figures such as Moses, Samson, and David. See Rosenberg, *Legacy of Rage*.

49. Krondorfer, "Hiding in the Plain View," 17–52. One of the few important exceptions was Maddy Carey's work that demonstrated how Jewish men in the first months of the Holocaust lost access to public spaces where male bonds and status were established but to a certain extent could recover masculine identities in the ghettos. See Carey, *Jewish Masculinity in the Holocaust*.

50. Sarah Imhoff, *Masculinity and the Making of American Judaism* (Bloomington: Indiana University Press, 2017).

51. Miriam Eve Mora, *Carrying a Big Schtick: Jewish Acculturation and Masculinity in the Twentieth Century* (Detroit: Wayne State University Press, 2024).

52. Patrick Farges, "'Muscle' Yekkes? Multiple German-Jewish Masculinities in Palestine and Israel after 1933," *Central European History* 51,

no. 3 (2018): 466–487; Sebastian Huebel, *Fighter, Worker, and Family Man: German-Jewish Men and Their Gendered Experiences in Nazi Germany, 1933–1941* (Toronto: University of Toronto Press, 2021).

53. Sarah Cole, *Modernism, Male Friendship, and the First World War* (Cambridge: Cambridge University Press, 2003); Santanu Das, *Touch and Intimacy in First World War Literature* (Cambridge: Cambridge University Press, 2005).

54. Lusty, "Introduction," 2. See Michael Gluzman, *Ha-guf ha-tsiyoni: Leumiyut, migdar u-miniyut ba-sifrut ha-israelit ha-hadasha* (Tel Aviv: Hakibbutz Hameuchad, 2007); Mikhal Dekel, *The Universal Jew: Masculinity, Modernity, and the Zionist Moment* (Evanston, IL: Northwestern University Press, 2011).

55. Wojciech Śmieja, *Nie/podległości i transformacje: Szkice o stuleciu męskiego niepokoju 1918–2018* (Katowice, Poland: Wydawnictwo Uniwersytetu Śląskiego, 2023); Adam Dziadek, *Formy męskości* (Warsaw: Wydawnictwo IBL PAN, 2018), three parts; Monika Szczepaniak, *Habitus żołnierski w literaturze i kulturze polskiej w kontekście Wielkiej Wojny* (Kraków: Universitas, 2017); Tomasz Tomasik, *Wojna-Męskość-Literatura* (Słupsk, Poland: Wydawnictwo Akademii Pomorskiej w Słupsku, 2013); Tomasz Kaliściak, *Płeć Pantofla: Odmieńcze męskości w polskiej prozie XIX i XX wieku* (Warsaw: Wydawnictwo IBL PAN, 2016); Filip Mazurkiewicz, *Siła i słabość: Studium upadku męskiej hegemonii w Polsce* (Warsaw: Wydawnictwo IBL PAN, 2019); Wojciech Śmieja, *Hegemonia i trauma: Literatura wobec dominujących fikcji męskości* (Warsaw: Wydawnictwo IBL PAN 2016). Maciej Duda's monograph on men supporting women's emancipation is one of a few historical works that study masculinity in Poland: Maciej Duda, *Emancypanci i emancypatorzy: Mężczyźni wspierający emancypację Polek w drugiej połowie XIX i na początku XX wieku* (Szczecin, Poland: Wydawnictwo Naukowe Uniwersytetu Szczecińskiego, 2017).

56. Sarah Ashwin, *Gender, State and Society in Soviet and Post-Soviet Russia* (London: Routledge, 2000); Barbara Evans Clements, Rebecca Friedman, and Dan Healey, eds., *Russian Masculinities in History and Culture* (New York: Palgrave, 2002); Rebecca Kay, *Men in Contemporary Russia: The Fallen Heroes of Post-Soviet Change?* (London: Ashgate, 2006); Maya Eichler, *Militarizing Men: Gender, Conscription, and War in Post-Soviet Russia* (Stanford, CA: Stanford University Press, 2012); Erica L. Fraser, *Military Masculinity and Postwar Recovery in the Soviet Union* (Toronto: University of Toronto Press, 2019); Alisson Leigh, *Picturing Russia's Men: Masculinity and Modernity in Nineteenth-Century Painting* (New York: Bloomsbury, 2020).

57. See Aída Hurtado and Mrinal Sinha, *Beyond Machismo: Inter-sectional Latino Masculinities* (Austin: University of Texas Press, 2016); Anthony Christian Ocampo, *Brown and Gay in LA: The Lives of Immigrant Sons* (New York: New York University Press, 2023); bell hooks, *We Real Cool: Black Men and Masculinity* (New York: Routledge, 2004).

58. Andersen and Wendt, introduction to *Masculinities and the Nation*, 2.

59. Graham Dawson, "The Blood Bedouin: Lawrence of Arabia, Imperial Adventure and the Imagining of English-British Masculinity," in Roper and Tosh, *Manful Assertions*, 118.

60. Reeser, *Masculinities in Theory*, 22–23.

61. Michael S. Kimmel and Michael A. Messner, introduction to *Men's Lives* (Boston: Allyn & Bacon, 2001), XVI.

62. Björn Krondorfer, "Conflicting Religious Ideals of Masculinity: On Godmen and Male Eunuchs" (presentation, Heinrich Böll Foundation, Berlin, Germany, December 13, 2007).

63. Israel Bartal, "Virility and Impotence: From Traditional Society to the Haskalah," in *Brother Keepers: New Perspectives on Jewish Masculinity*, ed. Harry Brod and Shawn Israel Zevit (Harriman, TN: Men's Studies, 2010), 84.

64. Emma Zohar, "Between Hope and Struggle: The Gender Struggle and the Jewish Socialist Parties in Interwar Poland," *East European Jewish Affairs* 52, no. 1 (2023): 48–66.

65. Moshe Rosman, *Categorically Jewish, Distinctly Polish: Polish Jewish History Reflected and Refracted* (London: Littman Library of Jewish Civilization, 2022), 110.

66. Carey, *Jewish Masculinity in the Holocaust*, 46; Krondorfer, "Hiding in the Plain View," 35–36.

67. Yohai Hakak, *Haredi Masculinities between the Yeshiva, the Army, Work, and Politics: The Sage, the Warrior, and the Entrepreneur* (Leiden, Netherlands: Brill, 2016), 21.

68. See Kijek, *Dzieci modernizmu*, 72–100, on modern Polish Orthodoxy.

69. Gilman, *Freud, Race and Gender*, 236. Historian Stefanie Schüler-Springorum demonstrated that the situation of Jewish men in Germany was much more complex and in certain aspects their masculinities in the nineteenth century differed little from non-Jewish ones. Before Prussia culturally dominated Germany in 1871, petite bourgeoise German Jewish men developed values and practices analogous with those of their non-Jewish counterparts. For example, they enjoyed the access to premarital sex with low-class women but also cherished the ideal of a

cohesive and loving bourgeois family. Toward the end of the nineteenth century, many German Jews embraced general masculine cultural codes of honor and defense readiness. According to Schüler-Springorum, the antisemitic attacks on Jewish masculine gender identity did not immediately lead to the internalization of idea of a weak and effeminate Jewish man. See Stefanie Schüler-Springorum, *Geschlecht und Differenz* (Paderborn, Germany: Ferdinand Schöningh, 2014), 67–109.

70. Bartal, "Virility and Impotence."

71. Lynne Segal, *Slow Motion: Changing Masculinities, Changing Men* (London: Palgrave MacMillan, 2008).

72. Elissa Mailänder, in Anna Hájková, Elissa Mailänder, Doris Bergen, Patrick Farges, and Atina Grossmann, "Forum: Holocaust and History of Gender and Sexuality," *German History* 36, no. 1 (2018), 84.

73. Huebel, *Fighter, Worker, and Family Man*, 76.

74. Merry Wiesner-Hanks, *Gender in History: Global Perspective* (Hoboken, NJ: Wiley-Blackwell, 2001), 7.

1. YESHIVA MEN

1. Ben-Zion Dinur, *Be-olam she-shaka: Zikhronot u-reshumot mi-derekh hayim* (Jerusalem: Mosad Bialik, 1958), 48–49. Dinur's memoirs pertain to years 1884–1914.

2. *Yeshiva*, plural *yeshivot*. *Litvak* is a Yiddish term for a Jew of historical greater Lithuania.

3. Boyarin, *Unheroic Conduct*.

4. As Yakir Englender demonstrated in his study of post-Holocaust Haredi musar and hagiography texts, ultra-Orthodoxy engages in searching for intramural dialogue, and rabbis introduce secular values portraying them as positive virtues. For example, he argues that the Slobodka movement in particular acknowledged and imitated the "ideal body" of a non-Jewish European culture. Yakir Englender, *The Male Body in Ultra-Orthodox Jewish Theology* (Eugene, OR: Pickwick Publications, 2021).

5. Ben-Zion Gold, *The Life of Jews in Poland before the Holocaust: A Memoir* (Lincoln: University of Nebraska Press, 2007), 62.

6. Autobiographies, as texts that address the ontology of self and the dialectics of truth and fiction, are a contested territory. They played a decisive role in the self-perception of the new Jewish intelligentsia. Moseley speaks of Orthodox autobiographies as revisionist and idealizing. Critical theory has deconstructed the autobiography as the embodiment

of a patriarchal gender order and an imperialist "locus of monumental Western selfhood." Marcus Moseley, *Being for Myself Alone: Origins of Jewish Autobiography* (Stanford, CA: Stanford University Press, 2006), 1–5, 377. The early Orthodox autobiographies include *Midor ledor* by Tsvi Hirsh Lipshitz (1901) and *Mekor Barukh* (1928) by Barukh Epstein. See Don Seeman and Rebecca Kobrin, "'Like One of the Whole Men': Learning, Gender and Autobiography in R. Barukh Epstein's *Mekor Barukh*," *Nashim: A Journal of Jewish Women's Studies & Gender Issues* 2 (1999): 52–94.

7. Mitnagdim or misnagdim is the common name for rabbinical opponents of the Hasidic movement, based largely in Lithuania, northern Belarus, and northeastern Poland, that is, the territory inhabited by Litvaks.

8. Immanuel Etkes, *Gaon of Vilna: Man and His Image* (Berkeley: University of California Press, 2002), 170–172.

9. Etkes.

10. Heb. *beit midrash*, plural *batey midrash*. Yiddish singular is *beis midrash*.

11. Shaul Stampfer, *Families, Rabbis and Education: Essays on Traditional Jewish Society in Eastern Europe* (Liverpool, UK: Liverpool University Press, 2010), 216–217.

12. Stampfer, 255–256. Plural of *rosh yeshiva is rashey yeshivot*.

13. Maskilim were the followers of the Haskalah, the Jewish Enlightenment. Haskalah sought to exploit the new possibilities of economic, social, and cultural integration that had become available to Jews. It favored the continued existence of Jewish society as a distinct entity and sought to promote its spiritual and cultural renewal. Both the yeshiva students and the maskilim perceived themselves as members of the masculine elite. Consequently, the blade of maskilic criticism was not directed against the yeshiva but against the heder specifically. While the *hadarim* (plural of *heder*) were strongly criticized by proponents of the Haskalah as backward and primitive, yeshivot never became an object of criticism by the maskilim. This attack was easier since it did not question the elite status of yeshiva graduates and did not shake the masculine hierarchies. Maskilim, while being reformers, still perceived themselves as part and parcel of eastern European Jewish societies and to a certain extent identified with yeshiva students. See Mordechai Zalkin, *Modernizing Jewish Education in Nineteenth-Century Eastern Europe: The School as the Shrine of the Jewish Enlightenment* (Leiden, Netherlands: Brill, 2016), 32–38.

14. The agitation was even stronger in interwar Poland. See Sholem B. Kowalsky, *From My Zaidy's House* (Lakewood, NJ: Israel Bookshop, 2000), 61–63, 80–81.

15. Stampfer, *Families, Rabbis and Education*, 252–261.

16. Stampfer, 272. See Glenn Dynner, *The Light of Learning: Hasidism in Poland on the Eve of the Holocaust* (Oxford: Oxford University Press, 2024). However, the Volozhin yeshiva was almost defunct in the mid-1930s; see "W sławnej jeszywie w Wołożynie," *Nasz Przegląd*, January 31, 1935, 3.

17. See Michelle Zimbalist Rosaldo and Louise Lamphere, eds., *Women, Culture and Society* (Stanford, CA: Stanford University Press, 1974).

18. See Biale, *Eros and the Jews*, 7–8.

19. Tamar Samogyi, *Die Schejnen und die Prosten: Untersuchungen zum Schönheitsideal der Ostjuden in Bezug auf Körper und Kleidung unter besonderer Berücksichtigung des Chassidismus* (Cologne, Germany: Reimer, 1982), 70–71.

20. Shlomo Tikochinski, *Lamdanut, musar ve-elitizm: Yeshivat Slobodka me-Lita le-Erets Israel* (Jerusalem: Zalman Shazar Center for Jewish History, 2016), 161–164.

21. Dinur, *Be-olam she-shaka*, 72.

22. Sara Reguer and Moshe Aron Reguer, *My Father's Journey: A Memoir of Lost Worlds of Jewish Lithuania* (Boston: Academic Studies, 2015), 65.

23. Reguer, 37.

24. Joseph Rolnik, *With Rake in Hand: Memoirs of a Yiddish Poet* (Syracuse, NY: Syracuse University Press, 2016), 82.

25. Yitshak Nissenbaum, "Be-yeshivot Bobruisk ve-Volozhin," in Immanuel Etkes and Shlomo Tikochinski, eds., *Yeshivot Lita: Prakey zikhornot* (Jerusalem: Zalman Shazar Center for Jewish History, 2004), 103–104; Moshe Eizenstadt, "Yeshivat Volozhin," in Etkes and Tikochinski, *Yeshivot lita*, 110–111; Efraim Moszwicki, "Me-zikhronotay me-'yeshiva' be-Volozhin," in Etkes and Tikochinski, *Yeshivot lita*, 127; Dinur, *Ba-olam she-shaka*, 71. In the interwar years, most mitnagdim yeshiva students did shave their beards, while students of Hasidic yeshivot did not. See Stampfer, *Families, Rabbis and Education*, 271.

26. Reguer, *My Father's Journey*, 99.

27. Reguer, 129–131.

28. Heb. *Mredot* or *mehumot*. Eizenstadt, "Yeshivat Volozhin," 119.

29. Moszwicki, "Me-zikhronotay me-'yeshiva' be-Volozhin," 127.

30. Moszwicki, 127–128.

31. Tikochinski, *Lamdanut, musar ve-elitizm*, 43–49.

32. Meir Bar-Ilan (Berlin), "Al yeshivat Volozhin ve-rashe'a," in Etkes and Tikochinski, *Yeshivot Lita*, 199.

33. Kimmel, *Manhood in America*; Anthony Rotundo, *American Manhood: Transformations in Masculinity from the Revolution to the Modern Era* (New York: Basic Books, 1994), 10–31.

34. Shaul Stampfer, *Lithuanian Yeshivot of the Nineteenth Century: Creating a Tradition of Learning* (Oxford: Littman Library of Jewish Civilization, 2012), 129.

35. Meir Sheli, "Resisey Telz," in Etkes and Tikochinski, *Yeshivot Lita*, 262.

36. Dinur, *Be-olam she-shaka*, 48, 101.

37. Stampfer, *Families, Rabbis and Education*, 29–30.

38. Tikochinski, *Lamdanut, musar, ve-elitizm*, 158–159; Asaf, "Shnot ha-limudim sheli ba-yeshivat Telz," 239.

39. See Tomasik, *Wojna-Męskość-Literatura*; Szczepaniak, *Habitus żołnierski w literaturze i kulturze polskiej.*

40. Reguer, *My Father's Journey*, 133.

41. Reguer, 76, 81.

42. Menachem Mendel Zlotkin, "Yeshivat Volozhin ba-tkufat Bialik," in Etkes and Tikochinski, *Yeshivot Lita*, 189.

43. Stampfer, *Families, Rabbis, and Education*, 226–227.

44. Yehuda Leib Don Yichye, "Ba-yeshivat Volozhin," in Etkes and Tikochinski, *Yeshivot Lita*, 155.

45. Gold, *The Life of Jews in Poland*, 100.

46. Moszwicki, "Me-zikhronotay me-'yeshiva' be-Volozhin," 125. Asir Yehuda Unterman, in Etkes and Tikochinski, *Yeshivot Lita*, 300–301. Yom Tov Levinski, "Al ha-yeshiva ha-gdola ba-Łomża lifney yovel shanim," in Etkes and Tikochinski, *Yeshivot Lita*, 350.

47. Bar-Ilan, "Al yeshivat Volozhin ve-rashe'a," 199.

48. Reguer, *My Father's Journey*, 75.

49. Yehoshua Leib Radus, "Yeshivat Slobodka," in Etkes and Tikochinski, *Yeshivot Lita*, 333.

50. Zlotkin, "Yeshivat Volozhin ba-tkufat Bialik," 187.

51. Don Yichye, "Ba-yeshivat Volozhin," 155.

52. Pinchas Turberg, "Ba-tsa'ati me-Volozhin," in Etkes and Tikochinski, *Yeshivot Lita*, 195.

53. See Immanuel Etkes, "Marriage and Torah Study among the Lomdim in Lithuania in the Nineteenth Century," in *The Jewish Family: Metaphor and Family*, ed. David Kraemer, 153–178 (New York: Oxford University Press, 1989).

54. Moszwicki, "Me-zikhronotay me-'yeshiva' be-Volozhin," 125.

55. Zvi Scharfstein, "From the Life of Our Brothers in Galicia: The Education of Daughters," *Ha-Olam*, September 29, 1910, 11–12, quoted in Rachel Manekin, *The Rebellion of the Daughters: Jewish Women Runaways in Habsburg Galicia* (Princeton, NJ: Princeton University Press, 2020).

56. Jakub Schall, *Dzieje Żydów na ziemiach polskich: Podręcznik dla szkół średnich* (Lviv, Poland: A. Bardach, 1926), 53.

57. Manekin, *The Rebellion of the Daughters.*

58. Stampfer, *Families, Rabbis and Education,* 147.

59. Saul M. Ginsburg and P. S. Marek, *Evrejskija narodnyja pesni v Rossii* (Saint Petersburg: Voskhod, 1901), quoted in Samogyi, *Die Schejnen und die Prosten,* 52.

60. Stampfer, *Families, Rabbis and Education,* 145–148.

61. Rolnik, *With Rake in Hand,* 84, 161.

62. Tikochinski, *Lamdanut, musar ve-elitizm,* 160.

63. Eizenstadt, "Yeshivat Volozhin," 108; Moszwicki, "Me-zikhronotay me-'yeshiva' be-Volozhin," 129.

64. Asaf, "Shnot ha-limudim sheli ba-yeshivat Telz," 231.

65. Sheli, "Resisey Telz," 231, 266.

66. Turberg, "Ba-tsa'ati me-Volozhin," 196. Other accounts speak of yeshiva students who engaged in private secular studies to enter the university after the yeshiva. See Shlomo Zaltsman, "Ba-yeshiva ba-Mir," in Etkes and Tikochinski, *Yeshivot Lita,* 317.

67. Don Yichye, "Ba-yeshivat Volozhin," 153.

68. Zalman Epstein, "Yeshivat volozhin," in Etkes and Tikochinski, *Yeshivot Lita,* 73.

69. Epstein, 73, 74.

70. Zlotkin, "Yeshivat Volozhin ba-tkufat Bialik," 185.

71. Dinur, *Be-olam she-shaka,* 85.

72. Zlotkin, "Yeshivat Volozhin ba-tkufat Bialik," 184–185.

73. B. Shulman, "Ha-ruah ha-maapkhanit ba-yeshivot Telz ve-Zhadov be-shanim 1906–1909," in Etkes and Tikochinski, *Yeshivot Lita,* 276.

74. Zaltsman, "Ba-yeshiva ba-Mir," 316.

75. Reguer, *My Father's Journey,* 47.

76. Stampfer, *Families, Rabbis and Education,* 147.

77. Dinur, *Be-olam she-shaka,* 79–80.

78. Zaltsman, "Ba-yeshiva ba-Mir," 316.

79. Shulman, "Ha-ruah ha-maapkhanit," 276–277.

80. Heb. *iluy,* plural *ilium,* Talmudic prodigy or genius; *matmid,* plural *matmidim,* a diligent student. Yechiel Yaakov Weinberg, *Le-prakim,* pages פח-פטת, quoted in Tikochinski, *Lamdanut, musar ve-elitizm,* 53.

81. Sheli, "Resisey Telz," 256.

82. Reguer, *My Father's Journey,* 69.

83. Stampfer, *Families, Rabbis and Education,* 262.

84. Tikochinski, *Lamdanut, musar ve-elitizm*, 153, 157.

85. Moszwicki, "Me-zikhronotay me-'yeshiva' be-Volozhin," 124–125.

86. See Theodore Bienenstok, "Social Life and Authority in the East European Jewish Shtetel Community," *Southwestern Journal of Anthropology* 6, no. 3 (1950): 238–254.

87. Moszwicki, "Me-zikhronotay me-'yeshiva' be-Volozhin," 120.

88. Rolnik, *With Rake in Hand*, 79.

89. Nissenbaum, "Be-yeshivot Bobruisk ve-Volozhin," 104.

90. Sheli, "Resisey Telz," 265.

91. Sheli, 265.

92. Dinur, *Be-olam she-shaka*, 58–59.

93. Samogyi, *Die Schejnen und die Prosten*, 91–93.

94. You are dark, dark / but full of charm / for someone you are ugly / for me you are beautiful. Ginsburg and Marek, *Evrejskija narodnyja pesni*, 33.

95. Riva Chirurg, Testimony ST.013, 11, Jewish Family and Children's Services CS Holocaust Center in San Francisco.

96. Rolnik, *With Rake in Hand*, 83.

97. Samogyi, *Die Schejnen und die Prosten*, 96.

98. Samogyi, 251.

99. Epstein, "Yeshivat volozhin," 75.

100. Epstein, 74.

101. Gold, *The Life of Jews in Poland*, 60.

102. Chirurg, Testimony ST.013, 11.

103. Stampfer, *Families, Rabbis and Education*, 273.

104. Epstein, "Yeshivat volozhin," 72.

105. Tikochinski, *Lamdanut, musar, ve-elitizm*, 157–158.

106. Reguer, *My Father's Journey*, 96.

107. Reguer, 129, 132.

108. Samogyi, *Die Schejnen und die Prosten*, 249.

109. The discourse of "degeneration of Eastern ghetto Jew" was particularly strong among the German-Jewish elite. See Todd Samuel Pressner, *Muscular Judaism: The Jewish Body and the Politics of Regeneration* (New York: Routledge, 2007), 24–65.

110. Nissenbaum, "Be-yeshivot Bobruisk ve-Volozhin," 103; Moszwicki, "Me-zikhronotay me-ha-'yeshiva' ba-volozhin," 120.

111. Moszwicki, "Me-zikhronotay me-'yeshiva' be-Volozhin," 120.

112. Reguer, *My Father's Journey*, 75. Reguer adds that the musar spirit later challenged the moments of relaxation.

113. Reguer, 76.

114. Reguer, 138–139.

115. Zaltsman, "Ba-yeshiva ba-Mir," 318.

116. Turberg, "Ba-tsa'ati me-Volozhin," 196.

117. Zlotkin, "Yeshivat Volozhin ba-tkufat Bialik," 189.

118. Levinski, "Al ha-yeshiva ha-gdola," 356.

119. Dinur, *Be-olam she-shaka*, 53.

120. Dinur, 59.

121. Bar Ilan, "Al yeshivat Volozhin ve-rashe'a," 209.

122. Nissenbaum, "Be-yeshivot Bobruisk ve-Volozhin," 104.

123. Eizenstadt, "Yeshivat Volozhin," 110, 119.

124. Dinur, *Be-olam she-shaka*, 83.

125. Dinur, 91.

126. Bar-Ilan, "Al yeshivat Volozhin ve-rashe'a," 209.

127. Reguer, *My Father's Journey*, 60.

128. Reguer, 61.

129. Shulman, "Ha-ruah ha-maapkhanit," 278.

130. Shulman, 287.

131. Mosse, *The Image of Man*, 7–27.

132. Niobe Way, "Boys' Friendships during Adolescence: Intimacy, Desire, and Loss," *Journal of Research on Adolescence* 23, no. 2 (2013), 201.

133. See, for example, Sarah Cole, *Modernism, Male Friendship, and the First World War* (Cambridge: Cambridge University Press, 2003); Kenneth Loiselle, *Brotherly Love: Freemasonry and Male Friendship in Enlightenment France* (Ithaca, NY: Cornell University Press, 2014); Thomas Kühne, *The Rise and Fall of Comradeship: Hitler's Soldiers, Male Bonding and Mass Violence in the Twentieth Century* (Cambridge: Cambridge University Press, 2017).

134. Reguer, *My Father's Journey*, 94.

135. Stampfer, *Family, Rabbis and Education*, 225.

136. Stampfer, 225–226.

137. Turberg, "Ba-tsa'ati me-Volozhin," 197.

138. Nissenbaum, "Be-yeshivot Bobruisk ve-Volozhin," 96; Eizenstadt, "Yeshivat Volozhin," 111.

139. Aba Blosher, "Bialik ba-Volozhin," in Etkes and Tikochinski, *Yeshivot Lita*, 165–167.

140. Turberg, "Ba-tsa'ati me-Volozhin," 197.

141. Rolnik, *With Rake in Hand*, 83.

142. Zlotkin, "Yeshivat Volozhin ba-tkufat Bialik," 182–183.

143. Bar Ilan, "Al yeshivat Volozhin ve-rashe'a," 200.

144. Dinur, *Be-olam she-shaka*, 70.

145. Reguer, *My Father's Journey*, 112.

146. Reguer, 125.

147. Compare: 1 Samuel 18:1–5, "Jonathan became one in spirit with David, and he loved him as himself."

148. Rolnik, *With Rake in Hand*, 93, 267.

149. Rolnik, 92–93.

150. Rolnik, 113.

151. Rolnik, 114.

152. Zaltsman, "Ba-yeshiva ba-Mir," 316–317.

153. *Ha-Olam*, September 26, October 3, and October 10, 1935, translated by Gabriel Laufer and accessed July 14, 2024, at https://keidaner.com/in-prison/?fbclid=IwAR3-KOdefV--b5mwkdWdreMMUx4pdolmXeeZAN NsZAOylWtK9_hqX1HR2Ic.

154. Reguer, *My Father's Journey*, 100.

155. Dinur, *Be-olam she-shaka*, 109.

156. Richard Godbeer, *The Overflowing of Friendship: Love between Men and the Creation of the American Republic* (Baltimore: Johns Hopkins University Press, 2009), 9.

2. A JEW AND HIS PENIS

1. Moshe Weissman, *The Midrash Says: The Book of Beraishis* (New York: Bnei Yaakov, 1980), 153.

2. Gilman, *Freud, Race and Gender*, 49.

3. Lawrence A. Hoffman, *Covenant of Blood: Circumcision and Gender in Rabbinic Judaism* (Chicago: University of Chicago Press, 1995); Elizabeth Wyner Mark, ed., *The Covenant of Circumcision: New Perspectives on an Ancient Jewish Rite* (Hanover, MA: Brandeis University Press, 2003); Robin Judd, *Contested Rituals: Circumcision, Kosher Butchering, and Jewish Political Life in Germany, 1843–1933* (Ithaca, NY: Cornell University Press, 2011).

4. Boyarin, *Unheroic Conduct*, 231–244.

5. Gilman, *Freud, Race and Gender*, 51–52.

6. Neil R. Davison writes, "The internalization of the construct [of an effeminate Jewish man] by so many influential Jewish figures suggests that gendered differences haunted the colonized psyches of Jewish men rather than being dismissed by them as the product of a European racial hatred." Davison, *Jewishness and Masculinity*, 8.

7. Sander Gilman, *Jewish Self-Hatred: Anti-Semitism and the Hidden Language of the Jews* (Baltimore: Johns Hopkins University Press, 1986), 4, quoted in Noelle Gallagher, "The Jew's Penis: Circumcision and Sexual Pathology in Eighteenth-Century England," *Medical Humanities* 49, no. 1 (2023): 70–82.

8. Gallagher, "The Jew's Penis."

9. Edward Dutlinger, "Żydzi w życiu i literaturze," *Jedność: Pismo poświęcone szerzeniu myśli polskiej wśród Żydów*, July 16, 1909, 2–3. *Jedność* stood for Jewish acculturation within the Polish society.

10. The *sandak* is the man who holds the baby boy during Jewish religious circumcision. The *mohel* is the man who performs the circumcision.

11. "Nokh a yud!," *Der Moment*, October 19, 1911, 3.

12. "Oyfn Krokhmalner pletsel iz geven yom-tovdig. Der yidisher olem hot gepravet dort a bris fun a 26-yorigen ger," *Haynt*, September 28, 1934, 11. The plural of *bris* is *brisim*.

13. "Vi heysen di kinder vos men hot mol geven in shtotisher pindel-hoyz," *Der Moment*, September 23, 1934, 10.

14. "Mazl tov gants Radzymin!," *Hayntige Nayes*, September 16, 1935, 3.

15. A. P., "Di nekhtige bris-mile-fayerung in Falenits. Toyzender gerer hasidim betayligen zikh in der simkhe," *Der Moment*, July 11, 1926, 4.

16. See, for instance, "Di 2 groyse simkhes bay Gerer rabin in Otwock," *Der Moment*, July 29, 1929, 5.

17. Regina Lilientalowa, *Dziecko żydowskie* (Kraków, Poland: Polska Akademia Umiejętności, 1927), 14–18.

18. "Der bris fun a 30-yorigen jungenman," *Der Moment*, February 1, 1922, 4.

19. "Bris mile fun a 20-yorigen bokher," *Haynt*, July 10, 1923, 3.

20. "Lodzer asimilator farlibt zikh in a vilner meydl," *Dos Naye Lebn*, October 3, 1928, 2.

21. "Bris-mile iber tsvey dervaksene brider," *Haynt*, July, 6, 1939, 5.

22. "A bris fun 60-yorigen hasidishen yud in Kroke," *Unzer Bialystok Ekspres*, May 19, 1936, 7.

23. "Mol-geven a 5-yerig yingele," *Haynt*, February 17, 1937, 5.

24. "Der oysterlisher bris fun a 13-yorikn bokhr," *Unzer Tsaytung*, October 27, 1935, 3.

25. "Zugeganevt bay tate-mame in yom kippur a kind un durkhgefirt a bris," *Der Moment*, October 8, 1928, 7.

26. "A kind in a bude," *Hayntige Nayes*, March 4, 1931, 1.

27. "Foter nisht gelozt mol zayn dos kind, vayl er iz in kaas oyf zayn mamen," *Hayntige Nayes*, October 30, 1935, 3.

28. "Origneler shvindel fun varshever aferisten. Men hot yidn me-khabed geven mit sandakues," *Haynt*, January 18, 1939, 5.

29. "Arestirt tsvey yuden, vos hoben geshvindelt mit . . . sandakues," *Der Moment*, July 6, 1934, 11.

30. See "Sandakues (a mayse she'haya)," *Der Moment*, July 21, 1916, 2; "Gevalt. Aferirn unzer barimten rav Dan," *Hayntige Nayes*, July 15, 1934, 3; "Provints-shpigel," *Haynt*, March 26, 1931, 4.

31. "A mayse mit a sandak," *Hayntige Nayes*, October 17, 1934, 1.

32. Sholem Ash, "Motke Ganef: Ertselung," *Haynt*, July 26, 1922, 8.

33. Ilonor, "Skąpiec. Z legend żydowskich," *Jedność*, August 26, 1910, 2–3.

34. Y. L. Perets, "In alt Khelem (a mayseleh)," *Der Fraynd*, March, 31, 1911.

35. "Oys moyre az men zol ir kind nisht mol zayn, a muter meshuge gevorn," *Der Moment*, February 16, 1934, 10.

36. The contributor in a local Yiddish newspaper criticized that babies of single Jewish mothers who gave birth in a Christian hospital were not circumcised and accused those Jewish women of "raising antisemites." "Dos kristlekhe shpitol un di yudishe kinder," *Nayer Morgen*, August 25, 1937, 3.

37. "Tsulib kargshaft lozt er nish mol zayn dos kind . . . ," *Kieltser Tsaytung*, November 13, 1936, 3.

38. "Kristlekhe muter khapt tsu dos kind bay ir yudishn man un lozt es nisht mol zayn," *Unzer Express*, September 18, 1933, 8.

39. Lipa Laykin, "Tsi ken fun a maydl vern a yingl," *Haynt*, August 21, 1908, 2.

40. Edmund Stein, "Judaizm a Hellenizm: Z powodu książki prof. Tadeusza Zielińskiego p.t. 'Hellenizm a Judaizm,'" *B'nai B'rith* (Kraków), February 1, 1929, 4–5.

41. Stein.

42. Regina Lilientalowa, *Precz z barbarzyństwem (rzecz o obrzezaniu)* (Warsaw: "Życie Wolne," 1928).

43. Lilientalowa, *Precz z barbarzyństwem*.

44. Herman Grynszpan, "Barbarzyństwa judaistyczne," *Myśl Niepodległa* 10, no. 78 (1908): 1421–1426.

45. Ludwik Krzywicki, *Dawne obrzezanie* (Warsaw: "Życie Wolne," 1928).

46. Ben-Zion Lieber, *Dos geshlekhts leben: A populer-visnshaftlikh bukh* (New York: Rational Living, 1927), 171–178.

47. Beniamin Rosenblum, *Uwagi nad teraźniejszym stanem starozakonnych pod względem policyjno-lekarskim* (Warsaw, n.p., 1842), 7–13.

48. T. Belke, "Kwestia nierządu publicznego," *Klinika, Tygodnik Lekarski*, November 11, 1869, 323. Analogous discussions appeared elsewhere in the world. See Daniel Poliak, "Metsitsah Be-Peh, Nineteenth Century New York Jewry, and the Board of Health," *Tradition: A Journal of Orthodox Jewish Thought* 44, no. 3 (2011): 39–52.

49. *Kurier Warszawski*, September 20, 1846, 1186.

50. Josef Ruff, *Wieczny związek: Obrzezanie ze stanowiska obrządkowego, chirurgicznego i higienicznego* (Warsaw, n.p., 1883).

51. Samuel Natan Kutna, *Sollen wir unsere Knäbelein beschneiden?* (Przemyśl, Poland: Robinsohn & Beglückter, 1903), 107.

52. Kutna, 66.

53. Kutna, 33.

54. "Nokh doktoyrim-tsuzamenfor fun 'TOZ,'" *Zdrowie Ludu-Folksgezunt*, July 1, 1928, 231.

55. "Popłoch wśród Żydów. Powtórne obrzezanie chłopców," *Expres Zagłębia*, May 4, 1934, 1.

56. I. Gott, "Di higyene bay yidn," *Dos naye lebn* (Kalisz), October 21, 1938, 5.

57. "Sharfe protest-rezolutsye fun rabanim-tsuzamenfor gegen tsvang-zontag-ru," *Der Moment*, January 8, 1932, 10.

58. "Der rabinat zol zushtetn di 'aktsye-gezelshaft' fun mohelim," *Der Moment*, January 30, 1935, 5. In the same time, the Jewish population of Warsaw grew from about 337,000 in 1914 to 375,000 in 1939.

59. Mordechai Lensky, *More derekh le-mohelim. Kurtse yedies fun anatomye, fizyologye un aseptik* (Warsaw: Kultur-sektsye bay der varshever kehile-fervaltung, 1931). The book appeared with Moshe Feldstein's foreword and new circumcision regulations adopted by the Warsaw kehillah.

60. "Tsi darfen mohelim fun der provints oykh bazitsen a legitimat-sye?," *Kalisher Wokh*, August 8, 1930, 2.

61. "Hayntige vokh geyt arayn in kraft der regulamin far mohelim," *Haynt*, December 18, 1930, 6.

62. "Groyse skandalen tsulib dem vos mohelim viln nisht mol zayn on geld," *Haynt*, January 18, 1935, 11.

63. "Bris mile fun a 27-yorigen ger," *Haynt*, March 11, 1927, 11.

64. "Ofene tribune," *Haynt*, March 12, 1912, 5.

65. "Grindung fun agudas hamohelim," *Haynt*, January 10, 1927, 6.

66. "Groyser skandal mit mohelim in varshe," *Unzer Tsaytung*, November 15, 1935, 5; "Der rabinat zol zushtetn di 'aktsye-gezelshaft' fun mohelim," *Der Moment*, January 30, 1935, 5.

67. "R. Moshe Feldshtayn hat a ta'ane tsu der agud'sher kehila fervaltung," *Haynt*, May 6, 1935, 5.

68. "Delegatsye fun varshever rabonim in regirungs-komisariat," *Unzer Express*, November 7, 1935, 9.

69. "Kristlelkhe eltern zenen mol zayer kind," *Hayntige Nayes*, April 7, 1930, 3.

70. "Setsatyoneler bris oyf Wolska," *Unzer Grodner Express*, February 18, 1931, 5.

71. Gershon Bacon, "Kfiya datit, hofesh bituy ve-zehut yehudit modernit ba-polin: Y. L. Peretz, Sholem Ash and the milah-scandal in Warsaw, 1908," in *Me-vilna le-yerushalayim: Mekhkarim be-toldotehem ve-tarbutam shel yehudey mizrakh eyropa, mugashim le-profesor Shmuel Verses*, 167–185 (Jerusalem: Magnes, 2002).

72. "W sprawie przymusu obrzędowego," *Nowa Gazeta*, October 12, 1908, 2.

73. "Varshever lebens-bildlekh," *Haynt*, October 13, 1908, 3.

74. For a detailed discussion, see Bacon, "Kfiya datit," 172–176.

75. "Der entfer fun rav Klepfish vegen aynshrayben in di geburts-bikher h. Alters nisht gemoltn zun," *Haynt*, July 28, 1927, 5.

76. Hersh Dovid Nomberg, "Notitsen. Der intsident mit h. Alters nicht gemoltn kind," *Der Moment*, July 21, 1927, 3.

77. "Tsi hot ratman Alter rekht nisht mol tsu zayn zayn zun?," *Haynt*, December 8, 1926, 5.

78. See Judd, *Contested Rituals*.

79. "Er mamitet zayn 'klerikaler' vayb, vos hot gegen zayn 'printsip' gelozt mol zayn zayer zun," *Der Moment*, March 31, 1935, 7.

80. "Groyse skandalen tsulib dem vos mohelim vilen nisht mol zayn on geld," *Haynt*, January 18, 1935, 11.

81. "Tsvey merkvurdige fale bay a rav," *Hayntige Nayes*, September 8, 1936, 3.

82. "A fraydenkerin lozt mol zayn kind nokh 9 hadoshim," *Hayntige Nayes*, April 29, 1930, 1.

83. "A yid farmishpet far mol zayn a kind," *Haynt*, February 28, 1922, 2; "Beshtraft der Minsker rav Sadovski derfar, vos er hot geyudisht zayn eynikel," *Unzer Express*, January 24, 1929, 3.

84. Yosef Opatoshu, "Printsipn," *Lubliner Tugblatt*, February 3, 1928, 4.

85. "Nowości warszawskie," *Kurjer Warszawski*, January 5, 1822, 1.

86. Polish: "Sanacja, sanacja, what is your female charm that so many circumcised young men follow you?" Sanacja was the political group ruling in Poland at the time.

87. "Mazal tov, r. Franciszek," *Grodner Moment*, September 29, 1929, 6.

88. "Sensacja w Radomsku," *Gazeta Radomskowska*, September 21, 1924, 6.

89. T.M. "Sensacje żydowskie," *Dziennik wileński*, January 18, 1936, 5.

90. Andrzej Niemojewski, *Dusza żydowska w zwierciadle Talmudu: Wydanie drugie poprawione* (Warsaw: self-published, 1920), 115–119.

91. Jan Ruff, "O reformę religijną żydostwa," *Rozwaga: Miesięcznik poświęcony idei zespolenia żydów z narodem polskim*, February 1, 1923, 165.

92. "Niezwykła sensacja miłosna w Piotrkowie. Jak b. sierżant-chrześcijanin został żydem," *Iskra: Dziennik polityczny, społeczny i literacki*, July 8, 1921.

93. Ignacy Charszewski, "Obrzezańcy, którzy obrzezują," *Dziennik Kujawski*, July 5, 10, and 12, 1932, unpaginated.

94. Ibid.

95. Ibid.

96. Adolf Nowaczyński, *Warta nad Wartą* (Poznań, Poland: Drukarnia Polska, 1937), 75.

97. Wanda Melcerowa, "Dziecko żydowskie rozpoczyna ziemską wędrówkę," *Wiadomości Literackie*, April 8, 1934, 1.

98. Tadeusz "Boy" Żeleński, *Obiad literacki* (Warsaw: Biblioteka Boya, 1934), 130.

99. "'Znak przymierza z Jehową' zlekceważyły tysiące Żydów warszawskich," *Nowa Rzeczpospolita*, August 10, 1938, 7.

100. Roman Brandstaetter, "Palestyńska Bereza," *5-ta rano*, August 7, 1936, 5.

101. "Vi azoy Leybele Kuzmir hot gevolt mol zayn a kristlekhen uzhendnik," *Hayntige Nayes*, January 24, 1932, 3.

3. BOYS SHOWING OFF

1. B. G., "Sport un natsyonale virde," *Nayer morgen*, August 2, 1936, 2.

2. "Lebens-geshikhte fun shapsel rotholc," *Hayntige Nayes*, April 10, 1938, 3.

3. Zelik Rusecki, "Yudishe shportler vos veren ferater," *Sport-tsaytung*, April 4, 1933.

4. Michael Brenner, "Warum Juden und Sport?," in Brenner and Reuveni, *Emanzipation durch Muskelkraft*, 8, 11. See also Robert Gawkowski and Jarosław Rokicki, "Stosunki polsko-żydowskie w sporcie II Rzeczpospolitej," in *Parlamentaryzm, konserwatyzm, nacjonalizm: Sefer jowel. Studia ofiarowane Profesorowi Szymonowi Rudnickiemu*, ed. Jolanta Żyndul, 221–240 (Warsaw: Wydawnictwo Sejmowe, 2010).

5. See Roni Gechtman, "Socialist Mass Politics through Sport: The Bund's Morgnshtern in Poland, 1926–1939," in "One Hundred Years of 'Muscular Judaism': Sport in Jewish History and Culture," special issue, *Journal of Sport History* 26, no. 2 (1999): 326–352; Jack Jacobs, "Jewish Workers' Sports Movements in Inter-War Poland: Shtern and Morgnshtern in Comparative Perspective," in *Jews, Sports and the Rites of Citizenship*, ed. Jack Kugelmass, 114–130 (Champaign: University of Illinois Press, 2007).

6. As Ulrike Brunotte writes, the encounter between Jewish studies and gender and queer studies produced an emphasis on antisemitic constructions of "soft" Jewish masculinity, homosexuality, and homophobia. Ulrike Brunotte, "'All Jews Are Womanly, but No Women Are Jews.' The 'Femininity' Game of Deception: Female Jew, Femme Fatale Orientale, and Belle Juive," in Ulrike Brunotte, Anna-Dorothea Ludewig, and Axel Stähler, eds., *Orientalism, Gender, and the Jews: Literary and Artistic Transformations of European National Discourses* (Oldenbourg, Germany: De Gruyter, 2015), 195–197.

7. Max Nordau, "Muskeljudentum," *Jüdische Turnzeitung*, June 1903, in Paul Mendes-Flohr and Yehuda Reinharz, eds., *The Jew in the Modern World: A Documentary History* (Oxford: Oxford University Press, 2010), 435.

8. Wildmann, *Der verändbare Körper*, 138–139; Max Mandelstamm, "Rede," in *Stenographisches Protokoll der Verhandlungen des II. Zionisten-Congresses* (Vienna: Verlag des Vereines "Erez Israel," 1898), 90.

9. Quoted in Wildmann, *Der verändbare Körper*, 144.

10. Wildmann, *Der verändbare Körper*, 153–156.

11. For example, when Daniela Gauding writes that the most popular Jewish strongman of the 1920s, Zishe Breitbart, "enjoyed a particular admiration among eastern European Jews in Poland and America precisely because he contradicted the image of a weak ghetto Jew on the world stage and acted as a proud Jew," she implies that eastern European Jews indeed perceived themselves as "weak ghetto Jews." Daniela Gauding, *Siegmund Sische Breitbart—Eisenkönig, stärkster Mann der Welt: Breitbart versus Hanussen* (Berlin: Hentrich & Hentrich, 2006). Historian Matthew Sherman suggests that Breitbart "exhibited the possibility for Jewish mobility, even emancipation, through corporeality and in that sense, he instilled hope and pride in a previously apathetic collective psyche," which supposedly characterized eastern European Jewry in particular. The question arises whether eastern European Jewish men indeed

deemed their psyche apathetic (and hence unmasculine) or whether it is Sherman who sees this feature as constitutive of eastern European Jewry. Sherman borrows his ideas from the vocabulary of the western European Zionist discourse and does not examine whether these ideas were at all discussed or existent in Poland and other countries of the region. Matthew J. Sherman, "Corporeality as Weapon: Siegmund Breitbart's Embodiment of Muskeljudentum," *German Politics and Society* 30, no. 2 (2012), 33.

12. "Shapsel: Lebens-geshikhte fun shapsel rotholc," *Hayntige Nayes*, April 3, 1938, 3.

13. André Rauch, "Wyzwanie sportowe a doświadczenie męskości," in Corbin, *Historia męskości*, 227, 251.

14. Rauch, 230–231.

15. When the Jewish wrestler Yaakov Fisher won the fight in the Warsaw circus, it was thanks to his "athletic art" rather than his brutal power. The press called Fisher "a shining master of the technique" and also noted the skills of other fighters. "Di nekhtiken kampfen in tsirk," *Unzer Express*, January 6, 1931, 7. In 1935, a journal of the sports club Maccabi printed gymnastics guidelines that were in line with the increasing quantification and subordination of masculine physical performance into regulations. M. Birger, "Trening wioślarski," *Hamakabi*, August 1, 1935, 2.

16. M. Hollender, "Farvos zenen die yuden gute bokser?," *Sport-tsaytung*, March 19, 1935, 3.

17. Tunkeler, "Mayn shvager hot entdekt dem sod," *Sport-tsaytung*, [1937?].

18. L. Wigman, "Boks, bronfen und yuden brengen aroys fun di keylim di lemberger antisemiten," *Sport-tsaytung*, March 21, 1939, 3.

19. See Rudy Koshar, "Seeing, Travelling and Consuming: An Introduction," in Rudy Koshar, ed., *Histories of Leisure* (Oxford: Oxford University Press, 2002), 1–24.

20. Shapsel Rotholc admired Polish-Catholic and Polish-Jewish performance wrestlers and circus strongmen Stanisław "Zbyszko" Cyganiewicz, Franciszek "Cyklop" Bieńkowski, and Zishe Breitbart. "Lebensgeshihkte fun shapsel rotholc," *Hayntige Nayes*, April 3, 1938, 3.

21. Rauch, "Wyzwanie sportowe," 238–250.

22. Sh. Danzig, "Vi azoy iz max krauser gevorn a mayster fun eyropa," *Sport-tsaytung*, May 14, 1935, 3.

23. See Jarosław Rokicki, *Żydowski ruch sportowy i turystyczny w Polsce w pierwszej połowie XX wieku* (Warsaw: n.p., 1994).

24. Zelik Rusecki, "Farvos zenen far unz farloyren di boks profesyonalisten," *Sport-tsaytung*, March 21, 1933, 9.

25. "Shapsel: Lebens-geshikhte fun shapsel rotholc," *Hayntige Nayes*, April 7, 1938, 3.

26. Al. Rekssa, "Gdzie djabeł nie może…," *Przegląd Sportowy*, July 28, 1934, 3; August 4, 1934, 3; August 8, 1934, 3; August 15, 1934, 3; August 18, 1934, 3.

27. "Shapsel: Lebens-geshikhte fun shapsel rotholc," *Hayntige Nayes*, April 5, 1938, 3.

28. Georges Vigarello, "Męskości sportowe," in Jaen-Jacques Courtine, ed., *Historia męskości*, vol. 3, *XX–XXI wiek: Męskość w kryzysie* (Gdańsk: słowo/obraz terytoria, 2021), 203–204.

29. Melech Ravitch, "Zishe Breitbarts kerper ligt shoyn in der erd," *Literarishe Bleter* 77 (October 23, 1925), 185.

30. See Sharon Gillerman, "Samson in Vienna: The Theatrics of Jewish Masculinity," *Jewish Social Studies* 9, no. 2 (2003): 65–98.

31. "A bezukh bay Breitbarts almone," *Der Moment*, November 16, 1925, 4; Izrael Kahan, "Der tumel vegn Zishe Breitbarts yerushe," *Yidische Zaitung*, January 1926, 9–10. Kahan was a Łódź journalist, but the article was published in Buenos Aires.

32. "Dziś w środę 27 b.m pierwszy występ Króla Żelaza Zygmunta Breitbarta," 1925, poster, Polona, https://polona.pl/item/ulotka-inc-dzis-w -srode-27-b-m-pierwszy-wystep-krola-zelaza-zygmunta-breitbarta,Mzg 3Mzk1ODg/1/#info:metadata.

33. "Bam yidishn ayzn-kenig (geshprekh mit zishe breitbart)," *Haynt*, March 3, 1925, 5.

34. Ravitch, "Zishe Breitbarts kerper," 185.

35. "Shimshon ha-gibor shel dorenu," *Ha-yom*, March 6, 1925, 5.

36. "Zishe Breitbart als 'Shimshon ha-giber' oyfn purim-bal fun der yidisher prese," *Haynt*, March 4, 1925, 6.

37. On the circus in Poland at the turn of the twentieth century, see Agnieszka Bińczycka, "Cyrk w Polsce na przełomie XIX i XX wieku i w okresie międzywojennym," in Grzegorz Kondrasiuk, ed., *Cyrk w świecie widowisk* (Lublin, Poland: Warsztaty Kultury w Lublinie, 2017), 111–134.

38. "Ayzn kenig Zishe Breitbart," *Der Moment*, February 27, 1925, 7.

39. "Cyrk Warszawski St. Mroczkowski 'Rusałka'" (Lublin, Poland: n.p., 1925?), Polona, https://polona.pl/item/afisz-inc-tylko-3-wystepy-nadzwyc zajnych-atrakcji-cyrku-warszawskiego-na-czele,Mzg3Mzk1OTY/0/#info: metadata.

40. "W środę d. 6-go września r.b. wieczór śmiechu i humoru … Dziś walczą 2 pary: 1 para francuska walka Brajtbard (sz. Wszechświat.) - Perkowski (szamp. Polski) …," flyer (Radom, Poland: n.p., 1925?), https://

polona2.pl/item/ulotka-incipit-w-srode-d-6-go-wrzesnia-r-b-wieczor
-smiechu-i-humoru-dzis,MTI4NDAyNTIx/0/#info:metadata.

41. "Yudisher atlet tsershtokhen mit mesers durkh huliganes," *Unzer Express*, November 18, 1935, 8. I assume that if the hooligans were non-Jews, their ethnic origin would be mentioned.

42. "Bam yidishn ayzn-kenig (geshprekh mit Zishe Breitbart)," *Haynt*, March 3, 1925, 5.

43. Tolie, "Oyfn literarishn purim-bal," *Dos naye lebn*, March 2, 1925, 2.

44. Ravitch, "Zishe Breitbarts kerper," 185.

45. "Di sensatsye mit Zishe Breitbartn in Lodz," *Haynt*, March 5, 1925, 3.

46. "Nowy popis atlety z Łodzi," *Echo Warszawskie*, March 24, 1924, 4.

47. "Shimshon ha-gibor shel dorenu," *Ha-yom*, March 6, 1925, 5.

48. Ravitch, "Zishe Breitbarts kerper," 185.

49. "Vi azoy iz Zishe Breitbart oyfgenumen gevorn oyf der 'linye,'" *Der Moment*, March 17, 1925, 9.

50. "Zishe Breitbart," *Haynt*, February 25, 1925, 6.

51. "Shimshon ha-gibor shel dorenu," *Ha-yom*, March 6, 1925, 5.

52. "Z cyrku," *Warszawianka*, March 3, 1925, 3.

53. "Lebens-geshikhte fun shapsel rotholc," *Hayntige Nayes*, April 7, 1938, 3.

54. Menachem Kipnis, "A Breitbart hot zikh im verglust tsu vern," *Haynt*, March 20, 1925, 8.

55. "Młodociany Breitbart," *Chwila*, October 10, 1927, 11.

56. Menachem Kipnis, "Bay a glezl kave . . . (a begegnish mit pan metsenas)," *Haynt*, March 5, 1925, 6.

57. "Słusznie," *Kabaret: Tygodnik satyryczno-humorystyczny*, no. 36 (1925), 3; "Nowy skandal z Breitbartem. Tym razem w Bielsku," *Dwa Grosze*, July 26, 1925, 8.

58. Adolf Nowaczyński, *Plewy i perły* (Warsaw: Drukarnia Archidiecezjalna, 1933), 79.

59. "Co mówi mistrz Pytlasiński o Breitbarcie?," *Dwa Grosze*, April 10, 1925, 1.

60. "Co mówi mistrz Pytlasiński o Breitbarcie?," *Dwa Grosze*, April 10, 1925, 1.

61. "And since he is Jewish as we are / we support him all the time / shouting among the goyim / that we [Jews] have our strongmen too." "Pani Feinbubowa o siłaczu, który sze nazywa Breitbart," *Kabaret: Tygodnik satyryczno-humorystyczny*, no. 20 (1925), 4.

62. "There goes Breitbart / the one who tears metal chains / a bunch of Jews runs after him / Like cockroaches! / Everyone grabs him where he wants / What reminds me / that this Breitbart is in fact / like a kind of a hooker." "Z bruku lwowskiego," *Kabaret: Tygodnik satyryczno-humorystyczny*, no. 21 (1925), 8.

63. "Polityk lwowski," *Kabaret: Tygodnik satyryczno-humorystyczny*, no. 33 (1925), 2.

64. "Żydowski awanturnik Breitbart," *Dwa Grosze*, June 5, 1925, 4.

65. Kahan, "Der tumel vegn Zishe Breitbarts yerushe," 9.

66. "Di sensatsye mit Zishe Breitbartn in Lodz," *Haynt*, March 5, 1925, 3.

67. Ravitch, "Zishe Breitbarts kerper," 185.

68. "Vos Breitbart hot betsolt shtoyern," *Haynt*, March 27, 1923, 2.

69. "Bam yidishn ayzn-kenig (geshprekh mit Zishe Breitbart)," *Haynt*, March 3, 1925, 5.

70. "Unzer Shapsel. Vi lebt der balibter bokser S. Rotholc?," *Yidishe Bilder*, October 1938, 15, 23.

71. "Sportowcy!," *5-ta rano*, October 10, 1934, 5.

72. S. Shaynkinder, "Vi azoy is oysgefalen der aroystrit fun di profesyo-nele bokser," *Sport-tsaytung*, March 21, 1933, 2.

73. "Drobiazgi," *Czas*, November 15, 1935, 6.

74. Diethlem Blecking, *Tempel aus Blättern der Phantasie: Skizzen zu Politik, Film, Literatur und Sport* (Norderstedt, Germany: BoD 2021), 57.

75. "Jak wygrał Szapsio Rotholc," *5-ta rano*, March 23, 1936, 5.

76. "Shapsel: Lebens-geshikhte fun shapsel rotholc," *Hayntige Nayes*, April 11, 1938, 3.

77. "Rotholc makht a tel fun Lendzion," *Sports-tsaytung*, February 7, 1939, 3.

78. "Co jest z Rotholcem?! . . . ," *5-ta rano*, March 12, 1936, 7.

79. "Młodszy brat Szapsia Rotholca," *5-ta rano*, January 10, 1935, 7.

80. "Prawda o Rotholcu," *5-ta rano*, February 7, 1935, 6.

81. "Shapsel: Lebens-geshichkte fun shapsel rotholc," *Hayntige Nayes*, April 15, 1938, 8.

82. Pacal Duret, *Les Jeunes et l'Identite masculine* (Paris: PUF, 1999), 36, quoted in Rauch, "Wyzwanie sportowe," 239.

83. Vigarello, "Męskości sportowe," 207.

84. "Dos poyzner publikum nemt zikh on far Rotholc's avele," *Sport-tsaytung*, April 3, 1934, 1.

85. Sh. Danzig, "Tsulib ayn kampf Rotholc-Nardecchia," *Sport-tsaytung*, March 29, 1939, 3.

86. "Shapsel: Lebens-geshichkte fun shapsel rotholc," *Hayntige Nayes*, April 1, 1938, 4.

87. *Przegląd Sportowy*, quoted in Henryk Lesser, "Jedyna godna odpowiedź żydowska," *Nowy Dziennik*, May 29, 1934, 7.

88. See Thierry Pillon, "Męskość robotnicza," in Courtine, *Historia męskości*, 268–281.

89. Aaron Belkin, *Bring Me Men: Military Masculinity and the Benign Facade of American Empire, 1898–2001* (New York: Oxford University Press, 2012), 1–6.

90. "Jak wygrał Szapsio Rotholc," *5-ta rano*, March 23, 1936, 5.

91. "Poylishe prese fodert, az Shapsel Rotholc zol foren tsu di oyropeishe maystershaft-kampfen keyn Dublin," *Unzer Byalisṭoker Ekspres*, April 12, 1939, 9.

92. "Jedyna godna odpowiedź żydowska," *Nowy Dziennik*, May 29, 1934, 7.

93. While Rotholc appeared as the author, it is possible that someone assisted him in writing the memoir or that the memoir was even ghostwritten.

94. Vigarello, "Męskości sportowe," 206–208.

95. "Shapsel: Lebens-geshichkte fun shapsel rotholc," *Hayntige Nayes*, April 1, 1938, 7.

96. Y. Bornshteyn, "Vu zenen di yudishe bokser?," *Sport-tsaytung*, October 4, 1933, 3.

97. "Shapsel: Lebens-gseshikhte fun shapsel rotholc," *Hayntige Nayes*, April 10, 1938, 3.

98. "Shapsel: Lebens-geshichkte fun shapsel rotholc," *Hayntige Nayes*, April 1, 1938, 7; April 3, 1938, 3.

99. "Shapsel: Lebens-geshichkte fun shapsel rotholc," *Hayntige Nayes*, April 10, 1938, 3.

100. "Shapsel: Lebens-geshichkte fun shapsel rotholc," *Hayntige Nayes*, April 10, 1938, 3.

101. Mora, *Carrying a Big Schtick*, 65.

102. "Shapsel: Lebens-geshichkte fun shapsel rotholc," *Hayntige Nayes*, April 3, 1938, 3.

103. "Prawda o Rotholcu," *5ta rano*, February 7, 1935, 6.

104. "Shapsel: Lebens-geshichkte fun shapsel rotholc," *Hayntige Nayes*, September 1, 1938, 3.

105. Y. B., "For ikh yo shoyn oyf di olimpiade, bin ich asur keyn mekane mayn gegner!," *Der Moment*, July 30, 1936, 5.

106. B. G., "Sport un natsyonale virde," *Nayer morgen*, August 2, 1936, 2.

107. "Shapsel: Lebens-geshikkhte fun shapsel rotholc," *Hayntige Nayes*, April 1, 1938, 7.

108. "Jedyna godna odpowiedź żydowska," *Nowy Dziennik*, May 29, 1934, 8.

109. Pinchas Katz, "Beni Leonard gib a patsh in varshe," *Forverts*, September 19, 1922, 3.

110. Charlie (K. Ferster), "Po zwycięstwie Maksa Baera (żyda) nad Carnerą," *Wróble na dachu*, no. 26 (1934), 4–5.

111. "WOZB pod znakiem swastyki?," *5ta rano*, February 14, 1935, 7. WOZB stands for Wielkopolski Oddział Związku Bokserskiego, or the Greater Poland Chapter of the Polish Boxing Association.

112. "Der varshever prayz-fayter Shapsel Rotholc brekht di bayne natsisher prayz-fayter in Berlin," *Forverts*, December 31, 1938, 8. Forverts quoted Rotholc's remarks from an unidentified Warsaw daily.

113. "Karjera Szapsy Rotholca: Krótka historia najpopularniejszego boksera," *5ta rano*, October 10, 1934, 5.

114. "Jedyna godna odpowiedź żydowska," *Nowy Dziennik*, May 29, 1934, 7.

115. *5a rano*, December 9, 1935, 3.

116. "Shapsel: Lebens-geshichkte fun shapsel rotholc," *Hayntige Nayes*, April 1, 1938, 7.

117. "Yidishe shportler foren keyn Berlin," *Hayntige Nayes*, July 29, 1936, 1.

118. Y. B., "For ikh yo shoyn oyf di olimpiade, bin ich asur keyn mekane mayn gegner! . . . ," *Der Moment*, July 30, 1936, 5.

119. "Rotholc vil vayter boksen," *Haynt*, November 2, 1936, 5.

120. "Co jest z Rotholcem?! . . . ," *5ta rano*, March 12, 1936, 7.

121. "Karjera Szapsy Rotholca: Krótka historia najpopularniejszego boksera," *5ta rano*, October 10, 1934, 5.

122. "20 nagród dla uczestników dorocznego plebiscytu: Kto jest naj-lepszym sportowcem polskim?," *Przegląd Sportowy*, January 13, 1934, 4; Jak wygrali Rotholc, Kajnar i Majchrzycki, "Po wielkim meczu pięściarzy polskich w Poznaniu," *Przegląd Sportowy*, May 5, 1934.

123. "Shapsel: Lebens-geshickhte fun shapsel rotholc," *Hayntige Nayes*, May 13, 1938, 7.

124. "Shapsel: Lebens-geshichkte fun shapsel rotholc," *Hayntige Nayes*, April 1, 1938, 4.

4. TENDER BONDS OF FRATERNAL AFFECTION

1. Harald Seewann, *Zirkel und Zionsstern. Bilder und Dokumente aus der versunkenen Welt der jüdisch-nationalen Korporationsstudententums: Ein Beitrag zur Geschichte des Zionismus auf akademischen Boden* (Graz, Austria, 1994), 4:119.

2. Sabrina Lausen, *Hüter ihrer Nationen: Studentische Verbindungen in Deutschland und Polen im 19. und frühen 20. Jahrhundert* (Cologne, Germany: Böhlau, 2020); Sonja Levsen, *Elite, Männlichkeit und Krieg: Tübinger*

und Cambridger Studenten 1900–1929 (Göttingen, Germany: Vandenhoeck & Ruprecht, 2006).

3. Alexandra Kurth, *Männer-Bünde-Rituale: Studentenverbindungen seit 1800* (Frankfurt: Campus, 2004), 131–135.

4. Saul Langans, *Żydzi a studja akademickie w Polsce w latach 1921–1931* (Lviv: Centrala Żydowskich Stowarzyszeń samopomocowych Środowiska Lwowskiego, 1935), 12–15.

5. There were regular fraternities in the cities where universities were located and "vacation fraternities" founded by students in their provincial hometowns as a way of carrying over the structures of student life into their vacations. Dietrich Hecht, "Jewish (Vacation) Fraternities in the Habsburg Monarchy: Kadimah and Geullah—Forward to Redemption," *Austrian Studies* 24 (2016) "Jews, Jewish Difference and Austrian Culture. Literary and Historical Perspectives," 32.

6. J. H., "O zmianę firm korporacji (na marginesie artykukułu pt. 'Korporacje i Stowarzyszenia,')" *Chwila*, May 21, 1926, 6.

7. Thomas Kühne, "Männergeschichte als Geschlechtergesichte," in Thomas Kühne, ed., *Männergeschichte als Geschlechtergesichte: Männlichkeit im Wandel der Moderne* (Frankfurt: Campus, 1996), 18.

8. Polish: Związek akademickich korporacyj syońskich; German: Verband zionistisch-akademischer Korporationen in Galizen; Hebrew: Histadruth Agudoth Ha-Akademayim ha-tsiyonim be-Galitsya.

9. "Dwa zjazdy," *Chwila*, January 24, 1930, 11.

10. Daniel Pater, "Żydowski Akademicki Ruch Korporacyjny w Polsce w latach 1898–1939," *Dzieje Najnowsze* 34, no. 3 (2002), 10.

11. *Sprawozdanie z działalności Związku Polskich Korporacji Akademickich za rok 1927*, Warsaw, 1928, 4, O 181, Archiwum Uniwersytetu Jagiellońskiego [AUJ].

12. Patryk Tomaszewski, *Polskie korporacje akademickie w latach 1918–1939* (Toruń, Poland: Wydawnictwo Uniwersytetu im. Mikołaja Kopernika, 2011), 138.

13. Seewann, *Zirkel und Zionsstern*, 1:195–198. Other sources mention much larger memberships. Lviv's Makabea had more than 250 registered members in 1927. Informacje dotyczące działalności akademickich korporacji żydowskich, f. 121, op. 3, sp. 103, k. 3, 7v, State Archive of Lviv Region (DALO), quoted in Ewa Bukowska-Marczak, *Przyjaciele, koledzy, wrogowie: Relacje pomiędzy polskimi, żydowskimi i ukraińskimi studentami Uniwersytetu Jana Kazimierza we Lwowie w okresie międzywojennym (1918–1939)* (Warsaw: Neriton, 2019), 94.

14. Żydowski Związek Akademicki "Hasmonea," invitation to "Uroczysty obchód dzesięciosemestrowy," 1913, reproduced in Seewann, *Zirkel und Zionsstern*, 2:146–150.

15. See Kühne, "Männergeschichte als Geschlechtergesichte," 18.

16. Letter to UJ Senate, October 1933, Bar Kochba, S II 795, AUJ.

17. Anatol Leszczyński, "Akademicka korporacja syjonistyczno-rewizjonistyczna Arnonia w Białymstoku 1934–1939," *Biuletyn Żydowskiego Instytutu Historycznego*, no. 1–3 (1994), 86.

18. Seth L. Wolitz, "Forging a Hero for a Jewish Stage: Goldfadn's 'Bar Kokhba,'" *Shofar* 20, no. 3 (2002), 62.

19. "Zjazd Seniorów Akademickich Korporacyj Sjonistyczych w Polsce," *Nowy Dziennik*, March 31, 1933, 11.

20. Mora, *Carrying a Big Schtick*, 69.

21. Attempts to bridge Polish-Catholic and Polish-Jewish fraternities were rare and were approached by Polish Catholics as a violation of ethnic separatism within the fraternal movement. When the Vilna fraternity Vilnensia invited Jewish frat brothers from the assimilationist Unitania for komers, they were later punished by exclusion from the union of Polish-Catholic fraternities. "Zjazd V-tej Rady Naczelnej Z.P.K.A.," *Wiadomości korporacyjne*, no. 9 (November 1930), 11.

22. Politician Stanisław Stomma recalled, "Members of the fraternities belonged to wealthy families and did not need to worry about their livelihood; their families took care of that." Stanisław Stomma, *Trudne lekcje historii* (Kraków: Znak, 1998), 61.

23. Tadeusz Doberski, "Wielkie reformy," *Wiadomości korporacyjne*, no. 9 (October–November 1930), 4–6.

24. *Komers* is singular; *komersy* is plural.

25. Wojciech Wasiutyński, "U podstaw rozwoju ruchu korporacyjnego," *Wiadomości korporacyjne*, no. 1 (November 1931), 15–16.

26. Aleksander Ołomucki, "The History of Academic Societies in Warsaw," in Seewann, *Zirkel und Zionsstern*, 4:291–296.

27. Odpowiedzi odnośnie do kwestionariusza przesłanego pismem pod L.2986/28 z kancelarji Rektoratu, S II 795, Ognisko, AUJ.

28. Związek to UJ Senate, December 10, 1926; Związek to UJ Senate, 1929, both in S II 795, AUJ. In 1929, two female students joined the seven-person board as treasurer and vice treasurer.

29. Chejruth to UJ Senate, 1930, S II 795, AUJ. When the number of members began to drop in 1932, three out of seven board members were female.

30. Bar Kochba to UJ Rector, June 8, 1934, S II 795, Bar Kochba, AUJ. For instance, in 1934, about 10 percent of the Bar Kochba fraternity was female.

31. Członkowie Stowarzyszenia, S II 795, Arlosorowja, AUJ.

32. Statut żydowskiej Korporacji Akademickiej "Emunah" w Krakowie, 1027, S II 796, ŻKA Emunah and ŻKA Kadimah, AUJ.

33. Leszczyński, "Akademicka korporacja syjonistyczno-rewizjonistyczna Arnonia," 87. Jabotinsky saw the Betar movement and his disciplined and strong New Jews as reanimations of King David's dynasty, metaphorically crowning them with his legacy. See Arye Naor, "The Leader as a Poet: The Political and Ideological Poetry of Ze'ev Jabotinsky," *Israel Affairs* 20, no. 2 (2014), 147.

34. "Uroczystości jubileuszowe 'Hebronji,'" *Trybuna Narodowa*, February 7, 1936, 7.

35. Yosef Krelman, "Betaryah (ma'mar sheni)," *Madrikh Betar*, December 1933, 47, quoted in Heller, *Jabotinsky's Children*, 182–183.

36. "Zjazd Seniorów Akademickich Korporacyj Sjonistyczych w Polsce," *Nowy Dziennik*, March 31, 1933, 11; Leszczyński, "Akademicka korporacja syjonistyczno-rewizjonistyczna Arnonia w Białymstoku 1934–1939," 89.

37. Marian Kasiński, "Wychowanie korporacyjne III: Cechy indywidualne polskiej idei korporacyjnej," *Korporant* no. 4 (June 1925), 12.

38. E. Bienenstock, "O szerszy horyzont" (głos w dyskusji), *Trybuna Akademicka*, November 1, 1929, 5–6.

39. Ludwik Krzywicki, *Wspomnienia* (Warsaw: Czytelnik, 1959), 3:298–300; Antoni Iwanowski recalled that Warsaw Zelotia gathered the "sons of the most influential Jewish families"; see Antoni Iwanowski, "Korporacja akademicka i moje pojedynki," *Polskie Korporacje Akademickie Biuletyn Zarządu SFPKA w Warszawie*, no. 14 (1997), 18.

40. Joshua Perec, "The Relationship between 'Aurora' and 'Zelotia,'" in Seewann, *Zirkel und Zionsstern*, 4:305.

41. Stanisław Urbańczyk, *Z miłości do wiedzy: Wspomnienia* (Kraków: Księgarnia Akademicka, 1999), 185, quoted in Tomaszewski, *Polskie korporacje akademickie w latach*, 361.

42. "Kronika korporacyjna," *Wiadomości korporacyjne*, no. 1 (December 1931), 18.

43. Janusz Kowalewski, "Sarmaci w papuzich piórach," *Życie akademickie*, quoted in Tadeusz Doberski, "Strach, strach . . . ," *Wiadomości korporacyjne*, no. 10 (December 1930), 4–6.

44. See Erwin Kowalski, *Dekiel i banda* (Poznań, Poland: Życie Uniwersyteckie, 1931).

45. Wacław, "Taniec z mieczykami," *Zarzewie Nowe*, no. 2 (November 1931), 10, quoted in Tomaszewski, *Polskie korporacje akademickie w latach*, 416.

46. "Po prostu nieporozumienie. Echa bójek korporanckich w Krakowie," *Myśl. Tygodnik proletariackich wolnomyślicieli*, March 11, 1928, 7.

47. B. Mosiężnik, "Katolickie czy żydowskie," *Trybuna Akademicka*, March 1, 1930, 6–7.

48. B. Mosiężnik, "Transfuzja krwi," *Trybuna Akademicka*, December 1, 1928, 12–13.

49. Norbert Elias, "Honour, Duelling and Membership of the Imperial Ruling Class: Being Judged Worthy to Give Satisfaction," in Norbert Elias and Michael Schroter, eds., *Studies on the Germans: Power Struggles and the Development of Habitus in the Nineteenth and Twentieth Centuries* (Dublin: University College Dublin Press, 2013), 49–134.

50. *Rocznik Korporacyjny 1828–1928* (Warsaw: ZPKA, 1928), 47; the resolution of Polish-Catholic fraternities corresponded with the so-called Waidhofener Resolution of 1896, which stipulated that Jews were excluded from executing honorary affairs against Christian German fraternity members.

51. "Walka z żydostwem," *Wiadomości korporacyjne*, no. 4–5 (January–February 1930), 21.

52. The Boziewicz code was adopted by the Warsaw Polish-Jewish fraternities Zelotia and Aurora; see Iwanowski, "Korporacja akademicka i moje pojedynki," 19. Like analogous regulations elsewhere in Europe, Boziewicz's code also did not consider women as actors who could stand in honor courts.

53. Izabela Mrzygłód, "Uniwersytety w cieniu kryzysu: Radykalizacja polityczna studentów Uniwersytetów Warszawskiego i Wiedeńskiego w okresie międzywojennym" (PhD diss., University of Warsaw, 2021), 218.

54. K. Turowski, *Historia Stowarzyszenia Katolickiej Młodzieży Akademickiej "Odrodzenie"* (Warsaw, 1987), 197, quoted in Tomaszewski, *Polskie korporacje akademickie w latach*, 290.

55. Adolf Nowaczyński, "Bluźnierstwo," *Myśl Narodowa* 20 (1924), 8, quoted in Pater, "Żydowski Akademicki Ruch Korporacyjny," 15.

56. V Zjazd P.K.A. w Warszawie, *Korporant*, no. 4 (1925), 3.

57. Untitled song, Śpiewnik korporacyjny, Materiały różne Korporacji Akademickich UJ i Związku Polskich Korporacji Akademickich, 1935–1939, O 182, AUJ.

58. Untitled song, *Śpiewnik korporacyjny*, AUJ, O 182, Materiały różne Korporacji Akademickich UJ i Związku Polskich Korporacji Akademic kich, 1935–1939, O 182, AUJ.

59. Unsigned and undated speech on the fifth anniversary of the Praetoria fraternity, probably around 1928, O 181, AUJ.

60. Marian Kasiński, "Wychowanie korporacyjne: Ustrój korporacyjny II," *Korporant*, no. 3 (May 1925), 9.

61. Emunah to UJ Senate, October 11, 1928, S II 796, Emunah, AUJ.

62. "Zaburzenia studenckie w Krakowie," *Akademik Polski: Ilustrowany dwutygodnik młodzieży*, no. 3 (1928), 5.

63. Momorjał, Konwent Seniorów Żydowskich Korporacji Aka-demickich, February 17, 1928, S II 796, Kadimah, AUJ.

64. Marek (Markus) Bolechower, declaration, SS II 796, Kadimah, AUJ.

65. *Rocznik Korporacyjny*, 84–85.

66. Potwierdzenie odbioru pisma Sekretariatu UJ na konferencję Przewodniczących Korp. w dniu 13 lutego 1928, February 13, 1928, S II 796, Kadimah, AUJ.

67. Protocol, UJ Rector Leon Marchlewski, March 15, 1928, S II 796, Kadimah, AUJ.

68. *Rocznik Korporacyjny*, 84–85.

69. Rector Marchlewski to Kadimah, April 30, 1928, S II 796, Kad-imah, AUJ.

70. Hecht, "Jewish (Vacation) Fraternities in the Habsburg Monar-chy," 38.

71. Hecht, 42.

72. "Akademickie burdy uliczne," *Wiek Nowy*, July 1, 1927, 10; "Lwów widownią przykrych zajść," *Chwila*, July 1, 1927, 1; "Lwów ponownie widownią skandalicznych zajść," *Chwila*, July 2, 1927, 3.

73. "Orgje brutalnośći. P. Rektora Siemiradzkiego to nie obchodzi . . . ," *Chwila*, July 5, 1927, 4.

74. Bukowska-Marczak, *Przyjaciele, koledzy, wrogowie*, 135.

75. Miriam Rürup, "Auf Kneipe und Fechtboden: Inszenierungen von Männlichkeit in jüdischen Studentenverbindungen in Kaiserreich und Weimarer Republik," in *Männer—Macht—Körper: Hegemoniale Männ-lichkeiten vom Mittelalter bis heute*, ed. Martin Dinges (Frankfurt: Campus, 2005), 142.

76. S. G., "W sprawie zajść krakowskich," *Wiadomości korporacyjne*, no. 2 (November 1929), 14.

77. Tadeusz Doberski, "Plaga," *Wiadomości korporacyjne*, no. 3 (Decem-ber 1929), 5–6.

78. Regulamin miejscowych sądów międzykorporacyjnych, O 181, AUJ.

79. "Po burzy," *Chwila*, July 8, 1927, 7.

80. Cwi Pragai (Preiger), "The Development of the Society and Its Internal Activities," in Seewann, *Zirkel und Zionsstern*, 4: 304.

81. Perec, "The Relationship between 'Aurora' and 'Zelotia,'" 309–310.

82. Pragai, "The Development of the Society," 304.

83. Jakób Schachter, *Sens żydowskiego korporantyzmu, Jednodniówka Jubieleuszowa S.K!S.R. 'El-Al' w Krakowie* (Kraków, 1937), 1, quoted in Tomaszewski, *Polskie korporacje akademickie w latach*, 396.

84. Joseph Menkes, "Erinnerungen eines Lemberger Zeloten," in Seewann, *Zirkel und Zionsstern*, 4:62–63.

85. Alfred Ajzyk Nimcovich, "Activities within University Zionist Movement," 301; Perec, "The Relationship between 'Aurora' and 'Zelotia,'" 310–312; Mosze Ring, "The Last Meeting of 'Aurora' in Warsaw," 313–317, all in Seewann, *Zirkel und Zionsstern*, vol. 4.

86. Unsigned and undated speech on the fifth anniversary of the Praetoria fraternity, probably around 1928, O 181, AUJ.

87. Mosse, *The Image of Man*, chap. 8.

88. Dawid Schreiber, "W dniu jubileuszu Makabei," unknown Jewish newspaper, February 5, 1934, 9.

89. "Żywa gazeta," *Chwila*, March 5, 1935, 7.

90. Związek Polskich Korporacji Akademickich oraz Krakowskie Koło Międzykorporacyjne 1927–1932, S II 775, AUJ, quoted in Tomaszewski, *Polskie korporacje akademickie w latach*, 395.

91. Wojciech Wasiutyński, "Praca społeczna korporanta," *Wiadomości korporacyjne*, no. 8 (May 1930), 3.

92. "Podstawy wychowania korporacyjnego," *Korporant*, no. 2 (April 1925), 5.

93. *Sprawozdanie z działalności Związku Polskich Korporacji Akademickich za rok 1927* (Warsaw: ZPKA1928), 12, 15, O 181, AUJ.

94. Essay by Stanisław Wysocki, member of Arkonja, around 1931, O 181, AUJ.

95. Essay by Stanisław Wysocki, member of Arkonja, around 1931, O 181, AUJ.

96. "Listy z kraju," *Trybuna Narodowa*, November 25, 1938, 8. El-Al was linked to the Emunah student fraternity.

97. "Dr Aleksander Hausman umarł," *Chwila*, January 15, 1931, 5.

98. "Listy z kraju," *Trybuna Narodowa*, no. 18 (May 5, 1939), 8.

99. Józef Prądzyński, "Szkoła rycerska," *Wiadomości korporacyjne*, no. 3–4 (March–April 1934), 2–3.

100. Ludwik Jaxa-Bykowski, "Kilka myśli o korporacjach w Polsce dzisiejszej," *Wiadomości korporacyjne*, no. 3–4 (March–April 1934), 11.

101. Statut Stowarzyszenia "Bar-Kochba," S II 795, Bar Kochba, AUJ.

102. Sprawozdanie z ogólnej działalności, undated, S II 795, Bar Kochba, AUJ.

103. Statut Żydowskiego Związku Akademickiego (Korporacji) Emunah w Krakowie, 1927, S II 796, Emunah, AUJ.

104. Emunah letter to UJ Senate, October 24, 1927, S II 796, Emunah, AUJ.

105. Sprawozdanie z działalności Ż.K!A. Kadimah w Krakowie, z semestru zimowego 1933/1934, SII 796, Kadimah, AUJ.

106. Essay by Stanisław Wysocki, member of Arkonja, around 1931, O 181, AUJ.

107. Władysław Medyński, "Wychowanie korporacyjne," *Wiadomości korporacyjne*, no. 8 (June 1928), 237.

108. "Rola wychowawcza ruchu korporacyjnego," *Kurier Poznański*, October 9, 1935.

109. Ulotka lwowskiej młodzieży akademickiej, f. 110, op. 4, sp. 423, k. 7, DALO, quoted in Bukowska-Marczak, *Przyjaciele, koledzy, wrogowie*, 105.

110. M. Czackis, "O syntezę intelektualisty i sportsmena," *Trybuna Akademicka*, November 1, 1931, 9.

111. Sprawozdanie z działalności Ż.K!A. Kadimah w Krakowie, March 1939, S II 796, Kadimah, AUJ.

112. Sprawozdania z działalności stowarzyszenia za r. akad. 1934/1935, February 26, 1935, S II 795, Bar Kochba, AUJ.

113. Sprawozdanie z ogólnej działalności Ż.K!A. UJ Emunah za rok akademicki 1935/1936, (Krakw, 1936), S II 796, Emunah, AUJ.

114. Sprawozdanie z działalności Ż.K!A. Kadimah w Krakowie, undated, probably 1935, S II 796, Kadimah, AUJ.

115. Wacław Wasiutyński, "Ojcostwo korporacyjne," *Wiadomości korporacyjne*, no. 1–2 (January/February 1931), 5–6.

116. Pragai, "The Development of the Society," 302–303.

117. Ołomucki, "The History of Academic Societies in Warsaw," 294–296.

118. Sprawozdanie z ogólnej działalności Ż.K!A. UJ Emunah za okres sprawozdawczy 1936/1937, S II 796, Emunah, AUJ.

119. Seewann, *Zirkel und Zionsstern*, 4:24–25.

120. M. Czackis, "O syntezę intelektualisty i sportsmena," *Trybuna Akademicka*, November 1, 1931, 9.

121. "W sezonie róż, chryzantem," Śpiewnik korporacyjny, AUJ, O 182, Materiały różne Korporacji Akademickich UJ i Związku Polskich Korporacji Akademickich, 1935–1939, O 182, AUJ.

122. Fraternity brothers indeed maintained long-lasting relationships. IGUL, an organization grouping former fraternity members from the Austro-Hungarian empire, existed until the 1980s.

123. Sprawozdanie z działalności Ż.K!A. Kadimah w Krakowie, March 1939, S II 796, Kadimah, AUJ.

124. Kronika, *Chwila*, December 9, 1931, 12.

125. Leszczyński, "Akademicka korporacja syjonistyczno-rewizjonistyczna Arnonia," 87.

126. Lech Muszyński, "Francuskie wspominki motocyklisty," *Wiadomości akademickie*, no. 2 (December 1931), 10–11.

127. Randall Collins, *Interaction Ritual Chains* (Princeton, NJ: Princeton University Press, 2004), 5–7.

128. Jewish Academic Sports Association, established in 1921, in Perec, "The Relationship between 'Aurora' and 'Zelotia,'" 308.

129. Sprawozdanie z walnego conventu Ż.K!A. Emunah, 1939, S II 796, Emunah, AUJ.

130. Sprawozdanie z działalności Ż.K!A. Kadimah w Krakowie w okresie od dnia 4. Marca 1934 do dnia 10.3.1935, March 10, 1935, S II 796, Kadimah, AUJ.

131. M. K., "Kolonje, campingi, trampy," *Chwila*, July 8, 1932.

132. Perec, "The Relationship between 'Aurora' and 'Zelotia,'" 308–309.

133. Sprawozdanie z działalności Ż.K!A. Kadimah w Krakowie, undated, probably 1936, S II 796, Kadimah, AUJ.

134. Sprawozdanie z działalności Ż.K!A. Kadimah w Krakowie, March 1939, S II 796, Kadimah, AUJ.

135. David Feigenberger, "The Essence of the Zionist Society in Poland," in Seewann, *Zirkel und Zionsstern*, 4:290.

136. "Rycerze z 'Unitanii' przed Sądem," *Nasz Przegląd*, January 12, 1930, 7.

137. Joseph Menkes, "Errinerungen eines Lemberger Zeloten," in Seewann, *Zirkel und Zionsstern*, 4:62.

138. Wacław Sikorski, "Sport a korporacje," *Korporant* 1 (March 1925), 21–22.

139. A. W., "O wychowaniu korporacyjnem," *Wiadomości korporacyjne*, no. 8 (July 1928), 276.

140. A. Płachciński, "Wielkie cięcie Prezesa," *Wiadomości korporacyjne*, no. 2 (December 1931), 19–21.

141. Rürup, "Auf Kneipe und Fechtboden," 144. Communal singing was central also for Fascist groups. See Roland Clark, "Collective Singing in Romanian Fascism," *Cultural and Social History: The Journal of the Social History Society* 10, no. 2 (2013): 251–271.

142. Untitled song, Śpiewnik korporacyjny, Materiały różne Korporacji Akademickich UJ i Związku Polskich Korporacji Akademickich, 1935–1939, O 182, AUJ.

143. Anthems reprinted in Seewann, *Zirkel und Zionsstern*, 1:227–228. Fraternities in other cities in eastern Europe were often much more explicit than Aurora and Zelotia members. For instance, Hasmonea in Czernowitz sang about "being in the same row as the Maccabees," and Barissia from Prague sang about "beating with sharp rapiers."

144. "Chociaż nas mało, jednak czynami / łeb skręcić hydrze potrafim; / choć droga nasza zalana łzami, My jednak do celu trafim! / Dumni przeszłością, silni jednością / Rychło u celu staniemy, / Bo walcząc wiarą, a nie podłością, / Zgnieść wroga łatwo możemy! / Dalej więc bracia! Do walki śmiało! Brońmy naszego zakonu! / A walcząc dzielnie, jak nam przystało / Ujrzymy mury Syonu!," *Kalendarzyk na rok 1905* (Tarnopil: Stowarzyszenie "Bar-Kochba," 1905).

145. Rürup, "Auf Kneipe und Fechtboden," 145–146.

146. This bifurcated masculinity order was noted by a Polish-Catholic frat brother who years later recalled, "The fraternity provided an opportunity for drinking, 'girls,' and arrogance, yet curbed in a certain manner." Wojciech Wasiutyński, *Prawą stroną labirtyntu* (Gdańsk, Poland: Exter, 1996), 84–55.

147. Untitled song, Śpiewnik korporacyjny, Materiały różne Korporacji Akademickich UJ i Związku Polskich Korporacji Akademickich, 1935–1939, O 182, AUJ.

148. Janusz Steliński, "Czara wikingów," *Wiadomości korporacyjne*, no. 4 (May 1932), 12–13.

149. "Hulanka," Śpiewnik korporacyjny, Materiały różne Korporacji Akademickich UJ i Związku Polskich Korporacji Akademickich, 1935–1939, O 182, AUJ.

150. Rürup, "Auf Kneipe und Fechtboden," 144.

151. Unsigned and undated speech on the fifth anniversary of the Praetoria fraternity, probably around 1928, O 181, AUJ.

152. Jan Niedziałkowski, "Wilno," *Wiadomości korporacyjne*, no. 2 (October 1928), 2–3.

153. *Wiadomości korporacyjne*, no. 6/7 (December 1928), 3.

154. Emunah letterhead, in Seewann, *Zirkel und Zionsstern*, 2:117.

155. "Jubileusz Bar-Kochby," *Echo*, October 5, 1934, 6.

156. "Listy z kraju," *Trybyna Narodowa*, March 20, 1936, 8.

157. Essay by Stanisław Wysocki, member of Arkonja, around 1931, O 181.

158. Leszczyński, "Akademicka korporacja syjonistyczno-rewizjonistyczna Arnonia," 89.

159. Raewyn W. Connell, *Masculinities* (Berkeley: University of California Press, 1995), 77. Connell and Messerschmidt, in their 2005 revision of the idea of marginalized masculinity, called for greater attention to the agency of marginalized groups and suggested that hegemony might be accomplished by incorporating responses of marginalized groups into the dominant gender order. Raewyn W. Connell and James W. Messerschmidt, "Hegemonic Masculinity: Rethinking the Concept," *Gender and Society* 19, no. 6 (2005): 829–859.

160. Rürup, "Auf Kneipe und Fechtboden," 154–155.

5. PULLING THE TRIGGER

1. Isaac Bashevis Singer, *Love and Exile* (New York: Doubleday, 1984), 83–85.

2. Ramon Hinojosa, "Doing Hegemony: Military, Men, and Constructing a Hegemonic Masculinity," *Journal of Men's Studies* 18, no. 2 (2010): 179–194.

3. Huebel, *Fighter, Worker, and Family Man*, 13.

4. Michał Friedman, 16793, USC Shoah Foundation Archive, segment 109.

5. See Jack Rosenberg, 32594, USC Shoah Foundation Archive.

6. Henryk Prajs, 29091, USC Shoah Foundation Archive, segments 46–53.

7. Uri Diamant, 40699, USC Shoah Foundation Archive.

8. Max Brett, 35732, USC Shoah Foundation Archive.

9. "Bezkres wędrówki," *Bezkres wędrówki: Jedniodniówka Związku Żydów Uczestników Walk o Niepodległość Polski Oddziału w Białymstoku*, 1935, 2.

10. "II Walny Zjazd Delegatów Związku," *Na Przełomie, Biuletyn Związku Żydów Uczestników Walk o Niedpodległość Polski*, March 1936, 4, 8.

11. Semion Goldin, *The Russian Army and the Jewish Population, 1914–1917: Libel, Persecution, Reaction* (Cham, Switzerland: Springer Nature, 2022); Derek J. Penslar, *Jews and the Military: A History* (Princeton, NJ: Princeton University Press, 2013); Michael Berger, *Eisernes Kreuz und Davidstern: Die Geschichte jüdischer Soldaten in deutschen Armeen* (Berlin: Trafo, 2006); Sarah Panter, *Jüdische Erfahrungen und Loyalitätskonflikte im Ersten Weltkrieg* (Göttingen, Germany: Vandenhoeck & Ruprecht, 2014).

12. Szczepaniak, *Habitus żołnierski w literaturze i kulturze polskiej*; Wojciech Śmieja, *Hegemonia i trauma: Literatura wobec dominujących fikcji męskości* (Warsaw: Instytut Badań Literackich, 2016).

13. David J. Fine, *Jewish Integration in the German Army in the First World War* (Berlin: De Gruyter, 2012).

14. Christa Hämmerle, *Ganze Männer? Gesellschaft, Geschlecht und Allgemeine Wehrpflicht in Österreich-Ungarn (1868–1914)* (Frankfurt: Campus, 2022); Christa Hämmerle, *Heimat/Front: Geschlechtergeschichte/n des Ersten Weltkriegs in Österreich-Ungarn* (Vienna: Böhlau, 2014); Christa Hämmerle, *Des Kaisers Knechte: Erinnerungen an die Rekrutenzeit im k. (u.) k. Heer 1868 bis 1914* (Vienna: Böhlau, 2011).

15. Jean-Paul Bertaud, "Męskość wojskowa," in Corbin, *Historia męskości*, 139–178.

16. "Żydzi, a służba wojskowa w Rosyi," *Jedność*, June 4, 1909, 7.

17. See Laura Engelstein, *The Resistible Rise of Antisemitism. Exemplary Cases from Russia, Ukraine, and Poland* (Waltham, MA: Brandeis University Press, 2020), 26–66.

18. "Żołnierze-żydzi," *Jedność*, June 12, 1909, 5.

19. B. Zimmermann, "Niebezpieczeństwa i nadzieje," *Moriah*, April 1, 1918, 237–242.

20. B. Zimmermann, "Niebezpieczeństwa i nadzieje," *Moriah*, April 1, 1918, 237–242.

21. See Karen Hagemann, "German Heroes: The Cult of the Death for the Fatherland in Nineteenth-Century Germany," in *Masculinities in Politics and War: Gendering Modern History*, ed. Stefan Dudink, Karen Hagemann, and John Tosh, 116–134 (Manchester, UK: Manchester University Press, 2004).

22. See Mordechai Zalkin, "Beyn 'bney elohim' l'bney adam.' Rabanim, bney yeshivot ve-gius le-tsava rusi ba-mea ha-teysha esre," in *Milhama ve-shalom ba-tarbut ha-yehudit*, ed. Avirel Bar-Levav, 165–222 (Jerusalem: Zalman Shazar Center for Jewish History, 2006).

23. Yohanan Petrovsky-Shtern, *Jews in the Russian Army, 1827–1917: Drafted into Modernity* (Cambridge: Cambridge University Press, 2008), 91–128. See a probably fictionalized account of one of these soldiers: Yehoshue Meyzakh, *Der yudisher soldat: A mayse nora vi a yudisher soldat iz durkhgegangen di sheva madurey ge'enom un iz le-soyf gliklekh gevorn* (Vilna: Druk un ferlag, 1910).

24. Eugene M. Avrutin, *Jews and the Imperial State: Identification Politics in Tsarist Russia* (Ithaca, NY: Cornell University Press, 2010), 61–69.

25. Abraham Lewin, *Kantonistn: Vegn der yidisher rekrutshine in Rusland in di tsaytn fun Tsar Nikolay dem ershtn 1827–1856* (Warsaw: Grafia, 1934); Shmuel Rotsztejn, *Kantonistn: Historish bild in dray taylen* (Łódź, Poland: Farlag Masora 1926).

26. Petrovsky-Shtern, *Jews in the Russian Army*, 16. Similar dynamics were common in France; see Bertaud, "Męskość wojskowa," 166–167.

27. Petrovsky-Shtern, *Jews in the Russian Army*, 60. See also Benjamin Nathans, *Beyond the Pale: The Jewish Encounter with Late Imperial Russia* (Berkeley: University of California Press, 2004), 23–80.

28. See Bruce W. Menning, *Bayonets before Bullets: The Imperial Russian Army, 1861–1914* (Bloomington: Indiana University Press, 1992), 21–29; Mark von Hagen, "The Limits of Reform: The Multiethnic Army Confronts Nationalism, 1874–1914," in David Schimmelpenninck van der Oye and Bruce W. Menning, eds., *Reforming the Tsar's Army: Military Innovation in Imperial Russia from Peter the Great to the Revolution* (Cambridge: Cambridge University Press, 2004), 34–55; Petrovsky-Shtern, *Jews in the Russian Army*, 129–166.

29. Petrovsky-Shtern, *Jews in the Russian Army*, 156–163.

30. Petrovsky-Shtern, 160–161.

31. Petrovsky-Shtern, 23.

32. Yohanan Petrovsky-Shtern, "Military Service in Russia," in *YIVO Encyclopedia of Jews in Eastern Europe*, https://yivoencyclopedia.org /article.aspx/Military_Service_in_Russia, accessed on February 27, 2025.

33. Fishel Bimko, *Rekrutn* (Warsaw: Di Tsayt, 1921).

34. Jacob Kreplak, *Fun kazerme un milkhome* (New York: Tsentral, 1927). Kreplak served in the tsarist army in the first decade of the twentieth century and, starting in 1915, published his stories in *Di Tsukunft* in New York.

35. Jillian Davidson, "A 'Secular Catastrophe' in Eastern Europe— World War One and the Reconstruction of Modern Jewish Memory," *Yearbook for European Jewish Literature Studies* 1, no. 1 (2014), 54–56.

36. See Salomon Judson, *Soldatchina* (Vilna, Poland: Vilner Ferlag fun B. Kletzkin, 1930); A. Kimmelfeld, *Mayn militer-dinst in rusland: A Tog bukh fun a yidishn soldat* (Los Angeles: Model Print Shop, 1916); Gershon Lewin, *Iberlebenishn: Epizodn un ayndrukn fun der rusish-yaponisher krig* (Vilna: Kletzkin Farlag, 1931); Gershon Lewin, *In velt krig* (Warsaw: Yehudiyah, 1923).

37. Steven E. Aschheim, *Brothers and Strangers: The East European Jew in German and German Jewish Consciousness, 1800–1923* (Madison: University of Wisconsin Press, 1982), 142.

38. For example, Beryl Segal remembered the anti-Jewish prejudice prior to 1914 but wrote that he "did not remember a single incident of racial discrimination" when he was drafted into the Russian army during World War I. Beryl Segal, "A Jew in the Russian Army during the First World War," *Rhode Island Jewish Historical Notes* 7 (1975), 119.

39. Michael Berger and Gideon Römer-Hillebrecht, eds., *Jüdische Soldaten–Jüdischer Widerstand in Deutschland und Frankreich* (Leiden, Netherlands: Brill, 2009); Michael Berger and Gideon Römer-Hillebrecht, eds., *Juden und Militär in Deutschland* (Baden-Baden, Germany: Nomos, 2009); Frank M. Schuster, *Zwischen allen Fronten: Osteuropäische Juden während des Ersten Weltkrieges (1914–1919)* (Cologne, Germany: Böhlau, 2004); David Engel, "World War I," in *YIVO Encyclopedia of Jews in Eastern Europe*, https://yivoencyclopedia.org/article.aspx/world_war_i, last accessed on February 27, 2025.

40. The Polish Legions, or Legiony Polskie, was a Polish military unit established in 1914 within the structures of the Austro-Hungarian army. The legions became identified as the key force behind Poland's independence in 1918. Polska Organizacja Wojskowa was a secret military unit active in the Russian-held Kingdom of Poland and later became a part of the Polish Legions.

41. Christhardt Henschel, "'Jeszcze nas straszą żywe upiory bez nosów . . .' Kilka uwag o miejscu kombatantów i inwalidów wojennych w społeczeństwie polskim 1918–1939," in *Margines społeczny Drugiej Rzecz pospolitej*, ed. Mateusz Rodak and Janusz Żarnowski, 103–118 (Warsaw: Instytut Historii PAN, 2013).

42. See Szczepaniak, *Habitus żołnierski w literaturze i kulturze polskiej.*

43. Władysław Steinhaus, *Pamiętnik legionisty bł. p. Władysława Steinhausa* (Kraków: Centralne Biuro Wydawnictw N. K. N., 1916), 9.

44. Ernst Hanisch, *Männlichkeiten: Eine andere Geschichte des 20. Jahrhunderts* (Vienna: Böhlau, 2005), 29–30.

45. Konrad Zieliński, "Jews, Poles, and the Legion," in Artur Tanikowski, ed., *Jew, Pole, Legionary: 1914–1920* (Warsaw: Museum of the History of Polish Jews, 2014); Marek Gałęzowski, *Na wzór Berka Joselewicza: Żołnierze i oficerowie pochodzenia żydowskiego w Legionach Polskich* (Warsaw: IPN, 2010); Jakub Schall, "Rozdział X. Żydzi w czasie wojny światowej i w legionach," in Norbert Getter, Jakub Schall, and Zygmunt Schipper, eds., *Żydzi bojownicy o niepodległość Polski* (Lwów: n.p., 1939), 86.

46. Petrovsky-Shtern, *Jews in the Russian Army*, 260.

47. Christhardt Henschel, *Jeder Bürger Soldat: Juden und das polnische Militär (1918–1939)* (Göttingen, Germany: Vandenhoeck & Ruprecht, 2023), 98.

48. Steinhaus, *Pamiętnik legionisty*, 19–20.

49. Steinhaus, 31, 55.

50. Steinhaus, 57.

51. Steinhaus, 8.

52. Steinhaus, 51–54.

53. Steinhaus, 69–71.

54. Steinhaus, 31.

55. Steinhaus, 34.

56. Steinhaus, 28.

57. See Thomas Kühne, *The Rise and Fall of Comradeship*.

58. Steinhaus, 68.

59. Bertold Merwin, *Z życia w Legionach* (Kraków: Biuro Wydawnictw N. K. N., 1918), 9, 59.

60. Merwin, 47–48.

61. Merwin, 60.

62. Merwin, 52–53.

63. Bogumił K. Rembowski, "Bohater Koty 182. Obywatel Icuś. Ze wspomnień oficera legionów," in Getter, Schall, and Schipper, *Żydzi bojownicy o niepodległość Polski*, 196–200.

64. Bronisław Laskownicki, "Na kanwie wspomnień," in Getter, Schall, and Schipper, *Żydzi bojownicy o niepodległości Polski*, 203–204.

65. Yankev Kahan, *Dray yor in poylishn militer (19.10.1919–22.11.1922)* (Tel Aviv: Ferlag Ha-Menorah, 1967).

66. Kahan, 103.

67. Kahan, 67.

68. Kahan, 43.

69. Kahan, 35.

70. Kahan, 35.

71. Kahan, 17.

72. Kahan, 18, 22.

73. Kahan, 99.

74. Kahan, 114.

75. Kahan, 41.

76. Kahan, 88.

77. Kahan, 60.

78. Stéphane Audoin-Rouzeau, "Armie i wojny-wyłom w samym sercu męskiego wzorca?," in Courtine, *Historia męskości*, 178.

79. See Julia Eichenberg, *Kämpfen für Frieden und Fürsorge: Polnische Veteranen des Ersten Weltkriegs und ihre internationale Kontakte* (Oldenburg, Germany: Wissenschaftsverlag, 2011), 171–222.

80. Kahan, *Dray yor in poylishn militer*, 40.

81. Kahan, 48.

82. Kahan, 58–59.

83. Audoin-Rouzeau, "Armie i wojny-wyłom," 175–177.

84. Kahan, 22.

85. Kahan, 80.

86. Kahan, 57.

87. Kahan, 30.

88. Kahan, 37.

89. Kahan, 141.

90. Michael Yosef Salem, *Bolshevikes bay di grenetsn fun poyln* (Łódź, Poland: Farlag S. Shapira, 1930), 3.

91. Kahan, *Dray yor in poylishn militer*, 66.

92. Kahan, 91.

93. Kahan, 53.

94. Kahan, 36.

95. Kahan, 25.

96. Ulrich Bröckling, *Disziplin: Soziologie und Geschichte militärischer Gehorsamsproduktion* (Munich: Brill, 1997), 11.

97. Kahan, *Dray yor in poylishn militer*, 55.

98. Kahan, 29, 32.

99. Kahan, 142.

100. Kahan, 24.

101. Kahan, 25–26.

102. Erving Goofman, *O pacjentach szpitali psychiatrycznych i mieszkańcach innych instytucji totalnych* (Gdańsk, Poland: Gdańskie Wydawnictwo Psychologiczne, 2011), 24.

103. See Remigiusz Kasprzycki, "Przemoc w przedwojennym Wojsku Polskim," *Studia Historyczne* 59 no. 4 (2016): 465–488.

104. Kahan, *Dray yor in poylishn militer*, 55.

105. See Dov Perlov, 19970, and Yehoshua Zwieback, 26047, both USC Shoah Foundation Archive.

106. Kahan, *Dray yor in poylishn militer*, 50.

107. Kahan, 31, 50.

108. Kahan, 39, 99.

109. Kahan, 56.

110. Kahan, 117.

111. Kahan, 39.

112. Kahan, 94.

113. Kahan, 21.

114. Kahan, 128, 144.

115. Salem, *Bolshevikes bay di grenetsn fun poyln*, 3, 5.

116. Salem, 5.

117. Salem, 7–8.

118. Salem, 9.

119. Salem, 12–13.

120. Getter, Schall, and Schipper, *Żydzi bojownicy o niepodległość Polski*, 309.

121. *Biuletyn Nr. 1 Okręgu Stołecznego Związku Żydów Uczestników Walk o Niepodległość Polski*, 1935–1936 (Warsaw: Okręg Stołeczny Związku Żydów Uczestników Walk o Niepodległość Polski, 1936), 7.

122. Jewish veterans in Poland performed enactments of military male gender norms in a way similar to their German Jewish counterparts. See Huebel, *Fighter, Worker, and Family Man*, 12–38.

123. Henschel, *Jeder Bürger Soldat*, 303.

124. In 1935, out of 578 members of the Warsaw chapter of ZŻUWoNP, more than a third (204) had a university education, and almost 300 were officers. *Biuletyn Nr. 1 Okręgu Stołecznego Związku Żydów Uczestników Walk o Niepodległość Polski*, 1935–1936, 8. The ideological roots of the Society of Jewish Fighters were in the Żagiew and Berek Joselewicz scouting associations, which attracted middle- and upper-class Jews acculturated to the Polish culture. In 1938, ZŻUWoNP had about 6,800 members. Henschel, *Jeder Bürger Soldat*, 304–305.

125. A. H. Rogowoj, "Droga kombatantów," *Na Przełomie*, March 1, 1936, 19, reprinted and translated from *Dos Yudishe Togblat*, January 6, 1936.

126. Letter of L. Hirszberg, the Board of the Jewish Community of Łódź to the chief rabbi of Kalisz, January 8, 1919, file 197, call no. 39/228/0. Łódzka Gmina Wyznaniowa Żydowska, Archiwum Państwowe w Łodzi.

127. Wojciech Śmieja, "Homo prostheticus czyli ciało zdemilitary-zowane: O dylogii powieściowej Jana Żyznowskiego," *Interalia: A Journal of Queer Studies* 10 (2015), 7.

128. J. B., "Sprawiedliwości," *Inwalida Żydowski*, February 1, 1927, 3.

129. "Statystyka inwalidów w Polsce," *Inwalida Żydowski*, November 1, 1934, 1.

130. Szczepaniak, *Habitus żołnierski w literaturze i kulturze polskiej*, 32.

131. Ludwik Schermant, "O własny dom . . . ," *Inwalida Żydowski*, November 1, 1926, 3–4.

132. Herman Schwarz, "Inwalidzkie bolączki," *Inwalida Żydowski*, June 1, 1928, 1.

133. L. S., "Jednością silni," *Inwalida Żydowski*, December 1, 1928, 1.

134. J. B., "Sprawiedliwości," *Inwalida Żydowski*, February 1, 1927, 3.

135. "Magistrat w Nowym Sączu krzywdzi żyd. inwalidów," *Inwalida Żydowski*, October 1, 1928, 4.

136. Jakób Bachner, "Męczarnie żyd. inwalidów," *Inwalida Żydowski*, December 1, 1926, 4.

137. "Męczarnie żydowskich inwalidów," *Inwalida Żydowski*, March 1, 1927, 6.

138. Jakób Bachner, "Leczenie żydowskich inwalidów wojennych w miejscach klimatycznych i kąpielowych na Górnym Śląsku," *Inwalida Żydowski*, June 1, 1930, 4–5.

139. "Śladami przelanej krwi," *Inwalida Żydowski*, June 1, 1929, 5–6.

140. Zwi Heller, "Cele i zadania Światowej organizacji żydowskich inwalidów, wdów i sierót wojennych," *Inwalida Żydowski*, November 1, 1928, 2–3.

141. Herman Schwarz, "Inwalidzkie bolączki," *Inwalida Żydowski*, February 1, 1929, 3.

142. "Nasze postulaty w Sejmie. Przemówienie posła Hellera na plenum Sejmu w dyskusji budżetowej dnia 8 lutego 1929," *Inwalida Żydowski*, March 1, 1929, 1.

143. Herman Schwarz, "Domagamy się pracy dla żyd. inwalidów wojen," *Inwalida Żydowski*, June 1, 1930, 1.

144. Ludwik Schermant, "O własny dom . . . ," *Inwalida Żydowski*, November 1, 1928, 4.

145. Ludwik Schermant, "O własny dom . . . ," *Inwalida Żydowski*, November 1, 1928, 4.

146. "Dziesięciolecie pracy organizacyjnej prezesa Jakóba Bachnera," *Inwalida Żydowski*, October 1, 1930, 1–2.

147. "Wieczornica chanukowa dla żołnierzy," *Na Przełomie*, February 1, 1935, 45.

148. Członkowie Żydowskiego Związku Inwalidów, Wdów i Sierot Wojennych podczas defilady, *Ilustrownay Kurier Codzienny*, May 3, 1935, call no. 1-P-2931-1, NAC.

149. "Uroczyste poświęcenie sztandaru Związku żyd. inwalidów, wdów i sierot woj. w Krakowie w dniu 24 lutego 1935," *Inwalida Żydowski*, January 1, 1935, 2–3.

150. "Po III. Walnym Zjeździe," *Inwalida Żydowski*, January 1, 1927, 1–3.

151. "Dzieje sztandaru oddziału krakowskiego," *Biuletyn Związku Żydów Uczestników Walk o Niepodległość Polski*, November 1938, 2–3.

152. Tadeusz Zubrzycki, *Żydzi w szeregach polskich 1914–1920* (Lviv: Grono Legionistów, 1924).

153. "II Walny Zjazd Delegatów Związku," *Na Przełomie. Biuletyn Związku Żydów Uczestników Walk o Niepodległość Polski*, March 1936, 7.

154. *III-ci Walny Zjazd Delegatów Związku Żydów Uczestników Walk o Niepodległość Polski w Krakowie, dnia 5 XII 1937 r. Referat ideowy Związku, wygłoszony przez kapitana rezerwy Prof. Dr. Zdzisława Zmigryder-Konopkę* (Warsaw: n.p., 1937), 10.

155. Henschel, *Jeder Bürger Soldat*, 290.

156. Henschel, 205–206.

157. Henschel, 206.

158. Henschel, 248–249.

159. Raport Dowództwa Okręgu Korpusu IV o żydach, February 3, 1926, call no. I.303.4.2687, Oddz. II SG, Centralne Archiwum Wojskowe (CAW, Central Military Archive in Warsaw), quoted in Henschel, *Jeder Bürger Soldat*.

160. Report about foreign nationalities in the Polish Army, October 18, 1923, call no. I.303.4.2710, Oddz. II SG, CAW; information report about national minorities in the Polish military, call no. I.371.7/A.25, undated, Samodzielny Referat Informacyjny (Independent Information Divison), CAW; report about nationalities and desertion, January 7, 1937, call no. I.371.9/A.143, SRI, all quoted in Henschel, *Jeder Bürger Soldat*, 222.

161. See Mateusz Rodak, *Mit a rzeczywistość. Przestępczość osób narodowości żydowskiej w II Rzeczpospolitej: Casus województwa lubelskiego* (Warsaw: Neriton, 2012), 97–02.

162. Jan Czekanowski, *Wstęp do historii Słowian: Perspektywy antropologiczne, etnograficzne, prehistoryczne i językoznawcze* (Lviv: Lwowska Biblioteka Slawistyczna, 1927), 41, quoted in Henschel, *Jeder Bürger Soldat*, 223.

163. Nationalities report (third quarter of 1926), October 15, 1926, call no. I.303.4.2684, Oddz. II SG, CAW, 114–153, quoted in Henschel, *Jeder Bürger Soldat*, 225.

164. Henschel, *Jeder Bürger Soldat*, 278–279.

165. Henschel, 275.

166. Pinkas Rosengarten, *Zapiski rabina Wojska Polskiego* (Warsaw: Stowarzyszenie Dokumentacji i Upowszechniania Dorobku Kulturalnego Żydów Europy Środkowej i Wschodniej "Pamięć Diaspory," 2001), 137, 139. Rosengarten was the rabbi of the Polish army formed in the Soviet Union in 1941.

167. Henschel, *Jeder Bürger Soldat*, 289.

168. M. Surits, *Militer-pflikht: Vos darf yederer visn vegn pobor, militer-dinst un ibungen?* (Warsaw: Kooperativ Vort, 1927).

169. Samuel Lipa Tennenbaum, *Zloczów Memoir 1939–1941: A Chronicle of Survival 1939–1941* (New York: Shengold, 1986), 72.

170. Zygmunt Sterngast, file 10478, 29/442 Sąd Okręgowy w Krakowie, Archiwum Narodowe w Krakowie.

171. Lejb Goldenberg, file 6430, 35/469 Sąd Okręgowy w Lublinie, AP Lublin.

172. Henschel, *Jeder Bürger Soldat*, 234–244.

173. Henschel, 237.

174. Tadeusz Mścisławski, *Wojsko polskie a żydzi: Bibljoteczka Żydoznawcza Towarzystwa Rozwój* (Warsaw: Towarzystwo Rozwój, 1923), 2:14.

175. "W armji narodowej nie ma miejsca dla żydów!," *Potęga Polski bez Żydów: Tygodnik społeczno-gospodarczy* (Poznań), October 18, 1936, 1, quoted in Henschel, *Jeder Bürger Soldat*, 232.

176. Kazimierz Kierski, *Kwestia żydowska* (Poznań: Związek Popierania Polskiego Stanu Posiadania, 1939), 77, quoted in Henschel, *Jeder Bürger Soldat*, 233.

177. *Kalendarz tygodnika humorystyczno-satyrycznego Szopka na rok 1924* (Warsaw: Spółka Wydawnicza Warszawska, 1924), 65.

178. Ute Frevert, *Die kasernierte Nation: Militärdienst und Zivilgesellschaft in Deutschland* (Munich: C. H. Beck, 2001), 241.

179. *Kabaret: Pismo satyryczno-humorystyczne*, no. 33 (1925), 4.

180. Dariusz Konstantynów, "Pogromy i inne akty przemocy fizycznej wobec Żydów w zwierciadle rysunków z prasy polskiej (1919–1939)," in *Pogromy Żydów na ziemiach polskich w XIX i XX wieku*, vol. 1, *Literatura i sztuka*, ed. Sławomir Buryła, 321–362 (Warsaw: Instytut Historii PAN, 2018).

181. *Szczutek*, no. 28 (1919), 5.

6. LEISURE AND TOIL

1. Nicolas Vallois and Sarah Imhoff, "'Floating Jews'—The Luftmentsh as an Economic Character," *Œconomia* 12, no. 2 (2022): 275–314. Vallois

and Imhoff quote from Jacob Lestchinsky, *Di ekonomishe lage fun yidn in poyln* (Berlin: n.p., 1931).

2. See Tadeusz Górski, "'Der Lodzer mensh' un der piotrkover gas," *Ilustrirter poylisher manchester*, May 1931, 14–15.

3. Vallois and Imhoff, "'Floating Jews,'" 30–34.

4. Connell and Messerchmidt, "Hegemonic Masculinity," 848.

5. See Benjamin Maria Baader, *Gender, Judaism, and Bourgeois Culture in Germany, 1800–1870* (Bloomington: Indiana University Press, 2006).

6. See Josep M. Armengol, "Gendering the Great Depression: Rethinking the Male Body in 1930s American Culture and Literature," *Journal of Gender Studies* 23, no. 1 (2014): 59–68.

7. Uwe Spiekermann, Paul Lerner, and Anne Schenderlein, "Jews, Consumer Culture, and Jewish Consumer Cultures: An Introduction," in Paul Lerner, Uwe Spiekermann, and Anne Schenderlein, eds., *Jewish Consumer Cultures in Nineteenth and Twentieth-Century Europe and North America* (Cham, Switzerland: Palgrave Macmillan, 2022), 4.

8. See Hanna Imbs, ed., *Miasto i kultura polska doby przemysłowej*, vols. 1–3 (Wrocław, Poland: Zakład Narodowy im. Ossolińskich, 1988–1993).

9. Joachim Zylberszpic, "Reforma czasu pracy," *Almanach Naszego Przeglądu*, 1939, 131–132.

10. Salo Baron, "Newer Emphases in Jewish History," *Jewish Social Studies* 25, no. 4 (1963): 245–258.

11. Around 50 percent were peasants, 30.2 percent were blue-collar workers, and 0.9 percent were "bourgeois." *100 lat Polski w liczbach* (Warsaw: GUS, 2018), fig. 45, quoting Janusz Żarnowski, *Społeczeństwo II Rzeczypospolitej. 1918–1939* (Warsaw: PWN, 1973).

12. In 1927, the Fareyn fun handel- un byuro-ongeshtelten (Union of Trade and Office Employees) was established to defend the rights of the growing community employed in these professions.

13. See Kimmel, *Manhood in America*, 7.

14. "Jak zostać milionerem," *Almanach Naszego Przeglądu*, 1937, 53–54.

15. A selection of books on that topic includes Tracey Deutsch, *Building a Housewife's Paradise: Gender, Politics, and American Grocery Stores in the Twentieth Century* (Chapel Hill: University of North Carolina Press, 2010); Erika Rappaport, *Shopping for Pleasure: Women in the Making of London's West End* (Princeton, NJ: Princeton University Press, 2001); Lori Anne Loeb, *Consuming Angels: Advertising and Victorian Women* (Oxford: Oxford University Press, 1994).

16. Mark A. Swiencicki, "Consuming Brotherhood: Men's Culture, Style and Recreation as Consumer Culture, 1880–1930," *Journal of Social History* 31, no. 4 (1998), 773.

17. Christopher Breward, *The Hidden Consumer: Masculinities, Fashion, and City Life, 1860–1914* (Manchester, UK: Manchester University Press, 1999).

18. On the economic crisis, see Jerzy Tomaszewski, "Położenie drobnych kupców żydowskich w Polsce w latach wielkiego kryzysu (1929–1935)," *Biuletyn Żydowskiego Instytutu Historycznego* 102, no. 2 (1977): 35–54; Emanuel Melzer, *No Way Out: The Politics of Polish Jewry 1935–1939* (Cincinnati: Hebrew Union College Press, 1987), 39–52.

19. Marta Dolecka and Dorota Raczkiewicz, "Bezrobocie w Polsce w okresie międzywojennym w kontekście jakości danych w spisach ludności," *Annales Universitatis Mariae Curie-Skłodowska. Sectio H Oeconomia* 48, no. 2 (2014), 54.

20. Connell and Messerschmidt, "Hegemonic Masculinity," 838.

21. Jill Greenfield, Sean O'Connell, and Chris Reid, "Fashioning Masculinity: Men Only, Consumption and the Development of the Marketing in the 1930s," *Twentieth Century British History* 10, no. 4 (1999), 459.

22. Graham Dawson, "The Blond Bedouin: Lawrence of Arabia, Imperial Adventure and the Imagining of English-British Masculinity," in Roper and Tosh, *Manful Assertions*, 118.

23. *Chwila: Dodatek ilustrowany*, February 9, 1930, 1.

24. *Chwila: Dodatek ilustrowany*, February 16, 1930, 1.

25. "Dwa lata," *Trybuna Akademicka*, March 1, 1928, 7.

26. *Almanach Naszego Przeglądu*, 1937, 172.

27. *Almanach Naszego Przeglądu*, 1937, 16.

28. *Almanach Naszego Przeglądu*, 1938, 113.

29. "Czy pani jest idealną żoną?," *Almanach Naszego Przeglądu*, 1938, 167–168.

30. "Di froy vil makhen dem man surprizen," *Velt-shpigl*, July 7, 1938, 18. See also "Tsi darf a froy endiken a universitet tsu kenen firen di hoyz-virtshaft?," *Ilustrirter poylisher manchester*, February 1930, 18–19.

31. "Unter di grininke boymelekh . . . ," *Idishe Bilder*, no. 6 (1937), 20.

32. For example, in *Śmiech do rana*, December 31, 1933, 1.

33. "Ziben ofenim vi tsu bazigen a froy," *Panorame*, October 29, 1937, 6. Improper household management was to lead to "man's unneeded expenses."

34. *Panorame*, January 7, 1938, 5.

35. "Kobieta w domu," *Ewa*, March 25, 1928, 9.

36. Greenfield, O'Connell, and Reid, "Fashioning Masculinity," 457.

37. "Mydło Kollontay," *Nowy Dziennik*, August, 13, 1987, 18.

38. *Ewa*, June 17, 1928, 8.

39. Greenfield, O'Connell, and Reid, "Fashioning Masculinity," 462.

40. Adam Świsłocki, "Pamflety na kobiety," *Współczesny Pan*, December 4, 1932, 2; "Kobiety nie walczą o dyplomy," *Współczesny Pan*, November, 1936, 6.

41. Aleksander Ołomucki, "Demokratyzacja wiedzy czy degradacja inteligencji," *Trybuna Akademicka*, September 1, 1927, 4–5; *Trybuna Akademicka*, October 1, 1927, 3–4.

42. Seweryn Cynsztang, "O reformę naszej pracy kulturalnej," *Trybuna Akademicka*, October 1927, 10–11.

43. On these dynamics in the Hapsburg Empire, see Susanne Korbel, *Auf die Tour! Jüdinnen und Juden in Singspielhalle, Kabarett und Varieté zwischen Habsburgermonarchie und Amerika um 1900* (Vienna: Böhlau, 2021).

44. Elchanan Lewin, "Degradacja mózgu (Kilka uwag na marginesie obecnej niedoli inteligencji)," *Trybuna Akademicka*, October 1, 1927, 15.

45. I. Oberzhanek, "Tsulib a por vayse hoyzn!," *Unzer tsaytung*, July 3, 1936, 3.

46. For example, Antoni Starzyński, "Prawo pierwszej nocy," *Współczesny Pan*, September 20, 1931, 1; Adam Świsłocki, "Ius primae noctis," *Współczesny Pan*, December 1934, 2.

47. Kenon Breazeale, "In Spite of Women: Esquire Magazine and the Construction of the Male Consumer," *Signs* 20 (1994), 1–22. See also Bill Osgerby, "A Pedigree of the Consuming Male: Masculinity, Consumption and the American 'Leisure Class,'" *Sociological Review* 51, no. 1 (2003): 57–85.

48. "Co nosi Pan w tym karnawale," *Bluszcz*, January 25, 1930, 21.

49. "Dla Pana," *ABC Mody*, March 1930, 2.

50. *ABC Mody*, March 1930, 5; "Zewsząd po trosze," *ABC Mody*, March 1930, 24.

51. "U naszych mistrzów," *ABC Mody*, March 1930, 13.

52. "Mundur Marszałka," *ABC Mody*, March 1930, 12.

53. *Współczesny Pan*, February 1936, 9. On sartorial debates in the context of Jewish Vienna see Jonathan Kaplan-Wajselbaum, *Jews in Suits. Men's Dress in Vienna, 1890–1938* (New York: Bloomsbury, 2023).

54. "Angielska moda dla Panów," *Almanach Naszego Przeglądu*, 1939, 209.

55. Paulinette (Paulina Appenszlak), "Moda anno 1938," *Almanach Naszego Przeglądu*, 1938, 151–152.

56. *Ilustrirter poylisher manchester*, February 1930, 3.

57. Greenfield, O'Connell, and Reid, "Fashioning Masculinity," 469.

58. Osgerby, "A Pedigree of the Consuming Male," 64.

59. "Co mężczyźni sądzą o modzie?," *Almanach Naszego Przeglądu*, 1938, 165–166.

60. "Co mężczyźni sądzą o modzie?," *Almanach Naszego Przeglądu*, 1938, 165–166.

61. "Mężczyzna zdobywa świat," *Współczesny Pan*, July 1, 1934, 1.

62. "Kobiety wynalazczynie," *Almanach Naszego Przeglądu*, 1938, 148.

63. *Almanach Naszego Przeglądu*, 1937, 236.

64. *Almanach Naszego Przeglądu*, 1938, 16.

65. *Di yidishe vokh*, March 21, 1913, 7.

66. *Chwila*, April 23, 1932, 2.

67. *Chwila*, December 27, 1938, 5.

68. "Unzer shapsel. Vi lebt der balibter bokser S. Rotholc?," *Idishe Bilder*, October 1938, 15–16.

69. *Pinsker Shtime*, March 28, 1930, 1.

70. *Di Panorame*, March 4, 1938, 2.

71. *Chwila*, February 26, 1934, 19.

72. *Di Idishe Vokh*, August 29, 1912, 1.

73. Helena Brzezińska, "Salon piękności dla panów," *Almanach Naszego Przeglądu*, 1938, 174.

74. *Nasz Przegląd*, December 24, 1927, 1.

75. *Nasz Przegląd*, November 23, 1927, 8.

76. *Almanach Naszego Przeglądu*, 1937, 99.

77. *Hayntige Nayes*, April 8, 1938, 7.

78. Paweł Klinger, "Dlaczego jest więcej wdów niż wdowców?," *Almanach Naszego Przeglądu*, 1937, 208–209.

79. *Nasz Przegląd*, December 9, 1932, 1.

80. *Di Panorame*, February 18, 1938, 4. A similar message sent an advertisement for the antirheumatic treatment of a Berlin doctor, August Märzke, in a Łódź Yiddish monthly. This ad included images of a broken man with crutches and a happy, healthy, elegant man pushing crutches away. *Ilustrirter poylisher manchester*, February 1930, 52.

81. Alain Corbin, "Przymus demonstrowania energii seksualnej," in Corbin, *Historia męskości*, 111–116.

82. *Di Idishe vokh*, April 25, 1913, 4.

83. *Di Idishe vokh*, April 25, 1913, 6.

84. *Tygodnik Żydowski*, May 7, 1937, 4.

85. For a short review, see Susan E. Cayleff, "'Prisoners of Their Own Feebleness': Women, Nerves and Western Medicine—A Historical Overview," *Social Science & Medicine* 26, no. 12 (1988), 1199–1208. For a full-length study, see Andrew Scull, *Hysteria: The Biography* (Oxford: Oxford University Press, 2009) and Mark S. Micale, *Hysterical Men: The Hidden History of Male Nervous Illness* (Cambridge, MA: Harvard University Press, 2008).

86. "Strach przed zdradą małżeńską," *Współczesny Pan*, September 4, 1932, 1.

87. *Pinsker Shtime*, February 19, 1932, 1.

88. *Ilustrirter poylisher manchester*, February 1930, 53.

89. *Di Idishe vokh*, March 7, 1913, 16.

90. *Hayntige Nayes*, January 4, 1935, 7.

91. Zygmunt Braude, "Narty," *Trybuna Akademicka*, November 1927, 34–35.

92. "Powrót do kobiecości," *Chwila*, February 13, 1929, 13.

93. Vivian, "Gdy jedziemy w góry . . . ," *Współczesny Pan*, August 2, 1931, 4.

94. On Jewish mountain leisure, see Urszula Madej-Krupitski, "Mapping Jewish Poland: Leisure Travel and Identity in the Interwar Period" (PhD diss., University of California Berkeley, 2020).

95. File 1008, collection 72/31/0 Zarząd Warszawskiego Oberpolicjmajstra, Archiwum Państwowe w Warszawie.

96. "Odczyt o motoryzacji w Klubie Towarzyskim," *Trybuna: Tygodnik Radomski*, January 20, 1939, 7.

97. *Trybuna: Tygodnik Radomski*, March 31, 1939, 14.

98. "Odczyt o motoryzacji," *Trybuna Radomska*, April 9, 1937, 5.

99. "Tegoroczny międzynarodowy raid samochodowy," *Nowy Dziennik*, March 20, 1928, 8.

100. Witkower, "Chłodne miasto," *Nowy Dziennik*, January 16, 1928, 5.

101. J. Orłowski, "Nieco o technice samochodowej," *Korporant* 6–7 (September–October 1925), 18–19.

102. *Ilustrirter poylisher manchester*, April 1931, 19.

103. *Velt-shpigel*, no. 14 (1929), 16.

104. *Der Mehabel*, February 14, 1936, 4.

105. L. D. Berkowicz, "Szofer," *Naród*, March 1, 1930, 32–42. Possibly the author was Yitskhok Dovid Berkowitz (Berkowicz) and his initials were misspelled.

106. *Nowy Dziennik*, January 1, 1935, 5.

107. "Heher ziben miliard papirosn roykhert man in eyn yor in poyln," *Dos yudishe vokhnblat*, September 28, 1928, 6.

108. V. Shalk, "Oyf sheyd-veg," *Di Tat*, May 17, 1939, 7.

109. I. Oberzhanek, "Tsulib a por vayse hoyzn!," *Unzer tsaytung*, July 3, 1936, 3.

110. *Kontratak*, September 20, 1938, 6.

111. *Dos Naye Leben*, April 11, 1922, 2.

112. "Historia papierosa," *Almanach Naszego Przeglądu*, 1939, 178.

113. Blanka Hollendrowa, "Kilka godzin w Zakopanem," *Nowy Dziennik*, June 10, 1928, 10.

114. "Er in shtot, zi oyf datshe," *Tararam*, August 3, 1934, 4.

115. "Oneg shabes," *Tararam*, June 1, 1934, 3.

116. "In kino," *Di Panorame*, September 24, 1937, 2.

117. "A shmues vegn libe zvishn a zeyde un on eyniklen," *Di Panorame*, January 14, 1938, 3.

118. *Di Panorame*, March 4, 1938, 1.

119. "Nowy typ mężczyzny," *Współczesny Pan*, February 1936, 10.

120. "Zboczenia płciowe," *Nasz Przegląd*, June 28, 1931, 14.

121. I. Oberzhanek, "Tsulib a por vayse hoyzn!," *Unzer tsaytung*, July 3, 1936, 3.

122. *Di Idishe vokh*, March 10, 1913, 6.

123. Translated from Yiddish, "Marianna has blond curls and blue eyes. But I am a Jewish boy and she is a non-Jewish girl." "Blonde loken hot Marianna," *Tararam*, June 29, 1934, 8.

124. "A radio," *Tararam*, June 1, 1934, 1.

125. Fabrice Virgili, "Męskość podszyta niepokojem, męskość agresywna," in Courtine, *Historia męskości*, 77–84.

126. On sexual assaults on house maids, see Izabella Moszczeńska, *Czego nie wiemy o naszych synach: Fakta i cyfry dla użytku rodziców* (Warsaw: Nasza Księgarnia, 1904); Joanna Kuciel-Frydryszak, *Służące do wszystkiego* (Warsaw: Marginesy, 2018).

127. "A kredens mit a pomotsnik," *Tararam*, May 11, 1934, 5.

128. "Ven a froy vil shpilen a platonishe libe," *Di Panorame*, January, 21, 1938, 7.

129. "A shmues vegn libe zvishn a zeyde un on eyniklen," *Di Panorame*, January 14, 1938, 3.

130. *Tararam*, May 11, 1934, 8.

131. *Di Panorame*, March 4, 1938, 1.

132. *Tararam*, July 27, 1934, 1.

133. "A brivel fun krinitse," *Tararam*, June, 1, 1934, 7.

134. "A brivel fun krinitse," *Tararam*, June 29, 1934, 2.

135. "Dos ershte datshe brivele," *Tararam*, May 27, 1934, 6.

136. "Az man shikt s'vayb keyn Ciechocinek," *Tararam*, May 27, 1934, 2.

137. B. Kovner, "Mayn vaybs ershter man," *Di Panorame*, March 4, 1938, 5.

138. Antoni Starzyński, "Salonowcy z ulicy Marszałkowskiej," *Współczesny Pan*, April 16, 1933, 1.

139. Klara Lewin, "Dos geyeg nokh mener," *Di Panorame*, February 25, 1938, 3.

140. Osgerby, "A Pedigree of the Consuming Male," 59–60.

7. HOMOSEXUAL MASCULINITIES

1. I understand sexual subjectivity following the approach of Deborah L. Tolman—that is, a "person's experience of herself as a sexual being, who feels entitled to sexual pleasure and sexual safety, who makes active sexual choices, and who has an identity as a sexual being." See Deborah L. Tolman, *Dilemmas of Desire: Teenage Girls Talk about Sexuality* (Cambridge, MA: Harvard University Press, 2005), 5–6.

2. David M. Halperin, *How to Do the History of Homosexuality?* (Chicago: University of Chicago Press, 2002), 1–7.

3. On the link between homosexuality and Jewishness in Germany, see Robert Deam Tobin, *Peripheral Desires: The German Discovery of Sex* (Philadelphia: University of Pennsylvania Press, 2016), 83; George L. Mosse, *Nationalism and Sexuality: Middle-Class Morality and Sexual Norms in Modern Europe* (Madison: University of Wisconsin Press, 1985); Mosse, *The Image of Man.*

4. Moshe Sluhovsky, introduction to Andreas Kraß, Moshe Sluhovsky, and Yuval Yonay, eds., *Queer Jewish Lives between Central Europe and Mandatory Palestine: Biographies and Geographies* (Bielefeld, Germany: Transcript, 2022), 8.

5. Weininger's *Geschlecht und Character* was translated into both Yiddish and Polish and republished several times.

6. Stanisława Paleolog, *Policja kobieca w Polsce (1925–1939)* (Warsaw: Biuro Programu "Niepodległa," 2020), 91–92.

7. Alfred Łaszowski, "Panowie wolą panów…," *Prosto z mostu: Tygodnik literacko-społeczny*, January 8, 1939, 2.

8. On Germany, see Robert Beachy, *Gay Berlin: Birthplace of a Modern Identity* (New York: Knopf, 2014); Florence Tamagne, *History of Homosexuality in Europe, Berlin, London, Paris 1919–1939* (New York: Algora, 2006).

9. In Germany there existed a homosexual rights organization, the Wissenschaftlich-humanitäres Komitee (Scientific-Humanitarian Committee, 1897), the Gemeinschaft der Eigenen (Community of the Unique, 1903), and several journals catering to homosexual men: *Der Eigene* (The unique) (1896–1932), *Die Freundschaft* (The friendship) (1919–1933), *Die Sonne* (The sun) (1920), and *Uranos* (1921–1923).

10. On the interwar developments in other European countries, see Lorenzo Banadusi, *The Enemy of the New Man: Homosexuality in Fascist Italy* (Madison: University of Wisconsin Press, 2012); Laurie Marhoefer, *Sex and the Weimar Republic: German Homosexual Emancipation and the Rise of the Nazis* (Toronto: University of Toronto Press, 2015); Anita Kurimay, *Queer Budapest, 1873–1961* (Chicago: University of Chicago Press, 2020); Dan Healey, *Homosexual Desire in Revolutionary Russia: The Regulation of Sexual and Gender Dissent* (Chicago: University of Chicago Press, 2001); Javier Fernández Galeano and Geoffroy Huard, "La homosexualidad masculina en el Occidente en el siglo XX," in Francisco Vázquez García, ed., *Historia de la homosexualidad masculina en Occidente* (Madrid: Los Libros de la Catarata, 2022).

11. Kamil Karczewski, "'For a Pole, It All Was a Great Abomination': Grassroots Homonationalism and State Homophobia à la Polonaise—A History Lesson from a Place between East and West," *Sexuality and Culture* 27 (2023), 207.

12. Shaun Jacob Halper, "Mordechai Langer (1894–1943) and the Birth of the Modern Jewish Homosexual" (PhD diss., University of California Berkeley, 2013), 1–6.

13. Valerie Purdie-Vaughns and Richard P. Eibach, "Intersectional Invisibility: The Distinctive Advantages and Disadvantages of Multiple Subordinate-Group Identities," *Sex Roles: A Journal of Research* 59, no. 5–6 (2008): 377–391.

14. Kamil Karczewski, "'Call Me by My Name': A 'Strange and Incomprehensible' Passion in the Polish Kresy of the 1920s," *Slavic Review* 81, no. 3 (2022): 631–652.

15. See Karczewski, 645–649.

16. *Statystyka Polski*, IX, no. 2 (Warsaw: Główny Urząd Statystyczny, 1930), 632, 644, 650, 670, 676.

17. File 1351 Aleksander Skuta, 29/442 Sąd Okręgowy w Krakowie, Archiwum Narodowe w Krakowie (ANK).

18. See Kamil Karczewski, "Transnational Flows of Knowledge and the Legalisation of Homosexuality in Interwar Poland," *Contemporary European History* 33 no. 3 (2024): 849–866.

19. J. Pruszynowski, "Mniejszości seksualne," *Głos poranny*, July 19, 1931. Dodatek społeczno-literacki, 1–2. Pruszynowski's text in the Socialist daily *Głos poranny* was one of the earliest appearances of terms like "sexual minorities" and "homosexual love."

20. For example, Richard von Krafft-Ebing, *Zboczenia umysłowe na tle zaburzeń płciowych* (Warsaw: A. i R. Kleinsinger, 1906); Friedrich Wilhelm Foerster, *Etyka płciowa i pedagogika: Nowe uzasadnienie prawd starych* (Warsaw: Gebethner i Wolff, 1911); Emile Jozan, *Dos seksuele lebn bay mener un froyen* (Warsaw: Farlag M. Goldfarb, 1934).

21. Konstanty Grodzki, *Poradnik Lekarski dla Mężczyzn* (Warsaw: Jan Breslauer, 1876), 27, 50, 82–159.

22. Friedrich Wilhelm Foerster, *Etyka płciowa i pedagogika* (Kraków: Gebethner i Wolff, 1911), 113–115.

23. Raphaël Saldo, *Miłość zboczona w świetle nauki* (Warsaw: S. Sikora, 1930), 11.

24. Stanisław Mikulski, *Homoseksualizm ze stanowiska medycyny i prawa* (Warsaw: Gazeta Lekarska, 1920).

25. File 431 Stanisław Pańczyszyn, 29/467 Prokuratura Sądu Okręgowego w Krakowie 1923–1939, ANK. On homosexuality and blackmail, see Martin Lücke, "Mann-männliche Prostitution und hegemoniale Männlichkeit im Kaiserreich," in *Männer—Macht—Körper: Hegemoniale Männlichkeiten vom Mittelalter bis heute*, ed. Martin Dinges (Frankfurt: Campus, 2005), 157–172.

26. File 530 Wawrzyniec Sikora, 29/467 Prokuratura Sądu Okręgowego w Krakowie 1923–1939, ANK.

27. *Ilustrowany Kurjer Codzienny*, October 10, 1929, 17.

28. *Ilustrowany Kurjer Codzienny*, August 4, 1928, 13.

29. *Ilustrowany Kurjer Codzienny*, December 29, 1930.

30. Paweł Klinger, *Vita sexualis: Prawda o życiu płciowym człowieka* (Warsaw: J. Przeworski, 1939), 451.

31. Klinger, 453.

32. Klinger, 410.

33. Klinger, 413.

34. Klinger, 415–416.

35. Tobin, *Peripheral Desires*, 93.

36. "Kronika," *Chwila*, May 4, 1934, 12.

37. "Sensatsyoneler arest fun a graf vos hot farfirt kleyne kinder," *Unzer tsaytung*, August 26, 1929, 3.

38. "Cudzołóstwo nie jest karalne," *5-ta rano*, December 12, 1932, 4.

39. Haim Sheptil, "Der nayer shtraf-kodeks," *Dos naye vort*, November 18, 1932, 3.

40. Paweł Klinger, "Każdy człowiek jest nieco 'zboczony,'" *Głos Poranny*, October 30, 1938, 9; N. M-n, "S'zaynen noytig seksuele reformen," *Dos naye lebn*, January 21, 1930, 2. The second article reported on Magnus Hirschfeld's agenda of reforming societal approaches to sexuality.

41. "60-lecie Magnusa Hirschfelda," *Nowy Dziennik*, May 18, 1928.

42. HBD, in Abraham Novershtern, ed., *Alilot neurim: Autobiografiot shel bney noar yehudim mi-polin beyn shtey milkhamot ha-olam* (Jerusalem: Zalman Shazar Center for Jewish History, 2011), 117.

43. HBD, 101.

44. HBD, 123–126.

45. HBD, 123–126.

46. HBD, 123–126.

47. See Karczewski, "'Call Me by My Name.'"

48. "Der Stormer," in Jeffrey Shandler, ed., *Awakening Lives: Autobiographies of Jewish Youth in Poland before the Holocaust* (New Haven, CT: Yale University Press, 2002), 236.

49. A. Greyno, in Shandler, *Awakening Lives*, 70.

50. Karczewski, "Transnational Flows of Knowledge," 11.

51. Tamagne, *History of Homosexuality*, 314–315.

52. "Di homoseksualisten hoben zikh banutst mit falshe dokumenten," *Der Moment*, December 9, 1927, 11.

53. "Z bagna stolicy," *Ilustrowany Kurjer Codzienny*, December 6, 1927, 6.

54. "Protses fun a beamten far homoseksualizm," *Haynt*, August 12, 1934, 7.

55. "Arestirt a degenerat," *Der Moment*, February 22, 1934, 6.

56. "Homoseksualist tsushtekht 12 mol mit a meser zayn 'kokhanke,'" *Unzer Express*, July 22, 1936, 9.

57. "Homoseksualizm," *Kovler shtime*, October 5, 1934, 4.

58. "Homoseksualista skazany na pół roku więzienia," *Nowy Dziennik*, September 30, 1928, 11.

59. "A homoseksueler farbrekher in Khelm," *Khelmer Folksblat*, July 26, 1929, 3.

60. File 2454 Stanisław Sitarz, 35/469 Sąd Okręgowy w Lublinie 1918–1944, Archiwum Państwowe w Lublinie.

61. File 1768 Józef Gruszczyński, collection 38/180 Sąd Okręgowy w Łodzi, Archiwum Państwowe w Łódzi. All quotes concerning the Gruszczyński case are from this file.

62. Józef Halperin used the nickname Józek in his memoir. Following his immigration to Palestine, he adopted the name Josef Arnon.

63. Estate of Josef Arnon (Józef Halperin), personal diary, July 17, 1926, 26; August 14, 1926, 59–60; November 25, 1926, 16, in file 35668, Ghetto Fighters House Archive.

64. Estate of Josef Arnon, May 22, 1926, 64.

65. Estate of Josef Arnon, January 16, 1926, 64.

66. Estate of Josef Arnon, July 6, 1926, 3.

67. Estate of Josef Arnon, July 12, 1926, 20.

68. Estate of Josef Arnon, July 12, 1926, 21.

69. Estate of Josef Arnon, September 26, 1926, 105–108.

70. Estate of Josef Arnon, July 6, 1926, 4; February 6, 1926, 25.

71. Estate of Josef Arnon, February 21, 1926, 35.

72. Estate of Josef Arnon, July 6, 1926, 6.

73. Estate of Josef Arnon, July 6, 1926, 9.

74. Estate of Josef Arnon, September 15, 1926, 97.

75. Estate of Josef Arnon, June 6, 1926, 75.

76. Estate of Josef Arnon, September 13, 1927, 19.

77. Estate of Josef Arnon, November 21, 1926, 13.

78. Estate of Josef Arnon, November 21, 1926, 13.

79. Estate of Josef Arnon, May 18, 1927, 88–89.

80. Estate of Josef Arnon, February 25, 1928, 33.

81. Estate of Josef Arnon, August 18, 1928, 8–9.

82. Estate of Josef Arnon, September 26, 1926, 105–108.

83. Estate of Josef Arnon, January 16, 1926, 20–21.

84. Estate of Josef Arnon, November 23, 1929, 77, 80.

85. Estate of Josef Arnon, September 15, 1929, 22.

86. Estate of Josef Arnon, November 21, 1926, 14.

87. Paweł Hertz and Marek Zagańczyk, eds., *Portret młodego artysty: Listy Józefa Rajnfelda do Jarosława Iwaszkiewicza, 1928 – 1938* (Warsaw: Tenten, 1997), 22–23, 26.

88. Hertz and Zagańczyk, 90–95.

89. Hertz and Zagańczyk, 52–53.

90. Hertz and Zagańczyk, 37.

91. Hertz and Zagańczyk, 135.

92. Hertz and Zagańczyk, 127.

93. Kutna, *Sollen wir unsere Knäbelein beschneiden?*, 33.

94. Ofri Ilany, "Naga nafots ba-mizrakh: Tiurim shel mishkav-zakhar ba-tkufat ha-mandat," *Zmanim* 131 (2015), 8–21; Ofri Ilany, "'An Oriental Vice': Representations of Sodomy in Early Zionist Discourse," in *National Politics and Sexuality in Transregional Perspective: The Homophobic Argument*, ed. Achim Rohde, Christina von Braun, and Stefanie Schüler-Springorum, 107–120 (New York: Routledge, 2018).

95. Aron Spiwak, "Uwagi i zdarzenia," *Trybuna Narodowa*, February 8, 1935, 3.

96. Arje Koczer, "Pamiętnik więźnia Syjonu," *Trybuna Narodowa*, May 5, 1939, 4.

97. Mateusz Mieses, *W kwestyi nienawiści rasowej* (Lviv, Poland: H. Alternberg, 1912), 92. See also Mieses's press contribution where he repeats the idea of Jewish ethical supremacy: Mateusz Mieses, "Święto Tory a święto Apollina," *Nasz Przegląd*, May 24, 1939, 9.

98. Edmund Stein, "Judaizm i hellenim," *Bnai Brith*, no. 2–3 (1929), 13–14.

99. Leon Gutman, "Powstanie Machabeuszy na tle kulturalnych przejawów epoki," *Chwila*, December 17, 1933, 9–10.

100. Halperin, *How to Do the History of Homosexuality?*, 1–5.

101. "Gwałty pruskie," *Górnik: Organ okręgowy okręgu Zagłębia … PPS*, December 20, 1907, 1–2; "Brudy junkrów pruskich," *Dziennik Śląski*, May 12, 1908, 1. This and similar articles linking Germanness with homosexuality appeared in Poland during the so-called Eulenburg affair in 1907–1909, when members of German noble elite were accused of homosexualism. See Wojciech Śmieja, *Homoseksualność i polska nowoczesność: Szkice o teorii, historii i literaturze* (Katowice, Poland: Wydawnictwo Uniwersytetu Śląskiego, 2015), 140; Wojciech Śmieja, "Wokół 'skandalicznego procesu' Oskara Wilde'a i 'afery Eulenburga'— Homoseksualne skandale przełomu XIX i XX wieku a polska opinia publiczna," *Studia Kulturowe*, vol. 2, 2011, 93–115; Wojciech Śmieja, "Skandal homoseksualny i polska opinia publiczna—'sprawa Eulenburga' na łamach wybranych tytułów prasy polskiej," *Teksty Drugie* no. 5 (2013): 311–329.

102. Quoted in Karczewski, "'For a Pole,'" 2002–2003.

103. Florence Tamagne, "Mutacje homoseksualne," in Courtine, *Historia męskości*, 324.

104. Ludwik Oberlender, "Współczesne ruchy nacjonalistyczne a antysemityzm," *Miesięcznik żydowski*, July–December 1932, 13–14.

105. "Na temat 'raubriterstwa teutońskiego,'" *Trybuna Narodowa*, December 2, 1938, 6. An analogous contextualization of homosexuality as "a German Nazi problem" could be found in Jewish publications across Eastern Europe. The Latvian *Batog* wrote of homosexuality as the "atmosphere" that ruled among Hitler's staff. See Y. Klinov, "Hitlers meshugene kaprizn," *Batog* (Riga), July 15, 1932, 3.

106. Paweł Klinger, "Każdy człowiek jest nieco 'zboczony,'" *Głos Poranny*, October 30, 1938, 9.

107. "Wychowanie młodzieży hitlerowskiej w świetle oficjalnej staty styki," *Chwila*, February 28, 1939, 8.

108. See Susanne zur Nieden, "Aufstieg und Fall des virilen Männerhelden: Der Skandal um Ernst Röhm und seine Ermordung," in Susanne zur Nieden, ed., *Homosexualität und Staatsräson: Männlichkeit, Homophobie und Politik in Deutschland 1900–1945* (Frankfurt: Campus, 2005), 147–192.

109. Jehuda Ohrenstein, "Bilans hitleryzmu," *Divrey Akiva*, July 20, 1934, 373–374.

110. "'Roehm Niemców sudeckich' Heinz Ruthe i jego działalność … niepolityczna," *Nasz Dziennik*, November 16, 1937, 7.

111. A. S. Lirik, "Hitlers lustknaben," *Haynt*, July 2, 1934, 3.

112. *Tararam*, July 13, 1934, 1.

113. "Homoseksualizm—choroba hitleryzmu," *Chwila*, August 21, 1934, 3.

114. "Tak wygląda naga prawda. Bez komentarzy … ," *Chwila*, June 10, 1937, 3; "Kobiety w życiu Hitlera," *Chwila*, November 28, 1934, 6.

115. Imhoff, *Masculinity and the Making of American Judaism*.

EPILOGUE

1. Carey, "Jewish Masculinity in the Holocaust," 76.

2. Carey, 87.

3. Huebel, *Fighter, Worker, and Family Man*.

4. See Imhoff, *Masculinity and the Making of American Judaism*; Mora, *Carrying a Big Schtick*.

5. See Marianne R. Sanua, *Going Greek: Jewish College Fraternities in the United States, 1895–1945* (Detroit: Wayne State University Press, 2018).

6. Kavod Masculinities Group, *Community Report Back*, undated, accessed May 30, 2023, https://docs.google.com/document/d/1paUMBHrF6 h2V9bI8pONiCEDdauhr1hSdGg7lxbclOAo/edit.

7. Raz Yosef, *Beyond Flesh: Queer Masculinities and Nationalism in Israeli Cinema* (New Brunswick, NJ: Rutgers University Press, 2004), 1.

8. Danny Kaplan, *The Men We Loved: Male Friendship and Nationalism in Israeli Culture* (New York: Berghahn Book, 2006).

9. See Hakak, *Haredi Masculinities between the Yeshiva, the Army, Work, and Politics.*

BIBLIOGRAPHY

PRIMARY SOURCES

Archives and Libraries

Archiwum Narodowe w Krakowie (ANK)
Archiwum Państwowe w Łodzi (APŁ)
Archiwum Państwowe w Lublinie (APL)
Archiwum Państwowe w Warszawie (APW)
Archiwum Uniwersytetu Jagiellońskiego (AUJ)
Berlin State Library
Centralne Archiwum Wojskowe in Warsaw (CAW)
Ghetto Fighters House Archive (Israel)
Jagiellonian Library in Kraków
Jewish Family and Children's Services Holocaust Center in San Francisco
National Library in Jerusalem
National Library in Warsaw
State Archive of Lviv Region (DALO)
USC Shoah Foundation Archive (Los Angeles)

Periodical Literature

5-ta rano. Bezpartyjny dziennik żydowski
Batog (Riga)
Bnai Brith
Chwila
Czas

Der Fraynd

Der Mehabel

Der Moment

Di Idishe Vokh

Di Panorame

Dos Naye Lebn (Kalisz)

Dos Yudishe Vokhnblat

Dwa Grosze

Dziennik Kujawski

Dziennik Wileński

Echo

Echo Warszawskie

Expres Zagłębia

Gazeta Radomskowska

Głos Poranny

Górnik. Organ okręgowy okręgu Zagłębia Dąbrowskiego PPS

Grodner Moment

Hamakabi

Haynt

Hayntige Nayes

Ha-Olam

Ha-yom

Idishe Bilder

Ilustrirter Poylisher Manchester

Ilustrowany Kurjer Codzienny

Inwalida Żydowski

Iskra: dziennik polityczny, społeczny i literacki

Jedność: Pismo poświęcone szerzeniu myśli polskiej wśród Żydów

Jüdische Turnzeitung

Kabaret. Tygodnik satyryczno-humorystyczny

Kalisher Vokh

Khelmer Folksblat

Kieltser Tsaytung

Klinika: Tygodnik Lekarski

Korporant

Kurier Poznański

Kurjer Warszawski

Literarishe Bleter

Lubliner Tugblatt

Miesięcznik Żydowski

Moriah

Myśl Niepodległa

Myśl. Tygodnik proletariackich wolnomyślicieli

Na Przełomie. Biuletyn Związku Żydów Uczestników Walk o Niedpodległość Polski

Nayer Morgen

Nasz Przegląd

Nowa Gazeta

Nowa Rzeczpospolita

Nowy Dziennik

Przegląd Sportowy

Rocznik Korporacyjny

Rozwaga. Miesięcznik poświęcony idei zespolenia żydów z narodem polskim

Sport-tsaytung

Szczutek

Tararam

Trybuna Akademicka

Trybuna Narodowa

Unzer Bialystoker Ekspres

Unzer Express

Unzer Grodner Express

Unzer Tsaytung

Velt-shpigel

Warszawianka

Wiadomości Akademickie

Wiadomości Korporacyjne

Wiadomości Literackie

Wiek Nowy

Wróble na dachu

Współczesny Pan

Zarzewie Nowe

Zdrowie Ludu-Folksgezunt

Życie Akademickie

Printed Primary Sources

Bimko, Fishel. *Rekrutn*. Warsaw: Di Tsayt, 1921.

Czekanowski, Jan. *Wstęp do historii Słowian: Perspektywy antropologiczne, etnograficzne, prehistoryczne i językoznawcze*. Lviv: Lwowska Biblioteka Slawistyczna 1927.

Dinur, Ben-Zion. *Be-olam she-shaka: Zikhronot u-reshumot mi-derekh hayim.* Jerusalem: Mosad Bialik, 1958.

Etkes, Immanuel, and Shlomo Tikochinski, eds. *Yeshivot Lita: Prakey zikhronot.* Jerusalem: Zalman Shazar Center for Jewish History, 2004.

Foerster, Friedrich Wilhelm. *Etyka płciowa i pedagogika.* Kraków: Gebethner i Wolff, 1911.

Getter, Norbert, Jakub Schall, and Zygmunt Schipper, eds. *Żydzi bojownicy o niepodległość Polski.* Lviv, n.p., 1939.

Gold, Ben-Zion. *The Life of Jews in Poland before the Holocaust: A Memoir.* Lincoln: University of Nebraska Press, 2007.

Goldstein, Bernard. *Twenty Years with the Jewish Labor Bund: A Memoir of Interwar Poland.* West Lafayette, IN: Purdue University Press, 2016.

Grodzki, Konstanty. *Poradnik Lekarski dla Mężczyzn.* Warsaw: Jan Breslauer, 1876.

Hertz, Paweł, and Marek Zagańczyk, eds. *Portret młodego artysty: Listy Józefa Rajnfelda do Jarosława Iwaszkiewicza. 1928–1938.* Warsaw: Tenten, 1997.

Jozan, Emile. *Dos seksuele lebn bay mener un froyen.* Warsaw: Farlag M. Goldfarb, 1934.

Judson, Salomon. *Soldatchina.* Vilna, Poland: Vilner Ferlag fun B. Kletzkin, 1930.

Kahan, Yankev. *Dray yor in poylishen militer (19.10.1919–22.11.1922).* Tel Aviv: Ferlag Ha-Menorah, 1967.

Kierski, Kazimierz. *Kwestia żydowska.* Poznań, Poland: Związek Popierania Polskiego Stanu Posiadania, 1939.

Kimmelfeld, A. *Mayn militer-dinst in rusland: A Tog bukh fun a yidishn soldat.* Los Angeles: Model Print Shop, 1916.

Klinger, Paweł. *Vita sexualis: Prawda o życiu płciowym człowieka.* Warsaw: J. Przeworski, 1939.

Kowalski, Erwin. *Dekiel i banda.* Poznań, Poland: Życie Uniwersyteckie, 1931.

Kowalsky, Sholem B. *From My Zaidy's House.* Lakewood, NJ: Israel Bookshop, 2000.

Kreplak, Jacob. *Fun kazerme un milkhome.* New York: Tsentral, 1927.

Krzywicki, Ludwik. *Dawne obrzezanie.* Warsaw: Życie Wolne, 1928.

———. *Wspomnienia.* Vol. 3. Warsaw: Czytelnik, 1959.

Kutna, Samuel Natan. *Sollen wir unsere Knäbelein beschneiden?* Przemyśl, Poland: Robinsohn & Beglückter, 1903.

Langans, Saul. *Żydzi a studja akademickie w Polsce w latach 1921–1931.* Lviv: Centrala Żydowskich Stowarzyszeń samopomocowych Środowiska Lwowskiego, 1935.

Lensky, Mordechai. *More derekh le-mohelim: Kurtse yedies fun anatomye, fizyologye un aseptik.* Warsaw: Kultur-sektsye bay der varshever kehile-fervaltung, 1931.

Leshchinsky, Yankev. *The Last Years of Polish Jewry,* vol. 1, *At the Edge of the Abyss: Essays, 1927–33.* Edited by Robert Brym, Cambridge: Open Book Publishers, 2023.

Lestchinsky, Jacob (Yankev Leshchinsky). *Di ekonomishe lage fun yidn in poyln.* Berlin: n.p., 1931.

Lewin, Abraham. *Kantonistn: Vegn der yidisher rekrutshine in Rusland in di tsaytn fun Tsar Nikolay dem ershtn 1827–1856.* Warsaw: Grafia, 1934.

Lewin, Gershon. *Iberlebenishn: Epizodn un ayndrukn fun der rusish-yaponisher krig.* Vilna, Poland: Kletzkin Farlag, 1931.

———. *In velt krig.* Warsaw: Yehudiyah, 1923.

Lieber, Ben-Zion. *Dos geshlekhts leben: A populer-visnshaftlikh bukh.* New York: Rational Living, 1927.

Lilientalowa, Regina. *Dziecko żydowskie.* Kraków: Polska Akademia Umiejętności, 1927.

Lilientalowa, Regina. *Precz z barbarzyństwem (rzecz o obrzezaniu).* Warsaw: "Życie Wolne," 1928.

Merwin, Bertold. *Z życia w Legionach.* Kraków: Biuro Wydawnictw N. K. N., 1918.

Meyzakh, Yehoshue. *Der yudisher soldat: A mayse nora vi a yudisher soldat iz durkhgegangen di sheva madurey ge'enom un iz le-soyf gliklekh gevorn.* Vilna, Poland: Druk un ferlag, 1910.

Mieses, Mateusz. *W kwestyi nienawiści rasowej.* Lviv, Poland: H. Alternberg, 1912.

Mikulski, Stanisław. *Homoseksualizm ze stanowiska medycyny i prawa.* Warsaw: Gazeta Lekarska, 1920.

Moszczeńska, Izabella. *Czego nie wiemy o naszych synach: Fakta i cyfry dla użytku rodziców.* Warsaw: Nasza Księgarnia, 1904.

Mścisławski, Tadeusz. *Wojsko polskie a żydzi: Bibljoteczka Żydoznawcza Towarzystwa Rozwój.* Vol. 2. Warsaw: Towarzystwo Rozwój, 1923.

Niemojewski, Andrzej. *Dusza żydowska w zwierciadle Talmudu: Wydanie drugie poprawione.* Warsaw, self-published, 1920.

Novershtern, Abraham, ed. *Alilot neurim: Autobiografiot shel bney noar yehudim mi-polin beyn shtey milkhamot ha-olam.* Jerusalem: Zalman Shazar Center for Jewish History, 2011.

Nowaczyński, Adolf. *Plewy i perły.* Warsaw: Drukarnia Archidiecezjalna, 1933.

———. *Warta nad Wartą.* Poznań, Poland: Drukarnia Polska, 1937.

Paleolog, Stanisława. *Policja kobieca w Polsce (1925–1939)*. Warsaw: Biuro Programu "Niepodległa," 2020.

Reguer, Sara, and Moshe Aron Reguer. *My Father's Journey: A Memoir of Lost Worlds of Jewish Lithuania*. Boston: Academic Studies, 2015.

Rolnik, Joseph. *With Rake in Hand: Memoirs of a Yiddish Poet*. Syracuse, NY: Syracuse University Press, 2016.

Rosenblum, Beniamin. *Uwagi nad teraźniejszym stanem starozakonnych pod względem policyjno-lekarskim*. Warsaw, n.p., 1842.

Rosengarten, Pinkas. *Zapiski rabina Wojska Polskiego*. Warsaw: Stowarzyszenie Dokumentacji i Upowszechniania Dorobku Kulturalnego Żydów Europy Środkowej i Wschodniej "Pamięć Diaspory," 2001.

Rotsztejn, Shmuel. *Kantonistn: Historish bild in dray taylen*. Łódź, Poland: Farlag Masora, 1926.

Ruff, Josef. *Wieczny związek: Obrzezanie ze stanowiska obrządkowego, chirurgicznego i higienicznego*. Warsaw, n.p., 1883.

Saldo, Raphaël. *Miłość zboczona w świetle nauki*. Warsaw: S. Sikora, 1930.

Salem, Michael Yosef. *Bolshevikes bay di grenetsn fun poyln*. Łódź, Poland: Farlag S. Shapira, 1930.

Schall, Jakub. *Dzieje Żydów na ziemiach polskich: Podręcznik dla szkół średnich*. Lviv, Poland: A. Bardach, 1926.

Seewann, Harald. *Zirkel und Zionsstern. Bilder und Dokumente aus der versunkenen Welt der jüdisch-nationalen Korporationsstudententums: Ein Beitrag zur Geschichte des Zionismus auf akademischen Boden*. 5 vols. Graz, Austria, 1990–1996.

Segal, Beryl. "A Jew in the Russian Army during the First World War." *Rhode Island Jewish Historical Notes* 7 (1975): 105–139.

Shandler, Jeffrey, ed. *Awakening Lives: Autobiographies of Jewish Youth in Poland before the Holocaust*. New Haven, CT: Yale University Press, 2002.

Singer, Isaac Bashevis. *Love and Exile*. New York: Doubleday, 1984.

Steinhaus, Władysław. *Pamiętnik legionisty bł. p. Władysława Steinhausa*. Kraków: Centralne Biuro Wydawnictw N. K. N., 1916.

Stenographisches Protokoll der Verhandlungen des II. Zionisten-Congresses. Vienna: Verein "Erez Israel," 1898.

Stomma, Stanisław. *Trudne lekcje historii*. Kraków: Znak, 1998.

Surits, M. *Militer-pflikht: Vos darf yederer visn vegn pobor, militer-dinst un ibungen?* Warsaw: Kooperativ Vort, 1927.

Tennenbaum, Samuel Lipa. *Złoczów Memoir 1939–1941: A Chronicle of Survival 1939–1941*. New York: Shengold Publishers, 1986.

Turowski, Konstanty. *Historia Stowarzyszenie Katolickiej Młodzieży Akademickiej "Odrodzenie."* Warsaw: Ośrodek Dokumentacji i Studiów Społecznych, 1987.

Urbańczyk, Stanisław. *Z miłości do wiedzy: Wspomnienia.* Kraków, 1999.

von Krafft-Ebing, Richard. *Zboczenia umysłowe na tle zaburzeń płciowych.* Warsaw: A. i R. Kleinsinger, 1906.

Wasiutyński, Wojciech. *Prawą stroną labiryntu.* Gdańsk, Poland: Exter, 1996.

Żeleński, Tadeusz "Boy." *Obiad literacki.* Warsaw: Biblioteka Boya, 1934.

SECONDARY SOURCES

Armengol, Josep M. "Gendering the Great Depression: Rethinking the Male Body in 1930s American Culture and Literature." *Journal of Gender Studies* 23, no. 1 (2014): 59–68.

Aschheim, Steven E. *Brothers and Strangers: The East European Jew in German and German Jewish Consciousness, 1800–1923.* Madison: University of Wisconsin Press, 1982.

Ashwin, Sarah. *Gender, State and Society in Soviet and Post-Soviet Russia.* London: Routledge, 2000.

Avrutin, Eugene M. *Jews and the Imperial State: Identification Politics in Tsarist Russia.* Ithaca, NY: Cornell University Press, 2010.

Baader, Benjamin Maria. *Gender, Judaism, and Bourgeois Culture in Germany, 1800–1870.* Bloomington: Indiana University Press, 2006.

Bacon, Gershon. "Kfiya datit, hofesh bituy ve-zehut yehudit modernit ba-polin: Y. L. Peretz, Sholem Ash and the milah-skandal in Warsaw, 1908." In *Me-vilna le-yerushalayim: Mihkarim be-toldotehem ve-tarbutam shel yehudei mizrah eropa, mugashim le-profesor Shmuel Verses,* 167–185. Jerusalem: Magnes, 2002.

Banadusi, Lorenzo. *The Enemy of the New Man: Homosexuality in Fascist Italy.* Madison: University of Wisconsin Press, 2012.

Baron, Salo. "Newer Emphases in Jewish History." *Jewish Social Studies* 25, no. 4 (1963): 245–258.

Bartal, Israel. "Virility and Impotence: From Traditional Society to the Haskalah." In *Brother Keepers: New Perspectives on Jewish Masculinity,* edited by Harry Brod and Shawn Israel Zevit, 76–88. Harriman, TN: Men's Studies, 2010.

Baskin, Judith R., ed. *Jewish Women in Historical Perspective.* Detroit: Wayne State University Press, 1998.

Beachy, Robert. *Gay Berlin: Birthplace of a Modern Identity*. New York: Knopf, 2014.

Belkin, Aaron. *Bring Me Men: Military Masculinity and the Benign Facade of American Empire, 1898–2001*. New York: Columbia University Press, 2012.

Bennet, Judith M. *History Matters: Patriarchy and the Challenge of Feminism*. Philadelphia: University of Pennsylvania Press, 2010.

Berger, Michael. *Eisernes Kreuz und Davidstern: Die Geschichte jüdischer Soldaten in deutschen Armeen*. Berlin: Trafo, 2006.

Berger, Michael, and Gideon Römer-Hillebrecht, eds. *Juden und Militär in Deutschland*. Baden-Baden, Germany: Nomos, 2009.

————, eds. *Jüdische Soldaten–Jüdischer Widerstand in Deutschland und Frankreich*. Leiden, Netherlands: Brill, 2009.

Biale, David. *Eros and the Jew: From Biblical Israel to Contemporary America*. Berkeley: University of California Press, 1997.

Bienenstok, Theodore. "Social Life and Authority in the East European Jewish Shtetel Community." *Southwestern Journal of Anthropology* 6, no. 3 (1950): 238–254.

Blecking, Diethlem. *Tempel aus Blättern der Phantasie: Skizzen zu Politik, Film, Literatur und Sport*. Norderstedt, Germany: BoD, 2021.

Bloom, Ethan. "Toward a Theory of the Modern Hebrew Handshake: The Conduct of Muscle Judaism." In *Jewish Masculinities: German Jews, Gender, and History*, edited by Benjamin Maria Baader, Sharon Gillerman, and Paul Lerner, 152–185. Bloomington: Indiana University Press, 2012.

Bord, Matan. "Creating the Labor-Zionist Family: Masculinity, Sexuality, and Marriage in Mandate Palestine." *Jewish Social Studies* 22, no. 3 (2017): 38–67.

Bourdieu, Pierre. *Masculine Domination*. Stanford, CA: Stanford University Press, 2001.

Boyarin, Daniel. *Unheroic Conduct: The Rise of Heterosexuality and the Invention of the Jewish Man*. Berkeley: University of California Press, 1997.

Breazeale, Kenon. "In Spite of Women: Esquire Magazine and the Construction of the Male Consumer." *Signs* 20 (1994): 1–22.

Breines, Paul. *Tough Jews, Political Fantasies and the Moral Dilemma of American Jewry*. New York: Basic Books, 1990.

Brenner, Michael, and Gideon Reuveni, eds. *Emanzipation durch Muskelkraft: Juden und Sport in Europa*. Göttingen, Germany: Vandhoeck & Rupprecht, 2006.

————. *Emancipation through Muscles: Jews and Sports in Europe*. Lincoln: University of Nebraska Press, 2006.

Breward, Christopher. *The Hidden Consumer: Masculinities, Fashion, and City Life, 1860–1914*. Manchester, UK: Manchester University Press, 1999.

Bröckling, Ulrich. *Disziplin: Soziologie und Geschichte militärischer Gehorsamsproduktion*. Munich: Brill, 1997.

Brunotte, Ulrike, Anna-Dorothea Ludewig, and Axel Stähler, eds. *Orientalism, Gender, and the Jews: Literary and Artistic Transformations of European National Discourses*. Oldenburg, Germany: De Gruyter, 2015.

Bukowska-Marczak, Ewa. *Przyjaciele, koledzy, wrogowie: Relacje pomiędzy polskimi, żydowskimi i ukraińskimi studentami Uniwersytetu Jana Kazimierza we Lwowie w okresie międzywojennym (1918–1939)*. Warsaw: Neriton, 2019.

Butler, Judith. *Gender Trouble: Feminism and the Subversion of Identity*. New York: Routledge, 1990.

Carey, Maddy. *Jewish Masculinity in the Holocaust: Between Destruction and Construction*. London: Bloomsbury Academic, 2017.

Cayleff, Susan E. "'Prisoners of Their Own Feebleness': Women, Nerves and Western Medicine—A Historical Overview." *Social Science & Medicine* 26, no. 12 (1988): 1199–1208.

Clark, Roland. "Collective Singing in Romanian Fascism." *Cultural and Social History: The Journal of the Social History Society* 10, no. 2 (2013): 251–271.

Cole, Sarah. *Modernism, Male Friendship, and the First World War*. Cambridge: Cambridge University Press, 2003.

Collins, Randall. *Interaction Ritual Chains*. Princeton, NJ: Princeton University Press, 2004.

Connell, Raewyn W. *Masculinities*. Berkeley: University of California Press, 1995.

Connell, Raewyn W., and James W. Messerschmidt. "Hegemonic Masculinity: Rethinking the Concept." *Gender and Society* 19, no. 6 (2005): 829–859.

Corbin, Alain, ed. *Historia męskości*. Vol. 2, *XIX wiek: Tryumf męskości*. Gdańsk, Poland: słowo-obraz-terytoria, 2020.

Cornwall, Andrea, and Nancy Lindisfarne, eds. *Dislocating Masculinity: Comparative Ethnographies*. London: Routledge, 1994.

Courtine, Jaen-Jacques, ed. *Historia męskości*. Vol. 3, *XX–XXI wiek: Męskość w kryzysie*. Gdańsk, Poland: słowo/obraz terytoria, 2020.

Das, Santanu. *Touch and Intimacy in First World War Literature*. Cambridge: Cambridge University Press, 2005.

David, Deborah S., and Robert Brannon. *The Forty-Nine Percent Majority: The Male Sex Role*. Boston: Addison-Wesley, 1976.

Davidson, Jillian. "A 'Secular Catastrophe' in Eastern Europe—World War One and the Reconstruction of Modern Jewish Memory." *Yearbook for European Jewish Literature Studies* 1, no. 1 (2014): 41–61.

Davison, Neil R. *Jewishness and Masculinity from the Modern to the Postmodern*. New York: Routledge, 2015.

Dekel, Mikhal. *The Universal Jew: Masculinity, Modernity, and the Zionist Moment*. Evanston, IL: Northwestern University Press, 2011.

Deutsch, Tracey. *Building a Housewife's Paradise: Gender, Politics, and American Grocery Stores in the Twentieth Century*. Chapel Hill: University of North Carolina Press, 2010.

Dolecka, Marta, and Dorota Raczkiewicz. "Bezrobocie w Polsce w okresie międzywojennym w kontekście jakości danych w spisach ludności." *Annales Universitatis Mariae Curie-Skłodowska. Sectio H Oeconomia* 48, no. 2 (2014): 49–58.

Dominguez Andersen, Pablo, and Simon Wendt, eds. *Masculinities and the Nation in the Modern World: Between Hegemony and Marginalization*. New York: Palgrave, 2015.

Duda, Maciej. *Emancypanci i emancypatorzy:. Mężczyźni wspierający emancypację Polek w drugiej połowie XIX i na początku XX wieku*. Szczecin, Poland: Wydawnictwo Naukowe Uniwersytetu Szczecińskiego, 2017.

Dynner, Glenn. *The Light of Learning: Hasidism in Poland on the Eve of the Holocaust*. Oxford: Oxford University Press, 2024.

Dziadek, Adam, ed. *Formy męskości*. Warsaw: Wydawnictwo IBL PAN, 2018.

Eichenberg, Julia. *Kämpfen für Frieden und Fürsorge: Polnische Veteranen des Ersten Weltkriegs und ihre internationale Kontakte*. Oldenburg, Germany: Wissenschaftsverlag, 2011.

Eichler, Maya. *Militarizing Men: Gender, Conscription, and War in Post-Soviet Russia*. Stanford, CA: Stanford University Press, 2012.

Elias, Norbert, and Michael Schroter, eds. *Studies on the Germans: Power Struggles and the Development of Habitus in the Nineteenth and Twentieth Centuries*. Dublin: University College Dublin Press, 2013.

Elior, Rachel. *The Unknown History of Jewish Women through the Ages—On Learning and Illiteracy: On Slavery and Liberty*. Berlin: De Gruyter, 2023.

Eliott, Karla. "Caring Masculinities: Theorizing an Emerging Concept." *Men and Masculinities* 19, no. 3 (2015): 240–259.

Engelstein, Laura. *The Resistible Rise of Antisemitism. Exemplary Cases from Russia, Ukraine, and Poland*. Waltham, MA: Brandeis University Press, 2020.

Englender, Yakir. *The Male Body in Ultra-Orthodox Jewish Theology*. Eugene, OR: Pickwick, 2021.

Etkes, Immanuel. *Gaon of Vilna: Man and His Image*. Berkeley: University of California Press, 2002.

———. "Marriage and Torah Study among the Lomdim in Lithuania in the Nineteenth Century." In *The Jewish Family: Metaphor and Family*, edited by David Kraemer, 153–178. New York: Oxford University Press, 1989.

Evans Clements, Barbara, Rebecca Friedman, and Dan Healey, eds. *Russian Masculinities in History and Culture*. New York: Palgrave, 2002.

Even-Zohar, Itamar. "The Emergence of a Native Hebrew Culture in Palestine 1882–1948." In *Essential Papers on Zionism*, edited by Jehuda Reinharz and Anita Shapira, 727–744. New York: New York University Press.

Fager, Ruth A. *Sweatshop Strife: Class, Ethnicity, and Gender in the Jewish Labour Movement of Toronto, 1900–1939*. Toronto: University of Toronto Press, 1992.

Farges, Patrick. "'Muscle' Yekkes? Multiple German-Jewish Masculinities in Palestine and Israel after 1933." *Central European History* 51 (2018): 466–487.

Fine, David J. *Jewish Integration in the German Army in the First World War*. Berlin: De Gruyter, 2012.

Fraser, Erica L. *Military Masculinity and Postwar Recovery in the Soviet Union*. Toronto: University of Toronto Press, 2019.

Freeze, ChaeRan, Paula Hyman, and Antony Polonsky, eds. *Jewish Women in Eastern Europe*. Cambridge: Littman Library of Jewish Civilization, 2007.

Freidenreich, Harriet Pass. *Female, Jewish, and Educated: The Lives of Central European University Women*. Bloomington: Indiana University Press, 2002.

Frevert, Ute. *Die kasernierte Nation: Militärdienst und Zivilgesellschaft in Deutschland*. Munich: C. H. Beck, 2001.

Friedman-Kasaba, Kathie. *Memories of Migration: Gender, Ethnicity, and Work in the Lives of Jewish and Italian Women in New York, 1870–1924*. Albany: State University of New York Press, 2002.

Gałęzowski, Marek. *Na wzór Berka Joselewicza: Żołnierze i oficerowie pochodzenia żydowskiego w Legionach Polskich*. Warsaw: IPN, 2010.

Gallagher, Noelle. "The Jew's Penis: Circumcision and Sexual Pathology in Eighteenth-Century England." *Medical Humanities* 2022:1–13.

Garncarska-Kadary, Bina. *Żydowska ludność pracująca w Polsce, 1918–1939.* Warsaw: Żydowski Instytut Historyczny, 2001.

Gauding, Daniela. *Siegmund Sische Breitbart—Eisenkönig, stärkster Mann der Welt: Breitbart versus Hanussen.* Berlin: Hentrich & Hentrich, 2006.

Gawkowski, Robert, and Jarosław Rokicki. "Stosunki polsko-żydowskie w sporcie II Rzeczpospolitej." In *Parlamentaryzm, konserwatyzm, nacjonalizm: Sefer jowel. Studia ofiarowane Profesorowi Szymonowi Rudnickiemu,* edited by Jolanta Żyndul, 221–240. Warsaw: Wydawnictwo Sejmowe, 2010.

Gechtman, Roni. "Socialist Mass Politics through Sport: The Bund's Morgnshtern in Poland, 1926–1939." In "One Hundred Years of 'Muscular Judaism': Sport in Jewish History and Culture," special issue, *Journal of Sport History* 26, no. 2 (1999): 326–352.

Gere, Anne Ruggles. *Intimate Practices: Literacy and Cultural Work in U.S. Women's Clubs, 1880–1920.* Champaign: University of Illinois Press, 1997.

Gillerman, Sharon. "Samson in Vienna: The Theatrics of Jewish Masculinity." *Jewish Social Studies* 9, no. 2 (2003): 65–98.

Gilman, Sander. *Freud, Race and Gender.* Princeton, NJ: Princeton University Press, 1993.

———. *Jewish Self-Hatred: Anti-Semitism and the Hidden Language of the Jews.* Baltimore: Johns Hopkins University Press, 1986.

Gilmore, David D. *Manhood in the Making: Cultural Concepts of Masculinity.* New Haven, CT: Yale University Press, 1990.

Gluzman, Michael. *Ha-guf ha-tsiyoni: Leumiyut, migdar u-miniyut ba-sifrut ha-israelit ha-hadasha.* Tel Aviv: Hakibbutz Hameuchad, 2007.

Godbeer, Richard. *The Overflowing of Friendship: Love between Men and the Creation of the American Republic.* Baltimore: Johns Hopkins University Press, 2009.

Goldin, Semion. *The Russian Army and the Jewish Population, 1914–1917: Libel, Persecution, Reaction.* Cham, Switzerland: Springer Nature, 2022.

Goofman, Erving. *O pacjentach szpitali psychiatrycznych i mieszkańcach innych instytucji totalnych.* Gdańsk, Poland: Gdańskie Wydawnictwo Psychologiczne, 2011.

Greenfield, Jill, Sean O'Connell, and Chris Reid. "Fashioning Masculinity: Men Only, Consumption and the Development of Marketing in the 1930s." *Twentieth Century British History* 10, no. 4 (1999): 457–476.

Grinberg, Ronnie A. "Neither 'Sissy' Boy nor Patrician Man: New York Intellectuals and the Construction of American Jewish Masculinity." *American Jewish History* 98, no. 3 (2014): 127–151.

Hagemann, Karen. "German Heroes: The Cult of the Death for the Fatherland in Nineteenth-Century Germany." In *Masculinities in Politics and War: Gendering Modern History*, edited by Stefan Dudink, Karen Hagemann, and John Tosh, 116–134. Manchester, UK: Manchester University Press, 2004.

Hájková, Anna, Elissa Mailänder, Doris Bergen, Patrick Farges, and Atina Grossmann. "Forum: Holocaust and History of Gender and Sexuality." *German History* 36, no. 1 (2018): 78–100.

Hakak, Yohai. *Haredi Masculinities between the Yeshiva, the Army, Work, and Politics: The Sage, the Warrior, and the Entrepreneur.* Leiden, Netherlands: Brill, 2016.

Halper, Shaun Jacob. "Mordechai Langer (1894–1943) and the Birth of the Modern Jewish Homosexual." PhD diss., University of California Berkeley, 2013.

Halperin, David M. *How to Do the History of Homosexuality?* Chicago: University of Chicago Press, 2002.

Hanisch, Ernst. *Männlichkeiten: Eine andere Geschichte des 20. Jahrhunderts.* Vienna: Böhlau, 2005.

Hämmerle, Christa. *Des Kaisers Knechte: Erinnerungen an die Rekrutenzeit im k. (u.) k. Heer 1868 bis 1914.* Vienna: Böhlau, 2011.

———. *Ganze Männer? Gesellschaft, Geschlecht und Allgemeine Wehrpflicht in Österreich-Ungarn (1868–1914).* Frankfurt: Campus, 2022.

———. *Heimat/Front: Geschlechtergeschichte/n des Ersten Weltkriegs in Österreich-Ungarn.* Vienna: Böhlau, 2014.

Healey, Dan. *Homosexual Desire in Revolutionary Russia: The Regulation of Sexual and Gender Dissent.* Chicago: University of Chicago Press, 2001.

Hearn, Jeff. *The Gender of Oppression: Men, Masculinity and the Critique of Marxism.* New York: St. Martin's Press, 1987.

Hecht, Dietrich. "Jewish (Vacation) Fraternities in the Habsburg Monarchy: Kadimah and Geullah—Forward to Redemption." *Austrian Studies* no. 24 (2016), "Jews, Jewish Difference and Austrian Culture. Literary and Historical Perspectives," special issue: 31–48.

Hein-Kircher, Heidi. "Debating Social Change and the Jewish Nation: The Polish-Jewish Weekly Ewa on Jewish Families and Birth Control (1928–1933)." *Journal of Family History* 48, no. 3 (2023): 278–292.

Heller, Daniel Kupfert. *Jabotinsky's Children: Polish Jews and the Rise of Right-Wing Zionism.* Princeton, NJ: Princeton University Press, 2017.

Henschel, Christhardt. *Jeder Bürger Soldat: Juden und das polnische Militär (1918–1939).* Göttingen, Germany: Vandenhoeck & Ruprecht, 2023.

———. "'Jeszcze nas straszą żywe upiory bez nosów…' Kilka uwag o miejscu kombatantów i inwalidów wojennych w społeczeństwie polskim 1918–1939." In *Margines społeczny Drugiej Rzeczpospolitej*, edited by Mateusz Rodak and Janusz Żarnowski, 103–118. Warsaw: Instytut Historii PAN, 2013.

Hinojosa, Ramon. "Doing Hegemony: Military, Men, and Constructing a Hegemonic Masculinity." *Journal of Men's Studies* 18, no. 2 (2010): 179–194.

Hirsch, Dafna, and Dana Grosswirth Kachtan. "Is 'Hegemonic Masculinity' Hegemonic as Masculinity? Two Israeli Case Studies." *Men and Masculinities* 21, no. 5 (2018): 687–708.

Hoffman, Lawrence A. *Covenant of Blood: Circumcision and Gender in Rabbinic Judaism*. Chicago: University of Chicago Press, 1995.

hooks, bell. *We Real Cool: Black Men and Masculinity*. New York: Routledge, 2004.

Huebel, Sebastian. *Fighter, Worker, and Family Man: German-Jewish Men and Their Gendered Experiences in Nazi Germany, 1933–1941*. Toronto: University of Toronto Press, 2021.

Hurtado, Aída, and Mrinal Sinha. *Beyond Machismo: Intersectional Latino Masculinities*. Austin: University of Texas Press, 2016.

Hyman, Paula. *Gender and Assimilation in Modern Jewish History: The Roles and Representation of Women*. Seattle: University of Washington Press, 1995.

Ilany, Ofri. "Naga nafots ba-mizrakh: Tiurim shel mishkav-zakhar ba-tkufat ha-mandat." *Zmanim* 131 (2015): 8–21.

———. "'An Oriental Vice': Representations of Sodomy in Early Zionist Discourse." In *National Politics and Sexuality in Transregional Perspective: The Homophobic Argument*, edited by Achim Rohde, Christina von Braun, and Stefanie Schüler-Springorum, 107–120. New York: Routledge, 2018.

Imbs, Hanna, ed. *Miasto i kultura polska doby przemysłowej*. Vols. 1–3. Wrocław, Poland: Zakład Narodowy im. Ossolińskich, 1988–1993.

Imhoff, Sarah. *Masculinity and the Making of American Judaism*. Bloomington: Indiana University Press, 2017.

Jacobs, Jack. "Jewish Workers' Sports Movements in Inter-War Poland: Shtern and Morgnshtern in Comparative Perspective." In *Jews, Sports and the Rites of Citizenship*, edited by Jack Kugelmass, 114–130. Champaign: University of Illinois Press, 2007.

Judd, Robin. *Contested Rituals: Circumcision, Kosher Butchering, and Jewish Political Life in Germany, 1843–1933*. Ithaca, NY: Cornell University Press, 2011.

Kaliściak, Tomasz. *Płeć Pantofla: Odmieńcze męskości w polskiej prozie XIX i XX wieku*. Warsaw: Wydawnictwo IBL PAN, 2016.

Kaplan, Danny. *The Men We Loved: Male Friendship and Nationalism in Israeli Culture*. New York: Berghahn Books, 2006.

Kaplan-Wajselbaum, Jonathan. *Jews in Suits. Men's Dress in Vienna, 1890–1938*. New York: Bloomsbury, 2023.

Karczewski, Kamil. "'Call Me by My Name': A 'Strange and Incomprehensible' Passion in the Polish Kresy of the 1920s." *Slavic Review* 81, no. 3 (2022): 631–652.

———. "'For a Pole, It All Was a Great Abomination': Grassroots Homonationalism and State Homophobia à la Polonaise—A History Lesson from a Place between East and West." *Sexuality and Culture* 27 (2023): 1996–2015.

———. "Transnational Flows of Knowledge and the Legalisation of Homosexuality in Interwar Poland." *Contemporary European History* 33 no. 3 (2024): 849–866.

Kay, Rebecca. *Men in Contemporary Russia: The Fallen Heroes of Post-Soviet Change?* London: Ashgate, 2006.

Kijek, Kamil. *Dzieci modernizmu: Świadomość, kultura i socjalizacja polityczna młodzieży żydowskiej w Polsce międzywojennej*. Wrocław, Poland: Wydawnictwo Uniwersytetu Wrocławskiego, 2017.

Kimmel, Michael S. *Manhood in America: A Cultural History*. New York: Free Press, 1996.

Kimmel, Michael S., and Michael A. Messner. *Men's Lives*. Boston: Allyn & Bacon, 2003.

Klapper, Melissa R. *Jewish Girls Coming of Age in America, 1860–1920*. New York: New York University Press, 2005.

Kondrasiuk, Grzegorz, ed. *Cyrk w świecie widowisk*. Lublin, Poland: Warsztaty Kultury w Lublinie, 2017.

Konstantynów, Dariusz. "Pogromy i inne akty przemocy fizycznej wobec Żydów w zwierciadle rysunków z prasy polskiej (1919–1939)." In *Pogromy Żydów na ziemiach polskich w XIX i XX wieku*, vol. 1, *Literatura i sztuka*, edited by Sławomir Buryła, 321–362. Warsaw: Instytut Historii PAN, 2018.

Korbel, Susanne. *Auf die Tour! Jüdinnen und Juden in Singspielhalle, Kabarett und Varieté zwischen Habsburgermonarchie und Amerika um 1900*. Vienna: Böhlau, 2021.

Koshar, Rudy, ed. *Histories of Leisure*. Oxford: Oxford University Press, 2002.

Kraß, Andreas, Moshe Sluhovsky, and Yuval Yonay, eds. *Queer Jewish Lives between Central Europe and Mandatory Palestine: Biographies and Geographies*. Bielefeld, Germany: Transcript, 2022.

Krondorfer, Björn. "Conflicting Religious Ideals of Masculinity: On God-men and Male Eunuchs." Presentation held at the Heinrich Böll Foundation, Berlin, Germany, December 13, 2007.

Krondorfer, Björn, and Ovidiu Creangă, eds. *The Holocaust and Masculinities: Critical Inquiries into the Presence and Absence of Men*. Albany: State University of New York Press, 2020.

Kuciel-Frydryszak, Joanna. *Służące do wszystkiego*. Warsaw: Marginesy, 2018.

Kühne, Thomas, ed. *Männergeschichte als Geschlechtergesichte: Männlichkeit im Wandel der Moderne*. Frankfurt: Campus, 1996.

———. *The Rise and Fall of Comradeship: Hitler's Soldiers, Male Bonding and Mass Violence in the Twentieth Century*. Cambridge: Cambridge University Press, 2017.

Kurimay, Anita. *Queer Budapest, 1873–1961*. Chicago: University of Chicago Press, 2020.

Kurth, Alexandra. *Männer-Bünde-Rituale: Studentenverbindungen seit 1800*. Frankfurt: Campus, 2004.

Landau, Moshe. *Mi'ut yehudi lokhem: Maavak yehudey polin ba-shanim 1918–1928*. Jerusalem: Zalman Shazar Center for Jewish History, 1986.

Lausen, Sabrina. *Hüter ihrer Nationen: Studentische Verbindungen in Deutschland und Polen im 19. und frühen 20. Jahrhundert*. Cologne, Germany: Böhlau, 2020.

Leigh, Alisson. *Picturing Russia's Men: Masculinity and Modernity in Nineteenth-Century Painting*. New York: Bloomsbury, 2020.

Leszczyński, Adam. *Ludowa historia Polski*. Warsaw: WAB, 2020.

Levsen, Sonja. *Elite, Männlichkeit und Krieg: Tübinger und Cambridger Studenten 1900–1929*. Göttingen, Germany: Vandenhoeck & Ruprecht, 2006.

Loeb, Lori Anne. *Consuming Angels: Advertising and Victorian Women*. Oxford: Oxford University Press, 1994.

Loiselle, Kenneth. *Brotherly Love: Freemasonry and Male Friendship in Enlightenment France*. Ithaca, NY: Cornell University Press, 2014.

Lücke, Martin. "Mann-männliche Prostitution und hegemoniale Männlichkeit im Kaiserreich." In *Männer—Macht—Körper: Hegemoniale Männlichkeiten vom Mittelalter bis heute*, edited by Martin Dinges, 157–172. Frankfurt: Campus, 2005.

Lusty, Natalya, and Julian Murphet, eds. *Modernism and Masculinity.* Cambridge: Cambridge University Press, 2014.

Lynd, Staughton. *Doing History from the Bottom Up: On E.P. Thompson, Howard Zinn, and Rebuilding the Labour Movement from Below.* Chicago: Haymarket Books, 2014.

Madej-Krupitski, Urszula. "Mapping Jewish Poland: Leisure Travel and Identity in the Interwar Period." PhD diss., University of California Berkeley, 2020.

Manekin, Rachel. *The Rebellion of the Daughters: Jewish Women Runaways in Habsburg Galicia.* Princeton, NJ: Princeton University Press, 2020.

Marhoefer, Laurie. *Sex and the Weimar Republic: German Homosexual Emancipation and the Rise of the Nazis.* Toronto: University of Toronto Press, 2015.

Mark, Elizabeth Wyner, ed. *The Covenant of Circumcision: New Perspectives on an Ancient Jewish Rite.* Hanover, MA: Brandeis University Press, 2003.

Martschukat, Jürgen, and Olaf Steglitz. *Geschichte der Männlichkeiten.* Frankfurt: Campus, 2018.

Mazurkiewicz, Filip. *Siła i słabość: Studium upadku męskiej hegemonii w Polsce.* Warsaw: Wydawnictwo IBL PAN, 2019.

Melzer, Emanuel. *No Way Out: The Politics of Polish Jewry, 1935–1939.* Cincinnati: Hebrew Union College Press, 1997.

Menning, Bruce W. *Bayonets before Bullets: The Imperial Russian Army, 1861–1914.* Bloomington: Indiana University Press, 1992.

Micale, Mark S. *Hysterical Men: The Hidden History of Male Nervous Illness.* Cambridge, MA: Harvard University Press, 2008.

Miller, Pavla. *Transformations of Patriarchy in the West, 1500–1900.* Bloomington: Indiana University Press, 1998.

Mora, Miriam Eve. *Carrying a Big Schtick: Jewish Acculturation and Masculinity in the Twentieth Century.* Detroit: Wayne State University Press, 2024.

Moseley, Marcus. *Being for Myself Alone: Origins of Jewish Autobiography.* Stanford, CA: Stanford University Press, 2006.

Moss, Kenneth. *An Unchosen People: Jewish Political Reckoning in Interwar Poland.* Cambridge, MA: Harvard University Press, 2021.

Mosse, George L. *The Image of Man: The Creation of Modern Masculinity.* Oxford: Oxford University Press, 1996.

———. *Nationalism and Sexuality: Middle-Class Morality and Sexual Norms in Modern Europe.* Madison: University of Wisconsin Press, 1985.

Mrzygłód, Izabela. "Uniwersytety w cieniu kryzysu: Radykalizacja politiczna studentów Uniwersytetów Warszawskiego i Wiedeńskiego w okresie międzywojennym." PhD diss., University of Warsaw, 2021.

Naor, Arye. "The Leader as a Poet: The Political and Ideological Poetry of Ze'ev Jabotinsky." *Israel Affairs* 20, no. 2 (2014): 161–181.

Nathans, Benjamin. *Beyond the Pale: The Jewish Encounter with Late Imperial Russia*. Berkeley: University of California Press, 2004.

Nordheimer Nur, Ofer. *Eros and Tragedy: Jewish Male Fantasies and the Masculine Revolution of Zionism*. Boston: Academic Studies, 2014.

Ocampo, Anthony Christian. *Brown and Gay in LA: The Lives of Immigrant Sons*. New York: New York University Press, 2023.

100 lat Polski w liczbach. Warsaw: GUS, 2018.

Osgerby, Bill. "A Pedigree of the Consuming Male: Masculinity, Consumption and the American 'Leisure Class.'" *Sociological Review* 51, no. 1 (2003): 57–85.

Panter, Sarah. *Jüdische Erfahrungen und Loyalitätskonflikte im Ersten Weltkrieg*. Göttingen, Germany: Vandenhoeck & Ruprecht, 2014.

Parsons, Talcott. *The Structure of Social Action*. New York: McGraw-Hill, 1937.

Parush, Iris. *Reading Jewish Women: Marginality and Modernization in Nineteenth-Century Eastern European Jewish Society*. Waltham, MA: Brandeis University Press, 2004.

Pater, Daniel. "Żydowski Akademicki Ruch Korporacyjny w Polsce w latach 1898–1939." *Dzieje Najnowsze* 34, no. 3 (2002): 3–20.

Penslar, Derek J. *Jews and the Military: A History*. Princeton, NJ: Princeton University Press, 2013.

Peskowitz, Miriam, and Laura Levitt. *Judaism since Gender*. New York: Routledge, 1996.

Petrovsky-Shtern, Yohanan. "The 'Jewish Policy' of the Late Imperial War Ministry: The Impact of the Russian Right." *KRITIKA: Explorations in Russian and Eurasian History* 2 (2002): 217–254.

———. *Jews in the Russian Army, 1827–1917: Drafted into Modernity*. Cambridge: Cambridge University Press, 2008.

Plach, Eva. "Feminism and Nationalism on the Pages of 'Ewa: Tygodnik,' 1928–1933." In *Polin: Studies in Polish Jewry*, vol. 18, *Jewish Women in Eastern Europe*, 241–263. Liverpool, UK: Liverpool University Press, 2005.

Pleck, Joseph. "The Gender Role Strain Paradigm: An Update." In *Toward a New Psychology of Men*, edited by Ronald F. Levant and William S. Polack, 11–32. New York: Basic Books, 1995.

———. *The Myth of Masculinity*. Cambridge, MA: MIT Press, 1981.

Poliak, Daniel. "Metsitsah Be-Peh, Nineteenth Century New York Jewry, and the Board of Health." *Tradition: A Journal of Orthodox Jewish Thought* 44, no. 3 (2011): 39–52.

Pressner, Todd Samuel. *Muscular Judaism: The Jewish Body and the Politics of Regeneration*. New York: Routledge, 2007.

Purdie-Vaughns, Valerie, and Richard P. Eibach. "Intersectional Invisibility: The Distinctive Advantages and Disadvantages of Multiple Subordinate-Group Identities." *Sex Roles: A Journal of Research* 59, no. 5–6 (2008): 377–391.

Rappaport, Erika. *Shopping for Pleasure: Women in the Making of London's West End*. Princeton, NJ: Princeton University Press, 2001.

Rauszer, Michał. *Bękarty pańszczyzny: Historia buntów chłopskich*. Warsaw: Wydawnictwo RM, 2020.

Raz, Yosef. *Beyond Flesh: Queer Masculinities and Nationalism in Israeli Cinema*. New Brunswick, NJ: Rutgers University Press, 2004.

Reeser, Todd W. *Masculinities in Theory: An Introduction*. Chichester, UK: Wiley, 2011.

Robinson, Stephanie Nicole. *History of Immigrant Female Students in Chicago Public Schools, 1900–1950*. New York: Peter Lang, 2004.

Rodak, Mateusz. *Mit a rzeczywistość. Przestępczość osób narodowości żydowskiej w II Rzeczpospolitej: Casus województwa lubelskiego*. Warsaw: Neriton, 2012.

Rokicki, Jarosław. *Żydowski ruch sportowy i turystyczny w Polsce w pierwszej połowie XX wieku*. Warsaw: n.p., 1994.

Roper, Michael, and John Tosh, eds. *Manful Assertions: Masculinities in Britain since 1800*. London: Routledge, 1991.

Rosenberg, Warren. *Legacy of Rage: Jewish Masculinity, Violence, and Culture*. Amherst: University of Massachusetts Press, 2001.

Rosman, Moshe. *Categorically Jewish, Distinctly Polish: Polish Jewish History Reflected and Refracted*. London: Littman Library of Jewish Civilization, 2022.

Rotundo, Anthony. *American Manhood: Transformations in Masculinity from the Revolution to the Modern Era*. New York: Basic Books, 1994.

Rürup, Miriam. "Auf Kneipe und Fechtboden: Inszenierungen von Männlichkeit in jüdischen Studentenverbindungen in Kaiserreich und Weimarer Republik." In *Männer—Macht—Körper: Hegemoniale Männlichkeiten vom Mittelalter bis heute*, edited by Martin Dinges, 141–156. Frankfurt: Campus, 2005.

Samogyi, Tamar. *Die Schejnen und die Prosten: Untersuchungen zum Schönheitsideal der Ostjuden in Bezug auf Körper und Kleidung unter besonderer Berücksichtigung des Chassidismus.* Cologne, Germany: Reimer, 1982.

Sanua, Marianne R. *Going Greek: Jewish College Fraternities in the United States, 1895–1945.* Detroit: Wayne State University Press, 2018.

Schimmelpenninck van der Oye, David, and Bruce W. Menning, eds. *Reforming the Tsar's Army: Military Innovation in Imperial Russia from Peter the Great to the Revolution.* Cambridge: Cambridge University Press, 2004.

Schmale, Wolfgang. *Geschichte der Männlichkeit in Europa 1450–2000.* Vienna: Böhlau, 2003.

Schüler-Springorum, Stefanie. *Geschlecht und Differenz.* Paderborn, Germany: Ferdinand Schöningh, 2014.

Schuster, Frank M. *Zwischen allen Fronten: Osteuropäische Juden während des Ersten Weltkrieges (1914–1919).* Cologne, Germany: Böhlau, 2004.

Scull, Andrew. *Hysteria: The Biography.* Oxford: Oxford University Press, 2009.

Seeman, Don, and Rebecca Kobrin. "'Like One of the Whole Men': Learning, Gender and Autobiography in R. Barukh Epstein's *Mekor Barukh.*" *Nashim: A Journal of Jewish Women's Studies & Gender Issues* 2 (1999) "Crossing into Modernity: Renegotiating Jewish Gender Identities," special issue: 52–94.

Segal, Lynne. *Slow Motion: Changing Masculinities, Changing Men.* London: Palgrave MacMillan, 2008.

Sherman, Matthew J. "Corporeality as Weapon: Siegmund Breitbart's Embodiment of Muskeljudentum." *German Politics and Society* 30, no. 2 (2012): 21–37.

Śmieja, Wojciech. *Hegemonia i trauma: Literatura wobec dominujących fikcji męskości.* Warsaw: Instytut Badań Literackich, 2016.

———. "Homo prostheticus czyli ciało zdemilitaryzowane: O dylogii powieściowej Jana Żyznowskiego." *Interalia: A Journal of Queer Studies* 10 (2015): 7–32.

———. *Homoseksualność i polska nowoczesność: Szkice o teorii, historii i literaturze.* Katowice, Poland: Wydawnictwo Uniwersytetu Śląskiego, 2015.

———. "Skandal homoseksualny i polska opinia publiczna—'sprawa Eulenburga' na łamach wybranych tytułów prasy polskiej," *Teksty Drugie* no. 5 (2013): 311–329.

———. "Wokół 'skandalicznego procesu' Oskara Wilde'a i 'afery Eulenburga'—Homoseksualne skandale przełomu XIX i XX wieku a polska opinia publiczna." *Studia Kulturowe* 2 (2011): 93–11.

———. *Nie/podległości i transformacje: Szkice o stuleciu męskiego niepokoju 1918–2018.* Katowice, Poland: Wydawnictwo Uniwersytetu Śląskiego, 2023.

———. *Po Męstwie. Historia polskiej męskości w XX wieku.* Wołowiec, Poland: Czarne, 2024.

Spiekermann, Uwe, Paul Lerner, and Anne Schenderlein, eds. *Jewish Consumer Cultures in Nineteenth and Twentieth-Century Europe and North America.* Cham, Switzerland: Palgrave Macmillan, 2022.

Stampfer, Shaul. *Families, Rabbis and Education: Essays on Traditional Jewish Society in Eastern Europe.* Liverpool, UK: Liverpool University Press, 2010.

———. *Lithuanian Yeshivot of the Nineteenth Century: Creating a Tradition of Learning.* Oxford: Littman Library of Jewish Civilization, 2012.

Swiencicki, Mark A. "Consuming Brotherhood: Men's Culture, Style and Recreation as Consumer Culture, 1880–1930." *Journal of Social History* 31, no. 4 (1998): 773–808.

Szczepaniak, Monika. *Habitus żołnierski w literaturze i kulturze polskiej w kontekście Wielkiej Wojny.* Kraków: Universitas, 2017.

Szuman, Alicja. "Przeobrażanie struktury społeczno-zawodowej ludności Polski w XX wieku." *Ruch Prawniczy, Ekonomiczny i Socjologiczny* 61, no. 3–4 (1999): 187–202.

Szymański, Marcin Jakub, and Błażej Torański. *Fabrykanci: Burzliwe dzieje łódzkich bogaczy.* Warsaw: Wydawnictwo Zona Zero, 2016.

Tamagne, Florence. *History of Homosexuality in Europe, Berlin, London, Paris 1919–1939.* New York: Algora, 2006.

Tanikowski, Artur, ed. *Jew, Pole, Legionary: 1914–1920.* Warsaw: Museum of the History of Polish Jews, 2014.

Tikochinski, Shlomo. *Lamdanut, musar ve-elitizm: Yeshivat Slobodka me-Lita le-Erets Israel.* Jerusalem: Zalman Shazar Center for Jewish History, 2016.

Tobin, Robert Deam. *Peripheral Desires: The German Discovery of Sex.* Philadelphia: University of Pennsylvania Press, 2016.

Tolman, Deborah L. *Dilemmas of Desire: Teenage Girls Talk about Sexuality.* Cambridge, MA: Harvard University Press, 2005.

Tomasik, Tomasz. *Wojna-Męskość-Literatura.* Słupsk, Poland: Wydawnictwo Naukowe Akademii Pomorskiej w Słupsku, 2013.

Tomaszewski, Jerzy. "Położenie drobnych kupców żydowskich w Polsce w latach wielkiego kryzysu (1929–1935)." *Biuletyn Żydowskiego Instytutu Historycznego* 102, no. 2 (1977): 35–54.

Tomaszewski, Patryk. *Polskie korporacje akademickie w latach 1918–1939.* Toruń, Poland: Wydawnictwo Uniwersytetu im. Mikołaja Kopernika, 2011.

Tosh, John. "The Old Adam and the New Man: Emerging Themes in the History of English Masculinities, 1750–1850." In *English Masculinities, 1660–1800,* edited by Tim Hitchcock and Michelle Cohen, 61–82. London: Longman, 1999.

Vallois, Nicolas, and Sarah Imhoff. "'Floating Jews'—The Luftmentsh as an Economic Character." *Œconomia* 12, no. 2 (2022): 275–314.

Vázquez García, Francisco, ed. *Historia de la homosexualidad masculina en Occidente.* Madrid: Los Libros de la Catarata, 2022.

Way, Niobe. "Boys' Friendships during Adolescence: Intimacy, Desire, and Loss." *Journal of Research on Adolescence* 23, no. 2 (2013): 201–213.

Weissman, Moshe. *The Midrash Says: The Book of Beraishis.* New York: Bnei Yaakov, 1980.

Wiesner-Hanks, Merry. *Gender in History: Global Perspectives.* Hoboken, NJ: Wiley-Blackwell, 2001.

Wildman, Daniel. *Der veränderbare Körper: Jüdische Turner, Männlichkeit und das Wiedergewinnen von Geschichte in Deutschland um 1900.* Tübingen, Germany: Mohr Siebeck, 2009.

Wolitz, Seth L. "Forging a Hero for a Jewish Stage: Goldfadn's 'Bar Kokhba.'" *Shofar* 20, no. 3 (2002): 53–65.

Yablonka, Ivan. *A History of Masculinity: From Patriarchy to Gender Justice.* London: Penguin, 2022.

Yona, Rona. *Niye kulanu halutsim: Tnuat ha-avoda ve-ha-aliya me-polin 1923–1936.* Jerusalem: Magnes, 2021.

Zalkin, Mordechai. "Beyn 'bney elohim' l'bney adam.' Rabanim, bney yeshivot ve-gius le-tsava rusi ba-mea ha-teysha esre." In *Milhama ve-shalom ba-tarbut ha-yehudit,* edited by Avirel Bar-Levav, 165–222. Jerusalem: Zalman Shazar Center for Jewish History, 2006.

———. *Modernizing Jewish Education in Nineteenth-Century Eastern Europe: The School as the Shrine of the Jewish Enlightenment.* Leiden, Netherlands: Brill, 2016.

Żarnowski, Janusz. *Społeczeństwo II Rzeczypospolitej. 1918–1939.* Warsaw: PWN, 1973.

Zimbalist Rosaldo, Michele, and Louise Lamphere, eds. *Women, Culture and Society.* Stanford, CA: Stanford University Press, 1974.

Zohar, Emma. "Between Hope and Struggle: The Gender Struggle and the Jewish Socialist Parties in Interwar Poland." *East European Jewish Affairs* 52, no. 1 (2023): 48–66.

zur Nieden, Susanne, ed. *Homosexualität und Staatsräson: Männlichkeit, Homophobie und Politik in Deutschland 1900–1945*. Frankfurt: Campus, 2005.

Zwicker Fetheringill, Lisa. "Performing Masculinity: Jewish Students and the Honor Code at German Universities." In *Jewish Masculinities: German Jews, Gender, and History*, edited by Benjamin Maria Baader, Sharon Gillerman, and Paul Lerner, 114–137. Bloomington: Indiana University Press, 2012.

Związek Sjońskich Korporacyj
Akademickich w Polsce, 147
Związek Żydow Uczestnikow Walk o
Niepodległości Polski, 208–213

Żydowskie Akademickie
Stowarzyszenie Sportowe, 173
Żydowski Związek Inwalidów, Wdów i
Sierot Wojennych, 208

MARIUSZ KALCZEWIAK is Professor of Jewish Studies at the University of Lucerne, Switzerland. He is author of *Polacos in Argentina: Polish Jews, Interwar Migration, and the Emergence of Transatlantic Jewish Culture* and coeditor of *The World beyond the West: Perspectives from Eastern Europe.*